Change and Continuity
in the
1992 Elections

William H. Young

1994

Change and Continuity in the 1992 Elections

Paul R. Abramson
Michigan State University

John H. Aldrich
Duke University

David W. Rohde
University of Florida

CQ
PRESS

A Division of Congressional Quarterly Inc.

Library of Congress Cataloging-in-Publication Data

Abramson, Paul R.
    Change and continuity in the 1992 elections / Paul R. Abramson, John H. Aldrich, David W. Rohde.
        p.   cm.
    Includes bibliographical references and index.
    ISBN 0-87187-821-6
    1. Presidents--United States--Election--1992.   2. United States. Congress--Elections, 1992.   3. United States.   Congress--Elections, 1993.   4. Elections--United States.   5. United States--Politics and government--1945-1989.   6. United States--Politics and government--1989-1993   I. Aldrich, John Herbert, 1947-   . II. Rohde, David W.   III. Title.
    JK526   1992i
    324.973'0928--dc20
                                                            94-837
                                                            CIP

To the memory of William H. Riker

Contents

Tables and Figures

Tables

Figures

Preface

This is our fourth book on American elections. Our first three examined Republican presidential victories, and we were beginning to wonder when we would ever get a chance to write about a Democrat winning the White House. When the Persian Gulf war ended in February 1991, we thought that our earliest opportunity would be after the 1996 election, in which some lucky Democrat might have the chance to run against Dan Quayle. We were wrong.

But we were not alone in believing that George Bush would be reelected. Most Americans believed this, including Bush. His error in judgment was politically costly, for it may have led him to ignore a prolonged economic slowdown that undermined his presidency. Moreover, the end of the cold war, which Bush proclaimed as a Republican foreign policy success, was a political bonus for the Democrats. With the end of the "Evil Empire," as Reagan had called the Soviet Union, the belief that the Republicans were better qualified to defend America and maintain the peace was no longer a major political asset. As Sen. Bob Dole of Kansas reminded Americans during the 1976 vice-presidential debate, all four major wars of the twentieth century—World War I, World War II, the Korean War and the Vietnam War—began under Democratic presidents. A Republican president, Dwight D. Eisenhower, ended the Korean War, and Richard Nixon, another Republican, withdrew American troops from Vietnam.

Even as Bush's approval ratings fell between early 1991 and the summer of 1992, most Americans continued to believe that he was doing a good job handling American foreign policy. But by the fall of 1992 very few Americans had foreign policy on their minds. Few Americans thought Bush was doing a good job dealing with the economy.

Throughout 1991, many Democratic politicians believed that Bush was invincible. The Democrats who were believed to be most likely to have a chance against him may have decided that those chances were too slim. Thus, Bill Clinton, the governor of one of the nation's smaller states (and the third poorest), faced a weak set of opponents, who lacked the money to sustain their nomination campaigns after early primary losses.

For years, political scientists had been writing about weakening party loyalties. But we scarcely expected the candidacy of H. Ross Perot. We never imagined that a Texas billionaire who had never before run for public office would win nearly one out of every five votes cast.

We did predict that the Democrats would win the presidency before the Republicans won control of the U.S. House of Representatives, but we never claimed that 1992 would be the year for our prediction to be fulfilled.

Even though social scientists cannot predict the specific behavior of individuals, there are more general questions that can be answered through a systematic study of elections. How do political rules affect the decisions of politicians to run for office and how do they affect their chances of winning? Do election campaigns influence voter behavior? Was the 1992 presidential election merely a rejection of Bush, or did it reflect a choice among policy alternatives? How do party loyalties, often acquired in childhood, affect voting choices?

We are above all interested in the implications of the 1992 elections for the American party system. Did past hopes for Republican dominance die with Bush's defeat, or do the Republicans still have the opportunity to reemerge from defeat and become America's majority party? Do the Democrats have prospects to become the dominant party in American politics again? Or has the party system broken down so much that partisanship no longer matters? Does the large vote for Perot herald the beginnings of a new political party that can effectively compete with the Democrats and the Republicans?

We also ask questions about congressional elections. Why, despite public disdain for Congress, do most incumbents who seek reelection win? Why is there so much change in presidential voting and so much continuity in congressional voting? Since World War II ended in 1945, partisan control of the White House has changed six times. Partisan control of the U.S. House of Representatives has changed four times, but it has not changed since the Democrats took control of the 84th Congress in 1955. The Democrats have now won twenty consecutive House elections. Why do the Democrats continually win control of the House? Does the election of a Democratic president actually put Democratic control at risk?

To answer these questions, one cannot view the 1992 elections as isolated events. Rather, one must examine the 1992 elections in their historical context. To do this, we have examined a broad range of evidence, from past election results to public opinion surveys of the electorate conducted since 1944.

We employ many sources, but we rely most heavily upon the 1992 survey of the American electorate conducted by the Survey Research Center and the Center for Political Studies of the University of Michigan as part of an ongoing project funded by the National Science Foundation. We use every one of the twenty-two election studies conducted by the Michigan SRC-CPS, often referred to as the National Election Studies (NES).

These surveys of the American electorate, which are disseminated by the Inter-university Consortium for Political and Social Research, can be analyzed by scholars throughout the United States. The ICPSR provided these data in late May of 1993. Unless otherwise indicated, all the tables and figures in Chapters 2, 4 through 8, and 10 are based upon surveys obtained through the ICPSR. The standard disclaimer holds: the consortium is not responsible for our analyses or interpretations.

Several institutions aided us financially. John Aldrich received support from a Duke University College of Arts and Social Sciences Research Grant. David Rohde received support from Michigan State University from the fund for Distinguished University Professors and from the University of Florida through the Manning J. Dauer Eminent Scholar Chair endowment. In addition, we received support from the departments of political science at Michigan State University, Duke University, and the University of Florida.

Many individuals helped us with this effort. Sara McLaughlin, the acting director of the Politometrics Laboratory at Michigan State University, helped to prepare the 1992 NES data for analysis, and Robert Orme assisted with the data analysis for Chapter 10. Phil Paolino at Duke University assisted with most of the data analysis in Chapters 6, 7, and 8, and additional assistance was provided by Jennifer Schultz. Walter Dean Burnham of the University of Texas provided us with his estimates of turnout among the politically eligible population; Rhodes Cook of *Congressional Quarterly Weekly Report* shared his knowledge about the 1992 Democratic nomination rules; David C. Leege of the University of Notre Dame sent us the coding procedures that he and his colleagues developed to study the political impact of religion; Martin O'Connell of the U.S. Bureau of the Census answered questions about the census survey of voter turnout; Tom Smith of the National Opinion Research Center provided early results from the 1993 General Social Survey; and Santa Traugott of the Center for Political Studies of the University of Michigan answered questions about the 1992 NES survey.

Others helped by commenting on several of these chapters. We are grateful to Dean Burnham for his comments on Chapter 4. At Michigan State University, Ada W. Finifter commented on Chapters 4 and 5, Joseph A. Schlesinger gave us insights that helped us write Chapter 3 and 11, and Jim Granato, Thomas H. Hammond, Paul S. Kearns, and Nicolas van de Walle gave us comments on Chapter 11. In addition, David C. Leege and an anonymous reviewer provided us with extensive suggestions.

And, we again remain thankful to the staff at CQ Press. We had valuable suggestions from David Tarr, Nancy Lammers, and Shana Wagger. We are grateful to Nola Healy Lynch for her careful editing of our manuscript and to Laura Carter for guiding our book through production.

Like our earlier books, this book was a collective enterprise, but we divided the labor. Paul Abramson had the primary responsibility for Chapters 3, 4, 5, and 11; John Aldrich for chapters 1, 6, 7, and 8; and David Rohde for Chapters 2, 9, and 10. We must also take some responsibility for the electoral outcome since we all voted for Clinton. Over the past four elections, this is the first time that we have all voted for the winner. (One of us voted for Reagan in 1980, so we have not always supported the losing candidates in the past.)

Last, we will comment on our dedication. Our first three books were dedicated to our children. We can now think about a time when our children may dedicate books to us. We have dedicated this book to the memory of the late William H. Riker of the University of Rochester, who influenced our thinking about politics in many ways.

Paul R. Abramson
John H. Aldrich
David W. Rohde

The 1992 Presidential Election Contest

Presidential elections in the United States are partly ritual, a reaffirmation of our democratic values. But they are far more than ritual. The office confers great powers upon the occupant, and those powers have expanded during the course of American history. It is precisely because of these immense powers that presidential elections have at times played a major role in the determination of public policy.

The 1860 election, which brought Abraham Lincoln and the Republicans to power and ousted a divided Democratic party, focused on whether slavery should be extended into the western territories. Following Lincoln's victory, eleven southern states attempted to secede from the Union, the Civil War erupted, and slavery itself was abolished. An antislavery plurality (Lincoln received only 40 percent of the popular vote) set in motion a chain of events that freed some 4 million African-Americans.

The 1896 election, in which the Republican William McKinley defeated the Democrat and Populist William Jennings Bryan, beat back the challenge of western and agrarian interests to the prevailing financial and industrial power of the East. Although Bryan mounted a strong campaign, winning 47 percent of the vote to McKinley's 51 percent, the election set a clear course for a policy of high tariffs and the continuation of the gold standard for American money.

The twentieth century also witnessed presidential elections that determined the direction of public policy. In 1936, the incumbent Democrat, Franklin D. Roosevelt, won 61 percent of the popular vote and his Republican opponent, Alfred E. Landon, only 37 percent, a margin that allowed the Democrats to continue and consolidate the economic, social, and welfare policies of the New Deal.

1

Lyndon B. Johnson's 1964 landslide victory over Republican Barry M. Goldwater provided the clearest set of policy alternatives of any election in this century. Johnson, who received 61 percent of the popular vote to Goldwater's 38 percent, saw his triumph as a mandate for his Great Society programs, the most far reaching social legislation enacted since World War II.

Goldwater offered "a choice, not an echo," advocating far more conservative social and economic policies than Johnson, but the voters rejected him. Ironically, the election also appeared to offer a choice between escalating American involvement in Vietnam and restraint. But American involvement in Vietnam expanded after the election, and four years later the Democrats lost the presidency.

What Did the 1992 Election Mean?

Only the future can determine the ultimate importance of the 1992 election. Some scholars argue that elections have become less important for deciding public policy, and there is doubtless some truth in their argument.[1] But presidential elections often do have important public policy consequences. Bill Clinton offered the public ambitious proposals to improve the economy and to reform the health care system and the welfare system. George Bush appeared to offer continuity, with relatively modest proposals for change. And although H. Ross Perot offered few specifics, he gave the public the chance to break from the traditional pattern of two-party governance.

Because more than three out of five voters chose either Clinton or Perot, the presidential election results strongly suggest that the electorate preferred change to continuity. Even this conclusion is controversial, however. Everett Carll Ladd, for example, argues that, "For all their concern about the performance of the country's economy and political institutions, Americans issued a call better understood in terms of restoration than of change."[2] Moreover, as the Democrats lost ten seats in the U.S. House of Representatives and merely held their own in the Senate, the elections provided little new congressional support for Clinton's programs.

Even if Congress fails to enact major reforms, the election will change the course of public policy in areas over which Clinton has more direct control. The most immediate effects of Clinton's policies were in the area of abortion rights. Within the first week of his presidency, Clinton used executive orders to lift the so-called gag rule, which had prevented federally funded clinics from providing information about abortion. He also lifted a ban against federally funded research using fetal tissue derived from abortions. Moreover, the Supreme Court had been within one vote of the majority needed to overturn *Roe v. Wade,* which prevents states from outlawing abortion. Clinton's election made it extremely unlikely that an opponent of *Roe v. Wade* would be appointed to the Supreme Court during his presidency. Clinton's first appointment to the Supreme Court was Ruth Bader Ginsburg, a pioneer in women's rights issues, whose main criticism of *Roe* was that the opinion could have been better argued. Antiabortion groups recognized that the 1992 election was a major defeat for their position.

Clinton was less successful in fulfilling his promise to end the prohibition against allowing homosexuals to serve openly in the armed forces. Although he could have lifted this ban by executive order, many military and congressional leaders strongly oppose allowing homosexuals to serve openly in the military, and Congress can reverse an executive order through legislation. After a six-month study, Clinton reached a compromise: recruits would not be asked their sexual orientation, men or women who publicly revealed their homosexuality would be dismissed from the military, and the military authorities would not investigate cases of suspected homosexuality. This "don't ask, don't tell, don't pursue" policy was condemned as a betrayal of principle by gay rights activists and as an assault on religious values by opponents.

Because it takes sixty votes to close off debate in the U.S. Senate, the failure of the Democrats to gain seats in the elections left them with fifty-seven senators, three short of a "filibuster-proof" majority. Failure to gain Senate seats proved costly, for it provided the Republicans a line of defense against Clinton's policies. In April 1993, for example, the forty-three Republicans in the Senate, on Minority Leader Bob Dole's (Kan.) initiative, blocked Clinton's economic stimulus package. But Dole failed to block legislation requiring states to allow voting-age citizens to register to vote when applying for driver's licenses and to allow voter registration by mail. The "motor voter" bill was passed in May 1993 because six Republican senators voted to end the stalling tactics that could have prevented this legislation from reaching a vote. Registration requirements are one of the main reasons that voting turnout is low in the United States; thus, legislation that facilitates registration may lead to increased participation in future elections. Bush had opposed motor voter registration and had vetoed similar legislation in his presidency, so the 1992 presidential election made this reform possible.

A Senate minority cannot use the filibuster to prevent a vote on tax legislation, but the Republicans were united in their opposition to Clinton's proposals for tax reform. In August 1993, Congress passed a greatly modified version of Clinton's proposals for deficit reduction. The final package included tax increases on American families with taxable incomes above $140,000 a year, a surtax on families with incomes above $250,000, slightly increased corporate taxes, increased taxes on Social Security benefits for couples earning at least $44,000, and a 4.3 cent per gallon gasoline tax. These increases, along with spending cuts, were designed to reduce the deficit over the next five years. Congressional Republicans unanimously opposed the plan. In the House of Representatives, 217 Democrats and the one independent voted in favor of the final package and 41 Democrats voted against it; all 175 Republicans voted no. The measure passed by a margin of 218 to 216. In the Senate, 50 Democrats voted in favor of the plan, and six against, and all 44 Republicans voted against it. The measure passed with Vice President Al Gore's tie-breaking vote. According to R. W. Apple, Jr., "Historians at the Library of Congress and elsewhere could remember no major piece of legislation at least since World War II that was passed without a single vote from the opposition." [3] Despite the partisan vote, and despite claims by both its supporters and its opponents, the changes in the compromise budget package were small compared with those implemented in 1981 by the Economic Recovery Act under Ronald Reagan. Even so, the budget package marked a clear change in public policy.

If Clinton succeeds in implementing health care reform or if he succeeds in reforming the welfare system, the election will clearly have had a major impact on American public policy. But even if he does not succeed, the election has already led to changes. Skeptics ask, "Do elections matter?" [4] The answer is, clearly, yes.

Presidential elections not only change the direction of public policy, they also change the direction of American politics.[5] The 1992 election can only present clues about the nature of American electoral politics. During the Republican presidential victories of the 1980s, many political scientists raised the possibility that a partisan realignment had occurred or was about to occur. In 1985, President Reagan himself proclaimed that a Republican realignment was at hand. "The other side would like to believe that our victory last November was due to something other than our philosophy," he asserted. "I just hope they keep believing that. There's a change happening in America. Realignment is real." [6]

In November 1984, Reagan had won 59 percent of the popular vote. Bush's election in 1988 (with 53 percent of the vote) raised the prospect of continued Republican dominance. But in 1992 Bush won only 37 percent of the popular vote, a 22-point decline from Reagan's high-water mark. Not only had the Republican winning streak of three straight victories been broken, but the Republican party suffered one of the greatest popular vote declines since the Civil War.

Obviously, the 1992 election calls into question any claims of a pro-Republican realignment. But Clinton's narrow popular vote victory (he earned only 43 percent of the popular vote) raises serious questions about future Democratic dominance. Over 20 million Americans voted for neither the Republicans nor the Democrats: 19.7 million alone voted for a multibillionaire making his first attempt at elective office. That nearly one-fifth of the voters rejected both major parties raises the possibility of a breakdown of past voting patterns, something that political scientists have called a dealignment.

What do the terms realignment and dealignment mean, and do they provide insight into understanding American politics today? Political scientists define realignment in different ways, but they are all influenced by the seminal writings of V. O. Key, Jr., who began by developing a theory of "critical" elections in which "new and durable electoral groupings are formed." [7] Elections like that of 1860, in which Lincoln's victory brought the Republicans to power; the election of 1896, in which McKinley's victory consolidated Republican dominance; and the 1932 election, which brought the Democrats under Roosevelt to power, are obvious choices for this label.

But Key later argued that realignments take place over a series of elections—a pattern he called "secular realignment." During these periods, "shifts in the partisan balance of power" occur.[8] In this view, the first Republican realignment might be seen as having begun in 1856, when the newly formed Republican party displaced the Whigs as the major competitor to the Democrats, and having been consolidated by Lincoln's reelection in 1864 and by Ulysses S. Grant's election in 1868. The realignment of the late nineteenth century may well have had its beginnings in 1892, a Democratic victory by Grover Cleveland in which the Populist party, headed by James B. Weaver, won 8.5 percent of the popular vote, won four states, and gained electoral votes in two others. The realignment may have been consolidated by McKinley's reelection against Bryan in 1900 and Theodore Roosevelt's victory in 1904. The New Deal realignment, forged by Franklin D. Roosevelt, may be seen as beginning in Herbert H. Hoover's 1928 triumph over Alfred E. Smith (the first Roman Catholic candidate to be nominated by the Democratic party). Although Smith was badly defeated, he carried two New England states, Massachusetts and Rhode Island, which later became among the most Democratic states in the nation.[9] As Key points out, the beginnings of a shift toward the Democrats can be seen in Smith's defeat.[10] The term New Deal was not coined until 1932. Yet the New Deal coalition was created not by the 1932 election but after it and was consolidated in Roosevelt's 1936 landslide over Landon and his 1940 defeat of Wendell Willkie.

Although scholars disagree about how long it takes to create a new partisan alignment, all agree that durability is an essential element of realignment. As James L. Sundquist writes, "Those who analyze alignment and realignment are probing beneath the immediate and transitory ups and downs of daily politics and periodic elections to discover fundamental shifts in the structure of the party system." According to Lawrence G. McMichael and Richard J. Trilling, a realignment is "a significant and durable change in the distribution of party support over relevant groups within the electorate." [11]

Past partisan realignments in the United States have had five basic characteristics. First, past party realignments have always involved changes in the regional bases of party support. Between 1852 and 1860, for example, the Republican party replaced the Whigs. In all of the elections between 1836 (when the Whigs first opposed Democrat Martin Van Buren) and 1852, the Whigs drew at least some of their electoral support from the slave states. The last Whig candidate to be elected, Zachary Taylor in 1848, won 72 of his 163 electoral votes from the fifteen slave states.[12] In his 1860 victory, Lincoln did not win a single electoral vote from the slave states, and in twelve of them the Republican party did not even compete. But Lincoln won all of the electors in seventeen of the eighteen free states, as well as a majority of the electoral votes in New Jersey. Subsequent realignments do not reveal this degree of regional polarization, but they all display regional shifts in party support.

Second, past party realignments appear to have involved changes in the social group bases of party support. Even during a period when a party becomes dominant, some social groups may be moving to the losing party. During the 1930s, for example, Roosevelt gained the support of industrial workers, but at the same time he lost support among business owners and professionals, who were moving toward the Republican party.

Third, past realignments have been characterized by the mobilization of new groups into the electorate. Between Calvin Coolidge's Republican landslide in 1924 and Roosevelt's third-term victory in 1940, turnout rose from 44 percent to 59 percent, a 15 percentage point increase. Although there were long-term forces pushing turnout upward, the sharp increase in voting between 1924 and 1928, and again between 1932 and 1936, resulted at least partly from the mobilization of new social groups. Ethnic groups that were predominantly Catholic were mobilized to support Smith in 1928, and industrial workers were mobilized to support Roosevelt in 1936.

Fourth, past realignments have occurred when new issues divided the electorate. The most obvious example is the emergence of the Republican party, which reformulated the controversy over slavery to form a winning coalition. By opposing the extension of slavery into the territories, Republicans divided the Democratic party. Northern Democrats, such as Stephen A. Douglas, were forced to concede that territorial legislatures could ban slavery, a position unacceptable to most southern Democrats. No issue since slavery has divided America as deeply, but subsequent realignments have always been based upon the division of the electorate over issues.

Last, most political scientists argue that partisan realignments occur when voters change not just their voting patterns but the way they think about the political parties. For example, in 1932 many voters who thought of themselves as Republicans may have voted against Hoover. Many of these voters returned to the Republican side in subsequent elections, but others began to think of themselves as Democrats. Likewise, in 1936 some voters who thought of themselves as Democrats may have voted against Roosevelt's policies. Some of these Democrats returned to the Democratic fold during subsequent elections, but others began to think of themselves as Republicans.

During the three Republican victories of the 1980s, some of these changes occurred. As we will see, there were shifts in the regional bases of party support and there were changes in the distribution of partisan loyalties among the electorate. There were further shifts among some social groups (especially southern whites) away from the Democratic party, and some argued that the Republicans were establishing a winning position on issues that gained votes in presidential elections. Despite these changes, however, the Republicans never emerged as the majority party among the electorate, although they came close to parity with the Democrats in the mid-1980s. Moreover, even though the Republicans gained control of the U.S. Senate between 1981 and 1987, they never came close to winning a majority in the U.S. House of Representatives. Clearly, if there was a realignment, it was incomplete, leading some scholars to speculate about the possibilities of a "split-level realignment," a pattern in which the Republicans became dominant in presidential elections while the Democratic dominance of the House of Representatives remained intact.[13]

Clinton's Democratic victory calls into serious question any thesis that a pro-Republican realignment has occurred. At the same time, Clinton's popular vote minority provides little comfort for the Democrats. And the large vote for Perot raises the prospects of a breakdown in the traditional party system. Thus, the term *dealignment,* introduced by Ronald Inglehart and Avram Hochstein in 1972, may provide a better description of current political realities. A dealignment is a condition in which old voting patterns break down without being replaced by new ones. Most scholars who use this term stress the weakening of party loyalties as a key component. As Russell J. Dalton, Paul Allen Beck, and Scott C. Flanagan point out, dealignment was originally viewed as a preliminary stage leading to a new partisan realignment. But, they argue, dealignment "may be a regular feature of electoral politics."[14]

As Dalton and Martin P. Wattenberg have written, "Whereas realignment involves people changing from one party to another, dealignment concerns people gradually moving away from all parties." Moreover, this pattern may pose dangers to democratic political stability. "Many scholars," Dalton and Wattenberg write, "express concern about potential dealignment trends because they fear the loss of the stabilizing, conserving equilibrium that party attachments provide to electoral systems." [15] Wattenberg argues that American presidential elections have become increasingly centered upon political candidates rather than parties. The large Perot vote, Dalton and Wattenberg argue, may well have come largely from voters who have few feelings—either positive or negative—toward the Republican and Democratic parties.[16]

Some scholars have argued that American politics has reached a new era that makes the entire concept of partisan realignment meaningless.[17] We disagree. As Walter Dean Burnham demonstrates, there are serious problems with these critiques, and studying realignment can still lead to important insights about American electoral change.[18] We believe that discarding the concept of realignment would be costly because realignment theories are valuable in making comparisons of the present with the past.

In fact, few scholars see any more than the potential for a reassertion of Democratic dominance in the 1992 election results. As Gerald M. Pomper writes, "There is no party realignment evident in the election, but there is an opportunity to consolidate Democratic gains and to move beyond their 1992 electoral minority.... The Perot vote clearly underlines voters' willingness to abandon partisan loyalties and receptivity to new appeals." [19] As the Democrats regained the White House by revitalizing at least some elements of the old New Deal coalition, Donald E. Stokes and John L. DiIulio, Jr., write that "it is therefore tempting to say that the Roosevelt alignment is still intact, although very old and very weak." Clearly, they write, no new alignment has replaced it. "In the absence of such a realignment, it is probably more accurate to say that we are experiencing a long period of *de*alignment." [20]

On the other hand, Guy Molyneux and William Schneider see prospects for a new alignment. "The failure of one party only opens the door to realignment," they write. "To establish a new majority, a party must succeed in governing." A great deal, they argue, depends on Perot voters, as the large Perot vote, they argue, signals the end of a Republican presidential majority that was born in 1968 and died in 1992. "That majority," they write, "has now collapsed.... To replace it, the Democrats can't simply revive the old Roosevelt coalition. They have to build something genuinely new." [21] And in their provocative book on the 1992 elections, James Ceaser and Andrew Busch argue that a new dimension—an "inside-outside" division between those in Washington and those outside—has emerged to overlap with traditional dimensions of political cleavage. They maintain that a large floating vote destabilizes any alignment in modern American politics. Although they argue that economic conditions were important in weakening Bush, they also contend that the end of the cold war helped to undermine Republican electoral dominance.[22]

Raising questions about prospects for alignment and dealignment leads to four basic questions that we will ask throughout our book. What happened to Republican presidential dominance? Did it end mainly because the electorate judged Bush a failure, or did the Republican coalition also contain conflicting components that contributed to his defeat? Can the winning coalition of the 1980s be restored?

Second, what are the prospects for the Democrats to build a presidential majority? Was Clinton's victory something genuinely new, or did his coalition resemble that of past Democratic winners? Was Clinton's win based upon his appeals on newly emerging issues, or was his victory largely a negative judgment about Bush?

Third, what does the large Perot vote signify? Why did Perot draw such impressive support, and what are Perot voters likely to do in future elections? Given that Clinton won only 43 percent of the vote, it will be difficult for him to win a two-person race in 1996 unless he wins nearly half of the 1992 Perot voters.[23] And as the Republicans won only 37 percent of the popular vote, they may need to win more than half of the 1992 Perot voters to regain the presidency. And we cannot discount the possibility that Perot himself will run again in 1996.

Last, why have the Democrats continued to dominate in congressional elections? The Democrats have now won the U.S. House of Representatives in twenty consecutive elections, by far the longest period of one-party dominance in U.S. history.[24] What is the basis for Democratic dominance in congressional elections, a dominance they maintained in 1992 despite reapportionment and redistricting that might have brought more substantial Republican gains?[25]

Survey Research Sampling

Our book relies heavily upon surveys of the American electorate. It draws upon telephone polls held during the election year, an exit poll conducted outside voting stations by Voter Research and Surveys, and interviews conducted in respondents' households by the Gallup Organization, the National Opinion Research Center, and the U.S. Bureau of the Census. But we rely for the most part upon nationwide interviews conducted mainly in respondents' households during the two months before and the two months after the 1992 election by the Survey Research Center and the Center for Political Studies (SRC-CPS) of the University of Michigan. The SRC has been conducting surveys of the American electorate in every presidential election since 1948, and of every midterm election since 1954; these surveys are generally known as the National Election Studies (NES). We are able to use the NES surveys to study the entire postwar period. Since 1952 the NES surveys have measured party identification and feelings of political efficacy. The CPS, founded in 1970, has developed valuable questions for measuring issue preferences. The NES data are the best and most comprehensive source of information about political attitudes and partisan loyalties of the American electorate.

Readers may question our reliance on the NES survey of 2,487 Americans, when there are some 178 million Americans of voting age.[26] Would we have obtained similar results if all adults had been surveyed?[27] The NES surveys use a procedure called multistage probability sampling to select the particular individuals to be interviewed. These procedures ensure that the final sample is very likely to represent the entire U.S. adult citizen population (except for Americans living in institutions, on military bases, or abroad).[28]

Given the probability procedures used to conduct the NES surveys, we are able to assess the likelihood that the results represent the entire U.S. resident citizen population. The 1992 survey sampled only about one American adult in 70,000, but, provided that the sample is drawn properly, the representativeness of a sample depends far more on the size of the sample than on the size of the population being sampled. For most purposes, samples of 1,500 are adequate to study the electorate. With a sample of this size, we can be fairly confident (confident to a level of .95) that the results we obtain fall within 3 percentage points of the results we would get if the entire adult population had been surveyed.[29] For example, when we find that 64 percent of the NES respondents named an economic problem as the most important problem facing the country, we can be fairly confident that between 61 percent (64-3) and 67 percent (64+3) of the entire electorate considered an economic problem to be most important. The actual result for the electorate could be less than 61 percent or more than 67 percent. But a confidence level of .95 means that the odds are 19 to 1 that the entire electorate falls within this range.

The range of confidence becomes wider when we look at subgroups of the electorate. When we examine groups of 500 respondents, the range of confidence grows to ±6 percentage points. Because the likelihood of error grows as our subsamples become smaller, we often supplement our analysis with reports of other surveys.

Somewhat more complicated procedures are necessary to determine whether the difference between groups is likely to reflect the relationship that would obtain if the entire population were surveyed. The probability that such differences reflect real differences in the total population is largely a function of the sample size of the groups being compared.[30] Generally speaking, when we compare the results based upon the entire 1992 NES survey with an earlier NES survey, a difference of 4 percentage points is sufficient to be reasonably confident that the differences are real. For example, in 1980, 56 percent of the electorate named an economic problem as the most important problem facing the country; as we saw in 1992, 64 percent did—an 8 percentage point difference. As this difference is greater than 4 points, we can be reasonably confident that the electorate was more likely to be most concerned about an economic problem in 1992.

When we compare subgroups of the electorate sampled in 1992 (or subgroups sampled in 1992 with subgroups sampled in earlier surveys), a larger percentage point difference is necessary for us to be reasonably confident that differences did not result from chance. For example, when we compare men with women a difference of about 6 points is necessary. When we compare blacks with whites, a difference of about 9 points is necessary, since only about 200 African-Americans are sampled in most NES surveys.

These numbers provide only a quick ballpark estimate of the chance that the reported results are likely to represent the entire population. Better estimates can be obtained by using formulas presented in many statistics textbooks. To make such calculations or even a ballpark estimate of the chance of error, the reader must know the size of the groups being compared. For this reason, we always report in our tables and figures either the number of cases upon which our results are based or the information necessary to approximate the number of cases.[31]

The 1992 Contest

Part 1 of our book follows the chronology of the campaign itself. We begin with the struggle to gain the Republican and Democratic presidential nominations. In 1992, for the first time since 1980, an incumbent president faced a challenge to gain his party's nomination. On the Democratic side, six major candidates sought the nomination.

Chapter 1 analyzes the nomination contests for both parties. First, we examine who chose to run, with the goal of understanding the regularities that govern presidential nomination contests. As we shall see, 1992 was unusual because many who were seen as the strongest potential Democratic candidates chose not to run. We examine the rules for selecting delegates—the 1992 Democratic rules might have made it more difficult for a single winner to emerge before the convention. We discuss Bush's nomination victory: although his nomination was never in doubt, his inept response to Pat Buchanan's challenge helped lay the groundwork for his general election defeat. We shall see how Clinton, through a combination of skill and luck, achieved his nomination victory well before the Democratic convention met to ratify his candidacy.

We examine the selection of the vice-presidential running mates and shall see why Bush chose to retain Dan Quayle on the ticket, despite evidence that Quayle was an electoral liability. And we analyze Clinton's choice of Sen. Al Gore of Tennessee: 1992 was the first time a presidential candidate chose a running mate from a neighboring state since Harry S Truman of Missouri ran with Alben W. Barkley of Kentucky in the 1948 election. We discuss the "noncandidacy" of H. Ross Perot and see how his presence as a potential candidate influenced the strategies of the major party contenders.

In Chapter 1 we pay particular attention to the party nominating conventions, for although they played no role in actually selecting the presidential and vice-presidential candidates, they were important in setting the tone for the general election campaign. The high level of unity at the Democratic convention aided Clinton's general election campaign, and Perot's declaration that he would not be a candidate, made hours before Clinton's acceptance speech to the Democratic convention, further aided Clinton. On the other hand, the "family values" theme of the Republican convention, along with a strong emphasis on religious values, may have weakened Bush's prospects for winning the general election.

Having won their party's nomination, Bush and Clinton faced the task of gaining the 270 electoral votes needed to win the general election. In Chapter 2, we look at the strategies of both candidates. Bush began the general election campaign trailing in the polls, just as he had four years earlier in his successful run against Michael S. Dukakis. But in 1988, Bush was a sitting vice president running mainly on Reagan's record. His attacks on Dukakis proved highly successful, partly because Dukakis's response was inept. In 1992, Bush had his own record to defend, and although he had many foreign policy successes, the public perceived Bush to have done little to improve economic conditions during a prolonged economic downturn. Clinton's campaign team had learned from Dukakis's mistakes; and they were quick to respond to Bush's negative attacks while stressing the need to improve the economy. Moreover, unlike Dukakis, Clinton developed a well-coordinated strategy designed to win a majority of the 538 electoral votes.

The general election campaign took a dramatic new turn with Perot's decision to reenter the presidential race. Perhaps because he participated in the three presidential debates, he achieved considerable legitimacy. We examine how both Bush and Clinton responded to the Perot challenge, and we also discuss Perot's unconventional campaign. We follow the race to the finish line between the last presidential debate and election day, and see how neither Bush's strategies nor the Perot candidacy could derail Clinton's general election victory. Last, we attempt to assess whether the general election campaign mattered, and we discuss how the new use of the mass media by all three candidates (especially Perot) may alter future general election campaigns.

Chapter 3 presents and interprets the election results. We first discuss the election rules and see how the electoral college system transformed Clinton's 43 percent of the popular vote into 69 percent of the electoral vote. We examine the overall pattern of results, showing how a pattern of Republican presidential dominance ended, at least temporarily. Because states are the building blocks upon which electoral vote majorities are based, the results are discussed state by state. We pay particular attention to electoral change in the South, because in the past half-century the South has been transformed from the most solidly Democratic region into the most Republican region in presidential elections. And we discuss what happened to the Republican electoral vote base and ask whether there ever was a Republican electoral vote advantage, let alone a Republican "lock" on the electoral vote. Although the Republicans may gain a slight advantage from the electoral college system, presidential elections are, increasingly, national contests. The present balance of political forces among the states reveals problems and opportunities for both of the major parties. The potential Republican realignment of the 1980s may have dissolved, but no clear pattern has replaced it.

Chapter 1

The Nomination Struggle

Operation Desert Storm, a military mission fought by an impressive alliance of forces nominally under United Nations leadership but practically under the leadership of the United States, was breathtakingly successful. After thirty-eight days of aerial bombardment, the allied forces launched a ground war that lasted one hundred hours. The allied forces overwhelmed a surprisingly ineffective, dispirited, and uncoordinated Iraqi army, forcing it out of Kuwait and back inside its own borders. American soldiers came home to a patriotic blitz of parades and welcomes unseen since the end of World War II. As commander in chief, President George Bush rode a wave of popularity; his approval ratings in the public reached record highs, touching 86 percent in early March 1991.[1] With the 1992 presidential primaries only a year away, his bid for renomination and reelection appeared secure. On the domestic side, the economy soured. Bush and his closest advisers believed that his foreign policy triumph would enable him to ride out the economic downturn, which they thought would be relatively slight and short-lived.

As the 1992 presidential campaign neared, Bush's popularity left the Democrats in disarray. Some strong potential contenders, such as Sen. Sam Nunn (Ga.), who had opposed the use of force in the Gulf, might reasonably have feared that the remarkable victory might affect their chances of nomination, let alone election, severely. Others who might make strong candidates looked at the polls and concluded that Bush's popularity was sufficiently high that it was better to wait for a more opportune time to run for the presidency. Gov. Mario M. Cuomo (N.Y.), whom some saw as the best chance for a Democratic victory, refused to declare his candidacy, although he also refused to end speculation that he might run.[2] In addition, the Reverend Jesse Jackson, Jr., who had run in 1984 and 1988, did not announce his candidacy, joining such other prominent "noncandidates" as Rep. Richard A. Gephardt (Mo.) and Sen. Al Gore (Tenn.), both of whom had run in 1988, and Sen. John D. "Jay" Rockefeller (W. Va.) who had been prominently mentioned as a possible candidate.[3] By late summer, it had begun to look as if no serious Democratic aspirant would run.

The economic downturn, however, proved to be neither slight nor short-lived. As national attention turned from the glow of victory in the Gulf to the pain of increasingly severe economic conditions, Bush's popularity fell, although even by the middle of October 1991, most polls registered approval ratings above 60 percent.[4] In time, not only would six Democrats begin the battle for their party's presidential nomination, but so, too, would opposition begin within the Republican party. Initial Republican attacks were launched not at the president but at his vice president, Dan Quayle. Often the butt of jokes over verbal gaffes, he was seen by some as a continuing liability. Bush, however, ended speculation among Republicans and pundits by announcing that the vice president would remain on the ticket. One virtue Quayle brought to the ticket was the support of hard-line conservatives who had never been comfortable with Bush, in place of Reagan, as their alleged champion. On the extreme far right, David Duke, a former member of the Ku Klux Klan and Nazi sympathizer, was a state representative from Louisiana. After his loss in a runoff election for governor on November 16, 1991, he threatened to challenge Bush for the nomination, but his campaign never really got started. Pat Buchanan's did. As a Republican speechwriter in the late 1960s and early 1970s, Buchanan coined some of the most famous lines for then Vice President Spiro T. Agnew. He went on to become a popular, if acerbic, newspaper columnist and television commentator. As a representative of the hard-line conservatives, he decided to give voice to their (and his) concerns and challenge Bush for president.

On the other side, the economic downturn helped invigorate the Democrats. So, too, did the surprising victory in the November 1991 special election for U.S. senator from Pennsylvania of Harris Wofford, who defeated Richard Thornburgh, a former attorney general in the Bush administration, by focusing his campaign on health care reform. (Sen. John Heinz had died in a plane crash that May.) As Bush appeared increasingly vulnerable (although the vulnerability was only relative to the apparent invincibility of only a few months earlier), the six-man field of Democratic contenders took shape. Former senator Paul Tsongas (Mass.) declared first. Having left the Senate in 1984 to fight cancer, his apparently successful battle left him eager to send the party and nation a message, at least, if not to win nomination outright. Former California governor Jerry Brown was a veteran of the 1976 and 1980 presidential nomination races who launched a campaign to contest against politics—and politicians—as usual. Gov. L. Douglas Wilder of Virginia became the third African-American candidate for the Democratic presidential nomination.[5] Unlike Jackson, he was a mainstream Democrat, but his campaign became mired in a political battle with Sen. Charles S. Robb in his home state, and he left the race in January 1992, before the campaign began in earnest. Sen. Tom Harkin (Iowa) ran as the closest to a traditional New Deal Democrat as any left in the party. Sen. Bob Kerrey (Neb.), who had previously served as governor, was a Congressional Medal of Honor winner who had been wounded in Vietnam. Both Harkin and Kerrey had voted against the authorization to use force against Iraq, as had all but ten of the fifty-five Democrats in the Senate. Last, there was the young but experienced governor of Arkansas and former Rhodes Scholar, Bill Clinton. *Newsweek*'s postelection reprise called them "six guys named Moe,"[6] unknowns, but these candidates all held, or had held, high elective office. Even so, many commentators concluded that the Democrats were not fielding their strongest candidates.

Four years earlier, the seven Democratic candidates had been called the "seven dwarfs." In 1992, just as four years earlier, these faceless candidates became recognized by the public as the media turned to cover the nominations. Unfortunately for Bush, Buchanan gained recognition, too. The result was that the 1992 nomination races turned out to be fascinating, dramatic, and at times even lurid.

Actually, with the possible exception of the surprisingly strong, if short-lived, showing of Buchanan, the 1992 nomination campaigns looked in many ways like their predecessors stretching back at least to 1972. The 1972 campaigns were the first nominations in what can be called the new nomination system, that is, the system in which nominations are dominated by campaigning for public support in a large number of primary campaigns spread over a four- or five-month period. Six party campaigns in this period were run without an incumbent seeking nomination. Each attracted a relatively large field of credentialed candidates. Each had seemed as if it could end without an outright nomination winner before the national nominating convention, but in fact, each—including 1992—ended with one candidate vanquishing all others before the convention opened. Four earlier contests featured an incumbent president who sought nomination. Each attracted a very small field of opponents to the president, if any. The incumbent won nomination each time, although in two (the 1976 Republican race between Gerald R. Ford and Ronald Reagan and the 1980 Democratic race between Jimmy Carter and Sen. Edward M. Kennedy), the races were long, difficult, and ultimately not decided until late in the season. Bush won renomination much as Richard M. Nixon had in 1972, facing what would prove to be relatively inconsequential opposition. In Bush's case, however, failure to recognize even the limited potential of Buchanan made the campaign last longer than it might otherwise have and set the stage for mistakes at the national nominating convention that may have cost Bush dearly in the fall.

The regular patterns to presidential nominations are, as we will show, not coincidental. The new nomination system imposes regularities, and we examine them carefully in the rest of this chapter. And yet, as we shall also see, each campaign has its own unique characteristics, such as the nature of the individual candidates and their appeals. In 1992, the candidates proved to be inventive in the techniques they used to appeal to the public, and the campaigns and their coverage in the media focused more (although not exclusively) on the substance of the campaign themes than, it seems, had been true during other recent nomination contests. We turn next to examine the first step of the nomination process, the decision of politicians to become—or not to become—presidential candidates. Then we examine the rules of the nomination system they face. We next consider how the candidates ran and why Bush and, especially, Clinton succeeded in their quests. Finally, we examine the first part of the independent candidacy of H. Ross Perot for president, his withdrawal on the eve of Clinton's acceptance speech, and the events at and impact of the two parties' national conventions.

Who Ran

We have already named the six Democrats and two Republicans who were running for presidential nomination as the new year began. These eight were the "serious" contenders. Many others declared themselves to be candidates. Some of these, including Larry Agrin, the Democratic mayor of Irvine, California, were able to attract modest media attention, but mostly as side pieces to stories about the two main partisan competitions. The eight major candidates were, as a set, very similar to the sets of serious contenders for prior presidential nominations under the new nomination system.

First, three of the eight candidates, Brown, Buchanan, and Tsongas, were not in office during the nomination campaign. Even discounting Buchanan, who had never held elective office, over one-quarter of the candidates were not in office (one-third if we count from the date of the first primary, since Wilder had withdrawn in January 1992). Under the new nomination system, anywhere from one-quarter to one-half of the candidates have been out of elective office at the time of their campaign. In 1988, for example, six of fourteen candidates were not in office during the campaign. The reason is simply that the demands of the contemporary presidential nomination campaign are very difficult to balance with the demands of high elective office. Indeed, some past contenders (for example, Sen. Gary Hart [D-Colo.] in 1986) chose not to run for reelection to make a presidential candidacy more feasible.

For much the same reason, there is a second similarity between these contenders and those of the recent past. None was up for reelection to a current office in 1992 except President Bush. Not only would the demands on time, energy, and resources be thereby stretched even further by two campaigns, but such candidates might eventually be forced to choose between the relatively high probability of winning reelection to a current office and the much longer odds of winning their party's presidential nomination and then the general election.

A third and even more important regularity is that all but Buchanan held or had recently held a high elective office. In 1992, the fields included one president, two current senators (one of whom had also served as governor), and two current governors. The other two candidates were a former senator and a former governor. Ambition theory, developed originally by Joseph A. Schlesinger to explain how personal ambition and the pattern and prestige of offices combine to shape political careers, predicts that those who run for office will tend to emerge from political offices that provide the strongest electoral base for such a campaign.[7] This base for the presidency includes the offices of vice president, senator, governor, and, of course, the presidency itself.

The regularity with which candidates emerge from offices with strong electoral bases is shown in Table 1-1. The distribution of backgrounds of the candidates of 1992 is very similar to that of all candidates for presidential nomination over the 1972-1992 period. In short, all but one of the candidates came from offices that provide a strong electoral base. Moreover, about three in ten were no longer in office, just as in 1992. Of those, the great majority had left office in favorable political circumstances, and most were not also up for reelection to their current office as they ran for president.[8]

Overall, then, the fields of candidates for the 1992 presidential nominations resembled in most respects those of the other campaigns in the new nomination system. Even if few other than Bush were household names, all, with the exception of Buchanan, came to the campaign with the kind of presidential resume one expects of serious contenders for this office. Having decided to run, these aspirants faced a complex web of rules and procedures defining the presidential nomination system. These rules greatly shape and constrain the strategic choices any presidential candidate faces.

The Rules

Two major sets of rules govern presidential nomination campaigns, and both underwent important changes between 1968 and 1972. These

Table 1-1   Current or Most Recent Office Held by Declared Candidates for President: Two Major Parties, 1972-1992

Office held [a]	Percentage of all candidates holding that office	Number 1972-1992	Number 1992
President	7%	5	1
Vice president	3	2	0
U.S. senator	40	28	3
U.S. representative	13	9	0
Governor	24	17	3
U.S. cabinet	3	2	0
Other	4	3	0
None	6	4	1
Total	100%	70	8

Sources: The list of candidates between 1972 and 1984 is found in *Congressional Quarterly's Guide to U.S. Elections*, 2d ed. (Washington, D.C.: Congressional Quarterly Inc., 1985), 376. The 1988 candidates are listed in Paul R. Abramson, John H. Aldrich, and David W. Rohde, *Change and Continuity in the 1988 Elections*, rev. ed., (Washington: CQ Press, 1991), 13-14.

[a] Office held at time of candidacy or office held most recently prior to candidacy.

rules regulate the way delegates are selected to attend the national conventions and how money is raised and allocated in presidential contests. After 1972, these rules were modified further. The basic shape of the rules governing nominations, however, remains intact, and thus we can speak of nominations as under a new system that began in 1972.

Delegate Selection Rules

Since 1832 no person has been elected president without first having been chosen by the votes of delegates at the national nominating conventions.[9] In principle, delegates can nominate anyone they want. In reality, they have rarely been that free. Most delegates these days are chosen by competition among presidential contenders in the states' primaries or caucuses. The candidates, in other words, campaign to get the public to select delegates who back them.

National convention delegates are chosen by the states' parties in one of two ways. One method is the primary election. A primary is an official election held by the state, in which voters choose which presidential candidate's delegates attend the national convention. Since these are run by the state, if a state holds a primary, it usually holds primaries for both political parties.[10] Especially in the larger states, then, presidential candidates campaign for popular support in much the same way as they do in the general election, by direct appeal to the public through often expensive and extensive media campaigns.

Other states use the caucus method for choosing delegates. Caucuses are elections run by political parties, and there is a great deal of variation from state to state. Although caucus procedures are often very complex, the most important action usually happens in the very first step, often at the precinct level. A precinct caucus is a meeting of those partisans who live in the precinct and are interested enough to attend. At the caucus, partisans declare their preference among presidential candidates. In the Democratic party at least, delegates who back the various presidential candidates are then chosen to attend the county, then district, then state, and finally national conventions in proportion to the presidential preferences of those at the precinct caucuses. Thus, at least in the Democratic party, the caucus is like a primary in that all Democrats in the state can go to the caucus and declare a preference for the presidential candidate of their choice, and delegates, when finally chosen, must reflect the results of that "vote." [11] However, caucuses differ from primaries in one crucial respect. Very few people attend caucuses. Turnout of 5 to 10 percent is unusually high. One reason for this low turnout is that participants must learn when and where caucuses are held, and they may have to learn the rules governing the caucus proceedings to participate effectively. Therefore, the costs of learning about the rules and the candidates are often significantly higher for caucus participants than for primary voters. In many cases, even precinct caucus meetings perform a great deal of party business, in addition to considering presidential candidates, so that caucus meetings can be lengthy. Moreover, there are many further steps and meetings required before one's expressed presidential preferences at precinct caucuses are translated into the actual selection of delegates to the national conventions, all of which are quite unlike the relatively short and simple act of voting in a presidential primary. As a result, the overall costs of caucus participation are often far higher than those of primary election participation.

Lower participation rates mean that, although candidates might run an electionlike campaign in a caucus state, the important thing is to find the candidate's supporters and get them to attend the caucus. Success in caucuses, therefore, often turns little on general popularity, media campaigning, and advertising and much more on a strong, well-financed campaign organization. Many attributed the Reverend Pat Robertson's strong second place finish in the Iowa Republican caucuses and the Reverend Jesse Jackson's victory in the Michigan Democratic caucuses in 1988, for example, to their strong state organizations rather than to their overall popularity in the electorate in those states.

There is one more crucial fact about delegate selection. It is a months-long process, although the national Democratic party has tried to shorten it. In 1992 the season began on February 10 and ended on June 2.[12] As a result, candidates can hope to use success in one primary or caucus to generate enthusiasm, media coverage, and, the candidate hopes, greater popular support in a later state's primary or caucus. The result is a long, rapidly changing, and some would say chaotic campaign. Whatever the case, it is a campaign run by the candidates through the media to obtain grass-roots support. The party and its leadership play a small role in the selection of a standard bearer. This public campaign makes the United States unusual. In most other democracies, party leaders play a much greater role in choosing the nominees. How did it happen that our party leaders play such a small role—and the public such a large role—in choosing nominees?

The basic shape of the Democratic delegate selection reforms was created in reaction to the tumultuous nomination campaign in 1968. In that year, Sens. Eugene J. McCarthy (Minn.) and Robert F. Kennedy (N.Y.) ran public, primary-oriented campaigns. Before the second primary, in Wisconsin, President Lyndon B. Johnson surprisingly announced that he would not seek renomination. Vice President Hubert H. Humphrey took his place as a candidate. Humphrey, however, made no *public* campaign, winning nomination without entering a primary. The controversial nomination split the Democratic party and led it to initiate reforms, including those designed to open the nomination process to more diverse candidacies and to more public participation.

The most obvious consequence of these reforms was the rapid increase in the use of primaries to select delegates. In 1968, seventeen states held Democratic presidential primaries. That figure jumped to twenty-three in 1972, climbed to thirty in 1976, and was thirty-one in 1980. In 1984, several states abandoned primaries and chose their delegates by party caucuses, and there were only twenty-five Democratic primaries used to selected delegates. In 1988, there was a return to the primary. Thirty-three states used primaries to select delegates to the Democratic party convention, and thirty-five states held such primaries on the Republican side. In 1992, thirty-five states (including Texas, which held a primary and a caucus) held primaries on the Democratic side, while thirty-eight did on the Republican side, selecting about two-thirds and three-quarters of all delegates, respectively.[13] Most delegates not selected in primaries have been chosen by caucuses. However, reforms have succeeded in making caucuses more open to public participation—more timely, better publicized, and, in short, more primarylike. Since 1976, for example, the Iowa caucuses have been the first delegate-selection proceedings in the nation. As such, they have become as widely covered in the media and as hotly contested and important to the candidates as any primary, although this was not true in 1992. With Harkin as a favorite son and with Buchanan needing organizational resources unavailable to him that early, neither parties' candidates contested the Iowa caucuses in 1992. As a result, the action began in earnest in the New Hampshire primary on February 18.

The important point in these changes has been the greater role played by the public. No candidate can avoid a public campaign. Indeed, the eventual nominees in all campaigns have won *because* they won in the primaries and caucuses. Moreover, candidates discovered not only that they needed to win in the primary season, but also that they could use early primary and caucus events as a launching pad toward prominence, resources, and victory, gathering, in the favored catchword, momentum.[14]

These reforms, and the nomination system they created, have been controversial. The most controversial result has been to move the locus of nomination power from the party leadership to the general public. Indeed, the proportion of elected and appointed party leaders who were even able to win seats at the convention declined massively in the Democratic party in 1972.[15] In order to bring party leaders back into the selection process, the Democratic party created the "superdelegate" seats, reserved for party and elected leaders, for the 1984 convention. In 1984 and 1988, about one in seven Democratic delegates was a superdelegate, and in 1992 that number grew to about one in five. Moreover, superdelegates were free to vote for whomever they chose, unbound by popular sentiment expressed in primaries, caucuses, or public opinion polls. In 1984, these superdelegates played a critical role in the nomination campaign of former vice president Walter F. Mondale, transforming a slim lead over Hart in delegates won in primaries and caucuses into a clear victory in total delegate support.[16]

The changes discussed so far have been initiated primarily by the Democratic party. The Republican party's nomination procedures have been revised by the party over this period, generally in a direction consistent with the Democratic party reforms. The Republican reforms, however, have been less extensive. For example, they did not create superdelegates, largely because their elected and party officials were strongly represented at the convention without needing to mandate their presence. Their campaign process closely resembles the Democratic one, therefore, in part because they have followed Democratic reform initiatives and in part because primaries are the product of state legislation. If a state decides to establish a primary, it will generally hold primaries for both parties.

In 1972, the largest number of delegates to be won on a single day was in June, at the end of the primary season. Over time, more and more states chose to schedule their primaries earlier in the season, a phenomenon called front loading. By 1988, sixteen states, many of them in the South, held their primaries on the same day, two weeks after the first primary in New Hampshire.[17] That day (March 13, 1988) was called

Super Tuesday, because more delegates were selected on that day than on any other.[18] In 1992, the concentration on a single date was reduced, but front loading actually increased. Seven states held their Democratic primary or caucuses on March 3, five more did so later that week, and eleven held theirs on March 10.[19] Of the fifty states and D.C., thirty-one held their primary or caucus in February or March, with the remaining twenty scattered over April, May, and early June.

The consequences of front loading of the delegate selection process are great for the candidates. The front loading of contests demands the front loading of resources. The candidate who begins the primary season with the most money on hand, the most developed campaign organizations nationally and in the various states, and the highest levels of name recognition, popular following, and media attention, is thereby greatly advantaged. As we noted earlier, the 1992 Democratic candidates were unusually late in declaring, and they began their quests with relatively little name recognition in the public. Clinton held the largest war chest and had the most developed campaign organization at the outset. This early base was to prove valuable to him. Tsongas, by contrast, was less able to capitalize on his surprisingly strong showing in the New Hampshire primary, because by the time he (and Buchanan on the other side) could take advantage of the resulting momentum, too many primaries and caucuses had already been held. Tsongas had to balance the competing demands of raising resources and winning votes in primaries and was unable to do both in the relatively brief time available.

Although the Democratic and Republican nomination procedures are similar in most respects, there are some differences. As we saw, the Democrats now set aside one-fifth of their seats for superdelegates, to ensure representation of party officials. The Republicans have traditionally selected party leaders as delegates, but the party does not have explicit rules that guarantee them seats. As we noted, there are usually a few states where the Republicans accept a state's primary procedures for selecting delegates, but where the Democratic party demands that the state party hold a caucus to select delegates.

The national Democratic party has refused to certify a state's primary as a valid method for selecting delegates when there is no procedure to prevent Republicans from easily voting in the Democratic primary (or Democrats from easily voting in the Republican primary). The Republicans accept these "open" primaries. Although a Democratic primary may still be held in such states, the results do not affect the selection of delegates, and their actual allocation is determined by Democratic caucuses.

The Democratic rules differ from the Republican procedures in another major respect. From 1976 on, the Democrats have refused to accept state rules in which the candidate who wins the most votes in a state primary or caucus automatically wins all of the state's delegates.[20] The Democrats require, instead, that all states follow some form of proportional representation in choosing convention delegates. Under pure proportional representation, a candidate's share of the delegates is the same as his or her share of the popular vote. In 1976, the party allowed states to use various procedures that gave the winner more than his or her proportionate share of the delegates. In 1980, the Democratic party banned these procedures, but in 1984 and 1988, it allowed the states to employ procedures to award successful candidates with more than their proportionate share of delegates. The Democratic party again banned such rules in 1992.

Most systems of proportional representation provide some threshold below which the candidate or party wins nothing. The lower the threshold, the greater the level of proportionality will be. In 1984, a Democratic candidate usually needed 20 percent of the vote in a state to win any delegates. Jackson's supporters argued that he was deprived of representation because the threshold was too high. Since then, the threshold has been 15 percent. Thus, in 1992, losing candidates could earn some delegates, as long as they won 15 percent of the popular vote. The Republicans, on the other hand, allow the popular vote winner to earn all the state's delegates. In such cases, of course, losing candidates wind up with no delegates at all. Buchanan, for example, won 23 percent of the total votes cast in Republican primaries, but he won only 4 percent of the delegates to the Republican convention. Brown, by contrast, won 21 percent of the total votes cast in Democratic primaries and won a much more proportionate 14 percent of the delegates to the Democratic convention, even though he received very little support among superdelegates.

Financial Rules

The 1970s also brought major changes in campaign financing procedures. The Federal Election Campaign Act of 1971 opened these reforms. The act was substantially amended in 1974 and 1976 and has been revised and interpreted in less important ways since then. In general, the major features of the reforms fall into three areas of immediate concern.[21]

First, individuals and groups (political action committees, or PACs) were severely limited in the contributions they could make to any campaign (to $1,000 per person and $5,000 per group). The old-style "fat cats" who gave thousands or even millions of dollars to a candidate were thereby cut off. Money would henceforth have to be raised in a massive, broad-based campaign, paralleling the candidates' broad-based campaign for votes.

Second, presidential nomination candidates could receive a dollar-for-dollar match of small ($250 or less), individual contributions, thus providing up to 50 percent of their campaign funding from federal coffers. While few receive anything close to half their funding from the government, the federal government has become a very important source of funds.

Third, presidential candidates who accept federal funding (as all major candidates for the two parties' nominations did in 1992) are subject to limits on what they can spend. In 1992, candidates could spend about $25 million on the primary season (plus some for fund-raising expenses). Moreover, there are limits to spending in each state. Because state limits add up to nearly three times the overall limit, candidates who raise the full amount of money have to plan carefully where to spend it.

Clearly, the candidates will spend the most in states crucial to their nomination prospects. The importance of early events, such as those in the New Hampshire and other early primaries, means that spending is often even more front loaded than delegate selection. In 1980, for example, the four leading candidates had spent three-quarters of the legal maximum before half the delegates were selected, and a similar pattern has held since then. Campaigns in Iowa and New Hampshire, both small states, required a disproportionate amount of money but still could be conducted on a "retail" basis (that is, by telephone and doorbell ringing, shaking hands at malls and factories, and so on). Larger states, or dates featuring several primaries—such as the March 3-10 period— mandate a "wholesale" campaign for votes, which looks much like the media-dominated general election campaign. There simply wasn't time to do otherwise.

The Campaigns

Bush's "Flawed" Triumph

George Bush was renominated without apparent difficulty. He won a clear majority of the vote in every primary (see Table 1-2), and he was assured a majority of convention delegates with his victories in the Indiana and North Carolina primaries on May 5.[22] Duke won only about 1 percent of the total votes cast in Republican primaries, and he won no delegates, although he did garner nearly 11 percent of the vote in Mississippi. Buchanan, not surprisingly, presented more formidable opposition. Overall, he accumulated slightly less than one-quarter of the Republican votes cast in the primary season, and seventy-eight (or 4 percent) of the delegates. He peaked early: his strongest showing was in the first primary, New Hampshire, in which he won 37 percent of the vote (to Bush's 53 percent). He consistently received one-fifth to one-quarter of the vote through the primaries in March, and then declined to a typical vote of about 15 percent.[23] Clearly, such vote totals, although they are impressive for an inexperienced candidate facing an incumbent president, fall well short of yielding anything like a serious run at the nomination.

As straightforward as Bush's march to victory was, in terms of votes and delegates garnered, the road to victory was bumpy. First, the president's apparent difficulty stemmed from the context of the nomination campaign. An incumbent president who had recently enjoyed very high approval ratings should be all but invulnerable, many believed, especially when his only serious opponent not only lacked a strong electoral base but had never before run for any elective office.

Second, the opposition to Bush came from the ideological and activist heart of the Republican party. A standard rule of thumb for assessing prospects for a general election campaign is that the candidate must begin with strong support within the party and then compete with the opposition party for independents and moderates who fall between the nominees ideologically. Competition within the party for nomination places the candidate's core support for the general election at risk. Perhaps more important, it places at risk the committed core of activists crucial for mobilizing the candidate's pool of potential voters in the fall. Reagan, for example, had won his elections by holding a very high percentage of support from identifiers with his party in the electorate, and by winning more than his fair share of independents and even those, the "Reagan Democrats," who identified (often weakly) with the opposition. He relied on the active and dedicated commitment of the various conservative movements that had risen to prominence in the 1970s and 1980s to help translate his popularity into votes. Movement conservatives were never sure that Bush was truly committed to their causes. Buchanan was very much the candidate of such movement conservatives, allowing them to express their uncertainty about Bush's commitment to their concerns and to "send him a message" by voting for Buchanan.

There was a third set of reasons that Bush's triumph appeared flawed. Bush (and his advisers) underestimated dissatisfaction in the nation in general; he underestimated dissatisfaction within his own party over his handling of domestic issues; he underestimated the extent and duration of the decline in the economy; he underestimated the ability of Buchanan to serve as focal point for expressing dissatisfaction; and he underestimated how long it would take him to set his campaign in motion once he began it. Of all of these problems, the most pressing was that he failed to begin his campaign until it was quite late. He used his State of the Union address, at the end of January 1992, to begin his campaign—only three weeks before the New Hampshire primary.

Buchanan used that delay to good effect, running for some time as virtually the only Republican candidate in New Hampshire. The structure of the primary calendar also played into Buchanan's hands. New

Table 1-2 Republican Primary Results, 1992

Date		State	Total Vote	Buchanan	Bush	Duke	Uncommitted	Other
Feb.	18	New Hampshire	174,165	65,087	92,233	—	—	16,845
	25	South Dakota	44,671	—	30,964	—	13,707	—
March	3	Colorado	195,690	58,753	132,100	—	—	4,837
	3	Georgia	453,990	162,085	291,905	—	—	—
	3	Maryland	240,021	71,647	168,374	—	—	—
	7	South Carolina	148,840	38,247	99,558	10,553	—	482
	10	Florida	893,463	285,386	608,077	—	—	—
	10	Louisiana	135,109	36,525	83,744	11,955	—	2,885
	10	Massachusetts	269,701	74,797	176,868	5,557	10,132	2,347
	10	Mississippi	154,708	25,891	111,794	16,426	—	597
	10	Oklahoma	217,721	57,933	151,612	5,672	—	2,504
	10	Rhode Island	15,636	4,967	9,853	326	444	46
	10	Tennessee	245,653	54,585	178,219	7,709	5,022	118
	10	Texas	797,146	190,572	556,280	20,255	27,936	2,103
	17	Illinois	831,140	186,915	634,588	—	23,809	9,637
	17	Michigan	449,133	112,122	301,948	10,688	23,809	566
	24	Connecticut	99,473	21,815	66,356	2,294	9,008	—
April	7	Kansas	213,196	31,494	132,131	3,837	35,450	10,284
	7	Minnesota	132,756	32,094	84,841	—	4,098	11,723[b]
	7	Wisconsin	482,248	78,516	364,507	12,867[a]	8,725	17,633
	28	Pennsylvania	1,008,777	233,912	774,865	—	—	—
May	5	Dist. of Col.	5,235	970	4,265	—	—	—
	5	Indiana	467,615	92,949	374,666	—	—	—
	5	North Carolina	283,571	55,420	200,387	—	27,764	—
	12	Nebraska	192,098	25,847	156,346	2,808	—	7,097
	12	West Virginia	124,157	18,067	99,994	—	—	6,096
	19	Oregon	304,159	57,730	203,957	6,667	—	35,805

19	Washington	129,655	13,273	86,839	1,501	—	28,042[b]
26	Arkansas	52,141	6,551	45,590	—	—	—
26	Idaho	115,502	15,167	73,297	—	27,038	—
26	Kentucky	101,119	—	75,371	—	25,748	—
June 2	Alabama	165,121	12,588	122,703	—	29,830	—
2	California	2,156,464	568,892	1,587,369	—	—	203
2	Montana	90,975	10,701	65,176	—	15,098	—
2	New Jersey	310,270	46,432	240,535	—	—	23,303[b]
2	New Mexico	86,967	7,871	55,522	—	23,574	—
2	Ohio	860,453	143,687	716,766	—	—	—
9	North Dakota	47,808	—	39,863	—	—	7,945[b]
	Total	12,696,547	2,899,488	9,199,463	119,115	287,383	191,098

[a] Duke withdrew from the race April 22.

[b] Write-in votes for Ross Perot totaled 2.7 percent of the Republican primary vote in Minnesota, 19.6 percent in Washington, 7.5 percent in New Jersey, and 8.1 percent in North Dakota.

— Indicates that the candidate or the uncommitted line was not listed on the ballot.

Source: Adapted from America Votes 20: A Handbook of Contemporary American Election Statistics, ed. Richard M. Scammon and Alice V. McGillivray (Washington, D.C.: Congressional Quarterly Inc., 1993), 52.

Hampshire voters have long been vehemently opposed to higher taxes, so that Bush's breaking of his 1988 campaign pledge, "Read my lips. No new taxes!" was especially costly among Republicans there. The state was also one of the most seriously affected by economic woes. Buchanan's campaign began eleven weeks before the primary. After a rocky start, he "found" his populist, economic message, and it began to work. Polls in the state that had Bush leading 64-14 dropped to 50-30 for the president by Christmas, and Buchanan would have another month to campaign alone.[24] This 20-point lead narrowed only slightly more, but the media interpreted—not implausibly—Bush's 53 to 37 percent win as a surprisingly strong showing for Buchanan (with Tsongas, winner of the Democratic primary, coming in third on the Republican side with nearly one vote in eleven).

The primary calendar continued to work to Buchanan's advantage, as the next few weeks' primaries would be concentrated primarily in the South. His "hot button," conservative issues message could effectively be added to his economic "doom-and-gloom" message, and the media attention accentuated his appeals. Yet his strong, if losing, effort in New Hampshire had its negative aspects. For one, it *did* get the president's attention, and Buchanan would be hotly contested and certainly never again be given the field alone. For another, media attention is not an undiluted positive. Attention was drawn to some of the negative sides to his campaign themes, and he was charged with racism and anti-semitism. After peaking at 32 percent in Florida and 36 percent in Georgia, Buchanan's popular support, even in the South, declined somewhat. Most of all, however, the inevitability of Bush's march to the nomination was clear, and Buchanan's campaign became ever more of a sidebar for the media. Because a Bush victory was certain, media attention focused first on the more competitive Democratic contest and, later, on Perot.

Clinton's Determination Pays Off

Bill Clinton began the campaign with a number of attributes that, while not necessarily visible to the public, would prove to serve him well. One was his dogged determination. He was first elected as Arkansas's governor in 1978 (having just turned thirty-two). His first term in office was unsuccessful, and he was defeated for reelection in 1980. He rethought his approach to politics, ran again in 1982, and served continuously as governor until his election to president. Along the way, he forged durable links with the state's legislature.

The governor's long experience in office acquainted him with state-level executives throughout the nation (for example, he was active in, and served as chair of, the National Governors' Association). Not only did many of these colleagues endorse his candidacy, but they helped him create the strongest campaign organization among the Democratic presidential contenders in 1992.[25] He had also played a major role in the Democratic Leadership Council, an organization of moderate Democrats who seek a more centrist position for the national Democratic party. One result of this long period of time in office and large number of contacts was that he was far more successful in attracting the support of superdelegates than his opponents, even before his chances for nomination became clear. His behind-the-scenes support is also illustrated by his having raised more money than any other Democratic candidate before the primary season. All of this helped build a base for organizing in virtually every state, and it helped smooth over the rough spots—and rough spots there were.

The lurid side of politics affected many candidates in 1992, but none more than "Slick Willie." That nickname, which originally referred to Clinton's apparent desire to be liked by everyone, became attached to what was more politely called Clinton's "character issue." He led in early polls in New Hampshire, but lost that lead to Tsongas when a series of allegations that reflected on his character surfaced in the media. Rumors of extramarital affairs bloomed with media coverage of allegations by Gennifer Flowers that she had had a long-running affair with Clinton. "Damage control" worked reasonably well, as Bill and Hillary Clinton appeared on CBS's "60 Minutes." Without admitting that he had had any affairs, the Clintons acknowledged that their marriage had weathered difficult moments and had grown stronger from the experience.

Shortly thereafter came revelations of what appeared to be efforts to evade the draft during the Vietnam War. Twelve days before the New Hampshire primary, the *Wall Street Journal* reported that Clinton, while on his Rhodes Scholarship at Oxford University, apparently promised to attend law school at the University of Arkansas and to enroll in officer training there, thereby allegedly delaying an expected draft notice. He entered Yale Law School instead, and he did not participate in ROTC. Although Clinton's lead in New Hampshire opinion polls was lost, pollsters discovered that voters appeared to be more concerned with issues, especially the economy, in the campaign than with ambiguous allegations, some about events that had taken place a quarter century earlier. By keeping his campaign focused on the economy as much as possible, Clinton was able to stop his fall in the polls and even rebound somewhat.

Tsongas had several advantages in the first primary. For one thing, he was raised in and still lived only a few miles from New Hampshire in Lowell, Massachusetts, a city as seriously affected by the economic downturn as the Granite State was. For another thing, he offered a no-nonsense, "tough medicine" approach to economic revitalization. His approach was also more conservative (and some would say more nearly Republican) than his rivals'. As a result, his platform was not only distinctive from those of his competitors, but it was also one that would play well in New Hampshire and in succeeding primaries, especially those to follow in the South.

The Iowa caucuses (when they are contested) and the New Hampshire primary are pivotal events in the new nomination system. Unknown candidates, or those expected to do poorly, who do well in these contests often launch a strong campaign on that basis, as George S. McGovern (1972), Carter (1976), and Hart (1984) exemplify. Front-runners who do not win these early contests suffer a severe setback, sometimes signaling the beginning of the end of their candidacies (as Edmund Muskie found in 1972), or forcing them to struggle mightily to reverse their setback (as Mondale did in 1984). The largest impact, however, is felt by less well known candidates who do not do well. A failed effort all but dooms their candidacies. New Hampshire, in particular, winnows a large field of contenders to two or three.

Table 1-3 presents the results for the Democratic caucuses and Table 1-4 presents the results for the Democratic primaries. As Table 1-3 shows, Harkin won 76 percent of the first round of the Iowa caucuses but, because this win was uncontested, it gave him no momentum. As the results in Table 1-4 show, Kerrey, Harkin, and Brown all did badly in New Hampshire. Brown was not hurt much by his poor showing, however, because he had not been expected to do well there. Although both Kerrey and Harkin tried to compete thereafter, each withdrew within the month, Kerrey on March 5 and Harkin on March 9.[26] Brown, who trailed all of these serious candidates, maintained his candidacy and even won two later primaries, Colorado on March 3 and Connecticut on March 24; he never did withdraw. His chances of winning, however, were never high in 1992, and his ability and willingness to continue reflected the unusual nature of his campaign, as we discuss later.

Tsongas (with 33 percent) and Clinton (with 25 percent) broke from the pack in New Hampshire. Clinton was obviously the most advantaged by the primary calendar, with primaries concentrated next in the South. Tsongas, with his rather more conservative economic message, was also advantaged relative to the rest of the field. The calendar gave Clinton one clear advantage over Tsongas, however. Fourteen primaries were held in the two weeks of March 3-17. Clinton's lead in organization, state-level leadership support, and money permitted him to run more effectively and broadly than Tsongas. For instance, Clinton had qualified for $1.4 million in federal matching funds in early February, nearly three times the amount Tsongas was eligible to receive.[27] The result was that Clinton won ten of these fourteen primaries (with over 50 percent of the vote in each), including such large states as Florida, Texas, Illinois, and Michigan, while Tsongas won only in Maryland, Massachusetts, and Rhode Island. With the primaries of March 17, then, Clinton had amassed a large number of victories and nearly half of the delegates he would need to win the nomination, while Tsongas had accumulated barely 20 percent of the necessary delegate support. Most of all, Tsongas was severely strapped for cash and had to choose whether to devote time to raising money or to put his efforts into winning votes and delegates. Doing the former would mean that he would fall even further behind in the delegate count before he could spend any newly raised money; yet he could not compete successfully for winning delegates without the necessary resources. Two days after decisive losses to Clinton in Illinois and Michigan, Tsongas faced the inevitable and suspended his campaign on March 19. Clinton's path to nomination was now essentially clear. After a narrow but surprising loss to Brown in Connecticut on March 24, Clinton would win all of the remaining twenty-two delegate-selection primaries, and he would secure a majority of delegates to the national convention after winning all six primaries on June 2.

Clinton fared decidedly better in primaries than in caucuses throughout the campaign. He won twenty-eight of the thirty-five states (including the District of Columbia) in which Democratic delegates were chosen by primaries. He won only four of the sixteen states in which such delegates were chosen by caucuses. Several factors account for Clinton's poorer showing in the caucus states. Most of the caucuses were held fairly early, before he had emerged as the overwhelming favorite. Brown, Harkin, and Tsongas also had strengths that aided them in caucus contests. In light of the higher information costs to voters for participation, it helps for the candidate to have strong organizational support (as Mondale had in 1984 and Jackson had in 1988) or the support of enthusiastic activists (as Jackson also had in 1988). Brown was able to win the Maine caucuses with the support of antinuclear groups, and Harkin won in Idaho and Minnesota partly because he was supported by organized labor. And Tsongas was aided in part by the stronger support he received from the more highly educated voters, for whom information costs are lower.[28]

Clinton ran a brilliant primary campaign, but he, like most winners, also benefited from good luck. First, the front-loaded primary calendar aided his campaign. Tsongas's neighboring-state victory in New Hampshire was discounted somewhat, if not as heavily as Harkin's uncontested home-state win. The next contested primary, Georgia's, had been rescheduled to the week before Super Tuesday, largely through the efforts of Clinton supporter Gov. Zell Miller. Clinton was able to gain an early victory as a result. As Ross K. Baker writes, "The front-loaded nature of the Democratic primary process was made to order for a moderate southerner like Clinton, with his splendid organization, his abundant funds, and his ability to establish very early that he was the man to beat." [29]

Table 1-3   Democratic First-Round Caucus Results, 1992

Caucus States	Turnout	Brown	Clinton	Harkin	Kerrey	Tsongas	Others	Uncommitted
Iowa (Feb. 10)	30,000*	1.6	2.8	**76.4**	2.5	4.1	0.6	12.0
Maine (Feb. 23)	13,500*	**30.3**	14.8	5.2	3.0	29.0	1.7	16.1
Idaho (March 3)	3,090	4.5	11.4	**29.7**	8.0	28.4	0.8	17.2
Minnesota (March 3)	50-60,000*	8.2	10.3	**26.7**	7.6	19.2	3.9	24.3
Utah (March 3)	31,638	28.4	18.3	4.0	10.9	**33.4**	2.7	2.3
Washington (March 3)	60,000*	18.6	12.6	8.2	3.4	**32.3**	1.5	23.2
American Samoa (March 3)	N.A.	–	4.3	–	8.7	–	–	**87.0**
North Dakota (March 5-19)	5,000*	7.5	**46.0**	6.8	1.2[a]	10.3	2.4	25.9
Arizona (March 7)	36,326	27.5	29.2	7.6	–	**34.4**	–	1.3[d]
Wyoming (March 7)	1,500*	23.0	**28.5**	14.2	–	11.7	0.4	22.3
Democrats abroad (March 7-9)	4,000*	12.2	26.6	6.9	–	**36.8**	17.5	–
Nevada (March 8)	6-7,000*	**34.4**	26.6	–[b]	–	19.6	–	19.4[d]
Delaware (March 10)	2,500*	19.5	20.8	–	–	**30.2**	–	29.6
Hawaii (March 10)	3,014	13.6	**51.5**	12.7	0.4	14.3	–	7.5
Missouri (March 10)	20-25,000*	5.7	**45.1**	–	–	10.2[c]	–	39.0
Texas (March 10)	N.A.	N.A.	N.A.	N.A.	N.A.	N.A.	N.A.	N.A.
Virgin Islands (March 28)	343	4.1	39.7	–	–	–	–	**56.3**
Vermont (March 31)	6,000*	**46.7**	16.8	–	–	9.3	2.2	25.0
Alaska (April 2)	1,100*	33.1	30.9	–	–	1.3	–	**34.7**
Virginia (April 11, 13)	N.A.	11.6	**52.1**	–	–	–	–	36.3
Guam (May 3)	1,000*	20.0	**49.0**	–	–	–	–	31.0

Source: Congressional Quarterly Weekly Report, July 4, 1992, 70.

Note: By and large, caucus results were compiled by the state parties and reflect either the share won of delegates to the next stage of the caucus process or a tally of the presidential preferences of caucus participants. No results were available from the March 10 precinct caucuses in Texas. In most cases, the turnout figures are estimates. The winner of each caucus event is indicated in boldface.

(Notes continue)

[a] Kerrey withdrew from the race March 5.

[b] Harkin withdrew from the race March 9.

[c] Tsongas suspended his campaign March 19.

[d] Vote for uncommitted and other was combined in tally.

*Turnout estimate.

— Indicates that the candidate was not listed on the caucus ballot or that his votes were not tabulated separately.

N.A. — not available.

Table 1-4   Democratic Primary Results, 1992

Date		State	Total Vote	Brown	Clinton	Harkin	Kerrey	Tsongas	Uncommitted	Other
Feb.	18	New Hampshire	167,819	13,654	41,522	17,057	18,575	55,638	—	21,373
	25	South Dakota	59,503	2,300	11,375	15,023	23,892	5,729	—	1,184
March	3	Colorado	239,643	69,073	64,470	5,866	29,572	61,360	5,356	3,946
	3	Georgia	454,631	36,808	259,907	9,479	22,033	109,148	17,256	—
	3	Maryland	567,243	46,500	189,905	32,899	27,035[a]	230,490	36,155	4,259
	7	South Carolina	116,414	6,961	73,221	7,657[b]	566	21,338	3,640	3,031
	10	Florida	1,123,857	139,569	570,566	13,587	12,011	388,124	—	42,390
	10	Louisiana	384,397	25,480	267,002	4,033	2,984	42,508	—	42,654
	10	Massachusetts	792,885	115,746	86,817	3,764	5,409	526,297	12,198	1,565
	10	Mississippi	191,357	18,396	139,893	2,509	1,660	15,538	11,796	25,972
	10	Oklahoma	416,129	69,624	293,266	14,015	13,252	—	—	2,090
	10	Rhode Island	50,709	9,541	10,762	319	469	26,825	703	432
	10	Tennessee	318,482	25,560	214,485	2,099	1,638	61,717	12,551	66,795
	10	Texas	1,482,975	118,923	972,151	19,617	20,298	285,191	—	9,826
	17	Illinois	1,504,130	220,346	776,829	30,710	10,916	387,891	67,612	2,955
	17	Michigan	585,972	151,400	297,280	6,265	3,219	97,017[c]	27,836	4,620
	24	Connecticut	173,119	64,472	61,698	1,919	1,169	33,811	5,430	7,568
April	7	Kansas	160,251	20,811	82,145	940	2,215	24,413	22,159	17,890[d]
	7	Minnesota*	204,170	62,474	63,584	4,077	1,191	43,588	11,366	20,087
	7	New York	1,007,726	264,278	412,349	11,535	11,147	288,330	—	26,488
	7	Wisconsin	772,596	266,207	287,356	5,395	3,044	168,619	15,487	21,534
	28	Pennsylvania	1,265,495	325,543	715,031	21,013	20,802	161,572	—	—
May	5	Dist. of Col.	61,904	4,444	45,716	—	—	6,452	5,292	—
	5	Indiana	476,849	102,379	301,905	—	14,350	58,215	—	—
	5	North Carolina	691,875	71,984	443,498	5,891	6,216	57,589	106,697	10,692
	12	Nebraska	150,587	31,673	68,562	4,239	—	10,707	24,714	10,692
	12	West Virginia	306,866	36,505	227,815	2,774	3,152	21,271	—	15,349

	Date	State								
	19	Oregon	354,332	110,494	159,802	—	—	37,139	—	46,897
	19	Washington*	147,981	34,111	62,171	1,858	1,489	18,981	—	29,371[d]
	26	Arkansas	502,617	55,234	342,017	—	—	—	90,710	14,656
	26	Idaho*	55,124	9,212	27,004	—	—	—	16,029	2,879
	26	Kentucky	370,578	30,709	207,804	7,136	3,242	18,097	103,590	—
June	2	Alabama	450,899	30,626	307,621	—	—	—	90,863	21,789
	2	California	2,863,609	1,150,460	1,359,112	—	33,935	212,522	—	107,580
	2	Montana	117,471	21,704	54,989	—	—	12,614	28,164	—
	2	New Jersey	392,626	79,877	243,741	—	—	45,191	—	23,817
	2	New Mexico	181,443	30,705	95,933	3,233	—	11,315	35,269	4,988
	2	Ohio	1,042,335	197,449	638,347	25,395	22,976	110,773	—	47,395
	9	North Dakota*	32,786	—	4,760[e]	—	—	—	—	28,026[d]
		Total	20,239,385	4,071,232	10,482,411	280,304	318,457	3,656,010	750,873	680,098

[a] Kerry withdrew from the race March 5.
[b] Harkin withdrew from the race March 9.
[c] Tsongas suspended his campaign March 19.
[d] Perot write-in votes totaled 2.1 percent of the Democratic primary vote in Minnesota, 19.1 percent in Washington, and 28.4 percent in North Dakota (which was the winning total).
[e] Clinton's vote in North Dakota came on write-ins.
* Indicates a nonbinding "beauty contest" primary.
— Indicates that the candidate or the uncommitted line was not listed on the ballot.

Source: Adapted from *America Votes 20: A Handbook of Contemporary American Election Statistics,* ed. Richard M. Scammon and Alice V. McGillivray (Washington, D.C.: Congressional Quarterly Inc., 1993), 53.

Second, Clinton was fortunate to face poorly funded opponents. Except for Brown, his major opponents withdrew early, despite some successes. Kerrey withdrew nine days after a primary win in South Dakota, and Harkin quit six days after winning the caucuses in Idaho and Minnesota. Tsongas suspended his campaign two days after finishing second in the Illinois and third in the Michigan primaries, even though he had won primary contests in New Hampshire, Maryland, Massachusetts, and Rhode Island as well as caucuses in Utah and Washington. Because Democrats who won at least 15 percent support received a proportional number of delegates, there were strong reasons for continuing to compete in order to deny Clinton a majority at the convention. Kerrey, Harkin, and Tsongas, however, simply did not have the funds to continue. And Brown, the only candidate to continue his efforts throughout the delegate selection season, was unacceptable to a vast majority of the superdelegates.

Clinton was also lucky not to have faced an African-American opponent, and especially fortunate that Jackson had decided not to make a third presidential bid. As a Southern Baptist and as a Democrat in the post-Voting Rights Act era, Clinton communicated effectively with black voters. According to exit poll results, 70 percent of the blacks who voted in the Democratic primaries supported Clinton, while only 15 percent voted for Brown and 8 percent for Tsongas.[30] Although black turnout in primaries was down substantially from 1988, 14 percent of all Democratic primary voters were black. According to our calculations, they contributed about one in five of the votes Clinton won in primaries.

Despite his good luck, Clinton's inexorable march to nomination looked easier on paper than it was in reality. First, the character issue would never completely be resolved in the spring, and it would, in fact, be revisited by Bush in the fall. Second, once Clinton became the only potential winner in the field, the focus turned to his standing for the fall campaign. In February, Clinton had closed to within a few points of Bush in public opinion polls. He could not gain further, however, for the rest of the primary season. This seemed an inauspicious sign, as approval ratings for Bush were declining. One problem was the seeming uncertainty among voters about who Clinton was. Was he the moderate southern Democrat his Southern Baptist roots and leadership role in the Democratic Leadership Council would suggest? Was he another "elitist, tax and spend, liberal" Democrat, as his education at Georgetown, Oxford, and Yale Universities and his support from liberal television and movie stars might suggest? Was he an outsider or an insider to politics in this year of disaffection with politics as usual? He had never served in Washington (having lost a bid for a House seat in 1974, the year after he finished law school), but he had spent virtually all of his adult life in political office (as Arkansas's attorney general from 1977 through 1979, and governor from 1979 through 1981 and then from 1983 through 1992). Perhaps if he had been the only alternative to Bush, his message for change, so effective in the fall, would have been as effective in the spring. First Brown and then Perot, however, laid claim to being the true outsider to politics and at least muddied the perception of Clinton as the alternative to Bush, the status quo, and politics as usual.

Although Brown was experienced by virtue of having served two terms as governor of California, among other political posts, and having run presidential nomination campaigns in 1976 and 1980, he ran as an outsider to Democratic and national politics. He argued that the current system of campaigning was corrupting and needed to be changed to reduce the impact of money, political action committees (PACs), and special interests. His campaign was innovative, relying almost exclusively on small donations made through an 800 number. He used cable television, talk radio, and other innovative techniques to get his message across. Running his campaign on a virtual shoestring, this most experienced of Democrats sounded fresh and novel, effectively capturing those most disaffected from, but still willing to participate in, the Democratic nomination process. Overall, he amassed one Democratic vote in five, showing a talent remarkably similar to Buchanan's ability to mobilize disaffected Republicans on the other side. But, with Brown obviously unable to win nomination, those disaffected from politics as usual found an even fresher candidate who seemed even more clearly an outsider in 1992: H. Ross Perot.

The (Non)candidacy of H. Ross Perot

Perot was a self-made billionaire who retained a folksy, populistic style. He became something of a folk hero through his long, if somewhat quixotic, efforts on behalf of POWs and MIAs from the Vietnam War and his overseeing of a dramatic rescue of employees of his firm who were held hostage in Iran. On February 16, two days before the New Hampshire primary, Perot launched one of the strangest and surprisingly successful presidential bids ever. Greatly extending some of the new campaign techniques of 1992, such as those used by Brown, Perot appeared on CNN's "Larry King Live" show two days before the New Hampshire primary. He said that if the public wanted him, he might serve as president. The way to show public support was to have volunteers place his name on the ballot in all fifty states. If they did, he would agree to be their candidate. He later backed this promise with a pledge to spend upwards of $100 million of his own money in support of the people's will.

Just how much of the subsequent campaign to get his name on all state ballots was truly volunteer is a subject of some dispute. It is nonetheless clear that the undeclared candidacy of this "nonpolitician" captured the imagination of many people. In a remarkably short time, organizations sprang up in every state to secure the necessary signatures (and comply with other aspects of state requirements) so that Perot would be a candidate on every state's ballot. The number of ordinary citizens who volunteered their time to his candidacy was remarkable. It is, in fact, possible that he ended up with the largest campaign organization—with many volunteers and huge lists of names of voters who were willing to sign petitions in support of his efforts—of any of the three major candidates for the general election. Perot's organization was not a political party, but it did fulfill comparable roles and tasks for a general election campaign in this era of candidate-centered campaigns.

By April, Perot was registering 20 percent of the likely vote in three-way polls among Bush, Clinton, and Perot. By May his probable vote exceeded one respondent in four. By the end of that month, his support exceeded Clinton's and neared Bush's. By the middle of June, his poll support surged into first place, noticeably ahead of Bush's and well ahead of Clinton's.

Perot used a variety of devices to get his message across, from morning news shows to late night talk radio. He promised to be independent of special interests, a promise made credible by his ability to supply massive sums from his own funds and by the design of his campaign organization—independent of PACs, interest groups, and the like (except that United We Stand, his own organization, was a PAC). He shunned the traditional aspects of campaigning. He refused to hold conventional press conferences. Until summer, he avoided the campaign experts and spin doctors, staples of today's conventional campaigns. In the fall, he would achieve success, against the predictions of experts, with a campaign that consisted primarily of half-hour or longer infomercials, showing only Perot and his flip charts.

Perot's message was that "politics as usual" was not working. Most especially, the system as currently designed was unable to solve the growing budget deficits, which were of greatest concern to him. He asserted that all kinds of problems, including deficits, could be fixed, but not under the current stagnant system. Solutions would be possible, if a different sort of president were sent to Washington, with the support of the people. Perot would agree to be that different sort of president, if the people wanted him; after the election, he would roll up his sleeves, "get under the hood," and fix the problems.

After several months of extensive and generally positive media attention, a bit more balanced scrutiny began. The media covered Perot so favorably partly because Clinton and Bush were leaving him alone. At first, neither quite knew what to make of the noncampaign, which many experienced politicians and pundits expected to be no more than a brief flurry. As Perot rose in the polls, however, it became clear that the two major party nominees (by now all but certain to be Clinton and Bush) would have to take him seriously. Clinton chose to avoid engaging Perot, both because he had to secure his own nomination and because he feared losing his position as the most viable agent of change in the fall. To win election he would need a good portion of the voters who were attracted to Perot. Bush did not have to worry about securing his renomination, nor could he present himself as the agent of change. Perot launched his most pointed barbs at Bush. With the media beginning to ask Perot for policy specifics, and with Perot approaching and then passing Bush in the polls, Bush began to criticize Perot. In June and early July, the two engaged in what seemed more like bickering than serious campaigning.

As it became clear that Perot would make it on most or all ballots, he began to plan for the general election campaign. He chose to illustrate his bi- or nonpartisan appeal and yet bring in some experienced hands to lead his campaign by securing the services of Ed Rollins, who had run Reagan's reelection campaign in 1984, and Hamilton Jordan, who had been Carter's chief of staff. Perot did not want to run an ordinary campaign, and he therefore never felt comfortable assigning Rollins and Jordan any genuine authority. After a series of gaffes, increasing pressure from Bush, and increasingly less positive coverage in the media, Perot effectively forced Rollins and Jordan to the sidelines and then out of his campaign. With his poll standings declining to create a near three-way tie, Perot called a press conference to announce that he was withdrawing from his undeclared candidacy. He said, in part, "Now that the Democratic party has revitalized itself, I have concluded that we cannot win in November and that the election will be decided in the House of Representatives." [31] In a slightly backhanded way, Perot seemed to be saying that the Democratic ticket would be the best way to achieve his objectives. Clinton had won nomination the night before and was to give his acceptance speech later that night.

The Conventions

National nominating conventions under the new nominating system have become primarily a method for the party to attract media attention to itself and its nominees. The structure of conventions has not changed. As in the past, the delegates vote on the rules that define the national party organization, on the acceptability of the credentials of delegates, on the party's platform, and on the nominees for president and vice president. Not since 1952, however, has a major party required more than a single roll call vote to select its presidential nominee, and the outcome of that vote has consistently been known in advance. Decisions about credentials, rules, platform, and the presidential nomination are generally concluded before the convention opens. Since important decisions are rarely made at conventions, they are therefore largely ceremonial. The party uses them as a means of showcasing some of its leading talent, and the presidential nominee hopes to use the convention as a means of reconciling any remaining divisions within the party and of launching the general election campaign. Indeed, a well-run convention typically increases the poll standing of the nominee, in part because he has the attention of the media and the nation for a week, largely uncontested by the opposition.[32] A well-run convention, from the party's and candidate's perspectives, is one that is carefully controlled to forestall surprises, provides no news other than the actual votes and the nominees' acceptance speeches, and presents these in prime time television viewing hours.

From 1968 to 1988, the Republicans usually ran conventions more efficiently and effectively than Democrats. As seeming testimony to political humorist Will Rogers's famous line, "I belong to no organized party. I am a Democrat," Democratic conventions were usually the less well organized and run. Most of the Republican nominations in this era were less divisive, making them more coronation events than decision-making bodies. The one exception was in 1976—the single presidential election the GOP lost during those years. The most obvious explanation is that a nomination either uncontested or decided early and with little controversy leads to a better-run convention and easier trail to victory in the fall. Under this logic, the Republican convention should, once again, have been the better run. In fact, the reverse was true.

The Democratic Convention

Clinton's organization, which had helped him weather the difficult moments in the spring, controlled the convention well. Whenever a storm cloud appeared, the organization headed it off. For example, Robert P. Casey, governor of the key state of Pennsylvania, came out in opposition to Clinton's pro-choice stance and wanted to make a televised, prime time, pro-life speech. Clinton's organization made sure that only speeches in support of the candidate and his positions would get prime time slots.

Clinton chose his running mate in advance, avoiding the controversy that has often arisen about selections made in the night after the presidential nomination voting. He also made an unconventional choice. Instead of seeking someone to balance the ticket, by virtue of coming from a different region or ideological wing of the party, he chose Al Gore. This fellow Southern Baptist (who was also educated at elite schools, but who had served in Vietnam) was even younger than Clinton. Both are of a younger generation than Bush (and Perot), products of the Vietnam, rather than World War II, era. This selection served to signal his apparent dedication to moderation within the party.[33]

Earlier, we noted the uncertainty in the public about just who Clinton was and what he stood for. His campaign had, of course, noted this as well. His organization discovered through focus groups that the public did not understand Clinton's background very well. Presenting the public with the story of his life—how his father had died before his birth; how he was raised under difficult circumstances; how his stepfather had an alcohol problem and sometimes abused the family; and how he lived with his grandparents so that his mother could earn a nursing degree— not only changed people's view of Clinton, but persuaded them to be much more strongly supportive of Clinton's candidacy. A film about his life was created to tell this story and was shown before his acceptance speech. It seemed to work before a prime-time television audience as effectively as before these focus groups.

The result of the convention—and Perot's timely withdrawal—was that Clinton got a substantial "convention bounce" in the polls. In three-way trial heats, Bush's standing remained virtually unchanged; the decline in Perot's support that followed his withdrawal went almost entirely to Clinton, giving Clinton a nearly 10-point lead over Bush. In two-way pairings, Clinton surged past Bush for the first time in 1992, jumping to a nearly 30-point lead. Most expected this convention bounce to come back down. Clinton and Gore, however, followed the convention with a highly successful, almost euphoric, bus tour. Still, Bush could well anticipate a convention bounce of his own. After all, under the new nomination system, only McGovern in 1972 had failed to receive any such bounce, and that convention had been divisive and had ended with an acceptance speech that was delayed until well after prime time.

The Republican Convention

Contrary to expectations, Bush received no significant postconvention bounce in the polls. Whatever the full set of reasons, one part of the explanation was that the Republican convention was not as well managed as most had been in the past. There was, of course, no division on matters subject to vote. Events connected with credentials, rules, platform, and the two nominations went just as expected. But the Christian Coalition, an organization that was a vestige of Pat Robertson's 1988 presidential campaign, had a greater than expected influence in drafting the Republican platform, and the final document was even more conservative on social issues than the 1988 Republican platform had been. Moreover, the convention was poorly managed by the Bush campaign, and the most conservative forces in the party got extensive prime time coverage.

It appeared to many viewers that the Republican party included too many extremist elements among its leadership. An earlier flap surrounding Quayle's comments about the "Murphy Brown" television show and "family values" resurfaced at the convention, and Marilyn Quayle's convention speech seemed to some to be part of an unfair attack on

Hillary Clinton. But the tone of Mrs. Quayle's speech might have passed largely unnoticed were it not for the general context in which the address was made. The Republican platform, as we have noted, was very conservative: it continued the party's stringent opposition to abortion (debate over that issue was prohibited at the convention), it opposed various measures advocated by gays and lesbians, it denounced government support for art deemed obscene or offensive, and it even included a plank criticizing Bush for supporting tax increases in 1990. Buchanan gave an opening night address that received prime time coverage. Instead of seeking assurances of a conciliatory address by his chief opponent, Bush's campaign had let Buchanan speak as he wanted.[34] Buchanan's speech stressed moral issues. He said, "There is a religious war going on in this country for the soul of America. It is a cultural war as critical to the kind of nation we shall be as the Cold War, itself, for this is a war for the soul of America. And in that struggle for the soul of America, [Bill] Clinton and [Hillary] Clinton are on the other side, and George Bush is on our side." [35] Later Pat Robertson delivered a speech that was harsh and strident. According to Walter Dean Burnham, "Both the Houston platform and the ... speeches by such leading apostles as Pat Buchanan and Pat Robertson projected a theological tone more in keeping, one would have thought, with Ecumenical Councils of the early Christian church than with a political party in a popularist country whose founding charter explicitly separates church and state." [36] Not only did this sequence of speeches and positions suggest that the Republican party might be far to the right of the American mainstream, it also seemed to suggest that Bush had lost control over his party and convention.

This view seemed consistent with the decision Bush had recently reached of asking his close friend, adviser, and then secretary of state, James Baker, to resign his cabinet position, take control of the campaign, and define a domestic agenda. All of these signs indicated that the candidate was in trouble and not in control of his own campaign, let alone his party or its convention. As a result, Bush would not receive the kind of bounce he had in 1988, in which he closed a 30-point gap opened after Dukakis's nomination. Instead, the gap between Clinton and Bush would be largely unaffected by the Republican convention. And thus, as the general election campaign opened for real, the race was seemingly reduced to a typical two-candidate contest, and Bush was trailing his opponent badly.

Chapter 2

The General Election Campaign

Once they have been nominated, candidates choose their general election campaign strategies based on their perceptions of what the electorate wants, of the relative strengths and weaknesses of their opponents and themselves, and of their chances of winning. A candidate who has a substantial lead in the polls may choose strategies that are very different from those used by a candidate who is far behind. A candidate who believes that his or her opponent has significant weaknesses is more likely to run an aggressive, attacking campaign than one who does not perceive such weaknesses.

Although George Bush may have appeared to be unbeatable at the peak of his popularity in 1991 and Bill Clinton may have appeared to be politically at death's door at various points during the primary season, by the time the conventions were completed and the general election planning was under way, it was clear that the presidential race would be no cakewalk for the incumbent. Clinton had built a substantial lead in the wake of the Democratic convention, and when the small pro-Bush bounce after the Republican convention did not close the gap, observers concluded that Bush's difficulties were not merely transient and that Clinton could actually win. This did not mean that a Democratic victory was certain. Rather it meant that unlike in 1984, when Walter F. Mondale faced the juggernaut of Ronald Reagan's reelection campaign, both campaign organizations and independent analysts could create plausible scenarios that ended in the victory of either major party candidate.

Part 2 will consider in detail the impact of particular factors (including issues and evaluations of Bush's job performance) on the voters' decisions. This chapter will provide an overview of the campaign—an account of its course and a description of the context within which strategic decisions were made.

The Strategic Context and Candidates' Choices

As we have said, candidates base their strategies on their perceptions of the political situation. One aspect of that situation is the track record of the parties in presidential elections, and that certainly did not offer an encouraging picture for the Democrats in 1992. From 1952 through 1988 there had been ten presidential elections, and the Republicans had won seven of them. The more recent results were even worse; from 1968 on, the Republicans had won five of the six elections. During this span the Democrats won one close race (1976), lost one close race (1968), lost once by a moderate margin (1988), and were buried in three electoral college landslides.

The nature of the American system for electing a president compels us to examine the state-by-state pattern of results. U.S. voters do not directly vote for president or vice president. Rather, they vote for a slate of electors pledged to support a presidential and a vice-presidential candidate. Moreover, in every state except Maine and Nebraska, the entire slate that receives the most votes is selected. In no state is a majority of the vote required. Since the 1972 election, Maine has used a system in which the plurality-vote winner for the whole state wins two electoral votes. In addition, the plurality-vote winner in each of Maine's two House districts receives that district's single electoral vote. Beginning in 1992, Nebraska allocated its five electoral votes in a similar manner: the statewide plurality-vote winner gained two votes, and each of the state's three congressional districts awarded one vote on a plurality basis.

If larger states used the district plan employed by Maine and Nebraska, the dynamics of the campaign would be different. For example, candidates might target specific congressional districts and would probably campaign in all large states, regardless of how well they were doing in the statewide polls. But given the winner-take-all rules employed in forty-eight states and the District of Columbia, candidates cannot safely ignore the pattern of past state results. And a state-by-state analysis of the five presidential elections from 1972 through 1988 indicates that the Democrats faced a daunting task to win enough states to compile the 270 electoral votes necessary for victory.[1]

As Figure 2-1 reveals, there were twenty-four states that voted Republican in every one of those elections. No state was equally loyal to the Democrats. (See Chapter 3 on long-term voting patterns.) Only the District of Columbia, with three electoral votes, supported the Democratic candidate every time; the twenty-four Republican states, on the

Figure 2-1 States That Voted Republican at Least Four out of Five Times, 1972-1988

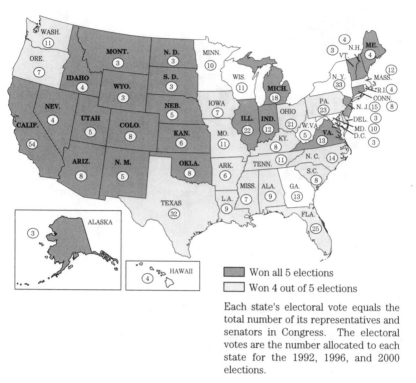

Won all 5 elections

Won 4 out of 5 elections

Each state's electoral vote equals the total number of its representatives and senators in Congress. The electoral votes are the number allocated to each state for the 1992, 1996, and 2000 elections.

Source: Election results based on *Presidential Elections Since 1789*, 5th ed. (Washington, D.C.: Congressional Quarterly Inc., 1991), 210-214.

other hand, had 221 electoral votes in 1992. These states alone would leave a Republican candidate only 49 votes short of victory. In addition, there were seventeen other states, with 212 electoral votes, that the GOP had carried in four of these five elections. Balancing these, the Democrats had won only Minnesota (with 10 votes) four times. Thus, if each state's political leanings were categorized on the basis of the last five elections, 13 electoral votes were likely to go Democratic and 433 were basically Republican. This pattern had led some analysts to talk of a "Republican lock" on the electoral college, implying that it was nearly impossible for the Democrats to win.

The underlying logic of an argument that the Republicans had a lock on victory in the electoral college was that the future would be like the past. However, political patterns can change, sometimes gradually and sometimes abruptly, so historical evidence must be considered

Figure 2-2 Clinton's Electoral Vote Strategy, 1992

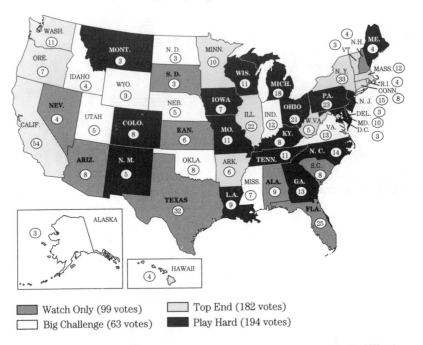

Watch Only (99 votes)   Top End (182 votes)
Big Challenge (63 votes)   Play Hard (194 votes)

Source: Based on information reported in Jules Witcover, "Democrats Crafted Winning Blueprint," *Lansing State Journal*, November 6, 1992, 3A.

carefully, with a sensitivity to possible shifts in context. There were features of the situation in 1992 that could give encouragement to both parties. The Democrats needed a strategy that would lead voters to depart from their pro-Republican leanings in presidential contests of the previous two decades, while the GOP had to convince those voters to choose the party again.

The Clinton campaign dealt with the Democrats' strategic disadvantage in the electoral college by facing the problem directly, in a departure from previous Democratic practice. In most recent campaigns, the Democrats never seemed to develop a deliberate electoral vote strategy, dealing instead with the electorate in terms of social and ethnic categories. The Clinton campaign realized that this approach was undesirable, and his staff devised a strategy targeting the electoral college early on. All states were put in one of four categories (see Figure 2-2).[2] First there were the "top end" states (thirteen plus the District of Columbia, with 182 votes) that they believed Clinton could win fairly easily.

It may seem surprising, but California, which had one-fifth of all the electoral votes needed to win the presidency, was viewed as an easy state for Clinton to capture, even though it had voted Republican in all six presidential elections since 1968. But polls in California showed Clinton with a more than 20-point lead, and by early September Bush himself had written off the state as unwinnable. Polls in two other large states, New York (which the Republicans and Democrats had split in the last six elections) and Illinois (which the GOP had won all six times in the same period), also showed Clinton with double-digit leads.

At the other end were two groups of Republican states: ten "big challenge" states that probably could not be won, and nine states to "watch only," in case opportunities developed. That left eighteen "play hard" states in the middle, totaling 194 electoral votes, which would decide the outcome of the election. It was in these states that the Clinton campaign would concentrate its efforts to pick the Republican lock. If the other calculations were right, less than half of the votes from the play-hard states were necessary for victory; carrying them all would yield a substantial 376-162 win.

The Clinton campaign organization also intended to avoid other mistakes of the past, learning from the previous experience of Republican as well as Democratic candidates. Speaking of the GOP, Clinton's campaign chairman, Mickey Kantor, said, "We've watched them and we've learned. . . . In the past, we've reinvented the wheel in every campaign, rather than taking people who made mistakes and learned from them. That's where the Republicans have done so well." [3] One mistake the Democrats resolved not to repeat was the Dukakis campaign's pattern of sitting on a big lead in the polls, refraining from vigorous responses to attacks launched by Bush and his allies. To be sure, Clinton's people were pleased that the polls after the Republican convention showed that they maintained a nationwide lead of 10 points or more over Bush, but they also recalled how Dukakis's lead had melted away in 1988 and how he had never recovered his momentum. In particular, they knew that as the trailing candidate, Bush would have to go on the attack, as he had four years earlier. When the attack came, the Democrats planned to respond vigorously and immediately. Their campaign operation in the "war room" in Little Rock, Arkansas, was structured to produce a response to Republican charges within hours.

Finally, the Clinton campaign team intended to maintain a focus on getting out their own message, and not simply get trapped into reacting to GOP charges. James Carville, the principal strategist, kept a small card posted on his desk in the War Room, one entry on which said "The economy, stupid!" This reminder of their strongest weapon against the president was more than just a slogan. Carville used many devices during the campaign to remind his team. For example, in early October he asked other members of the staff, "What place in Virginia is visited by more people than any other?" The correct answer was not the major tourist attractions, like Mount Vernon or Arlington National Cemetery; it was the Potomac Mills discount outlet mall. Carville used this fact to remind his people of the central place economic matters occupied in people's lives.[4]

For the Republicans, the situation was very different. As four years earlier, they were behind the Democratic ticket. Unlike 1988, however, Bush was the incumbent, with a record of his own to deal with, and in particular a weak economy to explain. Moreover, it was not clear on what basis the GOP should launch its offensive. Against Dukakis, the main themes were Bush's "no new taxes" pledge and the claim that the Democratic candidate was an extreme liberal whose values were not in accord with those of the American people. But Bush had agreed to a tax increase, and it was uncertain whether the "liberal" label could success- fully be hung on a southern Democrat. Before the Republican convention, Bush strategists began focusing on a number of issues they intended to use repeatedly against Clinton as the campaign unfolded. In the period right after the Democratic convention, Bush surrogates talked about Clinton's draft record and also charged that his economic plan would mean substantial tax increases for the average family. As the Republican convention approached, they planned to focus on Clinton's record as governor of Arkansas, which they thought would be fruitful because that state is poor and ranks low on many social and economic indicators.

Then, at the Republican convention and afterward, another theme was added to the campaign, partly through the choice of the Bush people and partly through activities of other convention participants. It was "traditional family values." The religious right was active and prominent at the convention—this segment had approximately 15 percent of the delegates and many speakers. Their catchphrase encompassed all of the social issues about which they cared so much: forestalling gay rights, reinstituting school prayer, and outlawing abortion. They vigorously pursued platform planks that were in accord with their views, and they were happy with the results. Ralph Reed, Jr., executive director of the Christian Coalition, told the convention: "We are here to celebrate a victory. . . . Within the past hour, the Republican party passed a pro-life, pro-family platform! The feminists threw everything they had at us! We won and they lost!"[5] Perhaps the strongest language was used by Pat Buchanan in his convention speech, as we have cited, when he declared that "there is a religious war . . . for the soul of America."[6]

These issues and others would serve as the basis for the Bush campaign's assault on Clinton's lead, for like four years earlier the GOP strategists recognized that presidential campaigns were about choices. Candidates had to give voters reasons to vote either for them or against their opponents. As had been the case four years earlier, Bush's ratings were poor, so the natural course was to "go negative" against his opponent. Unlike the Dukakis team, however, the Clinton people also recognized the strategic situation, and they intended to counter the Republicans. Moreover, the 1992 campaign would offer another new and uncertain element—the return of H. Ross Perot.

From Labor Day to the Debates

The Republicans: Searching for an Effective Theme

On September 7, Labor Day, the traditional opening day of presidential general election campaigns, the Bush campaign had cause for concern. In virtually every national poll, the president trailed Clinton by ten or more points; by this time four years earlier, Bush had already surged into the lead. The race was not yet lost, but Bush needed to find quickly some way to cut into the Democratic advantage. At the beginning, he tried both positive and negative themes, coupled with some traditional efforts to derive an advantage from incumbency. Bush announced that Homestead Air Force base in Florida, which had been scheduled by an independent commission for closing and was then badly damaged by Hurricane Andrew, would instead be rebuilt and kept open. Voters in South Dakota were told of a new subsidy for wheat exports, and the president announced approval of the sale of 150 F-16 fighters to Taiwan and 72 F-15 fighters to Saudi Arabia. Not at all coincidentally, the plane sales were announced in the cities where they would be built.

The main positive effort was a nationally televised speech to the Detroit Economic Club, which largely reiterated previous administration proposals to revive the economy. Bush dubbed his proposals an "agenda for American renewal" for his second term. The speech, which sought to draw attention to Bush's ideas and to draw contrasts with Clinton's plans, called for less spending, less regulation, and lower taxes. It was well received by commentators, although some contended that such a speech should have been delivered months earlier.

Consistent with earlier planning, however, most of the GOP campaign's themes were negative. One was a concerted attack on Clinton's draft record, launched principally by Bush surrogates. Senate Minority Leader Bob Dole challenged Clinton to "come clean" on the issue, Pat Buchanan charged directly that the Democratic candidate had "dodged the draft" and was therefore unfit to be commander in chief, and former president Ronald Reagan raised the matter at a campaign rally in California. When Bush was scheduled to address the national convention of the National Guard Association on September 15, many observers expected him to bring up the issue, but he merely alluded to it. When

Clinton came before the convention later the same day, he left out a segment of his speech that had been written to counter the anticipated Bush attack.

Over the next week, the Republicans tried to keep the issue alive with memos and statements, but they did not seem to be making much headway. Particularly disconcerting was the announcement by the Veterans of Foreign Wars, which had endorsed Reagan and Bush in the three previous campaigns, that they would endorse no candidate for president in 1992. Perhaps as a consequence, Bush raised the draft issue directly in an interview with conservative talk show host Rush Limbaugh. He attacked Clinton's "total failure to come clean with the American people" and said that the "fundamental difficulty is that he has not told the full truth, the whole truth, and nothing but the truth." [7]

Consistent with earlier plans, the Republican campaign also attacked Clinton's record as governor. On September 22, Bush campaigned in all six of the states that border on Arkansas, dubbing the Democrat "Governor Taxes" at one stop, and claiming that he was the type that "coddled criminals" at another. The president also criticized Clinton's record on the environment and on civil rights. The next day his campaign broadcast its first attack TV commercial of the campaign, with the same theme. The ad claimed that Clinton had increased spending sharply in Arkansas and had raised taxes on ordinary people to pay for the spending.

By late September, the Bush campaign had to deal with another issue: debates. The bipartisan Commission on Presidential Debates had proposed three 90-minute debates, employing a single moderator rather than the panel of reporters that had been used in previous years. Clinton had accepted the proposal, but the Bush organization had refused, claiming that the format for debates should be worked out between the candidates and expressing its preference for the traditional format. Having reached no agreement, the commission canceled the first debate, scheduled for September 23, and on that date proposed a new schedule and a meeting to negotiate on a format. The Republicans again refused, for they believed that the debates disadvantaged their candidate. As one aide said, "If you strategize the odds of who wins and who loses outside of flukes, we all come up with the same bottom line: He [Clinton] has more to gain, we have more to lose." [8]

Within a week, however, the Bush people had changed their minds, for the president challenged Clinton to debates on four consecutive Sunday nights, using two different formats. The Democrats accepted the challenge, but not the formats, and negotiations to work out the details began. By early October, things were set. There would be four debates—three presidential and one vice-presidential—spread out over nine days and using varying formats. Part of the reason for the Republicans' shift may have been their continued inability to gain ground in the polls; another may have been the possible reentry into the race by Perot.

Another response of the Bush campaign to the president's continued underdog status was to make its attacks on Clinton even stronger. Like many of the other negative issues in the campaign, this one was raised first by people other than the president. For a week in early October, Robert K. Dornan, a very conservative Republican representative from California, raised questions on the House floor about Clinton's anti-Vietnam War activities and about a trip he had made to Moscow when he was a Rhodes scholar in England in 1969. Dornan said in interviews that he believed that Clinton was a "dupe" of the Soviet secret police. During these attacks, Dornan was in daily contact with high-ranking people in the Bush campaign, who encouraged him to go ahead, and he visited the president to urge him to make an issue of these matters. Bush did so in an appearance on "Larry King Live," where he questioned Clinton's accounts of these matters. Bush, in subsequent interviews, went further and attacked Clinton for demonstrating against the war while overseas, and charged that he was lying about the visit to Moscow, although he offered no evidence to support these claims.[9]

Unfortunately, there was a good deal of negative reaction to this turn in the campaign among the public and the media, with charges of "red-baiting" and "McCarthyism" being lodged against the Republicans. Within two days, Bush dropped the Moscow trip issue, but he continued to attack Clinton for participating in antiwar demonstrations. All three network news shows led off with coverage of these attacks on October 9, but they all gave more weight to criticism of the president than to the charges. Polls in August had shown that there had been a negative response to the conservative, Christian right tone of the GOP convention. The charges against Clinton for his student activities seemed to reinforce the voters' feelings that the Republicans were to blame for turning the campaign in an undesirable direction. For example, a poll in Boston showed that "52 percent held the president responsible for a low-road campaign, while 15 percent said it was Clinton's fault."[10]

Thus on the eve of the first 1992 debate, the Bush campaign was in essentially the same position it had been in five weeks earlier. The campaign was half over, and Bush still trailed Clinton by double-digit margins in all major national polls. The debates now offered perhaps the best—and last—opportunity to turn things around. The Republicans hoped that their chances of doing this had improved with Perot's reentry into the race.

The Democrats: Defend and Attack

In early September, the Democratic campaign was doing well. Clinton had a good lead over Bush, but his campaign knew that could change. Clinton's people intended to respond vigorously to attacks, but they also wanted to convey a positive message, especially on their main issue, the economy. Over the previous couple of weeks, Clinton had sought to neutralize the draft issue, with limited success. There were apparent inconsistencies in his accounts, and the Republicans continued their efforts to maintain the salience of the issue. On Labor Day, Clinton appeared testy on the matter, blaming reporters for raising the latest questions, and urging them to exert as much effort in checking out Bush's veracity on the Iran-contra issue. By the end of the week, Clinton was seeking to avoid draft questions by canceling a news briefing and a press conference, meeting instead with three Detroit TV news anchors to answer questions about the economy. However, the issue would not go away, and new aspects continued to be the focus of news stories.

To avoid being on the defensive, the Democrats sought to present positions on a wide variety of domestic concerns. The campaign's earliest ads touted Clinton's economic plans, particularly the proposal to raise taxes on the wealthy. Another promised to revamp the welfare system, and in speeches Clinton discussed details of his plan to reform the health care system and proposed to revitalize the economy of rural America. Television ads also contended that Clinton and Gore were "a new generation of Democrats" who "don't think the way the old Democratic party did" because they held differing views on welfare reform, the death penalty, and government spending.

The Democratic campaign also developed a series of attacks on Bush and the Republican party. On the economy, Clinton repeatedly characterized the administration's policy as "trickle-down economics," under which the rich got tax cuts and the average citizen got nothing. Bush was blamed for presiding over an increase in unemployment, to a level that was "the highest in eight years." The Democrats also attacked on the debate issue. Clinton "accused his opponent of posturing behind 'macho talk,' but running away when it came time to 'go man to man.' " [11] By late September, Bush campaign appearances were visited by hecklers who were dressed in chicken suits and carried signs that said: "Chicken George Won't Debate." On a number of occasions the Republican candidate felt compelled to address the chicken of the moment, which was hardly a desirable image for a sitting president.

One of Clinton's strongest attacks contended that some actions of Bush and the GOP "give sanction to intolerance and bigotry." In a speech at the University of Notre Dame, he made specific reference to Pat Buchanan's remarks at the GOP convention. Clinton said that he was "appalled to hear … voices that proclaim that some families aren't real families, some Americans aren't 'real Americans,' " and he continued, "America doesn't need a religious war. America needs a reaffirmation of the values that, for most of us, are rooted in our religious faith." [12]

This response was Clinton's effort to defend himself against the attacks of the religious right and to build further support among groups that favored the positions that angered the right in the first place: working women, gay rights supporters, and young voters. Support for the Democratic ticket was strong among working women, owing partly to its support for abortion rights, although issues like the economy and family leave were also very important. Gay rights groups had favored Clinton during the primaries because he opposed discrimination against homosexuals, and he openly accepted their support. Particularly strong efforts were made to secure the support of the youngest segment of the electorate, which had strongly supported the GOP in previous campaigns. Clinton and Gore appeared frequently on college campuses and were interviewed on MTV. The effort appeared to be successful, for a poll in early October indicated that among eighteen-to-twenty-four-year-olds, Clinton was supported by 53 percent, whereas Bush earned 27 percent, and Perot had 15 percent. As was true in other groups, the support partly reflected economic concerns.

The few days before the first debate illustrate the mixed strategy of the Democrats. Clinton denounced the Bush campaign's criticism of his activities as a student in England. He characterized the attacks as "sad," "desperate," and "amazing," and said that "this campaign has sunk to a new level." [13] On the more positive side, the Democrats made public a list of 556 economists, including nine Nobel Prize winners, who supported his economic program over that of the president. (The Republicans countered with their own list of 110 economists who criticized the Clinton plan, although they did not necessarily endorse Bush's.)

The Democratic ticket had successfully weathered the first half of the campaign. The Democrats' lead was still intact, and they continued to adhere to their focused electoral-vote strategy by concentrating their purchase of television ads in about twenty of the most competitive states. The Republicans were forced to rely on more expensive national purchases of time. Election day was less than a month away, and success in the series of debates could solidify Clinton's support and virtually guarantee victory.

Perot: Once More into the Breach

Around the middle of September, Ross Perot began hinting that he might get back into the presidential race. During an appearance on the "Today Show," he said that the reason he was considering resuming his candidacy was that the networks were not willing to sell him air time to discuss his economic program unless he did so. A few days earlier, Perot supporters had succeeded in getting his name on the ballot in Arizona, the fiftieth state in which he was qualified as a candidate. The following week, on "CBS This Morning," Perot said that he had "made a mistake" when he withdrew and that the final decision about whether he would run rested with his "volunteers." [14] Federal campaign records show that he had given his volunteers a lot of help; since his July withdrawal, Perot had donated almost $7 million to the Perot Petition Committee.

Both the Bush and Clinton campaigns sent emissaries to a meeting of Perot supporters in Dallas late in the month, but neither organization was able to persuade them that it would be a mistake for Perot to get back into the race. Nor was their candidate dissuaded, and on October 1 Perot announced that he was resuming his quest for the presidency. He promised that his campaign would be unconventional, and he quickly made good on his promise when, a few days later, he appeared on a thirty-minute television commercial to outline for the electorate his views on the country's economic problems and on the federal deficit. This event was followed, a few days before the first debate—in which he had been included—by a set of three more conventional sixty-second commercials. All three focused on the size of the national debt and the fact that it would continue to grow unless something was done about it, although Perot did not outline any specific solutions.

The national polls at the time of his reentry showed Perot's support levels to be far below his earlier figures. Only about 10 percent of the respondents said they planned to vote for him, and his negative ratings were very high. Thus, for Perot, as for the other candidates, the debates were very important, for they offered a chance to recoup his lost support and to reinstate him as a major influence on the campaign.

The Debates: Nine Days of Drama

Round One: Perot's Resurgence

The first presidential debate was held in St. Louis on October 11. It employed the traditional format favored by the Bush campaign, in which a panel of three reporters asked questions of the candidates. Bush and Clinton had held practice debates during the preceding week, but Perot had passed up formal preparation. The Clinton forces had an extra concern because their candidate's recurring throat problems were back again, although hoarseness did not seem to hamper him significantly in the debate.

The opening question asked Perot and then the other candidates to discuss what separated each of them from the others. Perot argued that he was put on the ballot not by a major party but rather by "millions of people in 50 states all over this country who wanted a candidate that worked and belonged to nobody but them."[15] Clinton, going second, pressed the theme that he was the candidate who represented "real hope for change, a departure from trickle-down economics, a departure from tax-and-spend economics to invest-and-grow." Finally, Bush played to his strong suit and claimed that the "one thing that distinguishes is experience."

Fireworks developed early between Bush and Clinton when the former, responding to a question about issues of character, brought up his opponent's antiwar activities in England. Bush stated: "I think it's wrong to demonstrate against your country or organize demonstrations against your own country on foreign soil." Clinton responded by saying directly to Bush: "You have questioned my patriotism," and reminded the president that his own father, then a U.S. senator from Connecticut, had been a critic of Joseph McCarthy. McCarthy was a U.S. senator from Wisconsin who, during the early 1950s, had charged that many people in the federal government sympathized with the Communist party and were therefore un-American. These charges were widely believed to be unfounded. Clinton, in effect, claimed that Bush was using similar tactics. He said, "You were wrong to attack my patriotism. I was opposed to the war, but I love my country."

Another line of attack for Bush was taxes. He claimed, "Taxes spell out the biggest difference between us," and Clinton would "sock it to the working man." The Democrat responded, as he had before, that only the wealthy would see a tax increase. Clinton also went on the offensive, criticizing Bush for failing to create jobs. Perot was also critical of the administration for not encouraging defense industry conversion to high-technology peacetime jobs, but his main contrast with the other candidates was stylistic. Perot frequently produced laughter and applause from the audience with the kind of one-liners that had become his trademark.

The overnight polls indicated some disagreement about whether Perot had been the clear "winner" of the debate or whether he had been even with Clinton, but all showed that respondents had not rated Bush on top. Who won was not the important question, however. Rather, the issue of interest was how had the debate affected voting intentions. As the results from the Gallup/*USA Today*/CNN tracking poll show (see Figure 2-3), Perot support began moving up after the debate.[16] Apparently, his performance had begun to reverse the negative image he received as a result of his abrupt withdrawal from the race.

Round One and a Half: The Vice-Presidential Debate

Two days after the presidential candidates clashed, the only vice-presidential debate of the campaign was held in Atlanta. Here the format

Figure 2-3 National Poll Standings of the Candidates, Before and After
the Presidential Debates, October 1992

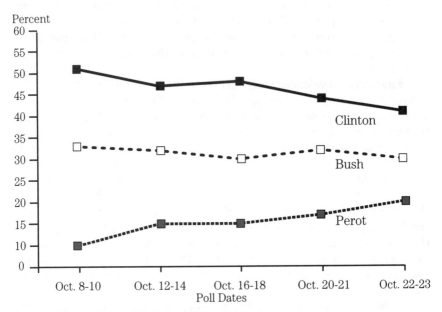

Source: Based on Gallup/*USA Today*/CNN tracking poll.

was the one the Democrats had favored, with a single moderator.
Proponents of the format had argued that it would have a more
interactive flow, and they were not disappointed. It was clear virtually
from the opening minute that Vice President Quayle intended to attack
Bill Clinton vigorously throughout the evening. In his opening remarks,
Quayle said that he was going to stress two things during the debate: that
Clinton's economic program would make the economy worse, and that
"Bill Clinton does not have the strength nor the character to be president
of the United States." [17] Quayle repeatedly returned to these themes,
especially the second one, saying that there was "a fundamental question
of trust and character" and claiming more than once that "Bill Clinton
has trouble telling the truth." At one point, he said to Gore that he was
"pulling a Clinton," and then went on, "You know what a Clinton is? . . .
He says one thing one day and another thing the next day."

Al Gore's strategy, like Quayle's, was to make the other party's
presidential candidate the target. He repeated the Democratic ticket's
attacks on "trickle-down economics," and said that "our country is in
trouble. We simply cannot continue this philosophy of giving huge tax
cuts to the very wealthy, raising taxes on middle-income families the way
Bush and Quayle have done and then waiting for it to work." Later he
talked about the Democrats' plan for health care reform and asked the

vice president, "Why has George Bush waited for three and a half years during this health insurance crisis before finally coming out with a proposal just before the election?" Gore also criticized the administration for a program that provided aid to Latin American countries to stimulate economic development, which he claimed subsidized the export of American manufacturing operations overseas. At one point he characterized Bush's attack on Clinton's antiwar activities as a "classic McCarthyite smear tactic."

The third participant in the debate was Perot's running mate, retired admiral James Stockdale. He was a former Vietnam prisoner of war with no political experience, and he was not well known to the country. He acknowledged this fact with his opening remarks, saying: "Who am I? Why am I here?" He talked of the Vietnam War as "the centerpiece of [his] life," and concluded the statement by claiming that "I have in my brain and my heart what it takes to lead America through tough times." As with his running mate, Stockdale was sometimes able to turn his inexperience and outsider status to his advantage. For example, after a particularly sharp exchange between Gore and Quayle, he said, "I think America is seeing right now why this nation is in gridlock." It became clear during the debate, however, that Stockdale was not nearly as familiar with the issues as his opponents were. At one point during a discussion of health care, the moderator returned to the admiral for further comment, and he responded, "I'm out of ammunition on this."

Despite the heat generated, and whatever entertainment value the evening provided, there was little evidence that the debate had affected the course of the race. Now attention turned again to the presidential candidates and their second meeting two days later.

Round Two: The Town Meeting

The debate in Richmond, Virginia, offered viewers still another format. This time questions came from a randomly selected group of undecided voters, in what had come to be known as a town meeting format. This setup was analogous to the talk show appearances that had been a prominent feature of the primary campaign, and it was a format in which Clinton had always done well. This night proved to be no exception.

Many observers had expected Bush to go on the attack in the same way Quayle had, but he did not. He may have been headed off by a question from a member of the audience, who asked the candidates to "focus on the issues and not the personalities and the mud." [18] Perot endorsed the idea, saying "Let's get off mud wrestling." Then came Bush's turn. He claimed that Clinton had started the negative attacks and that character was a legitimate issue, then he briefly criticized Clinton's antiwar activities. That largely exhausted his assaults for the evening. Clinton then said that he, too, had been concerned by the "tone and tenor of this campaign," and indicated that he would rather focus on his plans for change. One of Bush's aides later said that Bush had quickly realized that an aggressive style would not work. "He withdrew, he retreated. To try to engage aggressively would have made it a disaster. He did the only thing he could."

Whatever the reasons, the rest of the debate did concentrate on issues. To many observers, the debate did a good job of demonstrating contrasts between the candidates on those issues. This was especially true on the economy. For Perot, cutting the deficit was the top priority, while Clinton said that deficit reduction could not go too quickly because economic growth would suffer. Bush called for a balanced budget amendment, and said he opposed tax increases. Other contrasts came on international trade, school choice, and health care.

Style was where differences among the candidates were most apparent, and the basis on which postdebate analysts concluded that Clinton had secured an advantage. "Clinton seemed to revel in the format, making eye contact with questioners and loosening up his rhetoric and his body as he wandered near the audience. The emphasis on details was to his advantage." [19] Perot, on the other hand, was unable to offer many specific positions on issues that ranged far afield from his preferred topic of the deficit and the economy. Finally, Bush frequently seemed disconnected. Indeed, the camera caught him looking at his watch three times, as if he was interested only in when the evening's activities would end.

As the poll results in Figure 2-3 show, there was almost no change in the standings of the candidates after this debate, which was all that Clinton needed. The other candidates would have one more chance to gain ground in four days.

Round Three: Bush Has a Good Night

The final debate was held in East Lansing, Michigan, on October 19. It mixed the two formats preferred by the major party candidates, with a single moderator for the first half and a panel of reporters for the second. Bush made the most of the forum from the beginning, presenting his attack themes against Clinton more effectively than he had in the previous encounters. He focused on the Democratic candidate throughout the debate, challenging his record as governor, his credibility, and his taxation and spending plans. In his first response, for example, Bush said of his opponent: "When you hear him say we're going to tax only the rich, watch your wallet because his figures don't add up and he's going to sock it right to the middle-class taxpayer and lower, if he's going to pay for all the spending programs he proposes." [20] Later, when Clinton sought to make the point that he, personally, would be responsible for domestic policy in his administration, Bush offered an effective comeback. He said:

"That's what worries me, that he's going to be responsible. . . . He would do for the United States what he's done to Arkansas. We do not want to be the lowest of the low."

Clinton continued the strategy he had followed in the previous debates, trying to focus attention on the administration's alleged economic failings. As George Stephanopoulos, the Democratic campaign's communication director, said, the strategy was "really very simple. Answer the question—and then talk about the economy." [21] In this encounter, however, Clinton was frequently forced to defend his record. To the challenge against his governorship, Clinton contended that he had been responsible for causing a very poor state to make significant progress. When faced with a reporter's question about how his credibility had come into question because of his accounts of his efforts to avoid the draft, he admitted, "If I had it to do over, I might answer the questions a little better," and then contended that—like other presidents who had never served in the military—he could still send troops to war.

Ross Perot was more aggressive and critical of his opponents than he had been in the earlier debates. He indicated that being governor of a small state was not adequate qualification for the presidency, and he criticized Clinton's economic plan, saying, "It doesn't balance the budget." Perot attacked Bush for "coddling" Saddam Hussein before the Persian Gulf War and for mishandling the invasion of Panama and the subsequent capture of Panama's dictator, Manuel Noriega. He also contended, "Our country has sold out to foreign lobbyists," and he claimed that "the Republican dirty tricks group . . . went to extraordinary sick lengths" in investigating him and his family.

The remarkable series of debates was over. Most observers believed that Bush had done very well in the last debate, but the polls indicated that most of the benefits went to Perot. The data in Figure 2-3 show that over the four days after the third debate, the independent went up 5 points, while Clinton went down 7. Bush's standing showed no net change. Clinton still had a significant lead, but many possibilities now seemed open. Could Perot continue to gain ground? If so, could he win, or would he divide the anti-Bush vote and reelect the president? Or perhaps Perot had reached a ceiling, and Clinton could now solidify his victory. Two weeks remained in the campaign before the answers would be known.

To the Finish Line

As the polls we discussed showed, Bush had not increased his own standing during the debate period. Clinton's support had dropped 10 points, the same as Perot's rise. If Bush were to win, he had to draw voters to his side, and it became clear that the avenue the Republicans intended to follow was to launch even more negative attacks on Clinton. Indeed, the search for more ammunition in their assault led to an embarrassing incident in mid-October, when it was revealed that an assistant secretary of state had ordered the U.S. embassies in London and Oslo to conduct a search of their files for information on Bill Clinton's activities as a student in England. The search was to include data on his draft status and citizenship. Initially, the State Department claimed to be merely seeking to comply with a request from reporters under the Freedom of Information Act, but State was soon forced to admit that the search had violated its own regulations. Later information made clear that the search was made for political purposes and that Clinton's mother's files had also been searched; after the election it was even discovered that the British government (which favored Bush's reelection) had conducted a parallel search of its own files.

Despite this minor distraction, the Bush campaign moved ahead. Bush continued to upbraid Clinton on the prospect of tax increases, and on his "lousy" record as governor. Meanwhile, Quayle's chief of staff, William Kristol, again sought to raise the matter of Clinton's alleged extramarital involvement by reading to a Republican audience from transcripts of telephone tapes made by Gennifer Flowers. Bush also began assailing Perot, saying that he had "some nutty ideas" and had made some "crazy statements" about the president's dealings with Hussein.[22] Less than a week before election day, Bush trumpeted some positive news: the latest government figures showed a more substantial increase in the gross domestic product than expected.

The Clinton organization was concerned about Perot's gains, but the candidate continued to focus mainly on the president. He campaigned in the West, appealing to Republicans and independents for support. He hammered Bush on the economy and jobs, and criticized the administration in regard to the search of his and his mother's passport files. Democratic campaign commercials featured young people talking about having difficulties finding a job, and attacked the Republicans for permitting foreign corporations to operate in the United States without paying their fair share of taxes. Seeking a more positive tone, Clinton discussed his priorities for his first term, saying, "I did not enter this race for President to run my opponents down. . . . I entered this race to lift the American people up." [23]

Perot continued to run an unconventional campaign by making few personal appearances. Instead he bought a lot of television time, including the half-hour infomercials. In fact, by late October, Perot's spending on network television alone had already totaled more than $40 million.[24] In effect, Perot's only constraint was what he was prepared to spend. The two major party candidates had accepted public financing for their campaigns, so what they could spend was limited. Perot faced no limit.

His short commercials sought to reinforce his image as the candidate of the ordinary citizen. For example, one simply featured a letter of support from a veteran who had won a Purple Heart medal in Vietnam. In his thirty-minute infomercials Perot presented detailed strategies for tackling problems, including his plan for slashing the deficit.

In his personal statements, Perot was even more unusual, as he stepped up his charges of Republican dirty tricks. Specifically, he claimed in an interview with "60 Minutes" that there had been a GOP plot to embarrass his daughter just before her wedding by creating doctored photographs that portrayed her as a lesbian. In response, Marlin Fitzwater, the president's press secretary, characterized the charges as "crazy" and Perot as "paranoid." [25]

With only a few days to go, all of the polls indicated a tighter race between Bush and Clinton. The Democrat's formerly large lead had shrunk to single digits, and some polls showed the margin to be as close as 1 or 2 points, although Perot still hovered at or below 20 percent of the probable vote. With the tightening of the race, the rhetoric of the two leaders got even harsher. Bush continued to question whether Clinton could be trusted with power, and his characterizations of his opponents grew less civil. For example, referring to Clinton and Gore, he claimed, "My dog Millie knows more about foreign policy than these two bozos." [26] He also began referring to Senator Gore as "ozone man," and later simply "ozone," in a reference to Gore's allegedly extreme views on environmental issues.

Clinton sought to turn the attacks on him against the Republicans, urging the voters to reject "the politics of denial and division and blame which the Bush administration has visited on this country for too long." He, however, did not shrink from negative assaults of his own, as when he claimed, "This man [Bush] has no core convictions.... This is a guy here who would literally say or do anything to get elected." [27]

On the day before election day, all three presidential candidates made their last appeals to the electorate. After a three-day cross-country tour by Perot, which was his only traditional campaign trip since reentering the race, he ended with a disappointingly small rally in Dallas. There he criticized both Clinton and Bush. The president ended with a six-state trip, marking "the last day I will ever campaign for myself for president of the United States," and promising one of the "biggest surprises in political history." Clinton's campaign ended with a 4,000-mile swing on the final day that touched down in nine states and ended with a postmidnight rally in Little Rock. On that trip he claimed, "Tomorrow, we will drown out the negative voices that have held us back so long and build the America you deserve." [28] Now the three contenders could only wait to receive the electorate's verdict.

Did the Campaign Matter?

It is appropriate to ask whether the general election campaign made any difference, and the answer depends on the yardstick used to measure the campaign's effects. Did it determine the winner? Did it affect the choices of voters? Did it put issues and candidates' positions clearly before the voters? Were the issues that were addressed different from those that would have been otherwise considered? Did it produce events that will have a lasting impact on American politics?

Regarding the outcome, there is no evidence that the campaign made a difference. Clinton had established a substantial lead in the polls at the time of the Democratic convention, and he never relinquished that lead, although the race tightened up considerably after Perot's reentry. On the other hand, there is reason to believe that the campaign did have a significant impact on voters' choices. Over the final two months, the loyalties of a substantial proportion of the electorate shifted among the candidates, and even very late a considerable share of prospective voters indicated that they were undecided or weakly committed to their choice.

Data from the 1992 National Election Studies (NES) survey reinforces the conclusion that the general election campaign affected voters' choices (see Table 2-1). The table shows the percentage that reported voting for each of the three top candidates, controlling for the respondents' party identification and when he or she claimed to have made the vote choice.[29] Overall, only about 18 percent of the sample indicated that they knew all along how they were going to vote. On the other hand, almost 47 percent said they decided after the conventions, and 24 percent claimed they had made their choice in the preceding two weeks. Among this last group, the three candidates ran very close, and Perot's share just edged out Clinton's. One should also note that within each party identification category, those respondents who reported making their decisions later in the campaign were generally more likely to defect from their identification than those who had decided earlier.

Particularly noteworthy in Table 2-1 is the pattern of the Perot vote. The totals show that his share of the vote was much greater among those respondents who reported deciding later in the race. Very few said they knew all along that they would support Perot, but he received around a third of the vote among those who made their choice after the conventions. This pattern is indicative of Perot's success in renewing the support of a significant segment of the electorate after he returned to being a candidate.[30]

It can also be argued that the campaign gave rise to an issue agenda that was different from one that would have resulted from a different campaign. Specifically, the deficit received more attention because Perot

Table 2-1 Vote for President, by Time of Vote Decision and Party Identification, 1992

Party Identification	Vote	When Voter Decided			
		Knew All Along	Through Conventions	After Conventions Through Debates	Last Two Weeks or Later
Strong	Clinton	96	96	96	69
Democrat	Bush	4	2	0	10
	Perot	0	1	4	21
	(N)	(68)	(167)	(56)	(37)
Weak	Clinton	57	91	73	35
Democrat	Bush	41	6	8	20
	Perot	2	3	19	46
	(N)	(30)	(106)	(76)	(75)
Independent,	Clinton	85	81	65	60
leans	Bush	15	3	7	6
Democrat	Perot	0	15	29	34
	(N)	(22)	(69)	(76)	(57)
Independent,	Clinton	53	36	31	45
no partisan	Bush	43	19	16	24
leanings	Perot	4	45	54	31
	(N)	(14)	(38)	(33)	(53)
Independent,	Clinton	0	11	10	17
leans	Bush	95	66	47	52
Republican	Perot	5	23	44	32
	(N)	(31)	(60)	(44)	(68)
Weak	Clinton	0	16	23	19
Republican	Bush	97	73	37	41
	Perot	3	11	40	41
	(N)	(53)	(65)	(63)	(70)
Strong	Clinton	0	1	6	8
Republican	Bush	100	97	64	53
	Perot	0	2	30	40
	(N)	(83)	(73)	(29)	(32)
Total	Clinton	36	60	50	35
	Bush	63	31	21	29
	Perot	1	10	29	36
	(N)	(303)	(579)	(377)	(396)

Note: Numbers in parentheses are the total cases on which percentages are based. The numbers are weighted.

was in the race than would have been true otherwise. It is also probably true that his candidacy set the stage for greater spending cuts and larger tax increases to deal with the deficit than a two-candidate race would have.

Finally, the campaign of 1992 may have a lasting legacy for future races for the presidency. Clinton and Perot made frequent appearances on the talk show circuit. (The former was on five shows a total of forty-seven times in 1992 through the election, the latter thirty-three times. These numbers compare to sixteen appearances by Bush.)[31] Clinton also made frequent use of the town meeting format of the second presidential debate. Both these techniques permit a candidate to contact the electorate and respond to people's concerns without dealing with the established news media and without paying for television time. Most observers believe that the new formats mean that different questions are addressed, and it appears that voters respond positively to the new channels of communication; the conventional media have reacted less favorably. It seems likely that we will see more of this in the future, from both President Clinton and his prospective 1996 opponents.

Chapter 3

The Election Results

Although according to national polls the race had tightened during the last week of the campaign, Bill Clinton maintained a comfortable lead as election day, November 3, 1992, approached. All four television networks relied upon the same exit polls (Voter Research and Surveys), so their "calls" for each state came within minutes of each other. Perhaps in reaction to criticism that in the past three elections they had predicted the winner hours before the polls had closed in the West, CBS, NBC, and CNN waited until 10:48 p.m. (EST) to call the election, and ABC made its call two minutes later.

In the final tally, Clinton had carried thirty-two states and the District of Columbia, and George Bush had carried eighteen. H. Ross Perot finished second to Clinton in Maine and second to Bush in Utah, but he came in third in every other state and in the District of Columbia. Clinton won 44.9 million votes to Bush's 39.1 million, while Perot gained 19.7 million votes. Clinton won 43.0 percent of the votes cast, Bush gained 37.4 percent, Perot won 18.9 percent, and 0.6 percent of the votes were scattered among minor candidates. Clinton prevailed by a 5.6 percentage point margin over Bush. In 1980 Ronald Reagan had won by 9.7 points over Jimmy Carter, and in 1984 he had defeated Walter F. Mondale by a massive 18.2 points. In 1988, Bush prevailed over Dukakis by 7.7 points. The 1992 election was the closest contest since Carter defeated Gerald R. Ford by 2.1 points in 1976. Table 3-1 presents the official election results, by state, for the 1992 election.[1]

Clinton's electoral vote tally was impressive. As Map 3-1D of Figure 3-1 reveals, Clinton won 370 electoral votes to Bush's 168, and Perot won none. Even so, Clinton's electoral vote tally fell short of those of the three

Table 3-1 Official Presidential Election Results by States, 1992

State	Electoral Vote Dem.	Electoral Vote Rep.	Electoral Vote Other	Total Vote	Clinton (D)	Bush (R)	Perot	Other*	Plurality		Dem.	Rep.	Perot
Alabama		9		1,688,060	690,080	804,283	183,109	10,588	114,203	R	40.9%	47.6%	10.8%
Alaska		3		258,506	78,294	102,000	73,481	4,731	23,706	R	30.3%	39.5%	28.4%
Arizona		8		1,486,975	543,050	572,086	353,741	18,098	29,036	R	36.5%	38.5%	23.8%
Arkansas	6			950,653	505,823	337,324	99,132	8,374	168,499	D	53.2%	35.5%	10.4%
California	54			11,131,721	5,121,325	3,630,574	2,296,006	83,816	1,490,751	D	46.0%	32.6%	20.6%
Colorado	8			1,569,180	629,681	562,850	366,010	10,639	66,831	D	40.1%	35.9%	23.3%
Connecticut	8			1,616,332	682,318	578,313	348,771	6,930	104,005	D	42.2%	35.8%	21.6%
Delaware	3			289,735	126,054	102,313	59,213	2,155	23,741	D	43.5%	35.3%	20.4%
Florida		25		5,314,392	2,072,698	2,173,310	1,053,067	15,317	100,612	R	39.0%	40.9%	19.8%
Georgia	13			2,321,125	1,008,966	995,252	309,657	7,250	13,714	D	43.5%	42.9%	13.3%
Hawaii	4			372,842	179,310	136,822	53,003	3,707	42,488	D	48.1%	36.7%	14.2%
Idaho		4		482,142	137,013	202,645	130,395	12,089	65,632	R	28.4%	42.0%	27.0%
Illinois	22			5,050,157	2,453,350	1,734,096	840,515	22,196	719,254	D	48.6%	34.3%	16.6%
Indiana		12		2,305,871	848,420	989,375	455,934	12,142	140,955	R	36.8%	42.9%	19.8%
Iowa	7			1,354,607	586,353	504,891	253,468	9,895	81,462	D	43.3%	37.3%	18.7%
Kansas		6		1,157,335	390,434	449,951	312,358	4,592	59,517	R	33.7%	38.9%	27.0%
Kentucky	8			1,492,900	665,104	617,178	203,944	6,674	47,926	D	44.6%	41.3%	13.7%
Louisiana	9			1,790,017	815,971	733,386	211,478	29,182	82,585	D	45.6%	41.0%	11.8%
Maine	4			679,499	263,420	206,504	206,820	2,755	56,600	D	38.8%	30.4%	30.4%
Maryland	10			1,985,046	988,571	707,094	281,414	7,967	281,477	D	49.8%	35.6%	14.2%
Massachusetts	12			2,773,700	1,318,662	805,049	630,731	19,258	513,613	D	47.5%	29.0%	22.7%
Michigan	18			4,274,673	1,871,182	1,554,940	824,813	23,738	316,242	D	43.8%	36.4%	19.3%
Minnesota	10			2,347,948	1,020,997	747,841	562,506	16,604	273,156	D	43.5%	31.9%	24.0%
Mississippi		7		981,793	400,258	487,793	85,626	8,116	87,535	R	40.8%	49.7%	8.7%
Missouri	11			2,391,565	1,053,873	811,159	518,741	7,792	242,714	D	44.1%	33.9%	21.7%
Montana	3			410,611	154,507	144,207	107,225	4,672	10,300	D	37.6%	35.1%	26.1%

Nebraska		5	737,546	216,864	343,678	174,104	2,900	126,814	R	29.4%	46.6%	23.6%
Nevada	4		506,318	189,148	175,828	132,580	8,762	13,320	D	37.4%	34.7%	26.2%
New Hampshire	4		537,943	209,040	202,484	121,337	5,082	6,556	D	38.9%	37.6%	22.6%
New Jersey	15		3,343,594	1,436,206	1,356,865	521,829	28,694	79,341	D	43.0%	40.6%	15.6%
New Mexico	5		569,986	261,617	212,824	91,895	3,650	48,793	D	45.9%	37.3%	16.1%
New York	33		6,926,925	3,444,450	2,346,649	1,090,721	45,105	1,097,801	D	49.7%	33.9%	15.7%
North Carolina		14	2,611,850	1,114,042	1,134,661	357,864	5,283	20,619	R	42.7%	43.4%	13.7%
North Dakota		3	308,133	99,168	136,244	71,084	1,637	37,076	R	32.2%	44.2%	23.1%
Ohio	21		4,939,967	1,984,942	1,894,310	1,036,426	24,289	90,632	D	40.2%	38.3%	21.0%
Oklahoma		8	1,390,359	473,066	592,929	319,878	4,486	119,863	R	34.0%	42.6%	23.0%
Oregon	7		1,462,643	621,314	475,757	354,091	11,481	145,557	D	42.5%	32.5%	24.2%
Pennsylvania	23		4,959,810	2,239,164	1,791,841	902,667	26,138	447,323	D	45.1%	36.1%	18.2%
Rhode Island	4		453,477	213,299	131,601	105,045	3,532	81,698	D	47.0%	29.0%	23.2%
South Carolina		8	1,202,527	479,514	577,507	138,872	6,634	97,993	R	39.9%	48.0%	11.5%
South Dakota		3	336,254	124,888	136,718	73,295	1,353	11,830	R	37.1%	40.7%	21.8%
Tennessee	11		1,982,638	933,521	841,300	199,968	7,849	92,221	D	47.1%	42.4%	10.1%
Texas		32	6,154,018	2,281,815	2,496,071	1,354,781	21,351	214,256	R	37.1%	40.6%	22.0%
Utah		5	743,999	183,429	322,632	203,400	34,538	119,232	R	24.7%	43.4%	27.3%
Vermont	3		289,701	133,592	88,122	65,991	1,996	45,470	D	46.1%	30.4%	22.8%
Virginia		13	2,558,665	1,038,650	1,150,517	348,639	20,859	111,867	R	40.6%	45.0%	13.6%
Washington	11		2,288,230	993,037	731,234	541,780	22,179	261,803	D	43.4%	32.0%	23.7%
West Virginia	5		683,762	331,001	241,974	108,829	1,958	89,027	D	48.4%	35.4%	15.9%
Wisconsin	11		2,531,114	1,041,066	930,855	544,479	14,714	110,211	D	41.1%	36.8%	21.5%
Wyoming		3	200,598	68,160	79,347	51,263	1,828	11,187	R	34.0%	39.6%	25.6%
Dist. of Col.	3		227,572	192,619	20,698	9,681	4,574	171,921	D	84.6%	9.1%	4.3%
United States	370	168	104,425,014	44,909,326	39,103,882	19,741,657	670,149	5,805,444	D	43.0%	37.4%	18.9%

* Other includes Andre V. Marrou (Libertarian party), who received 291,627 votes, James Gritz (America First party), who received 107,014 votes, and a variety of other candidates.

Source: *America Votes 20: A Handbook of Contemporary American Election Statistics*, ed. Richard A. Scammon and Alice V. McGillivray (Washington, D.C.: Congressional Quarterly Inc., 1993), 7.

Figure 3-1 Electoral Votes by States, 1980-1992
Map 3-1A Electoral Votes by States, 1980

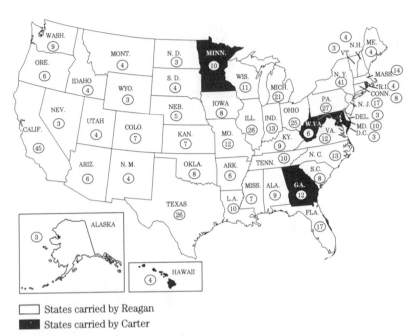

☐ States carried by Reagan
■ States carried by Carter

Note: Reagan won 489 electoral votes; Carter won 49 electoral votes.

previous Republican victories. In 1980, Reagan had captured forty-four states and 489 electoral votes (Map 3-1A), while in 1984 he had carried forty-nine states and 525 electoral votes (Map 3-1B). In 1988, Bush had carried forty states and 426 electoral votes (Map 3-1C).

The success of Clinton's electoral vote strategy (discussed in Chapter 2) is apparent. Clinton won all fourteen of the "top end" states (including the District of Columbia), earning 182 electoral votes. Among the eighteen "play hard" states in which he competed heavily, Clinton carried seventeen (all but North Carolina), thus gaining another 180 electoral votes. He won none of the ten "big challenge" states, which he had virtually conceded to Bush. But he narrowly won two of the nine "watch daily" states, New Hampshire and Nevada, picking up an additional eight electoral votes.

The Perot Vote and the Election Rules

Despite his solid electoral vote margin, Clinton had the third lowest popular vote percentage of any presidential winner since the current

Map 3-1B Electoral Votes by States, 1984

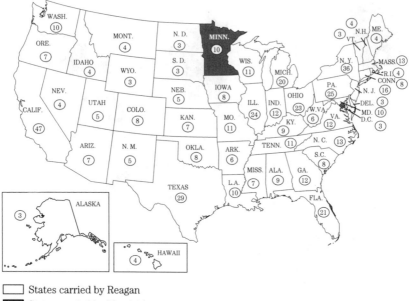

☐ States carried by Reagan
■ States carried by Mondale

Note: Reagan won 525 electoral votes; Mondale won 13 electoral votes.

presidential nomination system was developed in 1832. In the forty-one presidential elections from 1832 through 1992, only Abraham Lincoln in 1860 (with 39.8 percent of the popular vote) and Woodrow Wilson in 1912 (with 41.8 percent) won with a lower share of the popular vote. But Bush's popular vote tally was even more dismal. From 1832 through 1992, there were twenty-three contests in which the party controlling the White House ran its incumbent president. Eight of these incumbents were defeated; but only William Howard Taft (who won only 23.2 percent of the popular vote in 1912) fared worse than Bush. Taft lost to Wilson, but he also trailed Theodore Roosevelt, the Progressive candidate, who won 27.4 percent of the popular vote.

Just as Roosevelt's challenge reduced the Democratic and Republican share of the popular vote, Perot's popular vote tally drove down the vote share for both Clinton and Bush. Indeed, from a popular vote standpoint, Perot's third place challenge ranks only behind Theodore Roosevelt's 1912 candidacy and the 21.5 percent earned by Millard Fillmore, the Whig-American candidate, in 1856. Both Roosevelt and Fillmore, moreover, were past presidents.

Map 3-1C Electoral Votes by States, 1988

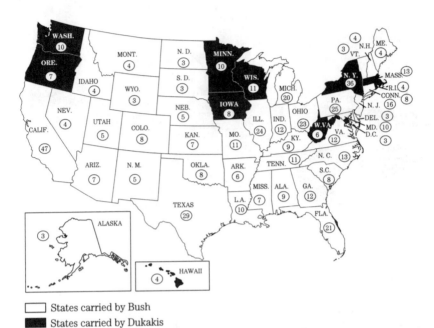

☐ States carried by Bush
■ States carried by Dukakis

Note: Bush won 426 electoral votes; Dukakis won 111 electoral votes. One of West Virginia's six electors voted for Bentsen.

Although Clinton might very well have won anyway in a direct popular vote contest, he was clearly the beneficiary of the U.S. electoral system. As we saw in Chapter 2, U.S. voters do not directly vote for president or vice president. Rather, they vote for a slate of electors pledged to support a presidential and vice-presidential candidate. Moreover, in every state except Maine and Nebraska, the slate that receives the most votes is selected. In no state is a majority of the vote required. In fact, Clinton (or, to be more precise, the slate of electors pledged to Clinton) won the majority of the vote only in the District of Columbia and Arkansas. Bush did not win a majority of the popular vote in a single state.

The plurality-vote winner-take-all system has a major consequence. It tends to transform a nationwide plurality of the popular vote into an absolute majority of the electoral votes. And it takes an absolute majority of the electoral votes for the electoral college to produce a winner. If there is no majority winner in the electoral college, the U.S. House of Representatives, voting by state delegation, chooses a winner among the three candidates with the largest number of electoral votes. But the

Map 3-1D Electoral Votes by States, 1992

■ States carried by Clinton
☐ States carried by Bush

Note: Clinton won 370 electoral votes; Bush won 168 electoral votes.
Sources: The results for 1980, 1984, and 1988 are from *Presidential Elections Since 1789*, 5th ed. (Washington, D.C.: Congressional Quarterly Inc., 1991), 212-214.

House has not chosen a president since 1824, mainly because the plurality-vote system is very likely to produce a majority winner in the electoral college. The majority vote winner is usually the presidential candidate with the most popular votes. Indeed, in thirty-nine of the forty-one elections held from 1832 through 1992, the candidate with the most popular votes has received an absolute majority of the electoral votes (the two exceptions were 1876 and 1888).[2] During this period there have been thirteen elections in which a candidate won only a plurality of the popular vote but an absolute majority of the electoral vote.[3]

This system takes a very heavy toll on third-party or independent candidates. A successful third-party candidate usually receives a far smaller share of the electoral vote than of the popular vote.[4] We can consider the fate of the three most successful independent or third-party candidates (in popular vote terms) since World War II, George C. Wallace (who won 13.5 percent of the vote in 1968), John B. Anderson (who won 6.6 percent in 1980), and Perot. Map 3-2A of Figure 3-2

Figure 3-2 Percentage of the Vote Received by Wallace in 1968, Anderson in 1980, and Perot in 1992

Map 3-2A Percentage of the Vote Received by Wallace in 1968

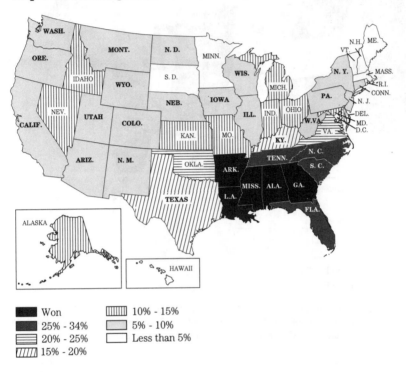

Won
25% - 34%
20% - 25%
15% - 20%
10% - 15%
5% - 10%
Less than 5%

presents Wallace's share of the vote by state in 1968, Map 3-2B shows Anderson's share in 1980, and Map 3-2C shows Perot's share in 1992. Clearly, there are regional differences in the Anderson and Perot vote. Both fared worst in the South, and both did somewhat better in New England than elsewhere. In addition, Perot did well in the mountain West and in Alaska. Perot, as we have noted, even finished second in two states. But neither Anderson nor Perot won a single electoral vote. Wallace, on the other hand, did much better. Even though he received a smaller share of the popular vote than Perot, he came in first in five states (winning a majority of the popular vote in Alabama and Mississippi), and gained 46 electoral votes (including one faithless elector from North Carolina). But even Wallace won only 8.5 percent of the electoral vote, less than his popular vote share.[5]

The U.S. plurality-vote system can be seen as a confirmation of Duverger's Law, a proposition advanced by Maurice Duverger in the early 1950s. According to Duverger, "the simple-majority single-ballot

Map 3-2B Percentage of Vote Received by Anderson, 1980

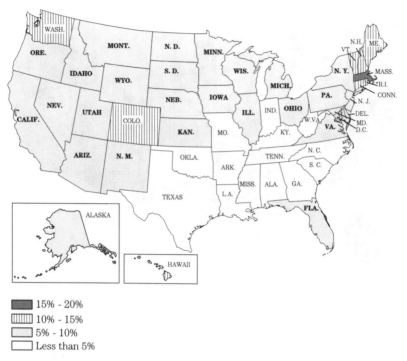

■ 15% - 20%
▥ 10% - 15%
▢ 5% - 10%
☐ Less than 5%

system favors the two-party system." In other words, a plurality-vote win system in which there are no runoff elections tends to favor the dominance of two political parties. Indeed, Duverger argued, "The American procedure corresponds to the usual machinery of the simple-majority single-ballot system. The absence of a second ballot and of further polls, particularly in the presidential election, constitutes in fact one of the historical reasons for the emergence and the maintenance of the two-party system." [6]

According to Duverger, this principle applies for two reasons. First, the plurality-vote system has a "mechanical" effect. Third-place parties may earn a large number of votes but fail to gain a plurality of the vote in many electoral units. Second, the plurality-vote system has a "psychological" effect. Some voters who prefer a party or candidate whom they think cannot win will cast a vote for their first choice among the major party candidates. This behavior is often called sophisticated or strategic voting. William Riker defines strategic voting as "voting contrary to one's immediate tastes in order to obtain an advantage in the long run." [7] As we shall demonstrate in Chapter 6, it seems highly

Map 3-2C Percentage of Vote Received by Perot, 1992

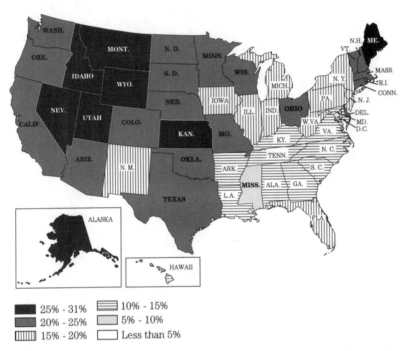

■ 25% - 31%	▤ 10% - 15%
■ 20% - 25%	▨ 5% - 10%
▥ 15% - 20%	☐ Less than 5%

Sources: The results for 1968 and 1980 are from *Presidential Elections Since 1789*, 5th ed.(Washington, D.C.: Congressional Quarterly Inc., 1991), 136,139. The 1992 results are from Richard M. Scammon and Alice V. McGillivray, *America Votes 20*, (Washington, D.C.: Congressional Quarterly Inc., 1993), 7.

likely that some voters who preferred Perot decided instead to vote for Clinton or Bush.

Of course, we cannot know what the results would have been if an alternative electoral system had been used, because some voters might have voted differently if the election rules had been different. But, as Gerald M. Pomper points out, the electoral college system does have one virtue: it produces a clear winner who is recognized as the legitimately elected president despite his minority count in the popular vote. Pomper argues that "The existing system, while hard to justify in democratic philosophy, [gives] the nation a clear, immediate, and legitimate verdict." [8] If the president were elected by a direct popular vote, a runoff election might be necessary.[9] Moreover, in 1992, the system probably produced a Condorcet winner, that is, a candidate who would have won in a head-to-head contest against any opponent.[10] As we will show in Chapter 6, it seems likely that Clinton would have won in a two-person race against either Bush or Perot.[11]

The Pattern of Results

The 1992 presidential election may be placed in perspective by comparing it with previous presidential elections and by studying the overall pattern of results. Three conclusions emerge. Despite his solid electoral college victory, Clinton's popular vote margin was very low, demonstrating potential vulnerability. Second, the Clinton victory ended, at least temporarily, a pattern of Republican dominance in postwar presidential elections. Last, Clinton's victory reinstated a pattern of volatility that began with Dwight D. Eisenhower's 1952 victory.

Clinton's popular vote tally, as we saw, was the third worst for a winning candidate since 1832. Unless there is a three-way contest in 1996, Clinton cannot win reelection merely by holding the voters he won in 1992. There is considerable evidence that the Perot vote would have split evenly between Clinton and Bush in 1992. Of course, some Perot voters would not have voted at all if he had not been on the ballot, and the remaining vote would not have been split evenly between Clinton and Bush in every state. Even so, it seems likely that the electoral vote outcome would have been similar even if Perot had not reentered the contest. But many of Perot's 19.7 million voters will vote again in 1996. In a two-candidate race, Clinton may need almost half of them to be reelected. How well he will fare among these voters is difficult to estimate, but they seem a more likely target than the 39.1 million voters who supported Bush. Back in 1972, Richard M. Nixon captured most of the 1968 Wallace voters, along with some who had voted for Hubert H. Humphrey, his 1968 Democratic rival. Although Nixon's landslide win in 1972 was hardly predictable, survey data did demonstrate that most Wallace voters preferred Nixon to Humphrey. Clinton has no such clear advantage among Perot voters.

All the same, Clinton overcame the Republican dominance in postwar presidential elections. Even with Clinton's win, however, the Republicans have won seven of the twelve elections since World War II, including five of the last seven. They have won the majority of the popular vote six times (1952, 1956, 1972, 1980, 1984, and 1988); the Democrats have won a majority only twice (1964 and 1976). The average (mean) level of Republican presidential support is 49.8 percent; the average level of Democratic support is only 45.6 percent. Moreover, during these elections, the Republican presidential candidates have won 41 million more votes than the Democrats—a total of 457,215,000 cast for Republican candidates and 415,845,000 cast for the Democrats.

Despite this Republican advantage, the postwar results reveal considerable volatility, and the changeability of the electorate was underscored by the 1992 result. Between 1952 and 1984, no party was able to win more than two elections in a row, although Bush's 1988 victory broke that pattern. The high level of change since World War II sets the postwar era in sharp contrast with most of American electoral history. Table 3-2 shows the presidential election results since 1832, the first year the candidate of the modern Democratic party, Andrew Jackson, ran for reelection. From 1832 through 1948 we find four periods in which a single party won a series of three or more elections. The Republicans won six consecutive elections from 1860 through 1880, although in 1876 Rutherford B. Hayes beat Samuel Tilden by a single electoral vote, and Tilden had a majority of the popular vote. The Republicans also won four elections from 1896 through 1908, as well as three from 1920 through 1928. The Democrats won five straight elections from 1932 through 1948.

After 1948, a period of volatility began. But although no party was able to manage three straight wins, until 1980 the winning party was able to pull off a second presidential victory. The Republicans won in 1952 and 1956, the Democrats in 1960 and 1964, and the Republicans in 1968 and 1972. In all these elections, the second win was bigger than the first. The Democrats won narrowly in 1976 but failed to hold the White House in 1980. The 1980 and 1984 Republican victories fit the earlier pattern, a win followed by a bigger win. But in 1988, with Bush's election, the Republicans won their third straight election, albeit with a smaller margin than in 1984. With Clinton's victory, political volatility returned.

The 1976 and 1980 elections are the only elections in the twentieth century in which two consecutive incumbent presidents lost. There were two similar periods in the nineteenth century, however. Four elections in a row were lost by the incumbent party from 1840 through 1852, a period of alternation between the Democrats and the Whigs, and again from 1884 through 1896, a period of alternation between the Republicans and the Democrats. Both of these intervals preceded major party realignments. After the Whig party's loss in 1852, the Republican party replaced it as the second major party. Although many Whigs, including Lincoln, became Republicans, the Republican party was not just the Whig party renamed. The Republicans had transformed the American political agenda by capitalizing upon opposition to extending slavery into the territories.[12] Their political base was different from that of the Whigs, for Republicans had no southern support. But they created a base in the Midwest, something the Whigs had never established.

The 1896 contest, the last in a series of four incumbent party losses, is usually viewed as a critical election because it solidified Republican dominance. Although the Republicans had won all but two of the elections after the Civil War, many of their victories were by narrow

Table 3-2   Presidential Election Results, 1832-1992

Election	Winning Candidate	Party of Winning Candidate	Success of Incumbent Political Party
1832	Andrew Jackson	Democrat	Won
1836	Martin Van Buren	Democrat	Won
1840	William H. Harrison	Whig	Lost
1844	James K. Polk	Democrat	Lost
1848	Zachary Taylor	Whig	Lost
1852	Franklin Pierce	Democrat	Lost
1856	James Buchanan	Democrat	Won
1860	Abraham Lincoln	Republican	Lost
1864	Abraham Lincoln	Republican	Won
1868	Ulysses S. Grant	Republican	Won
1872	Ulysses S. Grant	Republican	Won
1876	Rutherford B. Hayes	Republican	Won
1880	James A. Garfield	Republican	Won
1884	Grover Cleveland	Democrat	Lost
1888	Benjamin Harrison	Republican	Lost
1892	Grover Cleveland	Democrat	Lost
1896	William McKinley	Republican	Lost
1900	William McKinley	Republican	Won
1904	Theodore Roosevelt	Republican	Won
1908	William H. Taft	Republican	Won
1912	Woodrow Wilson	Democrat	Lost
1916	Woodrow Wilson	Democrat	Won
1920	Warren G. Harding	Republican	Lost
1924	Calvin Coolidge	Republican	Won
1928	Herbert C. Hoover	Republican	Won
1932	Franklin D. Roosevelt	Democrat	Lost
1936	Franklin D. Roosevelt	Democrat	Won
1940	Franklin D. Roosevelt	Democrat	Won
1944	Franklin D. Roosevelt	Democrat	Won
1948	Harry S Truman	Democrat	Won
1952	Dwight D. Eisenhower	Republican	Lost
1956	Dwight D. Eisenhower	Republican	Won
1960	John F. Kennedy	Democrat	Lost
1964	Lyndon B. Johnson	Democrat	Won
1968	Richard M. Nixon	Republican	Lost
1972	Richard M. Nixon	Republican	Won
1976	Jimmy Carter	Democrat	Lost
1980	Ronald Reagan	Republican	Lost
1984	Ronald Reagan	Republican	Won
1988	George Bush	Republican	Won
1992	Bill Clinton	Democrat	Lost

Source: Presidential Elections Since 1789, 5th ed. (Washington, D.C.: Congressional Quarterly Inc., 1991), 174-214.

margins. In 1896 the Republicans emerged as the clearly dominant party, gaining a solid hold in New York, Connecticut, New Jersey, and Indiana, states in which they frequently had lost in the 1876-1892 period. After William McKinley's defeat of William Jennings Bryan in 1896, the Republicans established a firmer base in the Midwest, New England, and mid-Atlantic states. They lost the presidency only in 1912, when, as we have noted, the GOP was split, and in 1916, when Wilson ran for reelection.

The Great Depression ended Republican dominance. The emergence of the Democrats as the majority party was not preceded by a series of incumbent losses. The Democratic coalition, forged in the mid-1930s, relied heavily upon the emerging industrial working class and at least partly upon the mobilization of new groups into the electorate.

As the emergence of the New Deal coalition demonstrates, a period of electoral volatility is not a necessary precondition for a partisan realignment. Nor, perhaps, is volatility a sufficient condition. In 1985, Ronald Reagan himself proclaimed that a Republican realignment had occurred. Political scientists were skeptical of this claim, mainly because of Democratic dominance in the U.S. House of Representatives, but some argued that a "split-level realignment" had occurred.[13] While Bush's 1988 electoral victory seemed to suggest an era of Republican dominance in presidential elections, Clinton's victory suggests that volatility has returned.

State-by-State Results

Politicians, journalists, and political scientists are fascinated by how presidential candidates fare in each state because states deliver the electoral votes needed to win the presidency. The presidential contest can be viewed as fifty-one separate elections, one for each state and one for the District of Columbia.

As we have seen, the candidate with the most votes in each state, with the exception of Maine and Nebraska, wins all of the state's electoral votes. In the two states that use a congressional district plan to allocate their electors, there are actually multiple contests: three in Maine (one for the two at-large electors and one for each of Maine's two districts) and four in Nebraska. Regardless of how a state decides to allocate its electors, the number of electors for each state is the sum of its senators (two) plus the number of representatives in the House. In 1992, the number of electors ranged from a low of three in Alaska, Delaware, Montana, North Dakota, South Dakota, Vermont, Wyoming, and the District of Columbia to a high of fifty-four in California. There are 538 electors and an absolute majority (270) is required for a candidate to be elected by the electoral college. In 1992 the ten largest states, which have between fourteen and fifty-four electors, had 54 percent of the total population, but they chose only 48 percent of the total electors. The twenty-three smallest states (including the District of Columbia), which have from three to seven electors, are all overrepresented in the electoral college. They make up 13 percent of the population, but they choose 19 percent of the electors.

In the actual election contest, however, the candidates focus on the larger states, unless polling data indicate they are unwinnable. Despite being underrepresented on a per capita basis, California still provides one-fifth of the electoral votes necessary to win the presidency. Even so, Bush quit campaigning in California in early September since the polls showed that Clinton had a commanding lead.

States are the building blocks of winning presidential coalitions, but state-by-state results can be overemphasized, and may even be misleading. First, as we saw, in thirty-nine of the forty-one presidential elections from 1832 through 1992, the candidate with the largest popular vote has also gained a majority of the electoral vote. Thus, candidates can win by gaining broad-based support throughout the nation, even though they must also consider their likelihood of winning specific states. Moreover, given the importance of national television coverage, candidates must run national campaigns. They can make special appeals to states and regions, but these appeals may be broadcast through the national media.

Second, comparing state-by-state results can be misleading because these comparisons may conceal change. To illustrate this point, we can compare the results of two of the closest postwar elections—John F. Kennedy's win over Nixon in 1960 and Carter's win over Ford in 1976. There are many striking parallels between these two Democratic victories. In 1960 and 1976 the Republicans did well in the West, and both Kennedy and Carter needed southern support to win.[14] Kennedy carried six of the eleven states of the old Confederacy (Arkansas, Georgia, Louisiana, North Carolina, South Carolina, and Texas), as well as 5 of Alabama's 11 electoral votes, for a total of 81 electoral votes. Carter carried ten of these states (all but Virginia) for a total of 118 electoral votes.

The demographic basis of Carter's support was quite different from Kennedy's, however. In 1960, only 29 percent of the African-American adults in the South were registered to vote, compared with 61 percent of the white adults. According to our analysis of survey data from the National Election Studies (NES), only one voter out of fifteen who supported Kennedy in the South was an African-American. After the Voting Rights Act of 1965, however, black registration increased. In 1976, 63 percent of the African-Americans in the South were registered to vote, compared with 68 percent of the whites.[15] We estimate that about one out of three southerners who voted for Carter was black. A comparison of

Figure 3-3 The Winner's Margin of Victory, 1980-1992

Map 3-3A Reagan's Margin of Victory over Carter, 1980

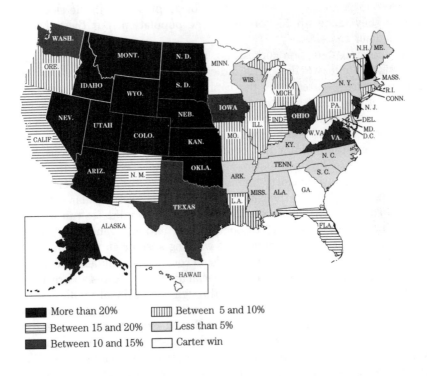

◾ More than 20%   ▥ Between 5 and 10%

▤ Between 15 and 20%   ▢ Less than 5%

◼ Between 10 and 15%   ▢ Carter win

state-by-state results conceals this massive change in the Democratic presidential coalition.

Third, state-by-state comparisons do not tell us why a presidential candidate received support. Of course, such changes can lead to interesting speculation, especially when dominant political issues are clearly related to regional differences. But it is also necessary to turn to surveys, as we do in Part 2, to understand the dynamics of electoral change.

With these qualifications in mind, we can turn to the state-by-state results. Figure 3-3 shows Reagan's margin of victory over Carter in 1980, Reagan's margin over Mondale in 1984, Bush's margin over Dukakis in 1988, and Clinton's margin over Bush in 1992. These maps clearly reveal differences between these three Republican victories, and they also demonstrate parallels between Bush's defeat in 1992 and his victory in 1988.

In 1980 Reagan did far better in the West than in other regions (Map 3-3A). We consider eighteen states as western from the standpoint of

Map 3-3B Reagan's Margin of Victory over Mondale, 1984

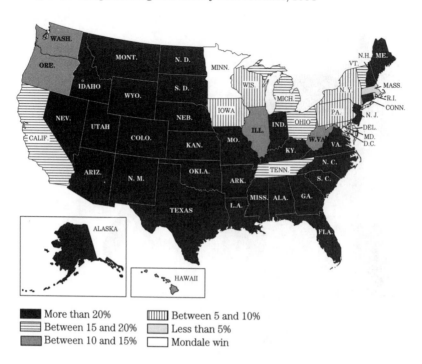

■ More than 20%   ▥ Between 5 and 10%
▤ Between 15 and 20%   ☐ Less than 5%
▨ Between 10 and 15%   ☐ Mondale win

presidential elections, and Reagan won thirteen of them by a margin of 20 points or more, while winning two other states by 15 to 20 points.[16]

In 1984 (Map 3-3B), the West no longer appeared distinctive. Reagan won by a larger overall margin in 1984, and he had impressive wins in many more states. Although Reagan still had a massive margin of victory in the West, he now carried seventeen states outside the West by a margin of 20 points or more. His biggest gains were in the South. In 1980 he had carried none of the eleven southern states by a 20-point margin. In 1984, he carried ten of them by a margin of at least 20 points, and he carried Tennessee by 16 points. Although southern blacks voted overwhelmingly for Mondale, his losses in the South were still massive. Whereas in 1980 Carter had won over one-third of the southern white vote, only about one white southern voter in four supported Mondale.

The 1988 results show a clear improvement for the Democrats (Map 3-3C). Dukakis won two New England states, gaining nearly half (49.9 percent) of the vote in this region. He carried three midwestern states. Dukakis fared slightly worse than Carter in the border states, where he won only West Virginia. Like Mondale, Dukakis lost all eleven southern states.

Map 3-3C Bush's Margin of Victory over Dukakis, 1988

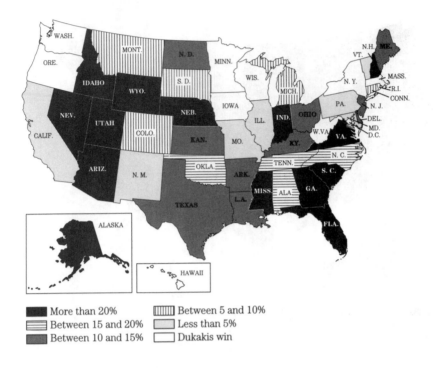

■ More than 20%	▥ Between 5 and 10%	
▤ Between 15 and 20%	□ Less than 5%	
■ Between 10 and 15%	□ Dukakis win	

Bush's overall margin of victory was much smaller than Reagan's margin over Mondale in 1984 and somewhat smaller than Reagan's margin over Carter. Moreover, Bush's regional strength differed from Reagan's. Bush's best region was the South, and he was far less dominant in the West than Reagan. Bush won five southern states by a margin of 20 points and three others by 15 to 20 points. He won the three remaining states by a margin of 10 to 15 points. Bush thus won every southern state by more than his national margin (7.7 points) and carried the South as a whole by 17.5 points over Dukakis.

In the eighteen states we view as western, Bush actually lost three states and won by less than 10 percentage points in five others, including California, which he carried by less than 5 percentage points. If we restrict our attention to the eight mountain states,[17] we find that Bush carried five by a margin of greater than 20 points, but he carried the remaining three by less than 10 points. The combined results for these states show a Bush margin of 16.8 points over Dukakis, slightly smaller than his margin in the South. Bush's overall margin in all eighteen western states was only 7.5 points, slightly *less* than his national margin.

Map 3-3D Clinton's Margin of Victory over Bush, 1992

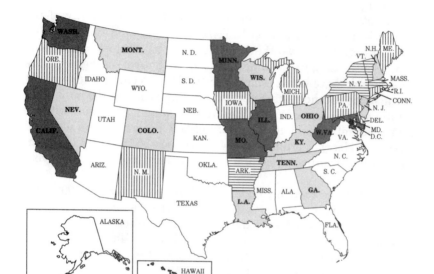

■ More than 20%   ▥ Between 5 and 10%
▤ Between 15 and 20%   ☐ Less than 5%
▨ Between 10 and 15%   ☐ Bush win

Sources: The results for 1980, 1984, and 1988 are from *Presidential Elections Since 1789*, 5th ed., (Washington, D.C.: Congressional Quarterly Inc., 1991), 139-141. The results for 1992 are from Richard M. Scammon and Alice V. McGillivray, *America Votes 20*, (Washington, D.C.: Congressional Quarterly Inc., 1993), 7.

In 1992, as in 1988, the South was the best region for the Republicans. As Map 3-3D shows, Clinton lost seven of the eleven southern states, and he won three others by less than 5 percentage points. For all eleven states, Bush won 42.6 percent of the popular vote, compared with 41.2 percent for Clinton. The Republican dominance of the West, which was already slipping by 1988, had disappeared. Among the eighteen states we classify as western, Clinton and Bush each won nine. Clinton even won four of the eight mountain states, although three of his wins were by less than 5 percentage points. But the mountain West was Perot's best region (see Map 2-C), and he won 25.2 percent of the vote there. Bush won 38.1 percent of the popular vote in these states, with Clinton winning 36.3 percent. But by winning by nearly 1.5 million votes over Bush in California, Clinton fared better in the eighteen western states than Bush. He carried 41.2 percent of all the western votes, compared with 35.6 percent for Bush.

His 5.6 percent margin over Bush in the West was the same as his national margin.

The South was the only region where Bush won a majority of the electoral vote. The South yielded 147 electoral votes, and Bush won 108 of them. Indeed, nearly two-thirds of Bush's total electoral votes came from the South. Despite fielding a ticket with two southerners, the Democrats would have won a clear majority of the electoral votes without carrying a single southern state. Lyndon B. Johnson was the only other Democratic winner since World War II who would have won without southern electoral votes, but Johnson, unlike Clinton, won an electoral vote landslide. Harry S Truman in 1948, Kennedy in 1960, and Carter in 1976 all needed southern electoral votes to earn their electoral vote majorities.

Indeed, it is instructive to compare Clinton's victory in 1992 with Jimmy Carter's victory in 1976. Although Carter actually won many southern states by a relatively narrow margin, his electoral vote victory depended very heavily upon southern electoral votes. Of the 297 electoral votes he won, 118 came from southern states. Of the 370 electoral votes that Clinton won, only 39 came from the South.

Clearly, the South has been transformed from the most Democratic region in presidential elections to the most Republican. As we shall see in Chapter 9, a similar but less dramatic shift has occurred in congressional voting. In congressional elections, regional differences between the parties, pronounced in the 1950s, were negligible by 1992. And, there has also been a decline in regional differences in presidential elections. Perhaps the most striking feature of the 1984, 1988, and 1992 elections is the relative absence of regional differences, which can be shown through statistical analysis.

Joseph A. Schlesinger has analyzed state-by-state variation in all the presidential elections from 1832 through 1988, and we have updated his analysis through 1992. His measure is the standard deviation among the states in the percentage of Democratic voting. In 1992, the state-by-state deviation was only 5.96 points, the fourth lowest in all twelve postwar elections. In 1988, the state-by-state deviation was only 5.60 points, the second lowest in postwar history, and in 1984 it was 5.84, the third lowest. State-by-state variation was somewhat higher in 1980 (7.95 points), placing that election in the middle range (fifth) among the postwar elections. But what is most striking in Schlesinger's analysis is the relatively low level of state-by-state variation in all twelve post-war elections. According to his analysis, all fifteen of the presidential elections from 1888 through 1944 displayed more state-by-state variation than any of the twelve postwar elections. To a very large extent, the decline in state-by-state variation results from the transformation of the South.[18]

Electoral Change in the Postwar South

The transformation of the South was a complex process, but the major reason for the change is simple. As V. O. Key, Jr., brilliantly demonstrated in *Southern Politics in State and Nation* (1949), the crucial factor in southern politics is race: "In its grand outlines the politics of the South revolves around the position of the Negro.... Whatever phase of the southern political process one seeks to understand, sooner or later the trail of inquiry leads back to the Negro." [19] And it is the changed position of the national Democratic party toward African-Americans that smashed Democratic dominance in the South. [20]

Between the end of Reconstruction and the end of World War II, the South was a Democratic stronghold. In fifteen of the seventeen elections from 1880 through 1944, all eleven southern states voted Democratic. In his 1920 victory over James M. Cox, Warren G. Harding narrowly carried Tennessee, but the ten remaining southern states voted Democratic. The only major southern defections occurred in 1928, when the Democrats ran Alfred E. Smith, a Roman Catholic. The Republican candidate, Hoover, won five southern states. Even so, six of the most solid southern states— Alabama, Arkansas, Georgia, Louisiana, Mississippi, and South Carolina— voted for Smith, even though all but Louisiana were overwhelmingly Protestant. [21] After southern blacks lost the right to vote in the South, the Republicans ceded these states to the Democrats. Although the Republicans, as the party of Lincoln, had black support in the North, they did not attempt to enforce the Fifteenth Amendment, which bans restrictions on voting on grounds of "race, color, or previous condition of servitude."

In 1932 a majority of African-Americans remained loyal to Hoover, although by 1936 Franklin D. Roosevelt won the support of northern blacks. Roosevelt made no effort to win the support of southern blacks, most of whom were effectively disenfranchised. Even as late as 1940 about 70 percent of the nation's blacks lived in the states of the Old Confederacy. Roosevelt carried all eleven of these states in all four of his elections. His 1944 victory, however, was the last contest in which the Democratic candidate carried all eleven southern states.

World War II led to a massive migration of African-Americans from the South, and by 1948 Truman, through his support of the Fair Employment Practices Commission, made explicit appeals to blacks. Truman's executive order ending segregation in the armed services, issued in July 1948, was also unpopular in the South. [22] These policies led to defections by the "Dixiecrats" and cost Truman four southern states (Alabama, Louisiana, Mississippi, and South Carolina). But Truman still won all seven of the remaining southern states. Adlai E. Stevenson deemphasized appeals to blacks, and he held most of the deep southern states, although Eisenhower made inroads. [23]

In 1952, Eisenhower captured Florida, Tennessee, Texas, and Virginia, and in 1956 he won all four of these states as well as Louisiana. In 1960, Kennedy also played down appeals to African-Americans, and southern support was essential in his win over Nixon (see Map 3-3A). By choosing Texan Lyndon B. Johnson as his running mate, Kennedy may have helped himself in the South. Clearly, Johnson's presence on the ticket helped Kennedy win Texas, which he carried by only a 2 percentage point margin.[24]

But if Johnson as running mate aided the Democrats in the South, Johnson as president played a different role. His support for the Civil Rights Act of 1964, as well as his explicit appeal to African-Americans, helped end Democratic dominance in the South. Goldwater, the Republican candidate, had voted against the Civil Rights Act, creating a sharp contrast between the presidential candidates. By 1968, Humphrey, who had long been a champion of black causes, carried only one southern state, Texas, which he won with only 41 percent of the vote. (He was probably aided by Wallace's candidacy, since Wallace gained 19 percent of the Texas vote.) Wallace's third-party candidacy carried Alabama, Arkansas, Georgia, Louisiana, and Mississippi, while Nixon carried the remaining five southern states. Nixon carried every southern state in 1972, and his margin of victory was somewhat greater in the South than outside the South. Although Carter won ten of the eleven southern states (all but Virginia), he carried a minority of the vote among white southerners.

In 1980, Reagan carried every southern state but Georgia, Carter's home state. In his 1984 reelection, he won every southern state, and his margin of victory was greater in the South than outside the South (Map 3-3B). In 1988, Bush carried all eleven southern states, and the South was his strongest region (see Map 3-3C). Although Clinton made some inroads in the South, Bush won seven of the eleven southern states, but he won North Carolina by less than 1 percentage point and Florida by less than 2 points (see Table 3-1). The 1976, 1980, and 1992 elections all demonstrate that the South can be a highly competitive region, at least when the Democrats field a presidential candidate from that region. All the same, the South emerged as the only predominantly Republican region in the 1992 election, and the transformation of the South is clearly the most dramatic regional change in postwar American politics.

Was There a Republican Electoral Vote Advantage?

The Republicans dominated presidential elections from 1972 through 1988. After his relatively narrow win over Humphrey in 1968, Nixon swept forty-nine states in his defeat of George S. McGovern four years later.

Although Carter won a narrow victory in 1976, the Republicans swept most states during the Reagan and Bush elections, winning forty-nine states in Reagan's 1984 triumph over Mondale (see Map 3-1B).

As a result of these victories the Republicans repeatedly carried many states over the course of these five elections (see Figure 2-1). Some scholars went so far as to argue that the Republicans held an electoral vote lock. According to Marjorie Randon Hershey, the Republicans won so many states during recent elections that they had "a clear and continuing advantage in recent presidential elections." [25] This advantage, Hershey argued, came mainly from the Republican strength in a large number of small states, which, as we have seen, are overrepresented in the electoral college. But Michael Nelson argued that the Republicans did not have an electoral vote advantage, and James C. Garand and T. Wayne Parent maintained that the electoral college was biased toward the Democrats.[26]

If there was a Republican bias in the electoral college in 1992, it was remarkably small. We can test for this possibility by asking what the results would have been if Bush and Clinton had each received the same share of the popular vote. As Clinton won by 5.6 percentage points, we can add 2.8 percentage points to Bush's vote in every state and subtract 2.8 percent from Clinton's. This hypothetical shift would move Colorado, Georgia, Kentucky, Louisiana, Montana, Nevada, New Hampshire, New Jersey, Ohio, Tennessee, and Wisconsin from the Clinton column to the Bush column, and Bush would have won with 275 electoral votes. In fact, Bush would have defeated Clinton even if Clinton led by a nationwide margin of 40.6 percent to 39.8 percent.

This is a very small bias. Of course, this hypothetical example does demonstrate that the electoral college can elect the plurality-vote loser, just as it did in 1876 and 1888.[27] The probability that a "wrong winner" will be elected is smaller than it was before World War II, however, since in those earlier elections the Democrats often won southern states by large popular vote margins.[28]

Today's elections are much more national in scope, and the electoral college provides no significant barrier to either party. Indeed, the last two elections show a very even balance. Figure 3-4 shows the combined results of the 1988 and 1992 presidential elections. We show the states won by Dukakis in 1988 and by Clinton in 1992, those won by Bush in 1988 and by Clinton in 1992, and those that Bush won in both elections.[29] The ten states (plus the District of Columbia) won by the Democrats in both contests will be worth 107 electoral votes in the 1996 and 2000 elections, and the eighteen states won by Bush in both elections will be worth 168. The remaining twenty-two states will be worth 263 electoral votes.

This mixture shows problems and opportunities for both parties. The results suggest that the Republicans now have strong prospects in

Figure 3-4 Results of the 1988 and 1992 Elections

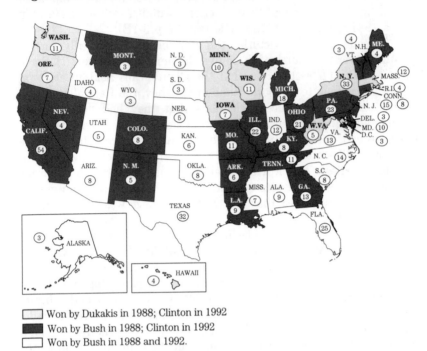

☐ Won by Dukakis in 1988; Clinton in 1992
■ Won by Bush in 1988; Clinton in 1992
☐ Won by Bush in 1988 and 1992.

Note: The electoral votes for states are the numbers for the 1992, 1996, and 2000 elections.
Sources: The 1988 results are from *Presidential Elections Since 1789*, 5th ed.(Washington, D.C.: Congressional Quarterly Inc., 1991), 214.

the South but that they may have "overinvested" resources in winning this region. For example, the conservative appeals that helped Bush carry these states may have cost him votes in California. The Democrats have demonstrated that they can win the presidency without the South, but many of their victories in the Midwest and West were in swing states that Clinton took by very narrow margins (see Map 3-3D). Moreover, an election in which the major party candidates carry the majority of the vote in only a single state can provide very little comfort for either political party. The potential Republican realignment of the 1980s may have dissolved, but no clear pattern has replaced it.

To assess future political prospects for the major political parties, as well as the electoral prospects for a new political movement, we must go beyond analyzing official voting statistics. To determine who voted, the way in which social coalitions have been transformed, and the issue preferences of the electorate, we must use surveys to analyze the political attitudes and behavior of individuals. Likewise, we must analyze surveys to study the extent to which the 1992 election was basically a rejection of Bush and the extent to which it was an endorsement of Clinton's policies. And we must study surveys to examine the way in which the basic partisan loyalties of the American electorate have changed during the postwar years. Part 2 of our study will use survey research data to examine the prospects for change and continuity in American electoral politics.

Voting Behavior in the 1992 Presidential Election

The collective decision reached on November 3, 1992, was the product of 183.5 million individual decisions.[1] Two choices faced American citizens eighteen years and older: whether to vote and, if they decided to vote, how to cast their ballots. How voters make up their minds is one of the most thoroughly studied subjects in political science—and one of the most controversial.[2]

Voting decisions can be studied from at least three theoretical perspectives. First, individuals may be viewed primarily as members of social groups. Voters belong to primary groups of family members and peers; secondary groups, such as private clubs, trade unions, and voluntary associations; and broader reference groups, such as social classes and ethnic groups. Understanding the political behavior of these groups is the key to understanding voters, according to the pioneers of this approach, Paul F. Lazarsfeld, Bernard R. Berelson, and their colleagues. Using their simple "index of political predisposition," they classified voters according to their religion (Catholic or Protestant), socioeconomic level, and residence (urban or rural) to predict how they would vote in the 1940 presidential election. Lazarsfeld and his colleagues maintained that "a person thinks, politically, as he is, socially. Social characteristics determine political preference."[3] This perspective is still very popular, although more so among sociologists than political scientists. The writings of Robert R. Alford, Richard F. Hamilton, and Seymour Martin Lipset provide excellent examples of this sociological approach.[4]

A second approach emphasizes psychological variables. To explain voting choices in the 1952 and 1956 presidential elections, Angus Campbell, Philip E. Converse, Warren E. Miller, and Donald E. Stokes, scholars at the University of Michigan Survey Research Center (SRC), developed a model of political behavior based upon social-psychological variables.[5] They focused on attitudes likely to have the greatest effect just before the moment of decision, particularly attitudes toward the candidates, parties, and issues. Party identification emerged as the major social-psychological variable that influences voting decisions. The Michigan approach is the most prevalent among political scientists, although many de-emphasize its psychological underpinnings. The writings of Philip E. Converse provide outstanding examples of this research tradition.[6]

A third approach draws heavily on the work of economists. According to this perspective, citizens weigh the cost of voting against the expected benefits of voting when deciding whether to go to the polls. And when deciding whom to choose on election day, voters calculate which candidate favors policies closest to their policy preferences. Citizens are thus viewed as rational actors who attempt to maximize their expected utility. Anthony Downs and William H. Riker helped to found this rational choice approach.[7] The writings of Riker, Peter C. Ordeshook, John A. Ferejohn, and Morris P. Fiorina provide excellent examples of this point of view.[8]

How, then, do voters decide? In our view none of these perspectives provides a complete answer. Although individuals belong to groups, they are not always influenced by their group memberships. Moreover, classifying voters by social groups does not explain why they are influenced by social forces. On the other hand, placing too much emphasis on psychological factors can lead us away from the political forces that shape voting behavior. The assumptions of economic rationality may lead to clearly testable propositions; however, the data used to test them are often weak, and the propositions that can be tested are often of limited importance.

Although taken separately, none of these perspectives adequately explains voting behavior, taken together they are largely complementary. Therefore, we have chosen an eclectic approach that draws upon insights from each viewpoint. Where appropriate, we employ sociological variables, but we also use social-psychological variables such as party identification and feelings of political efficacy. The rational choice approach guides our study of the way issues influence voting decisions.

Part 2 begins by examining the most important decision of all: whether to vote. One of the most profound changes in postwar American politics has been the decline of electoral participation. Although turnout grew fairly consistently between 1920 and 1960, it fell in 1964 and in each of the next four elections. Turnout rose slightly in 1984, but in 1988 it dropped to a postwar low. In the 1960 contest between John F. Kennedy and Richard Nixon, 63 percent of the adult population voted; in the 1988 contest between George Bush and Michael S. Dukakis, only 50 percent voted. In 1992, turnout rose by 5 percentage points, although it was still much lower than it had been in 1960. Turnout is somewhat higher in the United States than in Switzerland, but it is about 15 percentage points lower than turnout in Canada. And turnout is much higher in all the remaining industrialized democracies. But although turnout was low in the 1992 presidential election, it was not equally low among all social groups, and we examine group differences in detail. Drawing mainly upon a social-psychological perspective, Chapter 4 studies changes in attitudes that have contributed to the decline in electoral participation. We attempt to explain why turnout increased somewhat in 1992 and to assess the extent to which H. Ross Perot's campaign helped stimulate turnout. We also attempt to determine whether the increase in turnout helped Bill Clinton defeat George Bush. Finally, recognizing that overall levels of electoral participation are still very low in the United States, we attempt to determine whether low turnout threatens democracy itself.

In Chapter 5 we examine how social forces influence the vote. The National Election Studies (NES) surveys enable us to analyze the vote for Clinton, Bush, and Perot by race, gender, region, age, occupation, union membership, and religion. The impact of these social forces has changed considerably during the past half-century. Support for the Democratic party among the traditional New Deal coalition of white southerners, union members, the working class, and Catholics has eroded. Despite Clinton's victory, it seems unlikely that the old New Deal coalition can be restored.

Chapter 6 examines attitudes toward both the candidates and the issues. Because Clinton won in a three-person contest, it is possible that the outcome would have been different had Perot not been a candidate. Although Perot's campaign during the spring and summer may very well have influenced the choice of issues emphasized during the campaign, we show that his entry into the race on October 1 probably had no effect on the outcome. Had Perot not reentered the race, Clinton would still have been elected, although he would have won a clear majority of the popular vote. Moreover, we show that Clinton probably would have won in a head-to-head contest against *either* Bush or Perot. Turning to issues, we begin by examining the concerns of the electorate, and we show how the increased concern with economic issues diminished Bush's chances. We attempt to assess the extent to which voters based their votes upon their issue preferences. We pay special attention to the abortion controversy, not because it was the major issue for most voters, but because the NES survey clearly demonstrates that voters do not decide on the basis of issues unless they know where the candidates themselves stand on those issues. We pay special attention to the issue preferences of Perot voters.

We then turn to how presidential performance influences voting decisions. Recent research suggests that many voters decide how to vote on the basis of "retrospective" evaluations of incumbents. In other words, what incumbents have done in office—not what candidates promise to do if elected—affects how voters decide. In Chapter 7 we assess the role of retrospective evaluations in the last six presidential elections. Voters' evaluations of Gerald R. Ford's performance in 1976 played a major role in the election of Jimmy Carter, whereas four years later the voters' evaluations of Carter played a major role in the election of Ronald Reagan. To a very large extent, Bush's defeat in 1992 resulted from negative evaluations of his performance as president. We also pay special attention to the retrospective evaluations of Perot voters.

How closely do voters identify with a political party? And how does this identification shape issue preferences and retrospective evaluations of the incumbent and the incumbent party? Chapter 8 explores the impact of party loyalties on voting choices during the postwar era. Beginning in 1984 there was a shift in party loyalties to the Republican party; but that shift ended, and was possibly reversed, in 1992. Party loyalties played an important role in shaping issue preferences and evaluations of Bush. On the other hand, more than 19 million Americans voted for a candidate with no party label. Many of these Perot voters were Democrats or Republicans, although half were self-professed independents. We pay special attention to the party identification of Perot voters, for, as we have argued, no major party candidate can win in 1996 without drawing a substantial proportion of these 19 million voters.

Chapter 4

Who Voted?

Before discovering how people voted in the 1992 presidential election, we must answer a more basic question: Who voted? Only 55 percent of the adult population voted for president. Although there was a substantial increase in turnout over the 1988 contest, turnout in the United States remains lower than in any other industrialized democracy except Switzerland.[1] Did the increase in turnout help Bill Clinton? If nonvoters had participated in greater numbers, who would have been elected? Even though Clinton won by nearly 6 million votes over George Bush, the 74 million Americans who did not vote easily could have reelected Bush, or they could have chosen H. Ross Perot. In principle, nonvoters could have elected any alternative candidate, since many more Americans chose not to vote at all than voted for Clinton. Yet, it is unlikely that the surge in turnout accounted for Clinton's victory, and even less likely that increased turnout would have changed the outcome of the Clinton-Bush-Perot contest. Before we study turnout in the 1992 election, however, we must place the election in a broader historical context.[2]

Turnout from 1828 through 1916

Historical records can be used to determine how many people voted in presidential elections, and we can derive meaningful estimates of turnout for elections as early as 1828. Turnout is calculated by dividing the total number of votes cast for president by the voting-age population. But should the turnout denominator (that is, the voting-age population) include all persons old enough to vote, or should it include only those *eligible* to vote? The answer to this question greatly affects our estimate of turnout in all presidential elections through 1916, because few women were legally eligible to vote until 1920.

Although women gained the right to vote in the Wyoming Territory as early as 1869, even by the 1916 presidential election only eleven of the forty-eight states had enfranchised women, and these were mainly western states with small populations.[3] The Nineteenth Amendment, which granted women voting rights in all states, was ratified only a few months before the 1920 election. Because women were already voting in some states, it is difficult to estimate turnout before 1920. Clearly, women should be included in the turnout denominator in those states where they had the right to vote. Including them in those states where they could not vote leads to very low estimates of turnout.

Table 4-1 presents two sets of estimates of turnout between 1828 and 1916. The first column, compiled by Charles E. Johnson, Jr., calculates turnout by dividing the total number of votes cast for president by the voting-age population. The second, based upon Walter Dean Burnham's calculations, measures turnout by dividing the total presidential vote by the total number of Americans eligible to vote. Burnham excludes southern blacks before the Civil War, and from 1870 on he excludes aliens where they could not vote. But the major difference between Burnham's calculations and Johnson's is that Burnham excludes women from his turnout denominator in states where they could not vote.

Most political scientists would consider Burnham's calculations to be more revealing than Johnson's. For example, most political scientists argue that turnout was higher in the nineteenth century than it is today. But even if we reject this interpretation, both sets of estimates reveal the same pattern of change. There is clearly a large jump in turnout after 1836, for both the Democrats and the Whigs began to employ popular appeals to mobilize the electorate. Turnout jumped markedly in the 1840 election, the "Log Cabin and Hard Cider" campaign in which the Whig candidate, William Henry Harrison, the hero of Tippecanoe, defeated the incumbent Democrat, Martin Van Buren. Turnout waned after 1840, but it rose rapidly after the Republican party, founded in 1854, polarized the nation by taking a clear stand against the extension of slavery into the territories. In Abraham Lincoln's election in 1860, four white men out of five went to the polls.

Turnout waxed and waned after the Civil War, peaking in the 1876 contest between Rutherford B. Hayes, the Republican winner, and Samuel J. Tilden, the Democratic candidate. As a price of Hayes's contested victory, the Republicans agreed to end Reconstruction in the South. Having lost the protection of federal troops, many African-Americans were prevented from voting. Although some southern blacks could still vote in 1880, overall turnout among blacks

Table 4-1   Turnout in Presidential Elections, 1828-1916

Election Year	Winning Candidate	Party of Winning Candidate	Percentage of Voting-age Population Who Voted	Percentage Eligible to Vote Who Voted
1828	Andrew Jackson	Democrat	22.2	57.3
1832	Andrew Jackson	Democrat	20.6	56.7
1836	Martin Van Buren	Democrat	22.4	56.5
1840	William H. Harrison	Whig	31.9	80.3
1844	James K. Polk	Democrat	30.6	79.0
1848	Zachary Taylor	Whig	28.6	72.8
1852	Franklin Pierce	Democrat	27.3	69.5
1856	James Buchanan	Democrat	30.6	79.4
1860	Abraham Lincoln	Republican	31.5	81.8
1864[a]	Abraham Lincoln	Republican	24.4	76.3
1868	Ulysses S. Grant	Republican	31.7	80.9
1872	Ulysses S. Grant	Republican	32.0	72.1
1876	Rutherford B. Hayes	Republican	37.1	82.6
1880	James A. Garfield	Republican	36.2	80.6
1884	Grover Cleveland	Democrat	35.6	78.3
1888	Benjamin Harrison	Republican	36.3	80.5
1892	Grover Cleveland	Democrat	34.9	78.3
1896	William McKinley	Republican	36.8	79.7
1900	William McKinley	Republican	34.0	73.7
1904	Theodore Roosevelt	Republican	29.7	65.5
1908	William H. Taft	Republican	29.8	65.7
1912	Woodrow Wilson	Democrat	27.9	59.0
1916	Woodrow Wilson	Democrat	32.1	61.8

Sources: The estimates of turnout among the voting-age population are based upon Charles E. Johnson, Jr., *Nonvoting Americans,* ser. P-23, no. 102 (U.S. Department of Commerce, Bureau of the Census, Washington, D.C.: U.S. Government Printing Office, 1980), 2. The estimates of turnout among the population eligible to vote are based upon calculations by Walter Dean Burnham. Burnham's earlier estimates were published in U.S. Department of Commerce, Bureau of the Census, *Historical Statistics of the United States: Colonial Times to 1970,* ser. Y-27-78 (Washington, D.C.: U.S. Government Printing Office, 1975), 1071-1072. The results in this table, however, are based upon Burnham, "The Turnout Problem," in *Elections American Style,* ed. A. James Reichley (Washington, D.C.: Brookings Institution, 1987), 113-114.

[a] The estimate for the voting-age population is based upon the entire U.S. adult population. The estimate for the eligible population excludes the eleven Confederate states that did not take part in the election.

dropped sharply, which in turn reduced southern turnout. Turnout began to fall nationwide by 1892, but it rose in the 1896 contest between William Jennings Bryan (Democrat and Populist) and William McKinley, the Republican winner. Turnout dropped in the 1900 rerun between the same two men.

By the late nineteenth century, African-Americans were denied the franchise throughout the South, and poor whites often found it difficult to vote as well.[4] Throughout the country registration requirements, which were in part designed to reduce fraud, were introduced. Because individuals were responsible for getting their names on the registration rolls before the election, the procedure created an obstacle that reduced electoral participation.[5]

The introduction of the secret ballot also reduced turnout. Before this innovation, most voting in U.S. elections was public. Ballots were printed by the political parties; each party produced its own. Ballots differed in size and color, and any observer could see how each person voted. In 1856 Australia adopted a law calling for a secret ballot to be printed and administered by the government. The "Australian ballot" was first used statewide in the United States in Massachusetts in 1888. By the time of the 1896 election, nine out of ten states had followed Massachusetts's lead.[6] Although the secret ballot was introduced to reduce coercion and fraud, it also reduced turnout. When voting was public, men could sell their votes, but candidates were less willing to pay for a vote if they could not see it delivered. Ballot stuffing was also more difficult to manage when the state printed and distributed the ballot.

As Table 4-1 shows, turnout trailed off rapidly in the early twentieth century. By the time of the three-way contest among Woodrow Wilson (Democrat), William Howard Taft (Republican), and Theodore Roosevelt (Progressive), fewer than three out of five eligible Americans went to the polls. In 1916 turnout rose slightly, but just over three-fifths of eligible Americans voted, and only one-third of the total adult population went to the polls.

Turnout from 1920 through 1992

It is easier to calculate turnout after 1920, and we have provided estimates based upon Census Bureau statistics. Although there are alternative ways to measure the turnout denominator, they lead to relatively small differences in the overall estimate of turnout.[7]

In Table 4-2 we show the percentage of the voting-age population that voted for the Democratic, Republican, and minor party and independent candidates in the nineteen elections between 1920 and 1992. The table also shows the percentage that did not vote, as well as the overall size of the voting-age population. In Figure 4-1, we show the percentage of the voting-age population that voted in each of these nineteen elections.

As Table 4-2 shows, Clinton received the vote of only 24 percent of the voting-age population. Seventeen of the eighteen previous winners between 1920 and 1988 exceeded this total. Calvin Coolidge, the sole exception, won with a similar share in 1924. In fact, eight *losing* candidates (Wendell Willkie in 1940, Thomas E. Dewey in 1944, Adlai E. Stevenson in 1952 and 1956, Nixon in 1960, Barry M. Goldwater in 1964, Hubert H. Humphrey in 1968, and Ford in 1976) equaled or exceeded Clinton's share.

Clinton's low share results from two factors. First, he won only 43 percent of the total vote. Second, despite a substantial increase in turnout in 1992, turnout was still quite modest, even by American standards. But Bush did decidedly worse than Clinton. He received the votes of only 21 percent of the voting-age population. The only major party candidates to win a smaller share were James M. Cox in 1920 and John W. Davis in 1924. Bush gained about the same share as Hoover in 1932, Alfred M. Landon in 1936, and George S. McGovern in 1972.

As Figure 4-1 makes clear, turnout increased in seven of the ten elections from 1920 through 1960. Two of the exceptions—1944 and 1948—result from the social dislocations during and shortly after World War II. Specific political events explain why more people voted in certain elections. The jump in turnout from 1924 to 1928 resulted from the candidacy of Alfred E. Smith, the first Roman Catholic to receive a major party nomination, and the increase from 1932 to 1936 resulted from Franklin D. Roosevelt's efforts to mobilize the lower social strata, particularly the industrial working class. The extremely close contest between Nixon and the second Catholic candidate, John F. Kennedy, partly accounts for the high turnout in 1960. Turnout rose to 62.8 percent of the voting-age population and to 65.4 percent of the eligible population.[8] This was far below the percentage of eligible Americans that voted between 1840 and 1900, although it was the highest percentage of the voting-age population that had ever voted in a presidential election (see Table 4-1). Nonetheless, U.S. turnout in 1960 was still far below the average level of turnout attained in most Western democracies.

Although short-term factors account for the rise in turnout in specific elections, long-term changes were also driving turnout upward. The changing social characteristics of the electorate contributed to increasing turnout. For example, women who came of age to vote before the Nineteenth Amendment often failed to exercise their right to vote, but women who came of age after 1920 had higher turnout. These older women were gradually replaced by women who had the right to vote

Table 4-2   Percentage of Adults Who Voted for Each Major Presidential Candidate, 1920-1992

Election Year	Democratic Candidate		Republican Candidate		Other Candidates	Did Not Vote	Total Percent	Voting-age Population
1920	14.8	James M. Cox	26.2	Warren G. Harding	2.4	56.6	100	61,639,000
1924	12.7	John W. Davis	23.7	Calvin Coolidge	7.5	56.1	100	66,229,000
1928	21.1	Alfred E. Smith	30.1	Herbert C. Hoover	.6	48.2	100	71,100,000
1932	30.1	Franklin D. Roosevelt	20.8	Herbert C. Hoover	1.5	47.5	100	75,768,000
1936	34.6	Franklin D. Roosevelt	20.8	Alfred M. Landon	1.5	43.1	100	80,174,000
1940	32.2	Franklin D. Roosevelt	26.4	Wendell Willkie	.3	41.1	100	84,728,000
1944	29.9	Franklin D. Roosevelt	25.7	Thomas E. Dewey	.4	44.0	100	85,654,000
1948	25.3	Harry S Truman	23.0	Thomas E. Dewey	2.7	48.9	100	95,573,000
1952	27.3	Adlai E. Stevenson	34.0	Dwight D. Eisenhower	.3	38.4	100	99,929,000
1956	24.9	Adlai E. Stevenson	34.1	Dwight D. Eisenhower	.4	40.7	100	104,515,000
1960	31.2	John F. Kennedy	31.1	Richard M. Nixon	.5	37.2	100	109,672,000
1964	37.8	Lyndon B. Johnson	23.8	Barry M. Goldwater	.3	38.1	100	114,090,000
1968	26.0	Hubert H. Humphrey	26.4	Richard M. Nixon	8.4	39.1	100	120,285,000
1972	20.7	George S. McGovern	33.5	Richard M. Nixon	1.0	44.8	100	140,777,000
1976	26.8	Jimmy Carter	25.7	Gerald R. Ford	1.0	46.5	100	152,308,000
1980	21.6	Jimmy Carter	26.7	Ronald Reagan	4.3	47.4	100	164,595,000
1984	21.5	Walter F. Mondale	31.2	Ronald Reagan	.4	46.9	100	174,468,000
1988	22.9	Michael S. Dukakis	26.7	George Bush	.5	49.9	100	182,779,000
1992	23.8	Bill Clinton	20.7	George Bush	10.8	44.8	100	189,044,000

Sources: Results for 1920 through 1928 are based upon U.S. Department of Commerce, Bureau of the Census, *Statistical Abstract of the United States, 1972* (Washington, D.C.: U.S. Government Printing Office, 1972), 358, 373; results for 1932 through 1988 are based upon *Statistical Abstract of the United States, 1992* (Washington, D.C.: U.S. Government Printing Office, 1992), 251, 270. For 1992 the voting-age population is based upon U.S. Department of Commerce, Bureau of the Census, *Projections of the Population of Voting Age for States, November 1992*, ser. P-25, no. 1085 (Washington, D.C.: U.S. Government Printing Office, 1992), 1; the number of votes for each candidate and the total number of votes cast are based upon *America Votes 20: A Handbook of Contemporary American Election Statistics*, ed. Richard M. Scammon and Alice V. McGillivray (Washington, D.C.: Congressional Quarterly Inc., 1993), 7.

Note: The names of winning candidates are italicized.

Figure 4-1 Percentage of Voting-Age Population That Voted for President, 1920-1992

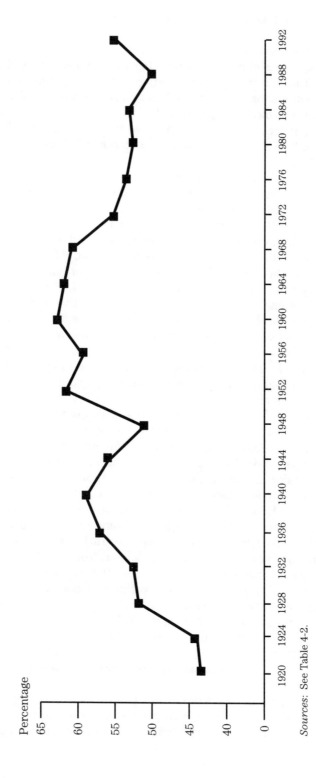

Sources: See Table 4-2.

when they reached voting age.[9] Because all states restricted voting to citizens, many immigrants failed to enter the electorate. But after 1921, as a result of restrictive immigration laws, the percentage of the population that was foreign born declined. Moreover, levels of formal education have been growing throughout the twentieth century, a change that has boosted turnout. Americans who have attained higher levels of education are much more likely to vote than those who have lower educational levels.

As Figure 4-1 shows, the trend toward increased turnout has been reversed since 1960. By 1960, the generational replacement among the female electorate had largely run its course. In the 1960s and 1970s, immigration laws were reformed, again increasing the noncitizen population. However, educational levels continued to rise, a change that might have been expected to increase turnout. After the passage of the Voting Rights Act of 1965, turnout rose dramatically among African-Americans in the South, and their return to the voting booth spurred voting among southern whites. Less restrictive registration requirements during the last three decades have made it easier to vote. Despite these changes, overall levels of turnout declined after 1960. Except for a small increase in participation from 1980 to 1984, turnout declined continuously from 1960 through 1988, and by 1988 only 50.1 percent of the voting-age population voted. We will explain why turnout declined later in this chapter.

In 1992, there were some efforts to increase turnout, and many were targeted at the young. The MTV network's "Rock the Vote" effort enlisted rock stars to encourage young Americans to vote, and there were voter registration drives on college campuses. On the other hand, neither of the major parties made a significant effort to increase turnout. The Clinton campaign focused far more on courting Democrats who had defected to Ronald Reagan and George Bush than on mobilizing participation among the disadvantaged. To some extent, Americans who were politically disaffected may have been attracted by Perot's candidacy, a possibility we explore later in this chapter. Voter participation increased, rising by 5.1 percentage points from 1988 to 1992. According to our estimates, 55.2 percent of the voting-age population voted. Among voting-age citizens, according to our estimates, 58.5 percent voted. Despite this increase, turnout was still 7.6 percentage points lower than it had been in the Kennedy-Nixon contest.

Turnout Among Social Groups

Although turnout was low in 1992, it was not equally low among all social groups. To compare turnout among social groups we will rely upon two main sources: the 1992 National Election Studies (NES) and the Current Population Survey conducted by the U.S. Bureau of the Census. With both studies, reported turnout is higher than actual turnout, although this bias is substantially greater for the NES survey. The NES survey includes only U.S. citizens. Among the 2,248 respondents questioned in the postelection interview, 76.2 percent said they voted for president, whereas only 58.5 percent of the politically eligible population voted.[10] A similar bias is found with previous reports of electoral participation based upon earlier NES presidential election surveys.

There are three basic reasons that the NES surveys exaggerate turnout. First, even though respondents are asked a question that supplies reasons for not voting, some nonvoters falsely claim to have voted.[11] Vote validation studies, in which the NES has directly checked registration and voting records, suggest that about 15 percent of the respondents who claim to have voted have not actually voted, whereas only a handful of actual voters say that they did not vote.[12] Second, the NES surveys do not perfectly represent the voting-age population. Lower socioeconomic groups, which have very low turnout, are underrepresented. Third, during presidential years the same respondents are interviewed both before and after the election. Being interviewed before an election provides a stimulus to vote and thus increases turnout among the NES sample.[13]

Wherever possible, we supplement our analyses with Census Bureau studies of turnout. Beginning in 1964, and for every subsequent midterm and presidential election, the Census Bureau has conducted a survey to determine who voted.[14] As a government agency, the bureau cannot ask some of the more important questions posed by political scientists. For example, the bureau asks no questions about political attitudes or religion. Also, these surveys cannot be used to determine *how* people voted. Asking any such questions would be inappropriate for a government agency.

Despite these limitations, Census Bureau studies have two major advantages. First, the bureau surveys the lower strata more effectively than the NES. This partly explains why the overall level of turnout in the Census Bureau studies is always much lower than reported turnout in the NES surveys.[15] In 1992, reported turnout in the Census Bureau survey was 61.3 percent, only 6 points higher than turnout among the voting-age population.[16] Second, the Census Bureau surveys are much larger than the NES surveys. In 1992, for example, the Current Population Survey conducted interviews in 57,000 households, and thus gathered information on about 106,000 individuals.[17] This large sample size allows us to make comparisons that are not practical with the NES surveys. For example, with the 1992 NES we have responses from only 119 black men and 166 black women. The Census Bureau survey provides information for approximately 5,300 black men and 6,600 black women.

Race, Gender, Region, Age

Table 4-3 compares reported turnout among basic social groups using the NES survey. Our analysis begins with a comparison of whites and African-Americans. As the table shows, whites were 8 percentage points more likely to report voting than blacks. According to the Census Bureau survey, reported turnout was 54.0 percent among blacks, while it was 63.6 percent among whites, nearly a 10-point difference. As we noted (note 12), all eight vote validation studies show that blacks are more likely than whites falsely to claim having voted, so it seems likely that racial differences are greater than these surveys suggest.[18] Indirect evidence about racial differences in turnout can be found from the exit polls conducted by Voter Research and Surveys on election day. Eleven percent of the voting-age population is black, but blacks made up only 8 percent of the exit poll sample.

Between 1988 and 1992 turnout increased more among whites than among blacks. The Census Bureau surveys register a 3.9 percentage point increase in reported turnout. Among whites, turnout rose 4.5 percentage points; among blacks, it rose only 2.5 points. The racial gap in turnout, which had fallen from 12.2 points in 1964 to 5.6 points in 1984, had increased to 7.6 points in 1988, and increased somewhat more in 1992.[19] Katherine Tate's analysis of the Black National Election Study surveys conducted in 1984 and 1988 suggests that the Rev. Jesse Jackson's 1984 campaign stimulated black turnout, but that in 1988 blacks who supported Jackson's primary bid were less likely to vote in the general election than those who favored Dukakis or other Democratic candidates.[20] In 1992, an election that had no black candidate to mobilize blacks in the primaries and a third-party candidate who was far more attractive to whites than to blacks, blacks responded very little to forces that increased turnout among whites.

Because relatively few African-Americans were sampled in the NES surveys, we will rely on census surveys to make comparisons among them. According to the census surveys, 56.7 percent of the black women, and 50.8 percent of the black men voted. In all previous presidential elections, the Census Bureau had found that southern blacks were less likely to vote than blacks outside the South, but in 1992 there were virtually no regional differences (reported turnout was 54.3 percent of the southern blacks and 53.8 percent among nonsouthern blacks).[21] The survey did find strong age differences, however. Young blacks were far less likely to vote than middle-aged blacks, or even blacks above the age of seventy-five (among whom 60.7 percent voted). Among all blacks between the ages of eighteen and twenty-four,

Table 4-3 Percentage That Reported Voting for President, by Social Group, 1992

Social Group	Voted	Did Not Vote	Total Percent	(N)
Total electorate	76	24	100	(2,248)
Electorate, by race				
African-American	70	30	100	(286)
White	78	22	100	(1,877)
Whites, by Hispanic identification				
Identify as Hispanic	64	36	100	(137)
Do not identify	79	21	100	(1,740)
Whites, by gender				
Females	78	22	100	(974)
Males	78	22	100	(903)
Whites, by region				
New England and Mid-Atlantic	80	20	100	(390)
North Central	82	18	100	(517)
South	69	31	100	(415)
Border	67	33	100	(152)
Mountain and Pacific	82	18	100	(404)
Whites, by birth cohort				
Before 1924	80	20	100	(233)
1924-1939	87	13	100	(307)
1940-1954	82	18	100	(504)
1955-1962	78	22	100	(428)
1963-1970	64	36	100	(316)
1971-1974	59	41	100	(91)
Whites, by social class				
Working class	71	29	100	(746)
Middle class	86	14	100	(844)
Farmers	71	29	100	(87)
Whites, by occupation of head of household				
Unskilled manual	71	29	100	(207)
Skilled, semiskilled manual	71	29	100	(539)
Clerical, sales, other white collar	81	19	100	(284)
Managerial	87	13	100	(325)
Professional and semiprofessional	92	8	100	(235)

(Table continues)

Table 4-3 Continued

Social Group	Voted	Did Not Vote	Total Percent	(N)
Whites, by level of education				
Eight grades or less	56	44	100	(97)
Some high school	48	52	100	(192)
High school graduate	74	26	100	(630)
Some college	85	15	100	(451)
College graduate	90	10	100	(312)
Advanced degree	97	3	100	(146)
Whites, by annual family income				
Less than $10,000	54	46	100	(172)
$10,000 to $14,999	64	36	100	(171)
$15,000 to $19,999	73	27	100	(120)
$20,000 to $24,999	71	29	100	(164)
$25,000 to $29,999	75	25	100	(140)
$30,000 to $34,999	82	18	100	(148)
$35,000 to $39,999	86	14	100	(118)
$40,000 to $49,999	87	13	100	(230)
$50,000 to $59,999	86	14	100	(162)
$60,000 to $74,999	91	9	100	(183)
$75,000 to $89,999	87	13	100	(89)
$90,000 and over	90	10	100	(112)
Whites, by union membership[a]				
Member	85	15	100	(323)
Nonmember	76	24	100	(1,548)
Whites, by religion				
Jewish	97	3	100	(41)
Catholic	82	18	100	(478)
Protestant	78	22	100	(1,041)
None, no preference	65	35	100	(289)
White Protestants, by whether born again				
Not born again	80	20	100	(547)
Born again	76	24	100	(460)
White Protestants, by religious commitment				
Medium or low	79	21	100	(306)
High	76	24	100	(590)
Very high	84	16	100	(145)

(Table continues)

Table 4-3 Continued

Social Group	Voted	Did Not Vote	Total Percent	(N)
White Protestants, by religious tradition				
Mainline	83	17	100	(432)
Evangelical	73	27	100	(434)
Whites, by social class and religion				
Working-class Catholics	78	22	100	(181)
Middle-class Catholics	87	13	100	(243)
Working-class Protestants	72	28	100	(423)
Middle-class Protestants	88	12	100	(443)

Note: Numbers are weighted.

[a] Whether respondent or family member belongs to a trade union.

reported turnout was only 36.6 percent; among black men of this age it was 31.9 percent.

As Table 4-3 shows, among whites, those who identified as Hispanics were less likely to vote than non-Hispanics, mainly because turnout was very low among Mexican-Americans.[22] The Census Bureau survey shows that only 28.9 percent of voting-age Hispanics voted, although this figure rises to 48.3 percent among Hispanics who were citizens. Compared with the 1988 Census Bureau survey, there was a 2-point increase in turnout among Hispanic citizens.[23]

Our table shows that white men and white women were equally likely to report voting. Surveys show that men consistently outvoted women in all presidential elections through 1976. By 1980, the Census Bureau surveys were showing no gender differences in turnout; in 1984, 1988, and 1992 women were slightly more likely to vote than men. In 1992, women were 2.1 percentage points more likely to vote than men. Among whites, women were only 1.9 percentage points more likely to vote than men. Between 1988 and 1992, turnout rose 4.7 points among white women and 4.3 points among white men. The 1980 election appears to mark a historic change, for the participation advantage among men was eliminated.

Of course, we do not need surveys to study turnout in the various regions of the country. Because the Census Bureau estimates the total voting-age population for each state, we can measure turnout merely by dividing the total number of votes cast for president within each state by its voting-age population. Turnout varied greatly from state to state, from a low of 41.9 percent in Hawaii to a high of 72.0 percent in Maine. Official statistics clearly show that turnout was lowest in the South, where only 46.5 percent of the voting-age population voted; outside of the South, 58.7 percent voted.

Official election statistics do not present results according to race, so we need surveys to study relative levels of turnout among whites and blacks within the regions. As Table 4-3 shows, white turnout in the South was lower than it was outside the South.[24] Sixty-nine percent of the whites in the South said that they voted; outside the South, 80 percent reporting voting. The Census Bureau survey also shows that turnout was low among white southerners. According to their survey, 60.8 percent of southern whites voted; outside the South, white turnout was 64.9 percent. The relatively low turnout in the South results partly from the low educational levels in that region.[25] But regional differences have declined dramatically during the past three decades. According to the 1964 census survey, southern whites were 15 percentage points less likely to vote than whites outside the South, and nonwhite southerners were 28 points less likely to vote than nonwhites outside the South.

The 1992 NES survey shows the same general pattern by age as previous surveys. Reported turnout was very low among the youngest age group (the group too young to have voted in 1988), but it was also low among young whites born from 1963 through 1970. Turnout was highest among the cohort born from 1924 through 1939, but it falls among the cohort born before 1924 (which entered the electorate before or during World War II). The Census Bureau survey reveals a similar pattern. Among whites aged eighteen through twenty, only 41.2 percent voted; among those from 21 through 24, 48.2 percent did. These figures show a 6.7 percent rise in turnout compared with eighteen- through twenty-year-olds in the 1988 election, and a 9.5 point increase among twenty-one- through twenty-four-year-olds. The census surveys show turnout continuing to rise with age, peaking at 75.4 percent among whites from 65 through 74. Turnout falls to 65.8 percent among whites seventy-five years old and older. There is little evidence that older Americans disengage from electoral politics. Rather, as Raymond E. Wolfinger and Steven J. Rosenstone show, low turnout among the elderly results from their relatively low level of formal education.[26]

Although the decline in turnout among the elderly is consistent with the relationship between level of education and turnout, the low turnout of the young is not. Young Americans have relatively high levels of formal education. However, as young Americans age, marry, have children, and develop community ties, their turnout tends to increase.

Social Class, Income, and Union Membership

As Table 4-3 shows, social class differences were pronounced in 1992, a finding consistent with the relationship of formal education to turnout. Middle-class whites (nonmanually employed workers and their dependents) were 15 percentage points more likely to report voting than working-class whites (manually employed workers and their dependents).[27] Farmers registered lower than average levels of turnout, but the number of farmers sampled is too small to lead to reliable conclusions. Although the distinction between the middle class and the working class is crude, it appears to capture a politically meaningful division, for when we further divide respondents according to occupation, we find that clerical, sales, and other white collar workers (the lowest level of the middle class) are markedly more likely to vote than skilled and semi-skilled manual workers.

Annual family income was also related to turnout, with reported electoral participation very low among whites with annual family incomes below $10,000 a year.[28] Turnout was very high among whites with annual family incomes of $60,000 and above. The Census Bureau survey also discovered a strong relationship between income and turnout. Among whites with annual family incomes below $10,000, reported turnout was only 37.6 percent; turnout rose to 52.4 percent among those with family incomes from $10,000 through $19,999, and was 69.3 percent among those with family incomes from $20,000 through $49,999; among whites with annual family incomes of $50,000 and above, 81.8 percent voted. Americans with high family incomes tend to have higher levels of formal education, and both education and income contribute to turnout; however, education has a greater impact on turnout than income does.[29]

Surveys over the years have found a weak and inconsistent relationship between union membership and turnout. Although being in a household with a union member may create organizational ties that stimulate turnout, members of union households tend to have somewhat lower levels of formal education. Nevertheless, as Table 4-3 reveals, in 1992 whites in union households were somewhat more likely to report voting than whites in households with no union members.

Religion

In most postwar elections, higher percentages of white Catholics than of white Protestants have voted, but these differences have eroded. As Table 4-3 reveals, in 1992 white Catholics were 4 percentage points more likely to report voting than white Protestants were. Jews have much higher levels of formal education than gentiles and have always had higher turnout. They registered very high reported turnout in the 1992 NES survey, but the number of Jews sampled is too small to reach reliable conclusions. Whites with no religious preference had lower than average turnout.

In recent elections, fundamentalist Protestant leaders have launched get-out-the-vote efforts to mobilize their followers, and we examined turnout among white Protestants in some detail. We found little evidence that mobilization efforts were successful in the 1992 election. We began by exploring differences among white Protestants with differing religious views. As we show in Table 4-3, reported turnout was somewhat lower among white Protestants who said they had been "born again" than among those who had not had this religious experience.[30] However, even these small differences result mainly from regional differences, since southern white Protestants are more likely to be born-again than those outside the South, and, as we saw above, turnout in the South is relatively low. Nearly three out of five southern white Protestants say they have been born again, whereas outside the South only two out of five have had this religious experience. Among southern white Protestants there are no differences in reported turnout among those who were born again and those who were not, but outside the South those who were not born again have slightly higher reported turnout.

David C. Leege and Lyman A. Kellstedt argue that religious commitment is an important dimension of political behavior. We classified white Protestants according to their level of commitment. To receive a score of "very high" on this measure respondents had to report praying several times a day, to attend church at least once a week, to say that religion provides "a great deal" of guidance in their daily lives, and to either believe that the Bible was literally true or that it was "the word of God."[31] White Protestants with a "very high" level of religious commitment were somewhat more likely to report voting than those with lower levels of religious commitment. Southern white Protestants are somewhat more likely to have very high levels of religious commitment than white Protestants outside the South. In the South one-sixth of the white Protestants score very high on our measure; outside the South, only one-eighth score very high. The turnout advantage among the strongly committed is somewhat greater when we take these regional differences into account, but even so turnout is not dramatically higher among the religiously committed. However, as we shall see in Chapters 5 and 10, religious commitment was strongly related to the way Protestants voted.

Beginning with 1990, the NES surveys included detailed questions that allow us to distinguish among Protestant denominations and allow us to conduct analyses of religious differences that could not have been made with earlier NES surveys. We can now divide white Protestants into four basic groups: Evangelicals, mainline Protestants, those with ambiguous affiliations, and nontraditional Protestants. Most white Protestants can be classified into the first two categories, which, according to Kenneth D.

Wald, make up almost half the adult population.[32] According to R. Stephen Warner, "The root of the [mainline] liberal position is the interpretation of Christ as a moral teacher who told disciples that they could best honor him by helping those in need." In contrast, Warner writes, "The evangelical position sees Jesus (as they prefer to call him) as one who offers salvation to anyone who confesses his name." Liberal or mainline Protestants stress sharing their abundance with the needy, while Evangelicals stress the importance of sharing their creed. Evangelicals, Warner argues, see the Bible as a source of revelation about Jesus, "treasure it and credit even its implausible stories.... Liberals argue that these stories are timebound, and they seek the deeper truths that are obscured by myth and use the Bible alongside other texts as a source of wisdom." [33]

As Table 4-3 reveals, white mainline Protestants were 10 percentage points more likely to report voting than white Evangelicals.[34] However, southern whites are more likely to be Evangelicals and less likely to be mainline Protestants than are whites outside the South. Six out of ten southern white Protestants are Evangelicals, while three out of ten belong to a mainline denomination; outside the South only three out of ten white Protestants belong to an Evangelical denomination, while just under half are mainline Protestants. Among southern whites, mainline Protestants were 18 percentage points more likely to report voting than Evangelicals; outside the South, they were only 4 percentage points more likely to vote. Evangelicals also tend to have lower levels of formal education. Just under two out of five white Evangelicals have had at least some college education; among white mainline Protestants, nearly three out of five have had at least some college education. Among white Protestants with at least some college education, the turnout advantage among mainline Protestants disappears, but among those who have not attended college mainline Protestants are somewhat more likely to report voting than Evangelicals. If we take into account that white mainline Protestants are more likely to live outside the South and that they tend to have higher levels of formal education, mainline Protestants still tend to vote more than Evangelicals, but the differences between the two groups are reduced substantially.

In Table 4-3 we also take a closer look at differences between white Protestants and Catholics, by showing the combined impact of social class and religion. Among middle-class whites, religion is not related to reported electoral participation. Among the working class, however, religion is related to turnout; working-class Catholics are 6 percentage points more likely to report voting than working-class Protestants.

Education

We found a strong relationship between formal education and turnout. As Wolfinger and Rosenstone demonstrate, education is the most important variable in explaining differences in turnout in the United States.[35] Better educated Americans have skills that reduce the information costs of voting and are also more likely to develop attitudes that contribute to political participation, especially feelings that citizens have a duty to vote and that they can influence the political process.

As Table 4-3 shows, among whites who had not graduated from high school only half said they had voted; among those who had graduated from high school 90 percent reported voting, and among those with advanced degrees 97 percent said that they voted.[36] The census survey also shows a very strong relationship between formal education and turnout. Among whites with no high school education, only 34.4 percent reported voting in the 1992 election; among whites with some high school, 41.8 percent voted; among those who had graduated from high school, 59.2 percent voted; among those with some college education, 71.0 percent voted; among those with a bachelor's degree, 82.6 percent voted; and among whites with an advanced degree, 86.4 percent said that they had voted.

Why Has Turnout Declined?

Clearly, turnout within educational groups must have declined so fast that the impact of rising educational levels was cancelled out. This suggests that the decline of turnout since 1960 results from the offsetting of some forces that stimulated turnout by others that depressed it. Analysts have studied the decline of turnout extensively. Some have focused on social factors, such as changing levels of formal education and the changing age distribution of the electorate. Some scholars have studied political attitudes, such as changes in partisan loyalties, as a major source of turnout change. Others have analyzed institutional changes, such as the easing of voter registration requirements. And, finally, some scholars have pointed to the behavior of political leaders, arguing that they are making less of an effort to mobilize the electorate. Some changes, such as the rise in educational levels and the easing of voter registration rules, should have increased turnout in national elections. Because turnout rates declined in spite of these forces, Richard A. Brody views the decline of turnout as a major puzzle for students of American politics.[37]

We began to explore this puzzle by examining the relationship of educational levels to reported turnout among whites in all presidential elections from 1952 through 1992. We divide whites into five educational levels: college graduate, some college, high school graduate, some high school, and eight grades or less. African-Americans have substantially lower levels of formal education than whites, and southern blacks have been enfranchised only since 1965. Therefore, including blacks in our analysis would substantially obscure the relationships we are studying.

The NES surveys show that white college graduates have maintained their high levels of turnout, and that they were as likely to vote in 1992 as in 1960, when overall turnout was highest. But turnout declined within all four of the remaining educational categories, and it dropped markedly among the three groups that had not attended college. Several studies of the Census Bureau surveys also suggest that turnout has decreased more among Americans who are relatively disadvantaged.[38] But there is considerable controversy about this conclusion. Ruy A. Teixeira's analysis of the census surveys shows a 10-point decline in turnout among college graduates from 1964 to 1988, although the drop was greater among the four lower educational categories; as with our analysis of NES data, the decline in turnout was greatest among respondents who had not attended college.[39] And Jan E. Leighley and Jonathan Nagler's analysis of census surveys shows a similar pattern. In addition, the studies by Teixeira and by Leighley and Nagler show that turnout declines were greater among manually employed workers. But Leighley and Nagler argue that the study of turnout inequalities should focus on differences in income, since the impact of government policies affects Americans differently according to their income levels. Their analyses suggest that the decline in turnout was consistent across all income categories.[40]

But it is the rise in educational levels among the electorate that creates the greatest problem in accounting for the puzzle of declining turnout. Although the increase in education among the electorate did not prevent the decline in turnout, it played a major role in slowing down the decline. From 1960 through 1992, the level of education among the white electorate rose substantially, an increase that resulted almost entirely from generational replacement.[41] According to the NES surveys, the percentage of the white electorate that had not graduated from high school fell from 47 percent in 1960 to 17 percent in 1992. During this same period, the percentage who had graduated from college rose from 11 percent to 24 percent. Between 1960 and 1992 reported turnout among the white electorate fell 6 percentage points. An estimate based upon a simple algebraic standardization procedure suggests that if educational levels had not increased, turnout would have declined 15 percentage points.[42] Although this procedure provides only a preliminary estimate of the impact of rising educational levels upon turnout, our analysis suggests that the overall decline of turnout would have been nearly two and a half times as great if educational levels had not risen.

Other social changes also tended to push turnout upward. In a comprehensive attempt to explain the decline of turnout between 1960 and 1988, Teixeira studies changes in reported electoral participation using the NES surveys. He finds that increases in income and the growth of white collar employment tended to retard the decline of turnout. But the increase in educational levels, according to Teixeira's estimates, is by far the most important of these changes, and its influence is three times as great as the impact of occupational and income changes combined.[43]

Steven J. Rosenstone and John Mark Hansen have also used the NES surveys to provide a comprehensive explanation of the decline in turnout during these years. Their analysis also demonstrates that the increase in formal education was the most important factor in preventing an even greater decline in voter participation. They also estimate the impact of the easing of voter registration requirements. They find that reported turnout declined 11 percentage points in the 1960s through the 1980s, but they estimate that turnout would have declined 16 points had it not been for the combined impact of rising educational levels and the liberalization of electoral laws.[44]

Although there were some social forces that slowed down the decline of electoral participation, there were others that contributed to its decline. After 1960, the electorate become younger, as the baby boom generation (generally defined as persons born from 1946 through 1964) entered the electorate. As we have seen, young Americans have relatively low levels of turnout. The proportion of Americans who were married declined, and, because married people are more likely to vote than unmarried people, this social change reduced turnout. And church attendance declined, reducing the ties of Americans to their communities. Teixeira identifies these three changes as major shifts that contributed to the decline of turnout, and argues that the decline of church attendance was the most important of these changes.[45] Rosenstone and Hansen also examine social changes that tended to reduce turnout, and their analysis suggests that a younger electorate was the most important social change reducing electoral participation.[46] Warren E. Miller argues that the decline of turnout results mainly from the entry of a post-New Deal generation (defined as Americans first eligible to vote in 1968) into the electorate.[47] This change, Miller argues, results not merely from the youth of these Americans but from generational differences that contribute to lower levels of electoral participation. During the late 1960s and the 1970s a series of events—the Vietnam War, Watergate, and the failed presidencies of Ford and Carter—Miller argues, created a generation that withdrew from electoral participation. We agree that generational replacement contributed to the decline of turnout, but analyses by Teixeira and by Rosenstone and Hansen suggest that Miller overestimated its impact.[48]

Most analysts of turnout agree that attitudinal change in the electorate contributed to the decline in electoral participation. Our own analysis has focused on the impact of attitudinal change, and we have examined the erosion of party loyalties and the decline of what George I. Balch and others have called feelings of external political efficacy.[49] These are the same two basic political attitudes studied by Teixeira in his first major analysis of the decline of turnout,[50] and they are among the political attitudes studied by Rosenstone and Hansen. We found these attitudinal changes to be major factors in the decline of turnout from 1960 through 1980, as did Teixeira.[51] We found these attitudinal changes to be somewhat less important when we extended our analysis to account for the decline in turnout from 1960 through 1984.[52] Attitudinal change became more important again when we extended our analysis to study the elections from 1960 through 1988, although it was not as important as it had been for the period that we had first studied.[53] The decline in partisan loyalties and the erosion of political efficacy played an important role in the decline of turnout among the white electorate from 1960 through 1992.

The measure of party identification we employ is based upon questions designed to gauge psychological attachment to a partisan reference group.[54] We will discuss how party identification contributes to the way people vote in Chapter 8. But party loyalties also contribute to *whether* people vote. Strong feelings of partisan identification contribute to psychological involvement in politics, as Angus Campbell and his colleagues argue.[55] Party loyalties also reduce the time and effort needed to decide how to vote, and thus reduce the costs of voting.[56] In every presidential election since 1952, strong partisans have been more likely to vote than those in any other partisan strength category. In every election since 1960, independents with no partisan leanings have been the least likely to vote.

The percentage of whites who strongly identified with the Republican or Democratic party dropped from 36 percent in 1960 and 1964 to 23 percent in 1980. Since then, it has rebounded; in 1988, 30 percent of whites were strong party identifiers. But partisan strength fell again in 1992, and only 27 percent of the whites were strong partisans. In all of the NES surveys from 1952 to 1964, the percentage of independents with no partisan leanings never rose above 9 percent. This figure rose to 14 percent in 1980, although it has fallen somewhat since then. In both 1988 and 1992, 12 percent of the whites were independents with no partisan leanings. For a detailed discussion of party identification and tables showing the distribution of party identification from 1952 through 1992, see Chapter 8.

Feelings of political effectiveness also contribute to electoral participation. Citizens may expect to gain benefits from voting if they believe that the government is responsive to their demands. Conversely, those who believe that political leaders will not or cannot respond to popular demands may see little reason to participate. In every presidential election since 1952, Americans with high feelings of political effectiveness have been the most likely to report voting, and those with low feelings of political effectiveness have been the least likely.

From 1960 to 1980 feelings of political effectiveness declined markedly. Scores on our measure are based upon responses to the following two statements: "I don't think public officials care much what people like me think" and "People like me do not have any say about what the government does." [57] In 1956 and 1960, 64 percent of the white electorate scored as highly efficacious. The decline in external political efficacy began in 1964. By 1980, only 39 percent scored high. Although feelings of political efficacy rose in 1984, they declined again in 1988. In 1988, only 38 percent of the whites scored as highly efficacious; in 1992, this figure rose only slightly to 40 percent. The percentage scoring low on our measure was only 15 percent in 1956 and 1960, but it rose fairly steadily through 1976. In 1980, 30 percent scored low. In 1984, fewer whites felt politically powerless, but in 1988, 37 percent scored low on our measure, and in 1992, 34 percent scored low.

Although feelings of partisan loyalty and feelings of political effectiveness are both related to turnout, in most NES surveys they have been only weakly related to each other. In 1992, the relationship between party identification and feelings of political effectiveness were stronger than in most surveys, with strong partisans having the highest feelings of political effectivness and independents with no partisan leanings the lowest. Table 4-4 examines the combined effect of these political attitudes upon the turnout of whites in the 1992 presidential election.

By reading down each column, we can see that feelings of political efficacy are related to reported electoral participation, regardless of levels of partisan strength. By reading across each row we can see that strong party identifiers are the most likely to vote, regardless of their level of political efficacy. Independents with no partisan leanings are always the least likely to vote, regardless of their feelings of political effectiveness. These attitudinal variables have a strong cumulative effect. Over nine out of ten strong partisans with high feelings of political efficacy say that they voted; among independents with no partisan leanings who score low on feelings of political efficacy, just over two out of five say that they voted. There are no consistent differences in reported turnout between weak partisans and independents who leaned toward a party.[58]

The decline in party loyalty and the erosion of political efficacy clearly contribute to the decline of turnout. A preliminary assessment of the impact of these factors can be derived through a simple algebraic standardization procedure. According to our calculations, the decline in feelings of party identification accounts for 31 percent of the decline of reported turnout among white Americans from 1960 through 1992, while the decline in feelings of political efficacy accounts for 81 percent of the decline.[59] Combined, the decline in party loyalty and the decline in political efficacy appear to account for 91 percent of the decline in reported turnout.

Table 4-4   Percentage of Whites Who Reported Voting for President, by Strength of Party Identification and Sense of External Political Efficacy, 1992

Scores on External Political Efficacy Index	Strength of Party Identification							
	Strong Partisan		Weak Partisan		Independent Who Leans Toward a Party		Independent with No Partisan Leaning	
	%	*(N)*	%	*(N)*	%	*(N)*	%	*(N)*
High	93	(240)	82	(237)	85	(195)	78	(68)
Medium	89	(117)	84	(163)	75	(151)	62	(54)
Low	77	(152)	65	(197)	63	(190)	45	(87)

Note: Numbers in parentheses are the totals upon which percentages are based. Numbers are weighted using the time series weight.

Our estimates clearly demonstrate that these attitudinal changes were important; but they are not final estimates of the impact of these changes. We do not claim to have solved the puzzle of declining participation, and we believe that comprehensive tests, such as those conducted by Teixeira and by Rosenstone and Hansen, are needed to study the 1992 NES results. As Teixeira demonstrates, a comprehensive estimate of the impact of attitudinal change must calculate the contribution of attitude change to the decline that would have occurred if there had been no social forces retarding the decline of turnout. In Teixeira's analysis, for example, the decline in party loyalties and the erosion of political efficacy accounted for 62 percent of the decline of turnout from 1960 through 1980. But these attitudinal changes accounted for only 38 percent of the larger decline that would have occurred if changes in educational levels, income, and occupational patterns had not slowed down the decline of turnout.

We analyzed the combined impact of rising educational levels, the erosion of feelings of political efficacy, and the decline of party loyalties upon levels of reported turnout among whites between 1960 and 1992. Our estimates suggest that attitude change accounted for 30 percent of the decline in electoral participation that would have occurred if rising educational levels had not slowed down the decline of turnout.[60]

A comprehensive assessment should take into account the impact of other attitudinal changes that may have contributed to the decline of turnout. Teixeira identifies a decline in campaign involvement through the media, along with the decline in feelings of political effectiveness, as the major attitudinal changes that have eroded turnout from 1960 through 1988.[61]

Rosenstone and Hansen also identify declining feelings of political efficacy as a cause of declining turnout, although they argue that the change in efficacy was not a major cause of the decline. Instead, they focus on the declining role of political parties in mobilizing the electorate, which they view as the major cause of turnout decline.[62] The key variable in their measure of party mobilization is whether respondents report being contacted by a political party.[63] Rosenstone and Hansen present a fascinating analysis that focuses on the effect of elite behavior on the participation of the electorate. But there are problems with their interpretation. The percentage of Americans who say they were contacted by a political party actually increased after the 1960 presidential election. In 1960, 22 percent of the electorate said they were contacted by a political party; in 1980, 32 percent said they were contacted. Yet turnout had declined substantially. In 1988, 24 percent said they had been contacted by a political party, virtually the same percentage as in 1960; yet turnout in 1988 reached a postwar low. In 1992, only 20 percent claimed to have been contacted by a political party.

Why Turnout Increased in 1992

As we saw, some of the major factors driving turnout downward during the past three decades did not change dramatically between 1988 and 1992. In fact, the percentage of whites with strong partisan loyalties actually declined somewhat, and feelings of external political efficacy increased very little. Moreover, contacts by political parties, which Rosenstone and Hansen identify as crucial in accounting for variation in turnout, fell somewhat from 1988 to 1992.[64]

Although mobilization efforts by political parties may have declined, Perot's candidacy may have boosted turnout. According to the Voter Research and Surveys exit poll, 14 percent of Perot's voters said that they would not have voted if Perot had not been on the ballot.[65] As we saw in Chapter 3, Perot won 19.7 million votes. If 14 percent of these voters had abstained, 2.8 million fewer Americans would have voted. Turnout would have been 53.7 percent rather than 55.2 percent, increasing 3.6 percentage points instead of 5.1 points. According to this logic, about 30 percent of the increase in turnout resulted from Perot's presence on the ballot.

This line of reasoning may underestimate Perot's impact, for his candidacy stimulated interest in the election. His appearance in the three presidential debates enlivened these confrontations. As we saw in Chapter 2, after the debates the percentage supporting Clinton in the public opinion polls declined (see Figure 2-3), creating the possibility of a close election. The NES surveys show that the percentage who thought that the election would be close increased in 1992 over 1988. In 1988, 74 percent of whites and 71 percent of African-Americans thought the election would be close; in 1992, 82 percent of whites thought the election would be close, although only 65 percent of African-Americans did.[66]

In most elections, voters who think the election will be close are more likely to vote than those who think the winner will win by a large margin. Even though these differences are usually not large, the percentage viewing the forthcoming election as close has varied greatly from contest to contest.[67] Orley Ashenfelter and Stanley Kelley, Jr., report that the single most important factor accounting for the decline of turnout between 1960 and 1972 was "the dramatic shift in voter expectations about the closeness of the race in these two elections." [68] In 1992 whites who thought the election would be close were somewhat more likely to vote than those who did not. Among whites who thought the election would be close ($N = 1532$), 79 percent said that they voted; among those who thought the winner would win by quite a bit ($N = 290$), 72 percent voted. As these differences are modest, and as the percentage of whites who thought the election would be close rose only 8 percentage points, increasing perceptions of closeness appear to contribute very little to the increase in turnout.

Analyzing perceptions of the election's closeness creates an interesting puzzle. Given that Perot had little chance of winning, one might have thought that voters who believed the election would be close would be more likely to vote for either Clinton or Bush, and not risk wasting their vote on a candidate who had very little chance of being elected. In fact, Perot gained a marginally larger share of the vote from whites who thought the election would be close. Among white voters who thought the election would be close ($N = 1203$), 40 percent voted for Clinton, 39 percent for Bush, and 22 percent for Perot. Among the 205 white voters who thought the winner would win by quite a bit, 56 percent voted for Clinton, 25 percent for Bush, and 19 percent voted for Perot.[69]

This puzzle may be partly explained by the finding that Perot voters were less likely to care who won the election.[70] Among whites who voted for Clinton, 86 percent said they cared "a good deal" who won the election, while among whites who voted for Bush, 85 percent cared; among those who voted for Perot, only 76 percent cared a good deal who won. Perot fared substantially better among whites who felt little concern about the electoral outcome. Among whites who cared "a good deal" who won the election ($N = 1202$), 43 percent voted for Clinton, 38 percent voted for Bush, and 19 percent voted for Perot. Among whites who did not care much who won ($N = 214$), 35 percent voted for Clinton, 34 percent voted for Bush, and 32 percent voted for Perot. As with previous elections, Americans who cared about the electoral outcome were much more likely to vote than those who did not care. Among whites who cared "a good deal" who won ($N = 1442$), 84 percent said that they voted; among those who did not "care much" ($N = 406$), only 54 percent voted. Despite the low turnout among Americans who did not care much who won, Perot may have mobilized Americans who do not generally care about elections, although changes in question wording make it difficult to compare these results with those for previous elections.

Perot may have also helped bring politically cynical voters to the polls. As is well documented, there has been a substantial decline in political trust during the last three decades.[71] In 1964, when trust among whites was highest, 77 percent of the whites said the government in Washington could be trusted to do what is right just about always or most of the time, and 74 percent of the blacks endorsed this view.[72] By 1980, only 25 percent of the whites and 26 percent of the blacks trusted the government. Although trust rebounded somewhat among whites in 1984, it fell after that.[73] In 1992, 29 percent of the whites and 26 percent of the blacks trusted the government to do what is right just about always or most of the time. Back in 1964, 63 percent of the whites and 69 percent of the blacks said that the government was run for the benefit of all.[74] By 1980, only 19 percent of the whites and 34 percent of the blacks held this view. Once again, trust rose among whites in 1984, but it fell after that. In 1992, 20 percent of the whites and 19 percent of the blacks said that the government was run for the benefit of all.

Despite this dramatic decline in political trust, this decline did not contribute to the decline of turnout, because in most elections Americans who are politically trusting and those who are politically cynical are equally likely to vote. In 1992, feelings of political trust were once again unrelated to voting participation. But Perot tended to do somewhat better among voters who were politically cynical than among those who trusted the government. Among white voters who trusted the government to do what is right just about always or most of the time ($N = 435$), 44 percent voted for Clinton, 40 percent for Bush, and 16 percent for Perot; among whites who thought it could be trusted only some of the time or none of the time ($N = 1,000$), Clinton won 41 percent of the vote, Bush won 35 percent, and Perot won 24 percent. Both Clinton and Perot fared better among voters who thought that the government was run for a "few big interests." Among whites who thought the government was run for the benefit of all ($N = 271$), 38 percent voted for Clinton, 43 percent voted for Bush, and 19 percent voted for Perot; among those who thought the government was run for a few big interests ($N = 1,111$), Clinton won 43 percent of the vote, Bush won 34 percent, and Perot won 22 percent.

Perot also fared somewhat better among whites with low feelings of political effectiveness. Among white voters with high feelings of political effectiveness ($N = 633$), 18 percent voted for Perot; among those who scored low on our measure ($N = 409$), 24 percent did. Perot fared much better among whites with relatively weak partisan loyalties, a group that generally has a low turnout. Among white voters who were strong party identifiers ($N = 438$), only 8 percent voted for Perot; among those who were weak party identifiers ($N = 478$), 23 percent voted for Perot; among independents who leaned toward a party ($N = 395$), 28 percent voted for Perot; and among independents with no partisan leanings ($N = 125$), 41 percent voted for Perot. And, as we will show, Perot fared somewhat better among respondents who said they had not voted in the 1988 election than among those who said they had voted in the Bush-Dukakis contest.

There were doubtless other factors that stimulated turnout in 1992. As James Ceaser and Andrew Busch point out, more money was spent on the 1992 election than on any previous contest, partly because Perot spent more than $60 million of his own money. As they also point out, there was more competition in congressional elections.[75]

Of course, we do not know whether the 5 percentage point rise in turnout is a blip, reflecting the peculiar nature of the 1992 contest, or whether it presages a reversal of the trend toward declining electoral participation. The passage of the "motor voter" registration bill in May 1993 will facilitate registration and thus may help increase electoral participation. And if Rosenstone and Hansen are correct, future turnout may depend largely upon the attempts by political elites to mobilize the electorate. But we should return to a basic fact: despite the increase in turnout in 1992, U.S. turnout remains very low by international standards.

Did Increased Turnout Matter?

For the last decade Democratic party leaders have debated the importance of increasing turnout. Some argued that low turnout was a major reason for the Democrats' presidential losses. The Democrats could win, they argued, if the party could mobilize disadvantaged Americans. In 1984, the Democrats and their supporters launched major get-out-the-vote efforts, but turnout rose less than a percentage point, and in 1988 turnout reached a postwar low. Other Democrats argued that the main problem the party faced was defections by its traditional supporters. Of course, attempting to increase turnout and attempting to win back defectors are not mutually exclusive strategies, but they can lead to contradictory tactics. For example, mobilizing African-Americans may not be cost-free if doing so leads to defections among white Democrats.

In fact, as James DeNardo has pointed out, from 1932 through 1976 there was only a very weak relationship between turnout and the percentage of the votes won by Democratic presidential candidates.[76] In our analyses of the 1980, 1984, and 1988 elections we argued that under most reasonable scenarios increased turnout would not have led to Democratic victories.[77] All the same, in 1992 increased turnout went hand in hand with a Democratic victory, although not an increased share in the total Democratic vote.

There is some evidence that increased turnout may have made a modest contribution to Clinton's victory. In the 1980, 1984, and 1992 elections, strong Republicans were more likely to vote than strong Democrats, and weak Republicans were more likely to vote than weak Democrats.[78] In Table 4-5 we show the percentage who report voting, according to both party identification and policy preferences. Turning first to party identification, we see that strong Republicans are only marginally more likely to report voting than strong Democrats, weak Republicans are only marginally more likely to vote than weak Democrats, and independents who lean toward the Republican party are only marginally more likely to vote than are independents who lean toward the Democratic party. In 1980, 1984, and 1988 the Republican turnout advantage was more marked, and accounted for about a 2 percentage point advantage for the Republicans in the major party vote. Partisan differences were all but eliminated in 1992, because the increase in turnout was somewhat greater among Democrats than among Republicans.

In Chapter 6 we will examine the issue preferences of the electorate. Our summary measure of issue preferences is based upon each voter's views on three issues—reducing government spending as opposed to providing more government services, increasing versus decreasing defense spending, and whether the government should guarantee each person a job and a good standard of living or should let people get ahead on their own. In 1980, there was no systematic relationship between issue preferences and turnout, although in both 1984 and 1988 respondents with pro-Republican views were somewhat more likely to vote than those with pro-Democratic views. In both 1984 and 1988, according to our estimates, these biases gave the Republicans about a 2 percentage point advantage in the major party vote. In Table 4-5 we show the percentage who said they voted according to scores on our balance of issues measure. Despite the mobilization of Democratic party identifiers, these biases were also found in 1992. Respondents with views on these issues that were closer to where Bush was seen to stand were somewhat more likely to vote than those with views closer to where Clinton was perceived to be.[79] But these differences are small, and, according to our estimates, cost Clinton less than 1 percentage point of the major party vote.

In Chapter 7 we shall study the retrospective evaluations of the electorate, and shall see that to a large extent the 1992 election was a

Table 4-5 Percentage That Reported Voting for President, by Party
Identification, Issue Preferences, and Retrospective
Evaluations, 1992

Attitude	Voted	Did Not Vote	Total Percent	(N)
Electorate, by party identification				
Strong Democrat	87	13	100	(387)
Weak Democrat	75	25	100	(395)
Independent, leans Democratic	73	27	100	(317)
Independent, no partisan leaning	60	40	100	(253)
Independent, leans Republican	75	25	100	(282)
Weak Republican	77	23	100	(335)
Strong Republican	89	11	100	(250)
Electorate, by scores on the balance of issues measure				
−3 (Most pro-Clinton)	80	20	100	(338)
−2	64	36	100	(160)
−1	80	20	100	(541)
0 (Neutral)	70	30	100	(160)
+1	84	16	100	(635)
+2	78	22	100	(60)
+3 (Most pro-Bush)	85	15	100	(112)
Electorate, by summary measure retrospective evaluations				
Strongly Democratic	84	16	100	(463)
Moderately Democratic	75	25	100	(498)
Leans Democratic	72	28	100	(252)
Neutral	72	28	100	(350)
Leans Republican	80	20	100	(339)
Moderately Republican	76	24	100	(73)
Strongly Republican	68	32	100	(10)

Note: Numbers are weighted.

negative judgment about Bush and the Republican party. Our summary
measure has three components: (a) an evaluation of Bush's performance
as president; (b) an assessment of how good a job the government was
doing solving the most important problem facing the country; and (c) a
judgment about which party would do a better job solving that problem.
In 1980 respondents who expressed negative views of the Democrats
were more likely to vote than those with positive views; given that

negative views prevailed, this bias hurt Carter. But in both 1984 and 1988 respondents with positive views of the Republicans were more likely to vote than those with negative views. In both elections, these biases gave the Republicans about a 2 percentage point advantage in the major party vote. As Table 4-5 shows, in 1992 the pro-Republican biases in turnout were eliminated. As only ten respondents expressed strongly pro-Republican evaluations, the relatively low turnout among this group must be treated with caution. However, respondents with moderately pro-Republican evaluations and those with moderately pro-Democratic evaluations were equally likely to vote, although those who leaned toward the Republican party were more likely to report voting than those who leaned toward the Democratic party.

Compared with the 1980, 1984, and 1988 surveys, 1992 results (see Table 4-5) suggest that the increase in turnout was modestly greater among Democratic identifiers and among those with negative views of the performance of Bush and the Republican party—a group that increased greatly in size from 1988 to 1992. But we may also gain some insight about the relative effects of mobilization and conversion by relying upon questions about how respondents voted in the 1988 presidential election.[80] The results must be treated with caution, since they are based upon the respondents' memories of behavior that occurred four years earlier. Among those who reported voting in the Bush-Dukakis contest, Bush won 62 percent of the major party vote; in fact, he won only 54 percent. Moreover, among those respondents who were old enough to have voted in 1988, and who remembered whether or not they voted, 69 percent claimed to have voted and only 31 percent said that they did not vote. Even if we assume that all the respondents who could not remember whether they voted were actually nonvoters, reported turnout among those old enough to have voted in 1988 was 64 percent. In fact, only 53 percent of the politically eligible population actually voted.

In Table 4-6, we first examine how respondents said they voted in 1992, according to how they said they voted in the Bush-Dukakis contest. More than nine out of ten respondents who said that they voted in 1988 also said that they voted in 1992, but Dukakis voters were somewhat more likely to report voting than Bush voters were. Clinton won a plurality among those who acknowledged that they had not voted in 1988, and among those who did not remember whether they voted; he beat Bush by more than two to one among those too young to have voted in 1988.

In the second part of Table 4-6 we examine how respondents had voted in 1988 according to how they said they voted in the Clinton-Bush-Perot contest. If these figures could be taken at face value, they would show us where Clinton's, Bush's, and Perot's votes came from. But as the reports about the way people voted in 1988 are biased toward Bush, these

Table 4-6 Whether and How Respondents Reported Voting in the 1988 and 1992 Elections

Whether and How Respondents Voted in 1992	Whether and How Respondents Voted in 1988					
	Dukakis	Bush	Other; Don't Remember Who	Did Not Vote	Don't Remember Whether	Too Young
Clinton	80%	22%	66%	18%	32%	32%
Bush	5	50	4	12	27	13
Perot	11	20	15	9	15	13
Did not vote	3	8	15	61	26	42
Total percent	99%	100%	100%	100%	100%	100%
(Number)	(493)	(820)	(30)	(591)	(174)	(113)

Whether and How Respondents Voted in 1988	Whether and How Respondents Voted in 1992			
	Clinton	Bush	Perot	Did Not Vote
Dukakis	50%	5%	17%	3%
Bush	23	72	52	12
Other; don't remember who	2	—[a]	1	1
Did not vote	14	12	16	67
Don't remember whether	7	8	8	8
Too young	5	2	5	9
Total percent	101%	99%	99%	100%
(Number)	(799)	(569)	(317)	(535)

Note: Numbers are weighted.
[a] Less than 1 percent.

results may exaggerate the share of the vote that Clinton, Bush, and Perot received from 1988 Bush voters and may underestimate the share of their vote that came from 1988 Dukakis voters. And as some of the respondents who claimed to have voted in 1988 may actually not have voted, these results may underestimate the impact of mobilization.[81] Given these biases, the percentages in this table should be interpreted with some caution. Still, it seems safe to say that about one in six of Clinton's votes came from 1988 Bush voters, whereas only about one in twenty of Bush's votes came from Dukakis voters. Perhaps one in four of

Clinton's votes in 1992 came from persons who did not vote in 1988, and about one out of twenty of his votes came from voters who were too young to have voted four years earlier. But it also seems likely that about one in four of Bush's votes came from 1988 nonvoters, although he appears to have won only one out of fifty of his votes from those too young to have voted in 1988. Perot probably drew just under half of his support from former Bush voters, and over a fourth of his vote from nonvoters. About one out of twenty of Perot's votes, like Clinton's, came from voters who had been too young to vote in 1988.

As can easily be demonstrated, each convert from your opponent is worth as much as two new voters.[82] Thus, even though Clinton probably received more votes from 1988 nonvoters than from 1988 Bush voters, Clinton benefited more from converting Bush voters than he gained from new voters. This becomes all the more apparent when one realizes that Bush and Perot also gained substantial support from 1988 nonvoters, whereas Bush gained only a handful of converts. Any 1988 voter who supported Perot was a convert, but the data suggest that Perot gained far more converts from 1988 Bush voters than he did from 1988 Dukakis voters.

In concluding that Clinton benefited more from conversion than mobilization, we are not discounting the potential benefits of get-out-the-vote efforts. These efforts are likely to make a difference in relatively close contests, and where such efforts are relatively low cost they are useful. Of course, newly registered citizens may fail to vote, and a party may mobilize new voters who wind up supporting its opponent. Therefore, partisan mobilization efforts must be carefully targeted. All the same, Clinton's campaign aimed far more at converting Reagan and Bush Democrats than it did at mobilizing new voters. Our analysis suggests that he succeeded.

Does Low Turnout Matter?

Despite the 5 percentage point increase in turnout in 1992, overall turnout remains low. There is little evidence that the increase in turnout played a major role in Clinton's victory. Nor do we see any plausible evidence that much higher levels of turnout would have altered the outcome of the election. As we shall see in Chapter 8, for example, Perot did substantially better among self-declared independents than among party identifiers, but even among independents Clinton won a plurality of the vote. And although 1988 Bush voters were somewhat less likely to vote in 1992 than 1988 Dukakis voters were, the difference is not large enough to account for Clinton's 5.6 percentage point margin of victory over Bush.

Given that increased turnout would not have altered the election's outcome, some may argue that low turnout does not matter. Some scholars point out that in most elections (although not in 1984, 1988, and 1992), the policy preferences of voters have been similar to the preferences of Americans who did not go to the polls. Turnout has been low in postwar elections, but, in most of them, the voters reflected the sentiments of the electorate as a whole.[83]

Despite this evidence, we cannot accept the conclusion that low turnout is unimportant. We are especially concerned that turnout is very low among disadvantaged Americans. There is some evidence that from the Johnson-Goldwater contest of 1964 through 1988, turnout declined more among the disadvantaged than among other groups. In 1992 turnout rose among all social groups, but the census surveys show that this increase was greater among whites than among African-Americans. Even if one disputes the conclusion that turnout has declined more among disadvantaged Americans, there is abundant evidence that Americans with lower levels of education and income are much less likely to vote than better educated Americans with higher income levels.

Some believe that turnout is low among the disadvantaged because political leaders structure policy alternatives in a way that provides disadvantaged Americans with little choice. Frances Fox Piven and Richard Cloward, for example, acknowledge that the policy preferences of voters and nonvoters are similar, but argue that this similarity results from the way elites have structured public policy choices. "Political attitudes would inevitably change over time," they argue, "if the allegiance of voters at the bottom became the object of partisan competition, for then politicians would be prodded to identify and articulate the grievances and aspirations of lower income voters in order to win their support, thus helping to give form and voice to a distinctive political class." [84]

We cannot accept this argument either, mainly because it is highly speculative, and there is little empirical evidence to support it. The difficulty in supporting this point of view may result from the nature of survey research, because questions about policy preferences are usually framed along the lines of controversy as defined by mainstream political leaders. Occasionally, however, surveys pose radical policy alternatives, and they often ask open-ended questions that allow respondents to state their policy preferences. We find little concrete evidence that low turnout leads current political leaders to ignore the policy preferences of the American electorate.

Nevertheless, low turnout among Americans can scarcely be healthy for a democracy. Even if low levels of turnout seldom affect electoral outcomes, they may undermine the legitimacy of elected political leaders. Moreover, the large bloc of nonparticipants in the electorate may be potentially dangerous, because this may mean that many Americans have weak ties to the established political leaders and parties. The prospects for electoral instability, and perhaps political instability, thus increase.[85] We do not argue that Perot posed a danger to political stability, although he certainly posed, and continues to pose, a danger to the established party system. As Table 4-6 shows, Clinton won a clear plurality of 1988 nonvoters, but Perot fared better among 1988 nonvoters than among those who had voted in the Bush-Dukakis contest. Moreover, the data suggest that Perot gained a larger share of his support from 1988 nonvoters than did either Clinton or Bush.

Does low turnout have implications for conclusions about whether a partisan alignment has occurred or is likely to occur? Low turnout in the 1980 election led some scholars to question whether Reagan's victory presaged a pro-Republican realignment. As Gerald M. Pomper argued at the time, "Elections that involve upheavals in party coalitions have certain hallmarks, such as popular enthusiasm." [86] Indeed, past realignments have been characterized by increases in turnout. As Table 4-1 shows, turnout rose markedly from 1852 to 1860, a period during which the Republican party was formed, replaced the Whigs, and gained control of the presidency. Turnout also rose for the Bryan-McKinley contest of 1896, which is generally considered a realigning election. As both Table 4-2 and Figure 4-1 show, turnout rose markedly after 1924, increasing in 1928 and again in 1936, a period when the Democrats emerged as the majority party.

Turnout did rise 5 percentage points in 1992. This increase, as we saw, was partly due to Perot's candidacy. There is no previous pattern to demonstrate a relationship between increased support for third-party or independent candidates and increased electoral participation. In 1912, Theodore Roosevelt ran the most successful third-party candidacy in U.S. history, substantially eclipsing the incumbent Republican president, William Howard Taft, in both the popular and the electoral vote. But there was nearly a 7-point decline in turnout among politically eligible Americans from 1908 to 1912. Roosevelt's strong third-party challenge left no lasting imprint on the American party system. But a strong independent candidacy combined with an increase in electoral participation may presage considerable instability in future elections.

Chapter 5

Social Forces and the Vote

One hundred four million Americans voted in 1992. Voting is an individual act, but group memberships influence voting choices because people who share social characteristics may share political interests. Group similarities in voting behavior also may reflect past political conditions. The partisan loyalties of African-Americans, for example, were first shaped by the Civil War; black loyalty to the Republican party, the party of Lincoln, lasted through the 1932 presidential election, although most blacks outside the South shifted to the Democrats by 1936. The steadily Democratic voting of southern whites, a product of the same historical conditions, lasted even longer, perhaps through 1960.

It is easy to see why group-based loyalties persist over time. Studies of preadult learning suggest that partisan loyalties are often transmitted from generation to generation. And because religion, ethnicity, and, to a lesser extent, social class are also transmitted from generation to generation, social divisions have considerable staying power. Moreover, the interaction of social group members with each other may reinforce similarities in political attitudes and behaviors.

Politicians often think in group terms. They recognize that to win they may need to mobilize the social groups that have supported their party in the past and that it is helpful to cut into their opponents' established bases of support. The Democrats think more in group terms than the Republicans do because the Democratic party has been a coalition of minorities since the 1930s. To win, the party has needed to earn high levels of support from the social groups that have traditionally made up its broad-based coalition.

The 1992 contest was unusual, however. Bill Clinton earned high levels of support from only two of the groups that made up the New Deal coalition—African-Americans and Jews. Most of the other groups that made up the New Deal coalition gave less than half of their vote to Clinton. But in the three-candidate contest of 1992, it took only 43 percent of the vote to win. In many respects, Democratic presidential losses during the past quarter century may be attributed to the party's failure to hold the basic loyalties of the social groups that made up the winning coalition forged by Franklin D. Roosevelt in the 1930s. In winning, Clinton only partly revitalized this coalition.

This chapter examines the voting patterns of social groups in the 1992 presidential election. To put the 1992 results in perspective, we examine the voting choices of key social groups during the entire postwar period. By studying the social bases of party support since 1944, we will examine the long-term trends that severely weakened the New Deal coalition, and we will better understand the distinctive character of Clinton's victory.

How Social Groups Voted in 1992

Our basic results are presented in Table 5-1, which shows how various social groups voted for president in 1992.[1] Excluding respondents for whom the direction of vote was not ascertained, the 1992 National Election Studies (NES) survey shows that 47.3 percent voted for Clinton, 33.6 percent for George Bush, 18.8 percent for H. Ross Perot, and 0.3 percent for other candidates. Although for Perot the results are within 0.1 percentage point of the actual vote, the NES survey shows Clinton doing 4.3 points better and Bush faring 3.8 points worse than the actual election results. This bias is somewhat more pronounced when we report the major party vote. Among major party voters in the 1992 NES survey, 58.4 percent report voting for Clinton. According to official election statistics, Clinton won 53.5 percent of the major party vote. Although this bias is not severe, it is somewhat greater than similar biases that exaggerate the winner's share of the vote in previous NES surveys, and our tables and figures somewhat overestimate Clinton's vote.[2]

Despite its tendency to exaggerate Clinton's vote, the 1992 NES survey, which is based upon 1,700 voters, is the single best source of survey data, especially when we study change over time. However, once we examine subsets of the electorate, the number of persons sampled in some social groups becomes rather small. Therefore, we supplement our analysis by referring to the exit poll of 15,490 voters conducted by Voter Research and Surveys (VRS) for the television networks[3] and by the final preelection Gallup telephone poll of 1,589 likely voters conducted during the two days before the election.[4]

Table 5-1 How Social Groups Voted for President, 1992
(in percentages)

Social Group	Clinton	Bush	Perot	Total Percent	(*N*)
Total electorate	47	34	19	100	(1,685)
Electorate, by race					
African-American	92	6	3	101	(194)
White	42	37	21	100	(1,441)
Whites, by Hispanic identification					
Identify as Hispanic	62	26	12	100	(85)
Do not identify	41	38	22	101	(1,356)
Whites, by gender					
Females	47	36	16	99	(749)
Males	36	37	26	99	(691)
Whites, by region					
New England and Mid-Atlantic	49	28	23	100	(307)
North Central	37	40	23	100	(421)
South	38	46	16	100	(282)
Border	49	37	14	100	(102)
Mountain and Pacific	42	33	25	100	(328)
Whites, by birth cohort					
Before 1924	51	39	10	100	(182)
1924-1939	45	38	17	100	(263)
1940-1954	45	33	22	100	(409)
1955-1962	31	45	24	100	(333)
1963-1970	39	30	31	101	(199)
1971-1974	53	24	24	101	(54)
Whites, by social class					
Working class	42	33	25	100	(522)
Middle class	41	38	21	100	(723)
Farmers	36	46	18	100	(62)
Whites, by occupation of head of household					
Unskilled manual	46	33	20	99	(148)
Skilled, semiskilled manual	40	33	26	99	(375)
Clerical, sales, other white collar	46	37	17	100	(227)
Managerial	35	37	29	101	(282)
Professional and semiprofessional	44	39	16	99	(213)

(Table continues)

Table 5-1   Continued

Social Group	Clinton	Bush	Perot	Total Percent	(N)
Whites, by level of education					
Eight grades or less	62	26	12	100	(54)
Some high school	46	37	16	100	(89)
High school graduate	44	35	21	100	(460)
Some college	39	33	28	100	(376)
College graduate	33	48	19	100	(279)
Advanced degree	51	36	13	100	(140)
Whites, by annual family income					
Less than $10,000	57	29	14	100	(94)
$10,000 to $14,999	57	29	14	100	(110)
$15,000 to $19,999	45	36	18	99	(85)
$20,000 to $24,999	51	28	21	100	(113)
$25,000 to $29,999	42	35	23	100	(104)
$30,000 to $34,999	43	35	22	100	(120)
$35,000 to $39,999	32	42	26	100	(100)
$40,000 to $49,999	38	39	24	101	(197)
$50,000 to $59,999	27	40	33	100	(136)
$60,000 to $74,999	40	38	22	100	(165)
$75,000 to $89,999	33	50	16	99	(76)
$90,000 and over	37	46	18	101	(101)
Whites, by union membership[a]					
Member	48	28	23	99	(270)
Nonmember	40	39	21	100	(1,166)
Whites, by religion					
Jewish	78	7	16	101	(40)
Catholic	48	29	23	100	(391)
Protestant	34	46	20	100	(801)
None, no preference	55	20	25	100	(185)
White Protestants, by whether born again					
Not born again	39	40	21	100	(429)
Born again	26	55	19	100	(344)
White Protestants, by religious commitment					
Medium or low	40	34	27	101	(236)
High	35	46	19	100	(445)
Very high	17	72	11	100	(120)

(Table continues)

Table 5-1   Continued

Social Group	Clinton	Bush	Perot	Total Percent	(N)
White Protestants, by religious tradition					
Mainline	35	39	25	99	(352)
Evangelical	32	53	15	100	(311)
Whites, by social class and religion					
Working-class Catholics	47	24	29	100	(140)
Middle-class Catholics	46	33	21	100	(210)
Working-class Protestants	38	41	21	100	(384)
Middle-class Protestants	31	48	21	100	(384)

Note: Percentages read across. The numbers are weighted. The twenty-four voters for whom direction of vote was not ascertained and the six voters who voted for other candidates have been excluded form these analyses.

[a] Whether respondent or family member belongs to a trade union.

Race, Gender, Region, and Age

Political differences between African-Americans and whites are far sharper than any other social cleavage.[5] According to the NES survey, 92 percent of the black voters supported Clinton; only 42 percent of the white voters did. According to the VRS exit poll, 82 percent of blacks voted for Clinton, while 39 percent of whites did. And the Gallup telephone poll revealed that 82 percent of the blacks interviewed supported Clinton, while only 40 percent of the whites did. Even though blacks make up only one-ninth of the electorate, and even though they have relatively low turnout, about one-fifth of Clinton's total vote came from black voters.[6] Few blacks voted for Perot. According to both the 1992 NES survey and the Gallup preelection survey, only about one African-American in fifty voted for Perot. Perot fared somewhat better among blacks in the VRS poll: 7 percent of African-Americans voted for Perot, whereas 20 percent of whites did.

Because race is such a profound social division, we examine whites and blacks separately.[7] Among African-Americans, as among whites, women were more likely to vote Democratic than men. According to the VRS poll, 86 percent of black women voted for Clinton, whereas only 77 percent of black men did. Unlike the pattern among whites, however, southern blacks were as likely to vote Democratic as blacks outside the South. And age differences among blacks, though not among whites, were negligible. Given the small number of African-Americans surveyed, we cannot comment further on differences among blacks. But one finding seems clear: within every social category we examine in Table 5-1, a large majority of blacks voted for Clinton.

Among whites, the small number who identified as Hispanic were much more likely to vote for Clinton than were non-Hispanics.[8] Even so, Bush won one out of four votes among white Hispanics, and Perot won nearly one out of seven. The VRS poll shows that for all Hispanics, 62 percent voted for Clinton, 25 percent voted for Bush, and 14 percent voted for Perot. Of course, the Hispanic community is diverse. Mexican-Americans identify themselves predominantly as Democratic, whereas the Cuban community in South Florida is heavily Republican. Unfortunately, not enough Hispanics are included in national survey samples to explore differences within this growing minority.

Gender differences in voting behavior have been pronounced in some European countries, but historically they have been weak in the United States.[9] In the 1980, 1984, and 1988 elections, women were less likely than men to vote Republican for president. Such differences led to much discussion of a "gender gap," and some feminists hoped that women would play a major role in defeating the Republicans. In 1988, George Bush and Michael S. Dukakis each won half of the women's vote, but Bush won a clear majority among men. Bush benefited from the gender gap in his 1988 election.

In 1992, Clinton benefited from the gender gap. As Table 5-1 reveals, Bush and Clinton split the major party vote among white men, while Clinton won a clear plurality among white women. Perot also fared substantially better among white men than among white women. The VRS poll reports that among white men Bush won a majority of the major party vote, edging Clinton by 41 percent to 37 percent; among white women, Clinton and Bush each won 41 percent. The VRS study also shows that Perot fared better among men than among women, gaining 22 percent of the vote among white men and 18 percent among white women. The final Gallup poll results are not presented with controls for race. They show that among women Clinton led Bush by 48 percent to 36 percent, and 10 percent supported Perot; among men, Clinton barely edged Bush 39 percent to 37 percent, and 19 percent supported Perot.

The gender gap may not have been decisive, because Clinton probably won a larger share of the male major party vote than Bush. Nonetheless, the popular vote would have been very close if the electorate had been restricted to men. Among women, Clinton would have scored a decisive victory, winning close to half of the popular votes cast, and a decisive majority of the major party vote.

As Everett Carll Ladd reports, the VRS exit poll reveals that the gender gap was greater among voters of higher socioeconomic status, and our analysis of the NES survey confirms this finding.[10] Among all whites, women were 11 percentage points more likely than men to vote for Clinton. Among whites with annual family incomes above $90,000, women were 17 points more likely to vote for Clinton. Differences are even more pronounced among men and women with higher levels of education. Among whites who held advanced degrees, women were 28 percent more likely to vote for Clinton than men. Among white women who held advanced degrees ($N = 64$), 67 percent voted for Clinton and only 28 percent voted for Bush.

As we did in our analyses of the 1984 and 1988 NES surveys, we found clear differences between women who were married and those who were single.[11] Single women, in particular, often believed that they had been harmed by Reagan and Bush's policies, and in 1992 the Republicans' emphasis on "family values" may have cost them votes among single women. Among all women who had never been married ($N = 115$), 69 percent voted for Clinton, while among married women ($N = 542$), only 46 percent did. However, these sharp differences result partly from the large number of single black women. Among white women who had never been married ($N = 83$), 59 percent voted for Clinton, while among white married women ($N = 481$), 42 percent did. Differences by marital status were also found among men. Among all men who had never been married ($N = 129$), 53 percent voted for Clinton, while among married men ($N = 570$), 37 percent did. These differences remained just as strong even when controls for race were introduced. Among white men who had never been married ($N = 112$), 48 percent voted for Clinton, while among white men who were married ($N = 504$), 32 percent did. Results for the VRS poll were reported for the total population. Among all unmarried voters, Clinton won 49 percent of the vote, Bush won 33 percent, and Perot gained 18 percent; among all married voters Clinton and Bush each won 40 percent of the vote, while Perot won 20 percent.

Our analysis in Chapter 3 shows that overall regional differences were relatively small. There were, however, pronounced regional differences among whites. As Table 5-1 reveals, among whites in the states of the old Confederacy, Bush won 46 percent of the vote, Clinton won 38 percent, and Perot won 16 percent. The South was the only region where Bush clearly won more white votes than Clinton, although according to the NES survey he narrowly edged out Clinton among whites in the north central states. The VRS exit poll suggests that the South was the only region where Bush won a majority of the white major party vote. According to this survey, Clinton won 34 percent of the southern white vote, Bush won 48 percent, and Perot won 18 percent. In the Midwest, Clinton and Bush each won 39 percent of the white vote, while Perot won 22 percent. Among whites in the West, Clinton narrowly edged Bush, winning 39 percent to 37 percent, while Perot gained 24 percent. Clinton's best region was the East, where he won 45 percent of the white vote, which compares with 36 percent for Bush and 19 percent for Perot.

In recent years, young Americans have been more likely to identify with the Republican party than older Americans,[12] and in the 1980, 1984, and 1988 elections the Democrats fared somewhat better among whites who reached voting age before or during World War II (those born before 1924). As Table 5-1 shows, Clinton, like Jimmy Carter in 1980, Walter F. Mondale in 1984, and Dukakis in 1988, did better among whites born before 1924 than among younger whites. As we saw in Chapter 2, the Clinton-Gore campaign made special efforts to appeal to young Americans. In fact, the NES survey shows that Clinton did best among the relatively small number of whites who reached voting age after the 1988 election. Perot, on the other hand, fared worst among whites born before 1924, and he also fared relatively poorly among whites born between 1924 and 1939. To some extent, Perot's relative success among younger voters results from their weaker levels of party identification, although age differences persist even when we take party loyalties into account.

The VRS poll also shows that Clinton did best among older voters. Among whites sixty years old and older, Clinton won a clear majority of the major party vote. Clinton gained 47 percent of the vote among older whites, Bush won 40 percent, and Perot gained only 13 percent. Among whites aged eighteen through twenty-nine, Clinton and Bush each won 38 percent of the vote, while Perot won 24 percent. Although the Gallup poll results do not introduce controls for race, they also show that Clinton did best among the elderly. Among likely voters sixty-five years old and older, 51 percent supported Clinton, 34 percent supported Bush, and only 8 percent supported Perot. However, the Gallup poll, unlike the two other surveys, shows Clinton doing relatively poorly among younger voters. Among likely voters from eighteen through twenty-nine years of age, 38 percent supported Clinton, 44 percent supported Bush, and 14 percent supported Perot. On balance, we would assign somewhat greater credence to the VRS poll, since the number of young respondents surveyed is substantially greater. However, all three polls support two basic findings: Clinton tended to fare best and Perot tended to fare worst among older voters.

Age group differences between Republicans and Democrats result from differences in the socialization of voters who entered the electorate at different historical periods.[13] Despite Democratic gains in the 1992 presidential elections, a majority of white party identifiers born between

1955 and 1970 are Republicans. The gradual replacement of relatively Democratic birth cohorts with younger, relatively Republican cohorts that entered the electorate in the 1970s and 1980s may lead to a gradual erosion in future Democratic support.

Social Class, Income, Education, and Union Membership

Traditionally, the Democratic party has done well among the relatively disadvantaged. It has done better among the working class, the poor, and voters with lower levels of formal education. Moreover, since the 1930s most union leaders have supported the Democratic party, and union members have traditionally been a mainstay of the Democratic presidential coalition. These bases of support persisted in 1992, but among all these groups there were substantial defections to Perot.

As we shall see, the weak relationship between social class and voting behavior is part of a long-term trend that has eroded class voting. Clinton was a moderate, and his support for the North American Free Trade Agreement led to lukewarm support by union leaders. On the other hand, he made strong class-based appeals during his campaign, promising to increase taxes on the wealthiest Americans. But Bush's appeals to traditional values may also have attracted working-class support.

When we examine social categories among whites, we find only five groups of whites that gave Clinton a clear majority of their votes (Hispanics, those with annual family incomes below $10,000, those earning between $10,000 and $15,000 a year, voters with less than a high school education, and Jews). Clinton did win a clear majority of the major party vote among working-class whites, but he also received half of the major party vote among the white middle class. Yet a fourth of the working-class whites and a fifth of the middle-class whites voted for Perot. Clinton did best among whites in families where the head of household was an unskilled manual worker, whereas Bush did best among families where the head of household held a managerial position.

Clinton clearly fared better among the poor than among the affluent. But, as Table 5-1 shows, the relationship between family income and electoral choice was relatively weak among white voters, mainly because Clinton won a clear majority of the vote only among the two lowest income categories. Among poor whites, only about three out of ten voted for Bush, while among the two most wealthy groups he won about half of the vote. Although Perot drew from all income categories, he tended to do best among whites with annual family incomes between $20,000 and $75,000 a year.

Income differences are sharper when the entire electorate is examined, because African-Americans are relatively poor and because the overwhelming majority of them voted for Clinton. For example, Table 5-1 shows that among the two lowest income categories, 57 percent of the whites voted for Clinton. But among all voters in these two groups ($N = 281$), 64 percent voted for Clinton. According to the VRS poll, Clinton won 59 percent of the vote among all voters with family incomes below $15,000 a year, but only 36 percent among those with family incomes of $75,000 and over. Among the wealthy, Bush won 48 percent of the vote. The exit poll reveals that Perot won substantial support among all income groups, but, as in the NES survey, he did somewhat better among the middle-income categories. The preelection Gallup poll found that 57 percent of the likely voters who had annual incomes below $20,000 supported Clinton, while only 29 percent favored Bush. Among those earning $50,000 or more a year, only 35 percent supported Clinton and 42 percent favored Bush. The Gallup survey found that Perot had the least support among the poor and the most among voters who had annual incomes of $50,000 and above, but the survey does not allow us to determine whether Perot's support dropped off among the more affluent.

Less educated whites were more likely to vote for Clinton than better educated whites. Among the small number of whites with an eighth-grade education or less he won a clear majority of the vote. But Table 5-1 also shows that Clinton did relatively well among whites with advanced degrees, among whom he won about half the total vote. Perot did worst among whites at the lowest and highest educational levels. The VRS poll reveals a similar pattern, although the results are presented without controls for race. Among all voters who had not graduated from high school, Clinton won 55 percent of the vote, Bush won 28 percent, and Perot gained 17 percent. Clinton's support tends to drop as educational levels rise, and among all college graduates he won 40 percent of the vote. But among voters with a postgraduate education, Clinton won 49 percent of the vote, Bush won 36 percent, and Perot won 15 percent. Moreover, as with the NES survey, Perot fared worst among voters at the highest and lowest educational categories.

Some scholars of American politics, such as Walter Dean Burnham and Everett Carll Ladd, argue that the Democrats now tend to fare better among upper and lower socioeconomic groups.[14] The results for both occupation and level of education support their thesis. The Democrats may be appealing to disadvantaged Americans because of their economic policies, while better educated Americans—and especially better educated women—may reject the interpretation of traditional values emphasized by the Republicans in recent elections.

Clinton clearly did better among union households. As Table 5-1 shows, he won nearly half the vote in white union households but only two-fifths of the vote among white nonunion households. Perot gained one-fifth of the vote among both union and nonunion households; the NES survey suggests he did slightly better among union households. The VRS exit poll reveals a similar pattern, although no controls for race are presented. Among union households, Clinton won 55 percent of the vote, Bush won 24 percent, and Perot won 21 percent. According to our calculations, the exit poll suggests that Clinton won only 40 percent of the vote from nonunion households, Bush won 38 percent, and Perot won 19 percent.

Religion

Religious differences, which partly reflect ethnic differences between Catholics and Protestants, have also played an important role in American politics.[15] Roman Catholics have tended to support the Democratic party, and white Protestants, especially outside the South, have tended to favor the Republicans. In all of Roosevelt's elections, and in every election through 1968, Jews strongly supported the Democratic presidential candidate. Even though Jewish support fell somewhat after that, an absolute majority of Jews voted Democratic in every subsequent election except 1980.

As Table 5-1 reveals, Clinton won nearly one-half the vote among white Catholics, while gaining only one-third of the vote among white Protestants. According to the VRS poll, 33 percent of white Protestants voted for Clinton, 46 percent for Bush, and 21 percent for Perot. Among white Catholics, Clinton won 42 percent, Bush 37 percent, and Perot 22 percent.[16]

Bush's appeals to traditional values, especially his opposition to abortion, may have had a special appeal to religious whites. As we saw in Chapter 1, the Republican platform was very conservative, advocating an absolute ban on abortions as well as explicitly rejecting proposals advocated by homosexual groups. The convention featured strident speeches by Pat Buchanan and the Rev. Pat Robertson. There was a great emphasis on "family values." As Ross K. Baker reports, many GOP professionals considered the family values focus of the convention to be a serious mistake.[17] But these appeals may have helped Bush among some religious groups.

As Table 5-1 shows, Bush fared better among white "born-again" Protestants than among other white Protestants; among those who identified as born again, Bush won a majority of the vote. Results for the VRS poll are reported for white born-again Christians. Among these voters, 61 percent voted for Bush, 23 percent supported Clinton, and 15 percent voted for Perot. As we saw in Chapter 4, white born-again Protestants are more likely to live in the South. Our analysis of the NES survey reveals that differences among Protestants are relatively small in the South. Among southern white Protestants who said they had been born again ($N = 115$), 57 percent voted for Bush; among those who said they had not been born again ($N = 77$), 52 percent voted for him. Outside the South, however, differences were substantial. Among white

Protestants outside the South who identified as born again ($N = 230$), 54 percent voted for Bush, whereas among those who had not had this religious experience ($N = 352$), only 37 percent did. As we noted in Chapter 4, David E. Leege and Lyman A. Kellstedt argue that religious commitment has a major impact on political behavior.[18] As Table 5-1 reveals, white Protestants with a very high level of religious commitment were much more likely to vote for Bush than were those with high or medium-low levels of commitment. As we noted, religious commitment is higher in the South, but the impact of commitment is strong even when we take regional differences into account. In both the South and the rest of the United States, Bush won 72 percent of the vote among white Protestants who pray several times a day, who attend church at least once a week, who say that religion provides "a great deal" of guidance in their daily lives, and who believe that the Bible is without error or is the "word of God." In both the South and the rest of the country, there was a substantial dropoff in support for Bush among white Protestants who did not meet all four of these conditions.

Bush also won a majority of the vote among white Protestants whom we classify as Evangelicals, although even among this group Clinton won nearly a third of the vote and Perot won 15 percent (see Table 5-1). But among the equally large group of white mainline Protestants, Bush won only two out of five votes, narrowly edging out Clinton, while Perot gained a fourth of the vote. Moreover, as we saw in Chapter 4, although these two Protestant groups are of equal size, white mainline Protestants were more likely to vote.

As we noted, white Evangelical Protestants are more likely to live in the South than are white mainline Protestants. Among southern whites, Bush fared only somewhat better among Evangelicals. Among white Evangelicals in the South ($N = 113$), Bush won 56 percent of the total vote, whereas among white mainline Protestants in the South ($N = 70$), he won 51 percent. Outside the South, differences were much greater. Among white Evangelicals outside the South ($N = 198$), Bush won 52 percent of the vote, while among white mainline Protestants ($N = 282$), he won only 37 percent.

Jews were clearly opposed to Bush. Bush's policies toward Israel may have alienated Jewish voters, and many were angered by Secretary of State James Baker's criticism of Jewish lobbying groups. Many Jews may have been further alienated from the Republican party by the speeches of Buchanan and Robertson at the Republican nominating convention: both argued that politics was about moral values, and many Jews want to ensure that the church and state remain separate. As Table 5-1 reveals, more than three out of four Jews voted for Clinton. Jews were less likely to vote for Perot than were white Protestants and Catholics, but they gave even less support to Bush. Because the NES survey interviewed only

40 Jewish voters, we must supplement this estimate with other surveys. The VRS exit poll provides data for about 600 Jewish voters. According to this survey, 78 percent voted for Clinton, 12 percent voted for Bush, and 10 percent voted for Perot.

Although Jews remain politically distinctive, the differences between Catholics and Protestants were relatively small. However, when religion and social class are combined, our ability to predict how people will vote is improved. Because working-class voters are more likely to vote Democratic than middle-class voters, and because Catholics are more likely to vote Democratic than Protestants, the tendency to vote Democratic is highest among those who are both working class and Catholic, and the Republicans do best among middle-class Protestants. In this three-candidate contest, Clinton won just under half the votes of white working-class Catholics, and only three out of ten votes among white middle-class Protestants. On the other hand, Bush won half the votes of white middle-class Protestants, but only a fourth of the votes of white working-class Catholics. There are five middle-class Protestants for every two working-class Catholics; although Bush fared better than Clinton among middle-class Protestants, his losses compared with 1988 were massive. Four years earlier two-thirds of white middle-class Protestants voted for Bush. Perot's relative success among white Catholics appears to result from the support of working-class Catholics.

How Social Groups Voted During the Postwar Years

Although there were sharp racial differences, and although Jews voted heavily Democratic, most other differences in voting behavior were relatively small in 1992. How does this election compare with earlier presidential elections? Were the relationships in 1992 atypical, or did they result from a long-term trend that has eroded the impact of social forces? To answer these questions we examine the voting behavior of social groups that have been an important part of the Democratic coalition during the postwar years. Our analysis begins with the 1944 presidential election contest between Roosevelt and Thomas E. Dewey and uses a simple measure of social cleavage to assess the impact of social forces over time.

In his lucid discussion of the logic of party coalitions, Robert Axelrod analyzes six basic groups that made up the Democratic presidential coalition: the poor, blacks (and other nonwhites), union members (and members of their families), Catholics (including other non-Protestants, such as Jews), and residents of the twelve largest metropolitan areas.[19] John R. Petrocik's more comprehensive study identifies fifteen coalition groups and classifies seven of them as predominantly Democratic: blacks, lower-status native southerners, middle- and upper-status southerners,

Jews, Polish and Irish Catholics, union members, and lower-status border state whites.[20] A more recent study, by Harold W. Stanley, William T. Bianco, and Richard G. Niemi, analyzes seven pro-Democratic groups: blacks, Catholics, Jews, females, native white southerners, members of union households, and the working class.[21] Our analysis focuses on race, region, union membership, social class, and religion.[22]

The contribution that a social group can make to a party's total coalition depends upon three factors: the relative size of the group in the total electorate, its level of turnout compared with that of the electorate as a whole, and its relative loyalty to a party.[23]

The larger a social group, the greater its contribution can be. African-Americans, for example, make up about 11 percent of the electorate, and the white working-class makes up 38 percent. Thus, the potential contribution of blacks to a political party is smaller than the potential contribution of working-class whites. The electoral power of blacks is diminished further by their relatively low turnout. However, because African-Americans vote overwhelmingly Democratic, their contribution to the party can be greater than their size would indicate. And the relative size of their contribution grows as whites desert the Democratic party.

Let us begin by examining racial differences, which we can trace back to 1944 by using the National Opinion Research Center (NORC) study for that year.[24] Figure 5-1 shows the percentage of white and black major party voters who voted Democratic for president from 1944 through 1992. Although most African-Americans voted Democratic from 1944 through 1960, a substantial minority voted Republican. The political mobilization of blacks spurred by the civil rights movement and the Republican candidacy of Barry M. Goldwater in 1964 ended this Republican voting, and the residual Republican loyalties of older blacks were discarded between 1962 and 1964.[25]

While the Democrats made substantial gains among African-Americans, they lost ground among whites. From 1944 through 1964, the Democrats gained an absolute majority of the white vote in two elections (1944 and 1964), and they gained a majority of the white major party vote in 1948. Since then, they have never won an absolute majority of the white vote, although they won about half of the white major party vote in 1992. However, even in a two-candidate contest the Democrats can win with just under half the white vote, as the 1960 and 1976 elections demonstrate.

The gap between the two trend lines in Figure 5-1 illustrates the overall difference in the Democratic vote between whites and blacks. Table 5-2 shows levels of "racial voting" in all thirteen elections; the table also presents four other measures of social cleavage.

From 1944 through 1960 racial voting ranged from a low of 12 to a high of 40. Although African-American support for the Democrats

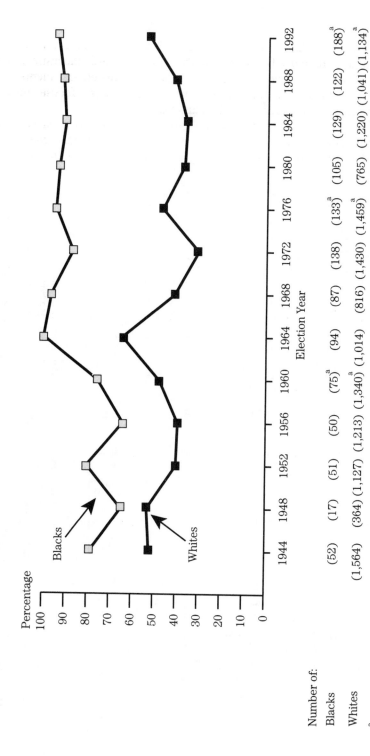

Figure 5-1 Major Party Voters Who Voted Democratic for President, by Race, 1944-1992 (in percentages)

Percentage

Election Year

Number of:

	1944	1948	1952	1956	1960	1964	1968	1972	1976	1980	1984	1988	1992
Blacks	(52)	(17)	(51)	(50)	(75)[a]	(94)	(87)	(138)	(133)[a]	(105)	(129)	(122)	(188)[a]
Whites	(1,564)	(364)	(1,127)	(1,213)	(1,340)[a]	(1,014)	(816)	(1,430)	(1,459)[a]	(765)	(1,220)	(1,041)	(1,134)[a]

[a] These numbers are weighted.

Table 5-2 Relationship of Social Characteristics to Presidential Voting, 1944-1992

	Election Year												
	1944	1948	1952	1956	1960	1964	1968	1972	1976	1980	1984	1988	1992
Racial voting [a]	27	12	40	25	23	36	56	57	48	56	54	51	41
Regional voting [b]													
Among whites	—	—	12	17	6	-11	-4	-13	1	1	-9	-5	-10
Among entire electorate (NES surveys)	—	—	9	15	4	-5	6	-3	7	3	3	2	0
Among entire electorate (official election results)	23	14	8	8	3	-13	-3	-11	5	2	-5	-7	-6
Union voting [c]													
Among whites	20	37	18	15	21	23	13	11	18	15	20	16	12
Among entire electorate	20	37	20	17	19	22	13	10	17	16	19	15	11
Class voting [d]													
Among whites	19	44	20	8	12	19	10	2	17	9	8	5	4
Among entire electorate	20	44	22	11	13	20	15	4	21	15	12	8	8
Religious voting [e]													
Among whites	25	21	18	10	48	21	30	13	15	10	16	18	20
Among entire electorate	24	19	15	10	46	16	21	8	11	3	9	11	10

Note: All calculations are based upon major party voters.

[a] Percentage of blacks who voted Democratic minus percentage of whites who voted Democratic.
[b] Percentage of southerners who voted Democratic minus percentage of voters outside the South who voted Democratic.
[c] Percentage of members of union households who voted Democratic minus percentage of members of households with no union members who voted Democratic.
[d] Percentage of working class that voted Democratic minus percentage of middle class that voted Democratic.
[e] Percentage of Catholics who voted Democratic minus percentage of Protestants who voted Democratic.

jumped in 1964, racial voting was held to 36 because a substantial majority of whites voted Democratic. But racial voting jumped to 56 in 1968 (to 61 if Wallace voters are included with Nixon voters), and it did not return to the pre-1968 level until the three-candidate contest of 1992. However, as very few blacks voted for Anderson in 1980 or for Perot in 1992, the racial voting score in these elections is higher if supporters of these independents are grouped with the Republicans. In 1980, racial voting rises from 56 to 59 points and in 1992 racial differences increase from 41 to 50 points.[26]

Not only did African-American loyalty to the Democratic party increase sharply after 1960, but black turnout rose dramatically from 1960 to 1968 because southern blacks (about half the black population during this period) were enfranchised. Moreover, the relative size of the black population increased somewhat during the postwar years. Between 1960, when postwar turnout was at its highest, and 1988, when postwar turnout reached its lowest level, turnout among whites dropped about 15 percentage points. Even though black turnout fell from its peak in 1968, black turnout was about 10 points higher in 1988 than in 1960. In 1992, as we saw, there was about a 5-point increase in white turnout, whereas turnout increased only about 2.5 points among blacks. Even though the differential between white and black turnout increased, relative levels of black turnout were far higher than in the years before the Voting Rights Act of 1965.

From 1948 through 1960, African-Americans never accounted for more than one Democratic voter out of twelve. In 1964, however, Lyndon B. Johnson received about one in seven of his votes from black voters, and blacks contributed a fifth of the Democratic totals in 1968 and 1972. In 1976, an election that saw Democratic gains among whites, the black total fell to just over one in seven. In 1980, Carter received about one in four of his total votes from blacks, and in the last three presidential elections about one Democratic vote in five came from blacks.

Region

The desertion of the Democratic party by white southerners is among the most dramatic changes in postwar American politics. As we saw in Chapter 3, regional differences can be analyzed using official election statistics. But official election returns are of limited utility in examining race-related differences in regional voting because election returns are not tabulated by race. Survey data allow us to document the dramatic shift in the voting behavior of white southerners.

As the data in Figure 5-2 reveal, white southerners were somewhat more Democratic than whites outside the South in the 1952 and 1956 contests between Dwight D. Eisenhower and Adlai E. Stevenson, as they were in the 1960 contest between John F. Kennedy and Richard M.

Figure 5-2 White Major Party Voters Who Voted Democratic for President, by Region, 1952-1992 (in percentages)

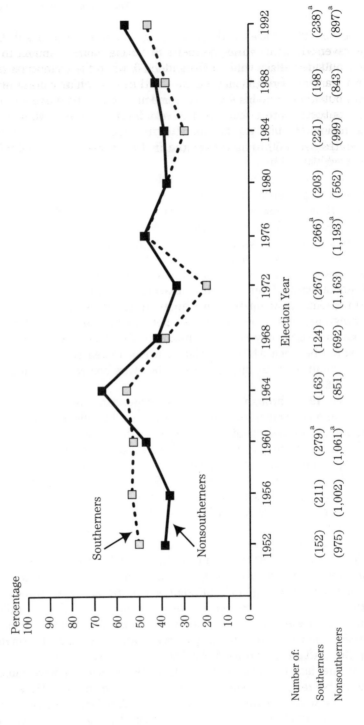

Number of:

	1952	1956	1960	1964	1968	1972	1976	1980	1984	1988	1992
Southerners	(152)	(211)	(279)[a]	(163)	(124)	(267)	(266)[a]	(203)	(221)	(198)	(238)[a]
Nonsoutherners	(975)	(1,002)	(1,061)[a]	(851)	(692)	(1,163)	(1,193)[a]	(562)	(999)	(843)	(897)[a]

[a]These numbers are weighted.

Nixon.[27] But in the next three presidential elections regional differences were reversed, with white southerners voting more Republican than whites outside the South. In 1976 and 1980, when the Democrats fielded Jimmy Carter of Georgia as their standard bearer, white southerners and whites outside the South voted very much alike. In both 1984 and 1988 white southerners were less likely to vote Democratic than whites in any other region. In 1992, the Democratic presidential and vice-presidential candidates were both from the South. Even so, as we saw, Bush did better among white southerners than among whites in any other region.

Regional differences in voting among whites from 1952 through 1992 are presented in Table 5-2. The negative signs for 1964, 1968, 1972, 1984, 1988, and 1992 reveal that the Democratic candidate fared better among white major party voters outside the South than he did among white southerners. As we saw in Chapter 3, Wallace did far better in the South than in any other region, whereas both Anderson and Perot fared worst in the South. If Wallace voters are included with Nixon voters, regional differences among whites increase markedly, moving from -4 to -12. Including Anderson voters with Reagan voters increases the Democratic advantage in the South from 1 to 3 points. And including Perot voters with Bush voters substantially reduces the Republican advantage among whites, so that regional voting moves from -10 to -5. However, even when we take Perot's relatively weak showing among southern whites into account, we find that the Clinton-Gore ticket fared worse among southern whites than among whites outside the South.

Table 5-2 also presents regional voting for the entire electorate. Here, however, we include two sets of estimates: (1) NES results from 1952 through 1992 and (2) results based upon official election statistics. Both sets of figures show that regional differences in voting have declined, but the NES surveys somewhat overestimated the Democratic advantage in the South in 1956 and somewhat underestimated the Republican advantage in 1964 and 1972. In 1968, 1984, and 1988, the NES surveys registered a slight Democratic advantage in the South, while official election statistics show that the Democrats actually fared better outside the South. In 1992, the NES results show the Republicans and Democrats faring equally in both regions, whereas the official election statistics demonstrate that the Republicans actually fared better in the South. Because most voters in both regions are white, it seems likely that the Republican advantage among white southerners in 1964, 1968, 1972, 1984, 1988, and 1992 was somewhat greater than the NES surveys reveal.

The mobilization of southern blacks and the defection of southern whites from the Democratic party dramatically transformed the demographic composition of the Democratic coalition in the South. Democratic presidential candidates from 1952 through 1960 never received more than one out of fifteen votes in the South from black voters. In 1964 nearly three out of ten of Johnson's southern votes came from blacks, and in 1968 Hubert H. Humphrey received nearly as many votes from southern blacks as from southern whites. In 1972, according to these data, George S. McGovern received more votes from southern blacks than from southern whites.

In 1976 African-American voters were crucial to Carter's success in the South. He received about one out of three of his southern votes from blacks in 1976 and again in 1980. In 1984, Mondale received about four in ten of his southern votes from blacks, and in 1988 about one out of three of the votes Dukakis received in the South came from blacks. According to the NES survey, about four out of ten of Clinton's southern votes came from African-Americans. Although this estimate is probably somewhat high,[28] it seems clear that Bush won more white votes than Clinton in three of the four southern states that Clinton carried—Georgia, Louisiana, and Tennessee.[29]

Union Membership

Figure 5-3 shows the percentage of white union members and nonmembers who voted Democratic for president from 1944 through 1992. In all six elections from 1944 through 1964, a majority of white union members (and members of their families) voted Democratic. In 1968 Humphrey received a slight majority of the major party vote cast by white union members, although his total would be cut to 43 percent if Wallace voters were included. The Democrats won 61 percent of the white union vote in 1976, when Carter narrowly defeated Ford. In 1988, Dukakis appears to have won a slight majority of the white union vote, although he fell well short of Carter's 1976 tally. In 1992, as we saw, Clinton won nearly half of the white union vote, although he won about three-fifths of the major party vote. Conversely, the Republicans have won a majority of the white union vote in only one of these thirteen elections, Nixon's 1972 landslide over McGovern.

Differences between union members and nonmembers are presented in Table 5-2. As Wallace did better among union members than nonmembers, including Wallace voters with union voters in 1968 reduces union voting from 13 to 10 points. Including Anderson voters with Reagan voters in 1980 has little effect on union voting (it falls from 15 points to 14 points). However, because Perot appears to have done better among union voters (a point confirmed by both the NES and the VRS polls), including Perot voters with Republicans in 1992 reduces union voting from 12 points to 8 points. We have also reported the results for the entire electorate, but, because blacks are as likely to live in union households as whites are, including blacks has little effect on our results.

The percentage of the total white electorate composed of white union members and their families declined during the postwar years. In 1952,

Figure 5-3 White Major Party Voters Who Voted Democratic for President, by Union Membership, 1944-1992 (in percentages)

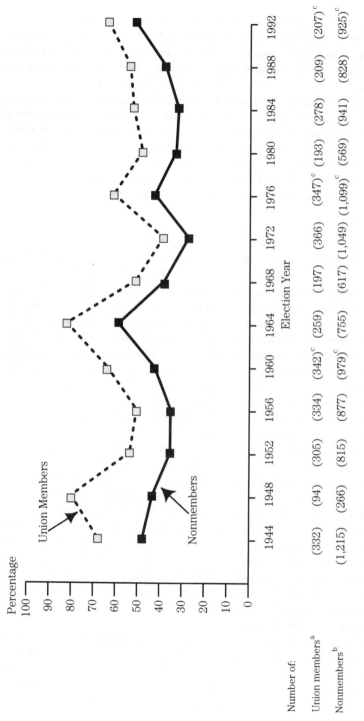

Number of:	1944	1948	1952	1956	1960	1964	1968	1972	1976	1980	1984	1988	1992
Union members[a]	(332)	(94)	(305)	(334)	(342)[c]	(259)	(197)	(366)	(347)[c]	(193)	(278)	(209)	(207)[c]
Nonmembers[b]	(1,215)	(266)	(815)	(877)	(979)[c]	(755)	(617)	(1,049)	(1,099)[c]	(569)	(941)	(828)	(925)[c]

[a] Union members or in household with union member.
[b] Not a union member and not in household with union member.
[c] These numbers are weighted.

for example, members of union households made up 25 percent of the electorate; by 1992, they made up only 15 percent. Turnout among white union households has declined at the same rate as turnout among nonunion whites. In addition, there has been a substantial decline in union support for Democratic presidential candidates. All these factors, as well as increased turnout among blacks, have reduced the total contribution of white union members to the Democratic presidential coalition. Through 1960, a third of the total Democratic vote came from white trade union members and members of their families. Between 1964 and 1984, only about one Democratic vote in four came from white union members. In both 1988 and 1992, about one in five Democratic presidential votes came from white trade union members.

Social Class

The broad cleavage in political behavior between manually employed workers (and their dependents) and nonmanually employed workers (and their dependents) is especially valuable for studying comparative voting behavior.[30] In every presidential election since 1936, the working class has voted more Democratic than the middle class. But, as Figure 5-4 shows, the percentage of working-class whites who have voted Democratic has varied considerably from election to election. It fell to its lowest level in 1972. Carter regained a majority of the white working-class vote in 1976, but he lost it four years later. The Democrats failed to win a majority of the white working class in both 1984 and 1988. In 1992, Clinton won only about two-fifths of the white working-class vote, although he did win a clear majority of the major party vote among working-class whites.

Although levels of class voting have varied since 1944, they are following a downward trend, as Table 5-2 reveals.[31] Class voting is even lower for 1968 (falling to 6) if Wallace voters are included with Nixon voters, because 15 percent of the white working-class voters supported Wallace, while only 10 percent of the white middle-class voters did. On the other hand, Anderson got relatively little support from the working class, and including Anderson voters with Reagan voters in 1980 raises class voting to 11. Perot appears to have done somewhat better among working-class whites than among middle-class whites. Including Perot voters with Bush voters all but eliminates class voting, and working-class whites become only 1 percentage point more likely to vote Democratic than middle-class whites.

Class voting trends are affected substantially if African-Americans are included in the analysis. Blacks are disproportionately working class and, as we have seen, they vote overwhelmingly Democratic. In all five of the last elections, including blacks increases class voting somewhat, and the overall trend toward declining class voting is dampened if we study

Figure 5-4 White Major Party Voters Who Voted Democratic for President, by Social Class, 1944-1992 (in percentages)

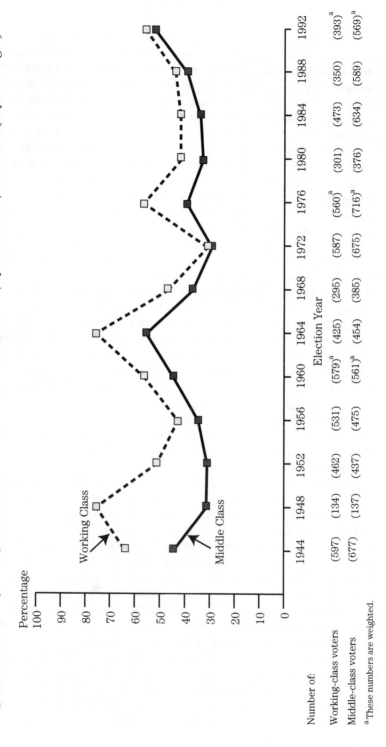

Number of:	1944	1948	1952	1956	1960	1964	1968	1972	1976	1980	1984	1988	1992
Working-class voters	(597)	(134)	(462)	(531)	(579)[a]	(425)	(295)	(587)	(560)[a]	(301)	(473)	(350)	(393)[a]
Middle-class voters	(677)	(137)	(437)	(475)	(561)[a]	(454)	(385)	(675)	(716)[a]	(376)	(634)	(589)	(569)[a]

[a] These numbers are weighted.

the entire electorate. However, black workers voted Democratic because they were black, not because they were working class. Most middle-class blacks also voted Democratic. In 1992, for example, among the seventy-one black middle-class voters in the NES survey, 89 percent voted for Clinton; among the ninety-two black working-class voters, 93 percent did. It seems reasonable, therefore, to focus on changing levels of class voting among the white electorate.

During the postwar years the proportion of the electorate made up of working-class whites has remained relatively constant, while the proportion made up of middle-class whites has grown. The percentage of whites in the agricultural sector declined dramatically. After 1960, turnout fell among whites of both social classes, but it fell more among the working class. As we saw in Chapter 4, only 76 percent of working-class whites claimed to have voted in 1992, while 86 percent of the white middle class did. Declining turnout and defections from the Democrats by working-class whites, along with increased turnout by blacks, have reduced the total contribution of working-class whites to the Democratic presidential coalition.

In 1948 and 1952 about half of the total Democratic presidential vote came from working-class whites, and from 1956 through 1964 more than four out of ten Democratic votes came from this social group. In 1968, the total white working-class contribution fell to 35 percent, and then to 32 percent in 1972. In 1976, with the rise of class voting, the white working class provided 39 percent of Carter's total vote, but in 1980 just over a third of Carter's total vote came from working-class whites. In 1984, 36 percent of Mondale's total support came from working-class whites. In 1988, only 28 percent of Dukakis's total support came from the white working class, and in 1992, 31 percent of Clinton's total vote came from working-class whites. The middle-class contribution to the Democratic presidential coalition amounted to fewer than three votes in ten in 1952, and just under one-third in 1956, stabilizing at just over one-third in the next five elections. In 1980, 33 percent of Carter's total vote came from middle-class whites. In 1984 Mondale received 39 percent of his vote from the white middle class, and in 1988 Dukakis gained 41 percent of his vote from this group. In 1992, 43 percent of Clinton's total vote came from middle-class whites, the highest total the Democrats have received from this group. In each of the last three presidential elections, the Democrats have received a larger share of the total vote from middle-class whites than from the white working class. The growing middle-class contribution to the Democratic presidential coalition results largely from two factors: first, the middle class is growing; and second, class differences are eroding. The decline in class differences in voting behavior may be part of a widespread phenomenon that is occuring in most advanced industrial democracies.[32]

Figure 5-5 White Major Party Voters Who Voted Democratic for President, by Religion, 1944-1992 (in percentages)

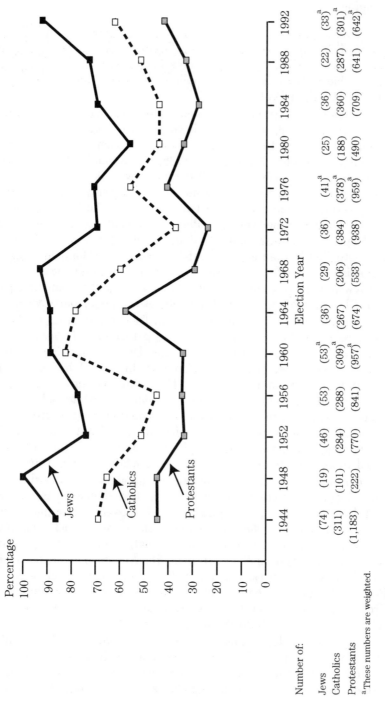

	1944	1948	1952	1956	1960	1964	1968	1972	1976	1980	1984	1988	1992
Number of:													
Jews	(74)	(19)	(46)	(53)	(53)[a]	(36)	(29)	(36)	(41)[a]	(25)	(36)	(22)	(33)[a]
Catholics	(311)	(101)	(284)	(288)	(309)[a]	(267)	(206)	(384)	(378)[a]	(188)	(360)	(287)	(301)[a]
Protestants	(1,183)	(222)	(770)	(841)	(957)[a]	(674)	(533)	(938)	(959)[a]	(490)	(709)	(641)	(642)[a]

[a] These numbers are weighted.

Religion

Voting differences among the major religious groups have also declined during the postwar years. Even so, as Figure 5-5 reveals, in every election since 1944, Jews have been more likely to vote Democratic than Catholics, and Catholics have been more likely to vote Democratic than Protestants.

A large majority of Jews voted Democratic in every election from 1944 through 1968, and although the Jewish vote for the Democrats dropped in Nixon's 1972 landslide, even McGovern won a majority of the Jewish vote. From 1972 through 1988, the Republicans won a sizable minority of the Jewish vote. In 1980, many Jews (like many gentiles) were dissatisfied with Carter's performance as president, and some resented the pressure he had exerted on Israel to accept the Camp David peace accord, which returned the Sinai Peninsula—captured by Israel in 1967—to Egypt. A substantial minority of Jews voted for Anderson, but Carter still outpolled Reagan among Jewish voters. Both Mondale in 1984 and Dukakis (whose wife, Kitty, was Jewish) in 1988 won a clear majority of the Jewish vote. And in 1992, the Jewish vote for the Democrats surged, with Clinton winning about 90 percent of the major party vote.[33]

A majority of white Catholics voted Democratic in six of the seven elections from 1944 through 1968. The percentage of Catholics voting Democratic peaked in 1960, when the Democrats fielded a Roman Catholic candidate, but it was also very high in Johnson's landslide victory four years later. Since then, Democratic voting among Catholics has declined precipitously. In 1968, a majority of white Catholics voted Democratic, although Humphrey's total would be reduced from 60 to 55 percent if Wallace voters were included. In 1992, Clinton won a majority of the major party vote among white Catholics (see Figure 5-5), but he failed to gain an absolute majority of the white Catholic vote.

Our simple measure of religious voting shows considerable change from election to election, and there was a clear downward trend through 1980 (see Table 5-2). Even though white Protestants were more likely to vote for Wallace in 1968 than white Catholics were, including Wallace voters in our totals has little effect on relative levels of religious voting (the measure falls from 30 to 29). Including Anderson voters has no effect on religious differences: religious voting remains at 9 points. In 1992, Perot did somewhat better among white Catholics than among white Protestants, and if Perot voters are included with Republican voters, religious voting falls from 20 to 14 points.

Including African-Americans in our calculations substantially reduces religious voting. Blacks are much more likely to be Protestant than Catholic, and including blacks adds a substantial number of Protestant Democrats. The effect of including blacks is greater from 1968 on because black turnout has been higher. In 1992 religious voting is reduced from 20 to 10 points if blacks are included.

White Catholics make up just over a fifth of the electorate, and this proportion has remained relatively constant during the postwar years. However, since 1960 turnout has declined more among white Catholics than among white Protestants. As Figure 5-5 shows, the proportion of Catholics voting for the Democrats has declined, although the Democratic share of the major party vote has crept upward since 1980. Even so, since 1976 the Democrats have not won an absolute majority of the white Catholic vote. In addition, increased turnout among blacks has tended to lower the overall contribution of white Catholics to the Democratic coalition.

According to our estimates based upon the NES surveys, Truman won about a third of his total vote from white Catholics. Stevenson won 29 percent of his total vote from white Catholics in 1952, but he gained only 25 percent of his vote from Catholics in 1956. In 1960, Kennedy received 37 percent of his total vote from white Roman Catholics, but the Catholic contribution fell to 28 percent when Johnson defeated Goldwater in 1964. In 1968, 30 percent of Humphrey's votes came from white Roman Catholics, but only 25 percent of McGovern's vote came from white Catholics. Just over a fourth of Carter's vote (26 percent) came from white Catholics in his 1976 victory, but in his loss to Reagan just over a fifth (22 percent) came from this source. Mondale received 28 percent of his total vote from white Catholics, and in 1988 Dukakis received 26 percent of his vote from this group. According to our estimates using the NES surveys, just under a fourth of Clinton's total vote (24 percent) came from white Catholics. Our recalculations based upon published results from the VRS exit poll show that just over a fifth of Clinton's total vote (21 percent) came from white Catholics.

The Jewish contribution to the Democratic coalition has declined, partly because Jews did not vote overwhelmingly Democratic from 1972 through 1988, and partly because the proportion of Jews in the electorate declined. From 1972 through 1988, Jews made up only about a twentieth of the total Democratic presidential coalition. Despite the upsurge in Jewish support for Clinton, the 1992 NES survey shows that Clinton received only 4 percent of his total votes from Jews. However, our estimates based upon published results from the VRS exit poll suggest that 7 percent of Clinton's total vote came from Jewish voters. But although Jews make up only 2.4 percent of the population, over three-fourths of the nation's Jews live in seven large states (New York, California, Florida, New Jersey, Pennsylvania, Massachusetts, and Illinois), which combine for 184 electoral votes.[34] New York has the largest proportion of Jews, and, according to the VRS exit poll in New York State, 17 percent of the voters were Jewish.

According to our estimates, a fourth of the votes Clinton received in New York State were cast by Jews.[35]

As the data in Figure 5-6 reveal, the effects of social class and religion are cumulative. In every election from 1944 through 1992, working-class Catholics have been more likely to vote Democratic than any other class-religion combination. In all thirteen elections, white middle-class Protestants have been the least likely to vote Democratic. They are more constant over time than any other group we have studied. An absolute majority voted Republican in every election from 1944 through 1988, and Bush won half of their total vote in the three-way contest of 1992.

The relative importance of social class and religion can be assessed by comparing the voting behavior of middle-class Catholics with that of working-class Protestants. Religion was more important than social class in predicting voting choices in 1944, 1956, 1960 (by a considerable margin), 1968, 1972, 1984, 1988, and 1992. Social class was more important than religion in 1948 (by a great margin), 1952, 1976, and 1980. And class and religion were equally important in 1964. However, during the last seven elections all these trend lines have tended to converge, suggesting that these traditional sources of social cleavage are declining in importance.

Why the New Deal Coalition Broke Down

Except for race, all of the social factors we have examined—region, union membership, social class, and religion—have declined in importance during the postwar years. The decline in regional differences directly parallels the increase in racial differences. As the national Democratic party strengthened its appeals to African-Americans during the 1960s, party leaders endorsed policies opposed by southern whites, and many of them deserted the Democratic party. The migration of northern whites to the South may have also reduced regional differences somewhat.

The Democratic party's appeals to blacks may have weakened its hold on white groups that traditionally supported it. Robert Huckfeldt and Carol Weitzel Kohfeld clearly demonstrate that Democratic appeals to blacks weakened the party's support among working-class whites.[36] But the erosion of Democratic support among union members, the working class, and Catholics results from other factors as well. During the postwar years, these groups have changed. Although union members do not hold high paying professional and managerial jobs, they have gained substantial economic advantages. Differences in income between the working class and the middle class have diminished. And Catholics, who often came from more recent immigrant groups than Protestants, have

Figure 5-6 White Major Party Voters Who Voted Democratic for President, by Social Class and Religion, 1944-1992 (in percentages)

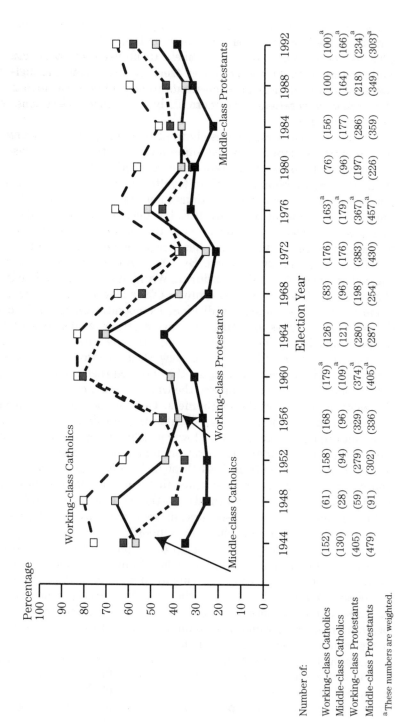

Number of:

	1944	1948	1952	1956	1960	1964	1968	1972	1976	1980	1984	1988	1992
Working-class Catholics	(152)	(61)	(158)	(168)	(179)[a]	(126)	(83)	(176)	(163)[a]	(76)	(156)	(100)	(100)[a]
Middle-class Catholics	(130)	(28)	(94)	(96)	(109)[a]	(121)	(96)	(176)	(179)[a]	(96)	(177)	(164)	(166)[a]
Working-class Protestants	(405)	(59)	(279)	(329)	(374)[a]	(280)	(198)	(383)	(367)[a]	(197)	(286)	(218)	(234)[a]
Middle-class Protestants	(479)	(91)	(302)	(336)	(405)[a]	(287)	(254)	(430)	(457)[a]	(226)	(359)	(349)	(303)[a]

[a]These numbers are weighted.

grown increasingly middle class as the proportion of second- and third-generation Catholic Americans has become larger. During the 1950s and 1960s white Catholics were more likely to be working class than were white Protestants. This is no longer true. In 1976, 1980, and 1984 they were just as likely as white Protestants to be middle class, and in 1988 and 1992 they were somewhat more likely to be middle class than white Protestants were.

Not only have these groups changed economically and socially, but the historical conditions that led union members, the working class, and Catholics to become Democrats have receded further into the past. While the transmission of partisan loyalties from generation to generation gives historically based coalitions some staying power, the ability of the family to transmit party loyalties has decreased as party identification has weakened.[37] Moreover, with the passage of time, the total proportion of the electorate that has directly experienced the Roosevelt years has progressively declined. By 1992, only one voter in eight had entered the electorate before or during World War II. New policy issues, often unrelated to the political conflicts of the New Deal, have tended to erode party loyalty among traditional Democratic groups. Edward G. Carmines and James A. Stimson provide strong evidence that race-related issues have been crucial in weakening the New Deal coalition.[38]

Despite the breakdown of the New Deal coalition, the Democrats managed to win in 1992. In doing so, they boosted their major party share of the vote among union members, the white working class, Jews, Roman Catholics, and even white southerners. Clinton focused his appeal on "middle America," and he paid as low a price as possible to gain the black vote. But the Democrats won with lower absolute levels of support among most of these groups than they had won in previous Democratic victories. In no previous election from 1944 through 1988 had the Democrats ever won without capturing *at least* three-fifths of the vote of white union members and *at least* two-thirds of the vote among working-class Catholics. Jews and African-Americans were the only two groups that provided Clinton with overwhelming support. But these are both small groups, and in addition to making up only one-ninth of the electorate, blacks have lower than average turnout. Clinton's victory is the first Democratic victory in which blacks made up more than 15 percent of the Democratic coalition. But in 1992 the white vote was split among three candidates. Our calculations suggest that it would be extremely difficult for the Democrats to win a two-candidate contest if blacks made up one-fifth or more of their total coalition.

Clinton's victory provides an opportunity to forge a new Democratic coalition, which may be based partly upon some of the components of the old New Deal coalition. Blacks and Jews are solidly Democratic, and union members provide a potential, if unreliable, basis of support. A successful coalition will need to gain a large share of the nearly twenty million Americans who voted for Perot. As we saw, from a demographic standpoint, Perot's supporters closely resembled the white electorate, although he gained relatively little support from southern whites and from Jews. Perhaps, as James Ceaser and Andrew Busch argue, new groups will be formed, based upon common issue positions rather than on the type of demographic categories that both politicians and political scientists employ.[39] Turning to the issue preferences of the electorate provides an opportunity to assess how a Democratic coalition can be forged, and may also suggest strategies the Republicans can employ to regain their domination of the presidency.

Chapter 6

Candidates, Issues, and the Vote

In Chapter 5, we discussed the relationship between various social forces and the vote. The impact of such forces on the vote is indirect. Even though the Democratic New Deal coalition was constructed from members of different groups, people who were members of these groups did not vote for Democrats simply because they were African-Americans, white southerners, union members, Roman Catholics, or Jews. Rather they more often than not voted Democratic because that party offered symbolic and substantive policies that appealed to the concerns of members of these groups, because the party nominated candidates who were attractive to members of these groups, and because the party's platforms and candidates were consistent enough that many voters developed long-term partisan loyalties. The long-term decline in the strength of class voting, for example, is evidence of the decreasing importance members of the working and middle classes assign to the differences between the parties on concerns that divide blue-collar and white-collar workers. And as we also saw, the changes in such voting patterns from election to election reflect differences in the attractiveness of the candidates and policies the two parties offer and the changing circumstances that have made the parties' appeals more or less important in any given election campaign. That race is the sharpest political division in American politics today does not mean that blacks vote Democratic simply because they are black; as Supreme Court Justice Clarence Thomas exemplifies, African-Americans may also identify with and vote for Republicans and may be conservative ideologically.

In this and the next two chapters, we examine some of the concerns that underlie voters' choices, connecting the indirect relationship between group membership and the vote. Even though, as we shall see, scholars and politicians disagree among themselves about what factors voters employ, and how they employ them, there is general consensus on several points. First, voters' attitudes or preferences determine their choices. There may be disagreement over exactly which attitudes shape behavior, but most agree that voters are not driven by unconscious forces. Rather, they deliberately choose to support the candidate or party they believe to be best. There is also general agreement that the most important attitudes in shaping the vote are attitudes toward the candidates, the issues, and the parties. This set of attitudes was first formulated and tested extensively by the authors of *The American Voter*, using data from what are now called the National Election Studies (NES) surveys. They based their conclusions primarily on data from a survey of the 1956 presidential election, a match between the Democrat Adlai E. Stevenson and the Republican (and this time incumbent) Dwight D. Eisenhower.

In this chapter, we first look briefly at the relationship between one measure of candidate evaluation and the vote. In this brief analysis we ignore two of the major components of the evaluation of the candidates: voters' perceptions of the candidates' personal qualities and voters' perceptions of the candidates' professional qualifications and competence to serve as president.[1] Still, there is a very powerful relationship between evaluations of candidates and the vote. It might seem obvious that voters support the candidate they like best, but the presence of a third candidate illustrates the complicated nature of voters' decision making. In 1992, it appears that some people may not have voted for the candidate they rated most highly, instead supporting one whom they thought had a better chance of winning, thus seeking to block the election of the candidate they liked least. Voters who do not vote for their first preference for these reasons are called sophisticated or strategic voters.[2]

In a three-way race, it is also possible for the candidate who wins with a plurality of the vote to have been opposed by the majority of the electorate who had divided their vote between the other two contenders. Thus, in a three-way race a candidate opposed by a majority may, by virtue of the rules governing presidential elections, nonetheless win. William H. Riker argues that Woodrow Wilson, the Democratic standard bearer in 1912, was such a candidate. A majority may have preferred William Howard Taft, the Republican incumbent, to Wilson, and a majority may have preferred Theodore Roosevelt, a former Republican president running under the Progressive or "Bull Moose" party label, to Wilson. With the vote for the other two candidates split, Wilson won with a plurality vote (that was approximately the same as Bill Clinton's in 1992), which became an electoral college majority by virtue of the states' winner-take-all rule.[3] We can use our measures of attitudes toward the candidates to investigate whether this appeared to happen in 1992; we show that apparently Clinton would have been the preferred candidate of a majority if he had run against either Bush or Perot alone.

We see the simple measure of attitudes toward the candidates as the most direct influence on the vote itself; attitudes toward the issues and the parties help to shape attitudes toward the candidates and, thus, the vote. We then turn to the first part of our investigation of the role of issues. After analyzing what problems most concerned the voters in 1992, we discuss the two forms of issue voting, which are referred to as voting based on prospective and retrospective issues. In this chapter, we investigate the impact of prospective issues. We consider one of the controversies about issue voting: how much information the public has about issues and candidates' positions on them. Our analysis of the impact of prospective issues on the vote is hampered by two problems— the NES surveys employed only three appropriate measures of such issue voting; and they failed to measure where the public believed Perot to stand on the issues. Nonetheless, we can provide some indication of the significance of prospective issues in 1992, and we can make some comparisons to their impact as shown in earlier election surveys. Chapter 7 examines retrospective issues and the vote, and Chapter 8 examines partisan identification and assesses the significance of parties and issues, together, on voting in 1992 and in earlier elections.

Attitudes Toward the Candidates

Overall Ratings of the Candidates

Voters faced three major choices in the 1992 election, which makes that election comparable to two other recent elections for which there are NES surveys, 1968 and 1980.[4] It seems reasonable to assume that voters support the candidate whom they believe would make the best president. This close relationship can be demonstrated by analysis of a measure in the NES surveys called the feeling thermometer. We have reproduced in Figure 6-1 the drawing shown to each respondent. This measure produces a scale that runs from 0 through 100 degrees, with zero indicating very "cold" or negative feelings, 50 indicating neutral feelings, and 100 indicating the "warmest" or most positive evaluation.

In the past, voters knew less about the third candidate than about the nominees of the two major parties. Therefore, fewer respondents ranked third candidates on the thermometer scales, and more of those rated them at the exact neutral point. For example, in the preelection measurement in 1980, 14 percent did not rate Anderson, about three times as many as did not rate Jimmy Carter or Ronald Reagan; in the postelection survey 9 percent failed to rate Anderson, but only 2 percent

Figure 6-1 The "Feeling Thermometer" Shown to Respondents When
They Are Asked to Rate Individuals and Groups

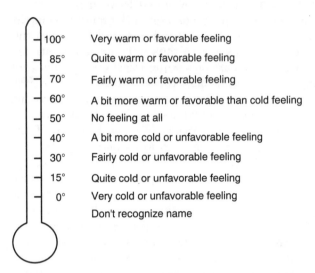

100°	Very warm or favorable feeling
85°	Quite warm or favorable feeling
70°	Fairly warm or favorable feeling
60°	A bit more warm or favorable than cold feeling
50°	No feeling at all
40°	A bit more cold or unfavorable feeling
30°	Fairly cold or unfavorable feeling
15°	Quite cold or unfavorable feeling
0°	Very cold or unfavorable feeling
	Don't recognize name

Source: 1992 National Election Studies Pre-Election Survey, Respondent Booklet.

or fewer failed to rate Carter or Reagan. Many respondents rated
Anderson at exactly the neutral point, twice as many as rated Reagan at
50 degrees and more than twice as many as rated Carter at 50 degrees. In
the 1992 preelection survey, 7 percent did not rate Perot, while only 2
percent did not rate Clinton and only 1 percent failed to rate Bush. By
the postelection survey, only 3 percent failed to rank Perot, and 1 percent
failed to rate Clinton or Bush. Although Perot gained widespread
recognition, a substantially greater proportion of the respondents rated
him at exactly the midpoint than rated Clinton and Bush at 50 degrees.
In the preelection survey, 24 percent rated Perot at 50 degrees, 15 percent
rated Clinton there, and 14 percent rated Bush there. Even in the
postelection survey, 23 percent rated Perot at the midpoint, whereas only
13 percent scored Clinton at the midpoint, and 15 percent placed Bush at
the midpoint.[5]

Were Voters "Sophisticated"?

The comparative ranking of the candidates on these scales is usually
a very accurate reflection of the vote. Table 6-1 reports the candidate
ranked highest by voters in the 1992 postelection survey and the
candidate they supported. Included as well are comparable figures from
the 1968 and 1980 NES surveys. In all three cases, those who rated a
major party nominee highest overwhelmingly voted for that candidate.

The lowest proportion was the 93 percent who rated Bush highest and voted for him in 1992. In all three cases, however, the third candidate fared more poorly. Of the 16 percent who rated Perot highest, only 77 percent actually voted for him, a proportion not as high as the comparable figure for Wallace in 1968 (85 percent), but considerably higher than the 57 percent received by Anderson in 1980. These results strongly suggest that at least some voters who preferred Perot strategically voted for Clinton or Bush.

The most obvious problem facing an independent or third-party candidate is how to attract more of a following, but there is a second obstacle: people find it hard to justify voting for their preferred candidate if they believe he or she has very little chance to win. Many people are unwilling to "waste" their vote. Perot apparently was aware of this fact and tried to counter it with the slogan, "Don't waste your vote on politics as usual."

The logic against "wasting" votes is a problem faced by third parties in many elections. There is strong evidence that some voters in Canada and Britain, for example, choose not to vote for the party they prefer.[6] Moreover, some voters in U.S. presidential nomination contests also vote for candidates who are not their first choice.[7]

In July 1992, Perot justified his withdrawal partly on the grounds that he could not win. Shortly before he withdrew from the race, Perot had been leading in the polls, but he argued that his candidacy might lead to a deadlock in which no candidate won a majority of the electoral vote. The U.S. House of Representatives would then need to elect the president, and the House had not chosen a president since it picked John Quincy Adams in 1825 (under the cloud of an alleged "corrupt bargain"). Having the House choose the president, Perot argued, would be "disruptive." Later, after he reentered the presidential contest, many Americans believed that Perot had no chance of winning. In part this view was fed by public opinion polls, and Gordon S. Black and Benjamin D. Black have used Voter Research and Surveys exit polls to suggest that Perot might have won a plurality of the popular vote if the polls had not contributed to this perception.[8]

Independent or third-party presidential candidates do not bear the imprimatur of one of the two major parties and the web of support that the label entails. Without a major party nomination, candidates find it difficult even to recruit a credible running mate. In 1968, Wallace picked a running mate, Gen. Curtis LeMay, whose lack of political experience led him to make statements in support of the possible use of nuclear weapons in Vietnam. James Stockdale, the highest-ranking American who had been a prisoner of war in North Vietnam, was Perot's running mate, and as we saw in Chapter 2, his lack of political experience was also a liability. Wallace, like Anderson in 1980, faced

Table 6-1   Candidate Thermometer Rankings and the Vote, 1968, 1980, and 1992 (in percentages)

First Place in Thermometer Rating	Voted for in 1968			Total Percent	(Number)
	Nixon	Humphrey	Wallace		
Nixon	96	2	2	100	(322)
Humphrey	2	97	1	100	(272)
Wallace	14	1	85	100	(79)
Nixon-Humphrey tie	45	53	2	100	(51)
Wallace-Nixon tie	[4]	—	[4]	—	(8)
Wallace-Humphrey tie	—	[3]	—	—	(3)
Three-way tie	[3]	[4]	—	—	(7)

First Place in Thermometer Rating	Voted for in 1980			Total Percent	(Number)
	Reagan	Carter	Anderson		
Reagan	97	2	1	100	(409)
Carter	3	97	—	100	(253)
Anderson	18	25	57	100	(111)
Reagan-Carter tie	40	60	—	100	(40)
Anderson-Reagan tie	88	3	9	100	(34)
Anderson-Carter tie	7	67	26	100	(27)
Three-way tie	24	64	12	100	(25)

First Place in Thermometer Rating	Voted for in 1992			Total Percent	(Number)[a]
	Bush	Clinton	Perot		
Bush	93	2	6	101	(485)
Clinton	2	95	3	100	(685)
Perot	10	13	77	100	(258)
Bush-Clinton tie	49	42	8	99	(72)
Perot-Bush tie	45	2	52	99	(48)
Perot-Clinton tie	5	57	38	100	(76)
Three-way tie	20	44	37	101	(27)

[a] Numbers are weighted.

great financial difficulties. Perot had no financial problems, which may partly account for his relatively high name recognition and popular vote success.

Perot was a very successful candidate, at least in popular vote terms. In a three-candidate race, it is always possible that the winning candidate might not have been elected if there had been only two candidates. As we saw, Riker argued that Wilson would not have won a two-candidate race against either Taft or Roosevelt. Wilson's victory was a triumph for a political scientist (as Wilson was before he became president of Princeton University and then governor of New Jersey), but not necessarily for political science. As there were no studies of the individual attitudes of American voters in 1912, we will never know whether Riker's conjectures about that election are correct.

By using the feeling thermometers employed in the 1992 NES survey, however, we can at least indirectly determine how Clinton would have done in a two-candidate race against Bush or Perot. Because these thermometer scores are so strongly related to the vote, they can be used to run three mock elections—one pairing Clinton against Bush, another pairing Clinton against Perot, and a third pairing Bush against Perot. We made head-to-head comparisons for all three combinations, using the thermometers in both the preelection and the postelection interviews conducted by the NES. Our results are presented in Table 6-2.

In the preelection poll, nearly half the electorate rated Clinton over Bush, while two out of five rated Bush over Clinton. In the postelection survey, Clinton was favored by just over half the electorate. These results are consistent with the Voter Research and Survey exit poll, which found that Perot voters would have split about evenly between Clinton and Bush if Perot had not been on the ballot. When we paired Clinton against Perot, a majority of the electorate ranked Clinton higher than Perot in the pre- and postelection interviews. Table 6-2 also suggests that Bush would have defeated Perot. Our main conclusion, therefore, is that Clinton would very likely have been the winner in any head-to-head contest. The electoral college did not yield a pernicious result. Most social choice theorists would agree with Condorcet that if there is an outcome that would be preferred by a majority over any other alternative, that outcome should be selected. In this sense, Clinton was a Condorcet winner.[9] Of course, there may be no candidate who would be the first choice in all head-to-head comparisons. For example, Clinton might have been preferred by a majority over Bush, Perot might have been preferred by a majority over Clinton, and Bush might have been preferred by a majority over Perot. And, even if there is a Condorcet winner, that candidate might not be elected. A third-party candidate, for example, might be preferred over either of the major party candidates and yet lose in a three-way race. These data provide no evidence that Perot was such a candidate. Although Clinton won just over two out of five votes, it appears that he was the Condorcet winner and that it would, therefore, be difficult to argue that his election was unfair.

Table 6-2   Comparative Thermometer Ratings of the Candidates, 1992 (Head-to-Head Comparisons, in percentages)

Clinton Versus Bush		Clinton Versus Perot		Bush Versus Perot	
A. Preelection Survey, Candidate Rated First					
Clinton	49	Clinton	56	Bush	51
Tie	12	Tie	14	Tie	12
Bush	40	Perot	30	Perot	36
Total %	101	Total %	100	Total %	99
(N)[a]	(2,425)	(N)[a]	(2,316)	(N)[a]	(2,319)
B. Postelection Survey, Candidate Rated First					
Clinton	53	Clinton	55	Bush	46
Tie	11	Tie	15	Tie	14
Bush	36	Perot	30	Perot	40
Total %	100	Total %	100	Total %	100
(N)[a]	(2,221)	(N)[a]	(2,180)	(N)[a]	(2,181)

[a] Numbers are weighted.

Retrospective and Prospective Evaluations

Behind these overall evaluations of the candidates are the public's attitudes toward the issues and toward parties, as well as more specific evaluations of the candidates. We begin by considering the role of issues in elections. Public policy concerns enter into the voting decision in two very different ways. In an election in which an incumbent is running, two questions become important: How has the incumbent president done on policy? And how likely is it that his opponent (or opponents) would do any better? Voting based on this form of policy appraisal is called retrospective voting and will be analyzed in Chapter 7. The second form of policy-based voting involves an examination of the policy platforms advanced by the candidates and an assessment of which candidate's policy promises are most similar to what the voter believes the government should be doing. Policy voting, therefore, involves comparing sets of promises and voting for the set that is most like the voter's own preferences. Voting based on these kinds of decisions may be referred to as prospective voting, for it involves examining the promises of the candidates about future actions. In this chapter, we examine prospective evaluations of the two major party candidates and how these evaluations relate to voter choice.

The three elections of the 1980s and the 1992 election show some remarkable similarities in prospective evaluations and voting. Perhaps the most important similarity is the perception of where the Democratic and Republican candidates stood on issues. In these four elections, the public saw clear differences between the major party nominees. In all cases, the public saw the Republican candidates as conservative on most issues, and most citizens scored them as more conservative than the voters rated themselves as being. And in all four elections the public saw the Democratic candidates as being liberal on most issues, and most citizens viewed them as more liberal than the voters rated themselves as being. As a result, many voters perceived a clear choice based on their understanding of the candidates' policy positions. The candidates presented, in the 1964 campaign slogan of Republican nominee Barry M. Goldwater, "a choice, not an echo." The *average* citizen, however, faced a difficult choice. For many, the Democratic nominees were considered to be as far to the left as the Republicans were to the right. On balance, the net effect of prospective issues was to give neither party a clear advantage.

There were also important differences among these elections. One of the most important of these was the mixture of issues that concerned the public. Each election presented its own mixture of policy concerns. Moreover, the general strategies of the candidates on issues differed in each election.[10] In 1980, Jimmy Carter's incumbency was marked by a general perception that he was unable to solve pressing concerns. Reagan attacked that weakness both directly (for example, by the question he posed to the public during his debate with Carter, "Are you better off today than you were four years ago?") and indirectly. The indirect attack was more future oriented. Reagan set forth a clear set of proposals designed to convince the public that he would be more likely to solve the nation's problems because he had his own proposals to end soaring inflation, to strengthen the United States militarily, and to regain respect and influence for the United States abroad.

In 1984, Reagan was perceived to be a far more successful president than Carter had been. He chose to run a campaign focused primarily on the theme of how much better things were by 1984 (as illustrated by his advertising slogan, "It's morning in America"). Mondale attacked that claim by arguing that Reagan's policies were unfair, and by pointing to the rapidly growing budget deficit. Reagan's counter to Mondale's pledge to increase taxes to reduce the deficit was that he, Reagan, would not raise taxes, and that Mondale would do so only to spend them on increased government programs (or, in his words, that Mondale was another "tax and spend, tax and spend" Democrat).

The 1988 campaign was more similar to the 1984 than to the 1980 campaign. Bush continued to run on the successes of the Reagan-Bush administration and promised no new taxes ("Read my lips," he said. "No new taxes!"). Dukakis initially attempted to portray the election as one about "competence" rather than "ideology," arguing that he had demonstrated his competence as governor of Massachusetts. By competent management, he would be able to solve the budget and trade deficit problems, for example. Bush, by implication, was less competent. Bush countered that it really was an election about ideology, that Dukakis was just another *liberal* Democrat from Massachusetts.

The 1992 election presented yet another type of campaign. Bush initially hoped to be able to run as the president who presided over the "new world order," the post-Soviet world, and he used the success of the Gulf war to augment his claim that he was a successful world leader. Clinton attacked the Bush administration on domestic issues, however, barely discussing foreign affairs at all. He sought to keep the electorate focused on the current economic woes, seeking to get the nation moving again. He also argued for substantial reforms of the health care system, and he raised a number of other issues that he expected to appeal to Democrats and to serve as the basis for action, should he become the first Democrat in the White House in twelve years. At the same time, he sought to portray himself as a moderate, not another "tax and spend" liberal Democrat. Thus, he emphasized that taxes would be raised on the wealthy but would be reduced for the middle class. Although he campaigned among African-Americans, he was conspicuously cool to the Reverend Jesse Jackson. His criticism of the rap singer Sister Souljah during a speech before a conference of the Rainbow Coalition (an organization Jackson had founded) was seen by many as a move to distance himself from Jackson.

The presence of Perot complicated the efforts of both major party candidates. Perot attacked the Bush administration and he focused his policy appeals on the budget deficit. He argued that, as an independent candidate and a proven manager, he could fix the deficit problem and build for the future.

Each of these general overviews of campaign strategies illustrates prospective and retrospective strategies. All incumbent party nominees were held accountable for the failings of the current administration by their challengers, and in 1984 and 1988 Reagan and Bush, respectively, emphasized Republican successes. Bush had hoped to be able to do so again in 1992. These were clearly retrospective strategies. But prospective promises also figured prominently in each contest. The challengers in all cases relied heavily on promises of what they would do in office, and all incumbent party candidates attacked those promises. If voters respond to the campaigns of the candidates, we might expect, therefore, to find that both retrospective and prospective policy concerns figure prominently in their decisions.[11]

The Concerns of the Electorate

The first question to ask about prospective voting is what kinds of concerns moved the public. The NES surveys ask, "What do you personally feel are the most important problems the government in Washington should try to take care of?" In Table 6-3, we have listed the percentage of responses to what respondents claimed was the single most important problem in broad categories of concerns over the six most recent elections.[12]

In 1992, the public was far more concerned about domestic issues than about foreign or defense policies. The very low levels of expressed concern about international problems undoubtedly reflects the ending of the cold war, as well as the receding memories of the rapid victory over Iraq in the Gulf war. The pattern also reflects the nature of the campaign, as the candidates (especially Clinton) focused very heavily on domestic concerns. In any event, only 3 percent cited some foreign or defense concern as the most important problem.[13]

The great majority of responses, therefore, concerned domestic issues. Of the two major categories of domestic issues, by far the more commonly cited was a concern about the economy. Indeed, nearly two in three who cited any problem as most important chose an economic problem as the single most important problem. In this sense, the public's concerns in 1992 were like those of 1976 and 1980. Over one in four, however, cited a social problem as most important, a percentage twice as large as that of 1976 and four times as large as that of 1980. Together, these two categories accounted for over nine in ten responses to this question. Very few cited problems in the "functioning of government" category, such as "gridlock," term limits or other reforms, or government corruption. Finally, in 1992, only 2 percent cited no problem at all.

The 17 percent who cited a social welfare problem in the social issues category is the largest percentage achieved in the surveys of the last six elections. Over a third of those responses (or 6 percent of all responses) cited health care as the specific problem they had in mind. The one in ten who named a problem of public order as most important were concerned (in roughly equal proportions) with drugs, crime and violence, and religious decay.[14]

While the economy was by far the dominant concern of the public, as it has been in every election since the end of American involvement in the Vietnam War, the particular concerns of the public in 1992 were quite different from those of earlier elections. Indeed, which aspect of the economy most concerns the public varies a great deal from election to election, as a reflection of differing economic conditions. For example, 1976 stood out as an economic period of "stagflation," with an unusual combination of high unemployment and high inflation, and these twin

Table 6-3 Most Important Problem as Seen by the Electorate, 1972-1992 (in percentages)

Problem	1972	1976	1980	1984	1988	1992
Economics	*27*	*76*	*56*	*49*	*45*	*64*
Unemployment/ recession	9	33	10	16	5	23
Inflation/prices	14	27	33	5	2	—ª
Deficit/govt. spending	1	9	3	19	32	16
Social issues	*34*	*14*	*7*	*13*	*38*	*28*
Social welfare	7	4	3	9	11	17
Public order	20	8	1	4	19	10
Foreign and defense	*31*	*4*	*32*	*34*	*10*	*3*
Foreign	4	3	9	17	6	2
Defense	1	1	8	17	3	1
Functioning of government (competence, corruption, trust, power)	*4*	*4*	*2*	*2*	*1*	*2*
All others	*4*	*3*	*3*	*3*	*6*	*2*
Total percent	100	101	100	101	100	100
(*N*)	(842)	(2,337)	(1,352)	(1,780)	(1,657)	(2,003)
"Missing"	(63)	(203)	(56)	(163)	(118)	(54)
Percent missing	7	7	4	7	7	2

Notes: Italicized entries are category totals. Foreign in 1972 includes 25 percent who cited Vietnam. Foreign in 1980 includes 15 percent who cited Iran. Questions asked of randomly selected half sample in 1972. Weighted numbers in 1976 and 1992. All of the subcategories are not included. The total percentages for the subcategories, therefore, will not equal the percentages for the main categories. In 1984, the total *N* is 1,943 because 46 respondents were not asked this question, being given a shortened postelection questionnaire. In 1992, the total *N* is 2,487, because 431 respondents either had no postelection interview or were given a shortened form via telephone.

ª Less than one percent.

problems were reflected in the concerns of the electorate. By 1980, unemployment was down, but inflation (and interest rates) were unusually high, and public concern about inflation was high. The lingering effects of a short but deep recession and dramatic increases in federal budget deficits are apparent in public reactions during 1984. The economic boom of the 1980s led few to be concerned about inflation or unemployment in 1988, but the ever-increasing budget deficits became the single most important concern to the public that year. The very low rate of inflation in 1992 was reflected in the very small percentage (actually 0.3 percent) who cited inflation or prices as their central concern, but the lingering recession, not as deep as in 1982 but longer lasting, was the major concern of nearly one in four. Budget deficits continued to grow into 1992, and they were the central focus of Perot's campaign. But only one in six cited the deficit as the most important problem, which is only half as many as in 1988.[15] The major reason for this change may be that a very large number of respondents in 1992 simply answered that the economy was their central concern ($N = 367$, or nearly 20 percent of those responding), without specifying any particular aspect of the economy or economic policy. This general unease was appropriate: the economy was no longer in a recession and inflation was very low, yet economists, politicians, and the media were as uneasy about the economy as the public.

The concerns of the electorate are the backdrop of the campaign. Concern about the economy, while hardly propitious for the incumbent president, did not translate into support for Clinton's economic programs, into a belief that Perot could fix the economy, or even into opposition to Bush, who had promised a new economic agenda. Nor does a person's concern translate into a vote for a favored candidate. A vote, after all, is a choice among alternatives. To investigate these questions, we must look at the voters' issue preferences and their perceptions of where candidates stood on the issues.

Issue Positions and Perceptions

Since 1972, the NES surveys have included a number of issue scales designed to measure the preferences of the electorate and voters' perceptions of the positions the candidates took on the issues.[16] The questions are therefore especially appropriate for examining prospective issue evaluations. We hasten to add, however, that voters' perceptions of where the incumbent party's nominee stands may well be based in part on what the president has done in office, as well as on the campaign promises he made as the party's nominee. The policy promises of the opposition party candidate may also be judged partly by what his party did when it last held the White House. Bush attempted to paint Clinton as another "tax and spend" Democrat, in the mold of Carter, Mondale, and Dukakis. Some respondents may have agreed and seen Clinton as taking positions similar to those of past Democratic administrations and nominees, even when Clinton did not endorse those policies. Nevertheless, the issue scales generally focus on prospective evaluations and are very different from those used to make the retrospective judgments examined in Chapter 7.

The issue scales will be used to examine several questions: What alternatives did the voters believe the candidates were offering? To

Figure 6-2 Example of a 7-Point Issue Scale: Jobs and Standard of
Living Guarantees

Question asked by interviewers:
"Some people feel the government in Washington should see to it that every
person has a job and a good standard of living." [For the first issue scale only, the
following is added: "Suppose these people are at one end of the scale at point 1."]
"Others think the government should just let each person get ahead on their
own." [For the first issue scale only, the interviewer says, "Suppose these people
are at the other end, at point 7. And of course, some other people have opinions
somewhere in between at points 2, 3, 4, 5, or 6."]
The interviewer refers the respondent to the appropriate page in the
respondent booklet (see scale below) and asks, "Where would you place yourself
on this scale, or haven't you thought much about this?"
If the respondent places himself or herself on the scale, the interviewer asks,
"Where would you place [George Bush, Bill Clinton] on this scale?"

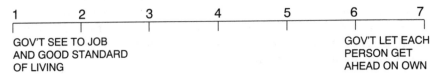

Job And Good Standard of Living

| 1 | 2 | 3 | 4 | 5 | 6 | 7 |

GOV'T SEE TO JOB
AND GOOD STANDARD
OF LIVING

GOV'T LET EACH
PERSON GET
AHEAD ON OWN

Source: 1992 National Election Studies Pre-Election Study, Questionnaire Survey Instrument and Respondent Booklet.

what extent did the voters have issue preferences of their own and
relatively clear perceptions of candidates' positions? Finally, how
strongly were voters' preferences and perceptions related to their choice
of candidates?

Figure 6-2 presents the text of one of the 7-point issue scale
questions, along with an example of an illustration presented to respondents as they considered their responses. Figure 6-3 shows the three issue
scales used in the 1992 NES survey. The figure presents the average
(median) position of the respondents (labeled "self") and the average
(median) perception of the positions of Bush and Clinton.[17] Note that,
unlike in past NES surveys, only three issue scales were included.
Fortunately, these three scales were asked in other surveys, so that we
can make some limited comparisons to other elections. Because Perot
reentered the presidential contest only after the 1992 NES survey was
under way, the NES did not ask respondents where they believed Perot
stood on the issues.[18] The three issue scales used in 1992 probe the
respondents' own preferences and perceptions of the major party nominees on whether government spending should be reduced or increased in

providing for greater social services; whether defense spending should be increased or decreased; and the jobs scale as shown in Figure 6-2.[19]

These issues were selected because they were controversial and generally measured longstanding partisan divisions. As a result, the average citizen comes out looking reasonably moderate on these issues—in each case, between the positions corresponding to the average placements of the two candidates. The average respondent was just to the liberal side of the midpoint of 4 on the government services and spending scale. This position for the average respondent is the same as in 1988, and nearly the same as in the two preceding elections. On the other domestic issue, the jobs and standard of living guarantees scale, the average respondent in 1992 was about halfway between 4 and 5. This is, once again, similar to the positions of the average respondent in the three elections of the 1980s.[20] Whether the electorate believes that defense spending should increase or decrease seems to depend on the context of the times, unlike the two previous issues. In 1980, the average respondent stood beyond point 5, reflecting the fact that all candidates thought that greater defense spending was needed; the election campaign took place during the Iranian hostage crisis and in the first year of the Soviet invasion of Afghanistan. In 1984 and 1988, the average respondent apparently thought defense spending was just right, adopting almost exactly the midpoint. In 1992, with the end of the cold war, the collapse of the former Soviet Union, and victory in the Gulf war, the average respondent thought defense spending should decrease (taking a position halfway between 3 and 4).

The average citizen saw clear differences between the positions of the major party candidates on each scale. On each, Bush was seen to be, on average, clearly to the right of the midpoint, and Clinton was placed to the left. The average perceptions of the two candidates were almost two full points apart on the two domestic issues and over a point and a half apart on the defense spending scale. This pattern of consistent and substantial differences in perceptions of the two parties' nominees is typical of all the surveys, especially of the Reagan-Bush elections; indeed, on virtually all 7-point issue scales presented, the Republican candidate has been to the right of the midpoint, the Democrat to the left. While there are slight differences between 1988 and 1992 on the placements of the candidates, the more remarkable point is how very consistently the electorate has perceived the Democratic candidates and the Republican candidates in recent elections. Thus, the distance between Bush and his 1988 and 1992 opponents is quite similar. This clear perception of differences between the nominees of the two parties applies to five of the six elections in this period. The only exception is 1976: although Ford was consistently seen as more conservative than Carter (and they were generally seen to stand on either side of the

Figure 6-3 Median Self-Placement of the Electorate and the Electorate's Placement of Bush and Clinton on Issue Scales, 1992

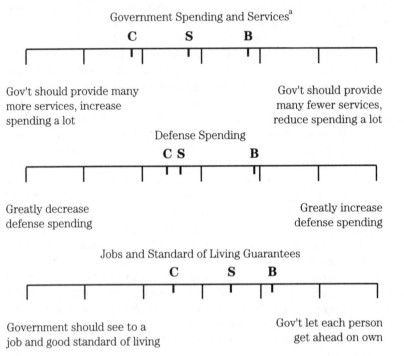

Government Spending and Services[a]

C S B

Gov't should provide many more services, increase spending a lot

Gov't should provide many fewer services, reduce spending a lot

Defense Spending

C S   B

Greatly decrease defense spending

Greatly increase defense spending

Jobs and Standard of Living Guarantees

C S B

Government should see to a job and good standard of living

Gov't let each person get ahead on own

Note: S=median self-placement of electorate; C=median placement of Clinton; B=median placement of Bush.

[a]Reversed from actual scoring to make a "liberal" response closer to 1 and a conservative response closer to 7.

midpoint), the overall perception in that election was that both candidates were moderate.

The average citizen stood between Bush and Clinton on all three issues. On the scales for government services and spending and the government provision of jobs and a good standard of living, in fact, the average citizen was almost halfway between the positions of the two candidates. On defense spending, however, the average citizen was within one-third of a point from the average perception of Clinton's position, and a point and a third from Bush's. Thus, the average respondent was a full point closer to the average placement of Clinton than to the average placement of Bush. It is very difficult to make general statements from so few issues. But if all issues were like the two domestic ones, the typical citizen would see a clear difference between the two candidates but would have little basis on which to choose, since Clinton was as far to the average citizen's left as Bush was to the average citizen's right. If, however, most issues were like the defense spending scale, the typical citizen would see a clear difference between the two candidates' offerings and would clearly favor Clinton's position.

If these were the only three issues in the election, we would conclude that Clinton had a clear advantage, by virtue of his platform as perceived by the electorate, and would win, if voting were based exclusively on prospective issue voting. Alternatively, these data might suggest that neither candidate had a clear advantage on domestic issues, but that Clinton had the clear edge—for the first time for the Democratic nominee in recent elections—on foreign and defense issues. How great an advantage that was would depend on the relative priority voters placed on foreign issues. Our analysis strongly suggests that prospective issue voters were much more likely to consider domestic than foreign or defense issues. Therefore, the advantage Clinton held on the defense spending issue would not be especially valuable, while more salient domestic issues appear to give neither candidate any significant advantage in seeking the support of prospective issue voters. Of course, we must look beyond the preferences and perceptions of the respondents before we can assess the role of these issues in electoral choice.

Issue Voting Criteria

The Problem

Since voting is an individual action, we must look at the preferences of individuals to see whether prospective issues influenced their vote. In fact, the question of prospective voting is controversial. The authors of the classic study of the American electorate, *The American Voter*, point out that the public is often ill informed about public policy and may not be able to vote on the basis of issues.[21] They asked what information voters would need before an issue could influence the decision of how to vote, and they specified three conditions. First, the voters must hold an opinion on the issue; second, they must see what the government is doing on the issue; and third, they must see a difference between the policies of the two major parties. According to their analysis, only about one-quarter to one-third of the electorate in 1956 could meet these three conditions.

Although it is impossible to replicate their analysis, we can adapt their procedures to the 1992 electorate. In some ways, more recent NES data focus more directly on the actual choice citizens must make, a choice among the candidates. The first criterion is whether the respondent claims to have an opinion on the issue. This is measured by whether respondents placed themselves on the issue scale. (If they did not, they were asked no more questions about the issue.) Second, the respondents should have some perception of the positions taken by the candidates on an issue. This was measured by whether they could place both major party candidates on that issue.[22] Although some voters might perceive the position of one candidate and vote on that basis, prospective voting involves a comparison among alternatives, so the expressed ability to perceive the stands of the contenders seems a minimal requirement of prospective issue voting. Third, the voter must see a difference between the positions of the candidates. Failing to see a difference means that the voter perceived no choice on the issue.

A voter might be able to satisfy these criteria but misperceive the offerings of the candidates. This leads to a fourth condition that we are able to measure more systematically than was possible in 1956. Does the respondent accurately perceive the *relative* positions of the two major party candidates—that is, see Bush as more "conservative" than Clinton? This criterion does not demand that the voter have an accurate perception of what the candidate proposes, but it does expect the voter to see that Clinton, for instance, favored more spending on social services like education and health care than Bush did.[23]

The Data

In Table 6-4 we report the percentages of the sample that met the four criteria on the three issue scales used in 1992. We also show the average proportion that met these criteria for all three scales and compare those averages to comparable averages for all issue scales used in the five preceding elections.[24] Because the three issue scales used in 1992 were also used in the three elections of the 1980s, we have also included the averages for those elections over the same three issue scales. As can be seen in column I of Table 6-4, most people felt capable of placing themselves on the issue scales, and this capability was common to all six election years.[25]

Fewer people could place both the candidates and themselves on an issue scale than could place just themselves, as can be seen in column II of Table 6-4. Nonetheless, seven in ten respondents met these two criteria in 1992. Notice that there was relatively little variation across issues: 68 to 76 percent met these criteria on each issue scale. The relatively consistent ability to satisfy the criteria is similar to what obtained in 1984 but different from findings in earlier elections. In 1980, for instance, there were three issue scales on which fewer than half placed themselves and both candidates.

As can be seen in column III of Table 6-4, two-thirds of the sample met the first two criteria and also saw a difference between the positions of Bush and Clinton, and there was again little variation among these three issues. The 1992 result is similar to the comparison for the same issues in 1984 and slightly higher than that for 1980 and 1988; it is

Table 6-4 Four Criteria for Issue Voting, 1992, and Comparisons with 1972-1988 Presidential Elections (in percentages)

Issue Scale	Percentage of Sample Who:			
	I. Placed Self on Scale	II. Placed both Candidates on Scale[a]	III. Saw Differences Between Clinton and Bush	IV. Saw Clinton More Liberal Than Bush
Government spending/services	82	68	63	50
Defense spending	87	69	68	52
Jobs and standard of living	87	76	68	53
Average [b]				
1992 (3)	85	71	66	52
1988 (3) [c]	84	70	60	49
1984 (3) [c]	86	76	67	59
1980 (3) [c]	84	68	60	51
1988 (7)	86	66	52	43
1984 (7)	84	73	62	53
1980 (9)	82	61	51	43
1976 (9)	84	58	39	26
1972 (8)	90	65	49	41

Note: Columns II, III, and IV compare the Democratic and Republican nominees (Anderson excluded in 1980).

[a] If respondent could not place self on scale, respondent was not questioned further on that issue.

[b] Number in parentheses is the number of issue scales included in average for each election year survey.

[c] Indicates averages for the three issues scales used in 1992.

noticeably higher than the averages for all issues asked in all prior election years.[26]

More striking, perhaps, is the variation in these percentages from election to election. The figures in column III of Table 6-4 indicate that 1992 was most similar to 1984. The 1980 and 1988 elections yielded only somewhat smaller percentages, but the figures for 1976 are especially low. What are we to conclude about these differences in the ability of the electorate to satisfy the criteria and thus to be able to vote on the basis of issues? It seems highly unlikely that the ability of the public to comprehend the electoral process varies so greatly from election to election. Note that there is very little difference among elections in self-placement on issue scales. Rather, the differences are due to perceptions of the candidates' positions. The differences between the election of 1976 and the elections of 1984 and 1992 first appears in the ability to place both candidates on the scales. Perhaps 1976 had relatively low scores because Ford had not run for president before and had been the incumbent for only two years, while Carter was a relatively unknown challenger. And, perhaps other elections had higher scores because the incumbent party's candidate had served four or more years in the presidency or the vice presidency. The differences become especially pronounced, however, in the electorate's ability to characterize the candidates' positions. In 1984, the candidates adopted particularly distinctive positions on issues, and this relative clarity was picked up by the electorate. Our comparisons are based on fewer issues, but the same seems to be true in 1992. In 1972, 1980, and 1988, the candidates were only slightly less distinct, and the electorate saw the differences only slightly less clearly. In 1976, by contrast, Ford and Carter were generally described as moderates, albeit moderately conservative and moderately liberal, respectively. The electorate reacted to the relative lack of differences.

In sum, we support Morris P. Fiorina's argument that failure to satisfy the criteria for issue voting does not mean that the electorate has ill-formed preferences and perceptions.[27] Rather, the electorate's ability to perceive differences between the candidates varies because political conditions differ from election to election, and these differences result mainly from differences in the strategies candidates follow. Thus, the "quality" of the responses to these issue questions is based in part on how clearly the candidates articulate their issue positions and on how distinctly the alternative policy platforms are as presented to the public.

The data in column IV reflect the ability of the electorate to discern distinctions between the candidates' policy offerings. Averaging these issues together, we see that in 1992 more than half of the respondents saw Clinton as more liberal than Bush. The 1992 data look much like those of 1980 and 1988 in these terms and on these issues, while 1984 is the high water mark in meeting the criteria on these issues. In light of the comparisons and the data from additional issues in the earlier elections, it seems likely that, had more issue scales been included in the 1992 survey, the results would have shown 1992 to be similar to most preceding elections. In this case, the 1976 election stands out in very sharp contrast, as barely more than one in four voters could assess the relative positions of the two candidates.

The data in Table 6-4 suggest that the potential for prospective issue voting was relatively high in 1992. Therefore, we might expect these issues to be closely related to voter choice. We will examine voter choice on these issues in two ways. First, how often did people vote for the closer candidate on each issue? Second, how strongly related to the vote is the set of all issues taken together?

Apparent Issue Voting in 1992

Issue Criteria and Voting on Each Issue

The first question is to what extent did people who were closer to a candidate on a given issue actually vote for that candidate? That is, how strong is apparent issue voting?[28] In Table 6-5 we report the proportion of major party voters who voted for Bush by where they placed themselves on the issue scales. We divided the seven points into the set of positions that were closer to where the average citizen placed Bush and Clinton (see Figure 6-2). Many individuals, of course, placed the candidates at different positions than the public did on average. Using average perceptions, however, reduces the effect of individuals' rationalizing their perceptions of candidates to be consistent with their own vote, rather than voting for the candidate whose views are actually closer to their own.[29]

As can be seen in Table 6-5, there is a strong relationship between the voters' issue positions and the candidate they supported on the three issues. Those who adopted positions at the "liberal" end of each scale were very unlikely to vote for Bush. If we define liberal as adopting position 1 or 2, then the highest proportion of support Bush received was the one in five who scored 2 on the defense spending scale, while only the very small number who adopted point 7 on that scale were "conservative" (that is, at point 6 or 7) on any scale and failed to give Bush a majority of their votes. Those with moderate views on each issue fell in between these two extremes of support. Indeed, there is a strong relationship between being close to Bush or Clinton on the two domestic scales and voting for the nearer candidate. While the relationship is weaker on the defense spending scale, those who thought spending should be reduced were quite unlikely to support the incumbent; they voted for him in significantly

Table 6-5   Major Party Voters Who Voted for Bush, by 7-Point Issue Scales, 1992 (in percentages)

Issue scale	Closer to Median Perception of Clinton				Closer to Median Perception of Bush			(N)
	1	2	3	4	5	6	7	
Government spending/services (N)	4 (97)	4 (105)	25 (230)	35 (367)	65 (185)	78 (121)	73 (74)	(1,179)
Defense spending (N)	11 (101)	20 (183)	40 (303)	56 (409)	51 (154)	55 (44)	45 (37)	(1,231)
Jobs and standard of living (N)	13 (106)	16 (100)	24 (170)	39 (257)	49 (259)	60 (180)	69 (164)	(1,236)

Note: The Government spending/services scale is reversed from actual scoring to make a "liberal" response closer to 1 and a conservative response closer to 7. Numbers in parentheses are the totals upon which percentages are based. Numbers are weighted.

lower proportions than those who thought spending was about right or should be increased.[30] Given the lower concern over foreign than domestic issues in 1992, the somewhat weaker relationship on defense spending is not unexpected. Over these three issues, then, there is a substantial relationship between the public's opinions and their perceptions of candidates on prospective issues.

The information in Table 6-6 can be summarized to illustrate what happened when voters met the various conditions for issue voting. In the first column of Table 6-6, we report the percentage of major party voters who placed themselves closer to the average perception of Clinton or Bush and who voted for the closer candidate. To be more specific, the denominator is the total number of major party voters who placed themselves closer to the electorate's perception of Bush or Clinton. The numerator is the total number of major party voters who were both closer to Bush and voted for him plus the total number of major party voters who were both closer to Clinton and voted for him.

If voting were unrelated to issue positions, we would expect 50 percent to vote for the closer candidate on average. In 1992, 62 percent voted for the closer candidate. This is a higher percentage on average than in 1976, but it is about the same as, or slightly lower than, in other elections. This percentage for 1992 is lowest on defense spending, again possibly reflecting that year's lower concern over defense and foreign policy than over domestic issues.

These figures do not tell the whole story, however, for those who placed themselves on an issue but failed to meet some other criterion were unlikely to have cast a vote based on that issue. In the second column of Table 6-6, we report the percentage of those who voted for the closer candidate on each issue, of the voters who met all four conditions on that issue. The third column reports the percentage that voted for the closer candidate, of the voters who failed to meet at least one of the three remaining conditions.

Those who met all four conditions were much more likely to vote for the closer candidate on any issue. Indeed, there is relatively little difference, on average, across all six elections (although the three issue comparisons indicate that the percentages for 1992 were lower than those for the elections of the 1980s). In each case, at least seven of ten such voters supported the closer candidate. For those who failed to meet the last three of the conditions on issue voting, in contrast, voting was essentially random with respect to the issues.

The strong similarity of all six election averages in the second and third columns suggests that issue voting seems more prevalent in some elections than others because elections differ with respect to the number of people who clearly perceive differences between the candidates. In all elections, at least seven in ten who satisfied all four conditions voted

Table 6-6   Apparent Issue Voting, 1992, and Comparisons with 1972-
1988 (in percentages)

Issue Scale	Percent of Voters Who Voted for Closer Candidate and:		
	Placed Self on Issue Scale	Met All Four Issue Voting Criteria	Placed Self but Failed to Meet All Three Other Criteria
Government spending/ services	62	71	45
Defense spending	59	65	47
Jobs and standard of living	66	74	51
Averages[a]			
1992 (3)	62	70	48
1988 (3)[b]	64	80	41
1984 (3)[b]	69	76	46
1980 (3)[b]	67	77	51
1988 (7)	62	71	45
1984 (7)	65	73	46
1980 (9)	63	71	48
1976 (9)	57	70	50
1972 (8)	66	76	55

Note: An "apparent issue vote" is a vote for the candidate closer to one's position on an issue scale. The closer candidate is determined by comparing self-placement to the median placements of the two candidates on the scale as a whole. Respondents who did not place themselves or who were equidistant from the two candidates are excluded from the calculations.

[a] Number in parentheses is the number of issue scales included in the average for each election year survey.
[b] Averages for the same three issues scales as used in 1992.

consistently with their issue preferences; in all elections, those who did not satisfy all the conditions on perceptions of candidates voted essentially randomly with respect to individual issues. As we saw earlier, the degree to which such perceptions vary from election to election depends more on the strategies of the candidates than on the qualities of the voters. Therefore, the relatively low percentage of apparent issue voting in 1976, for instance, results from the perception of small differences between the two rather moderate candidates. The large magnitude of apparent issue voting in 1984 results from the remarkable clarity with which most people saw the positions of Reagan and Mondale. The figures for the 1992 election fall in between.

The Balance of Issues Measure

Prospective issue voting means that voters compare the full set of policy proposals made by the candidates. As we have noted, each issue is fairly strongly related to the vote so we might expect the set of all three issues to be strongly related to the vote as well. To examine this relationship, we constructed an overall assessment of the issue scales, what we call the balance of issues measure. We did so by giving individuals a score of +1 if their positions on an issue scale were closer to the average perception of Bush, a −1 if their positions were closer to the average perception of Clinton, and a score of 0 if they had no preference on an issue. These scores for all three issue scales were added up together, creating a measure that ranged from −3 to +3. For instance, respondents who were closer to the average perception of Clinton's positions on the three scales received a score of −3. A negative score indicated that the respondent was, on balance, closer to the public's perception of Clinton, while a positive score indicated the respondent was, overall, closer to the public's perception of Bush.[31]

As can be seen in Table 6-7A, about one in six received a score of −3, or were closer to Clinton on all three issues, whereas only one in eighteen were closer to Bush on all three.[32] Similarly, one in twelve received a score of −2, but one in thirty received a score of +2.[33] Most received a score of −1 (27 percent) or +1 (31 percent), leaving one in twelve at the neutral position. Overall, a majority (52 percent) were, on balance, closer to Clinton, and 40 percent were closer to Bush. Clinton's advantage came primarily from the defense spending scale; the average citizen was placed nearly halfway between Clinton and Bush on the two domestic scales. Although Clinton had a clear advantage, that advantage came primarily from an issue scale that evoked relatively little concern.

This balance of issues measure was, indeed, strongly related to the vote, as the findings for the individual issues would suggest (see Table 6-7B). Clinton won 84 percent of the major party vote from those with a score of −3, 80 percent from those with a score of −2, and 67 percent from those with a score of −1. He also won a strong majority (62 percent) from those with a score of 0. Conversely, Bush did much better among those who were on balance closer to him, receiving 63, 35, and 74 percent of the vote from those with scores of +1, +2 (of which there were very few), and +3, respectively. Clinton received 75 percent of the vote from those closer to where the public saw him standing on all three issues, and Bush received 62 percent from those closer to where he was seen to stand. Overall, 69 percent of major party voters voted for the closer candidate on this summary measure. This percentage is higher

Table 6-7 Distribution of the Electorate on the Net Balance of Issues Measure and Major Party Vote, 1992

	Net Balance of Issues								
	Strongly Democratic	Moderately Democratic	Slightly Democratic	Neutral	Slightly Republican	Moderately Republican	Strongly Republican	Total Percent	(N)
A. Distribution of Responses									
	17%	8	27	8	31	3	6	100%	(2,206)
B. Percentage of Major Party Voters Who Voted for Clinton									
	84	80	67	62	37	65	26		
(N)	(221)	(90)	(344)	(88)	(404)	(42)	(76)		

Note: Numbers are weighted.

than that for any individual issue (see Table 6-5), which suggests that voters weighed the full platforms of the candidates, at least as measured by these three issues, and therefore supported a candidate who was the closer overall. The relationship between the balance of issues measure and the major party vote is quite strong and seemingly comparable to that found in prior elections, although, having only three scales, we cannot make precise comparisons.

The Abortion Issue

We give special attention to the public policy controversy about abortion, for two reasons. First, abortion is an especially divisive issue, and the Republican national platform took a strong "pro-life" stand. Bush had supported "right-to-life" groups in several ways; for example, he maintained a rule (often called the "gag rule" by its opponents) that prohibited federally funded clinics from providing information about abortion. He continued a ban, originally imposed by the Reagan administration, against federally funded research using fetal tissue derived from abortions.[34] And it seemed very likely that if he were reelected, Bush would attempt to appoint Supreme Court justices who would vote to overturn the *Roe v. Wade* decision. Clinton's views did not satisfy the strongest "pro-choice" advocates. For example, he favored laws requiring minors to notify their parents before having an abortion. But he was clearly committed to ending the gag rule, allowing federal funding for research with fetal tissue derived from abortions, and upholding *Roe v. Wade* by appointing a justice who would sustain that decision.

The second reason for examining this issue is that it is the only policy question beyond those already considered about which respondents were asked not only their own views but also what they thought Bush and Clinton's positions were. Respondents were provided the following four alternatives:

1. By law, abortion should never be permitted.
2. The law should permit abortion only in the case of rape, incest, or when the woman's life is in danger.
3. The law should permit abortion for reasons *other than* rape, incest, or danger to the woman's life, but only after the need for the abortion has been clearly established.
4. By law, a woman should always be able to obtain an abortion as a matter of personal choice.

The electorate's responses were clearly toward the pro-choice end of the measure. Among the 2,413 respondents who chose among these four alternatives, 47 percent said that abortion should be a matter of personal choice. Fourteen percent were willing to allow abortions for reasons other than rape, incest, or danger to the woman's life, while 28 percent said abortion should be allowed only under those conditions. Only 11 percent said that abortion should never be permitted.

Among major party voters, there was a strong relationship between a voter's opinion and the way he or she voted. Table 6-8 presents the percentage of major party voters who voted for Bush according to their view on the abortion issue. Nearly 99 percent of the respondents had an opinion on this issue, and the top row shows whether they voted for Bush.[35] As the table shows, Bush received a narrow majority of the vote among those who thought abortion should never be permitted. Among those who thought the decision to have an abortion should be a matter of personal choice, nearly three out of four voted for Clinton.

Because the survey asked respondents what they thought Bush and Clinton's positions were, we can see if the basic issue-voting criteria apply. If they do, we can expect to find a very strong relationship between the respondents' positions and how they voted if they met three additional conditions, beyond having an opinion on this issue themselves. First, they would have to have an opinion about where the candidates stood on the issue. Second, they would have to see a difference between the positions of Bush and Clinton. Third, to cast a policy-related vote reflecting the actual positions of the candidates, they would have to recognize that Clinton held a more pro-choice position than Bush. Three out of five respondents met all of these conditions.

Among voters who met all of these conditions, there was a very strong relationship between policy preferences and voting.[36] We see this relationship by reading across the second row of Table 6-8. Among major party voters who thought that abortions should never be allowed, over three out of four voted for Bush. Among those who thought that the decision to have an abortion should be a matter of personal choice, over four out of five voted for Clinton.

The final row of Table 6-8 shows the relationship of issue preferences and the vote among voters who did *not* see Clinton as more pro-choice than Bush. Among such voters, there is a much weaker relationship. In fact, voters who were pro-choice were more likely to vote for Bush than those who held a right-to-life position.

These results do not prove that policy preferences shape voting decisions. Some voters may project the position they favor themselves onto the candidate they favor. But it does appear that unless all the basic conditions for issue voting are present, issue voting does not occur. When the conditions are present, there can be a strong relationship between the position voters hold and their choice between the major party candidates.

Table 6-8 Percentage of Major Party Voters Who Voted for Bush, by Opinion About Abortion, and What They Believe Bush and Clinton's Positions Are, 1992

	Respondent's Position on Abortion							
	Abortion Should Never Be Permitted		Abortion Should Be Permitted Only in the Case of Rape, Incest, or for Health of the Woman		Abortion Should Be Permitted for Other Reasons, but Only if a Need is Established		Abortion Should Be a Matter of Personal Choice	
	%	(N)	%	(N)	%	(N)	%	(N)
All major party voters	56	(129)	56	(375)	52	(189)	27	(642)
Major party voters who placed both candidates, who saw a difference between them, and who saw Clinton as more "pro-choice" than Bush	76	(81)	65	(249)	47	(124)	18	(468)
Major party voters who did not meet all three of these conditions	22	(47)	37	(125)	59	(66)	50	(175)

Note: Numbers in parentheses are the totals upon which the percentages are based. The numbers are weighted.

The Issue Preferences of Perot Voters

Our discussion of issue preferences has focused on the major party vote. As we saw, the NES did not measure the electorate's views about where Perot stood on the issues.[37] Thus, we cannot determine whether Perot voters were apparent issue voters. We can, however, compare the issue preferences of Perot voters with those of major party voters.

Perot voters had the same basic concerns as Clinton voters. As we saw, 64 percent of all respondents named the economy as the most important problem facing the country, and among voters this figure rises to 67 percent. Among Clinton voters, 70 percent saw the economy as the most important problem, while 69 percent of Perot voters named the economy. Even among Bush voters, 62 percent saw the economy as the most important problem. Thirty-two percent of the Bush voters named a social problem as the most important one facing the country, while only 23 percent of Clinton voters and 22 percent of Perot voters named a social problem. Despite Perot's criticism of the government process, only 5 percent of those who voted for him specified the functioning of government as the most important problem, only slightly more than the 2 percent found among the major party voters. In short, Perot voters did not appear to have distinctive policy concerns.

Perot voters, like major party voters, saw clear policy differences between the major party candidates, although they did not see them to be as different as Republican and Democratic voters did. On the government services and spending question, Bush voters placed Bush and Clinton 2.29 points apart, and Clinton voters saw a 2.30-point difference. Perot voters saw a 1.84-point difference between the two major party candidates. All voters saw less of a difference between Bush and Clinton on the defense spending scale. The difference for Bush voters was 1.72; it was 1.75 for Clinton voters; and Perot voters saw a 1.66-point difference on this scale. When asked to place Bush and Clinton on the job guarantee scale, Bush voters placed the major party candidates 2.18 points apart, while Clinton voters saw a 2.35-point difference. Perot voters still saw a clear difference between Bush and Clinton, but scored them only 1.53 points apart.

It seems likely that at least some Perot voters supported him because they failed to see as much of a policy difference between Bush and Clinton as major party voters did. And, of course, Perot encouraged them by trying to persuade them that it made very little difference whether Bush or Clinton won. Nonetheless, most Perot voters did see clear policy differences between the major party candidates.

When asked to locate their own position on the issue scales, Perot voters consistently fell in between the Clinton and Bush voters. On the government services and spending question, the average Perot voter was only somewhat closer to Bush voters than he or she was to Clinton voters. On the defense spending scale, the average Perot voter was somewhat closer to the average Clinton voter. And on the question about government job guarantees, the average Perot voter was clearly closer to the average Bush voter than to the average Clinton voter.

Perot tended to fare best among voters who scored toward the middle on the balance of issues measure, although he did slightly better among voters who were pro-Republican than among those who were pro-Democratic. As Perot voters tend to be somewhat more conservative than Clinton voters, they may be a difficult target for the Democrats. But they are not as conservative as Republicans, so the GOP may find it no easier to gather their support. Moreover, Perot voters are much more pro-choice than the average Bush voter. For example, among voters who thought that abortions should never be permitted ($N = 147$), only 13 percent voted for Perot; among those who thought a woman should always have the right to an abortion ($N = 817$), 21 percent voted for him. Perot voters may be targets of opportunity for both the Democrats and Republicans in 1994 and 1996. But on the basis of their issue preferences, they may be a difficult target to identify.

Conclusion

Although it is difficult to locate any distinctive issue positions among Perot voters, these findings suggest that for major party voters prospective issues were quite important in the 1992 election. Even so, studying prospective issues alone cannot account for Clinton's victory. Those for whom prospective issues gave a clear choice voted consistently with those issues. Most people, however, were located between the candidates as the electorate saw them. Indeed, on all issues, most people were relatively moderate, and the candidates were seen as more liberal and more conservative, respectively. In 1980, Carter lost because he fared worse than he had in 1976 among voters who were slightly Democratic, neutral, or in any of the pro-Republican categories. In 1984, Mondale did even worse among all these groups but the slightly pro-Democratic one. This line of reasoning suggests that people voted against an unpopular incumbent in 1980, unless issues pushed strongly in his direction; they voted for a popular incumbent in 1984, unless issues strongly impelled them otherwise. In 1988, Dukakis did about as well among pro-Republican voters as Mondale had, and he did slightly better among the slightly and strongly pro-Democratic voters.

In 1992, while the balance of issues measure was strongly related to the vote, Clinton did better at every negative score than Bush did at the same positive score. Moreover, Clinton won a large majority among those (admittedly rather few) who were closer to neither candidate. This line of reasoning suggests that voters took prospective issues into account in 1992, but that they also took other factors into consideration. In the next chapter, we will see that the second form of policy voting, that based on retrospective evaluations, was among those other factors, as it has been in all five of the previous presidential elections.

Chapter 7

Presidential Performance and Candidate Choice

George Bush, as we saw in Chapter 1, at first expected to tread an easy path to the nomination and reelection. The victories in the cold war and Persian Gulf war had happened on his watch; both were highly regarded foreign policy triumphs for which he could claim credit. In the wake of victory in the Gulf, his approval ratings soared. With so many approving the way he handled his job, and with clear and important events undergirding that approval, he reasoned in 1991 that voters would decide in 1992 that "one good term deserves another." But in the year after the Gulf war, the economy declined into a recession which ended only with painfully slow growth. Bill Clinton and H. Ross Perot attacked this vulnerability in Bush's record, and with good reason. As we shall see, very few approved of the way Bush handled the economy. The other candidates' argument was that Bush's term had not been good enough to deserve another. Instead, they argued, voters should "throw the rascal out" of office, turning to a new administration that each promised would perform better than Bush's. Bush, on the other hand, could argue that even if there were economic problems, the economy had been worse under Jimmy Carter, the last Democratic president.

Such appeals to the performance of the incumbent administration, appeals about the successes or failures of earlier administrations, and assessments of what previous performance indicates about the future are attempts to benefit from retrospective evaluations. Retrospective evaluations are concerns about policy, but they differ significantly from the prospective evaluations we considered in the last chapter. Retrospective evaluations are, as the name suggests, concerned about the past. While the past may be prologue to the future, retrospective evaluations also focus on outcomes, with what actually happened, rather than on the policy means for achieving outcomes—the heart of prospective evaluations.

In this chapter, we focus on the same kinds of concerns as the candidates did, looking at peace, prosperity, and the public's approval of the incumbent. We shall see that these three assessments, in particular, played a powerful role in shaping not only the candidates' strategies but also voters' attitudes toward the candidates and the parties and their choices on election day.

What Is Retrospective Voting?

An individual who voted for the incumbent party's candidate because the incumbent was, in the voter's opinion, a successful president is said to have cast a retrospective vote. A voter who votes for the opposition because, in the voter's opinion, the incumbent has been *un*successful has also cast a retrospective vote. In other words, retrospective voting decisions are based on evaluations of the course of politics over the last term in office and on evaluations of how much the incumbent should be held responsible for what good or ill occurred. V. O. Key, Jr., popularized this argument by suggesting that the voter might be "a rational god of vengeance and of reward." [1]

Obviously, the more closely the candidate of one party can be tied to the actions of the incumbent, the more likely it is that voters will decide retrospectively. The incumbent president cannot escape such evaluations, and the incumbent vice president is often identified with (and often identifies himself with) the administration's performance. In twenty of the twenty-four presidential elections since 1900 (all but 1908, 1920, 1928, and 1952), an incumbent president or vice president stood for election.

In the perspective offered by Key, retrospective voters are oriented toward outcomes. They also evaluate the performance of the incumbent only, all but ignoring the opposition. Further, the retrospective voter evaluates what has been done, paying little attention to what the candidates promise to do in the future.

Anthony Downs presents a different picture of retrospective voting.[2] He argues that voters look to the past to understand what the incumbent party's candidate will do in the future. According to Downs, parties are basically consistent in their goals, methods, and ideologies over time. Therefore, the past performance of both parties' candidates, but especially that of the incumbent, may prove relevant for making predictions about their future conduct. Because it takes time and effort to evaluate campaign promises and because promises are just words, the voters find it faster, easier, and safer to use past performance to project the administration's actions for the next four years. Downs also emphasizes that retrospective evaluations are used to make comparisons between the alternatives standing for election. Key sees a retrospective referendum on the incumbent's party alone. Downs believes that retrospective evaluations are used to make comparisons between the candidates as well as to provide a guide to the future. In 1992, for example, Bush attempted to tie Clinton to past Democratic presidents, especially Carter. Clinton and Perot pointed to the budget deficits and to the state of the economy as evidence that Bush could not govern effectively, and each argued that he would solve those problems. Thus, all of the candidates encouraged voters to make comparative retrospective evaluations.

Another view of retrospective voting is advanced by Morris P. Fiorina. His view is in many respects an elaboration and extension of Downs's thesis. In Fiorina's view, party identification plays a central role. He argues that "citizens monitor party promises and performances over time, encapsulate their observations in a summary judgment termed 'party identification,' and rely on this core of previous experience when they assign responsibility for current societal conditions and evaluate ambiguous platforms designed to deal with uncertain futures." [3] We will return to Fiorina's views on partisanship in the next chapter.

Retrospective voting and voting according to issue positions, as analyzed in Chapter 6, differ significantly. The difference lies in how concerned people are with societal outcomes and how concerned they are with the means to achieve desired outcomes. For example, everyone prefers economic prosperity. The disagreement among political decision makers lies in how best to achieve it. At the voters' level, however, the central question is whether people care only about achieving prosperity or whether they care, or even are able to judge, how to achieve this desired goal. Perhaps they looked at high inflation and interest rates in 1980 and said, "We tried Carter's approach, and it failed. Let's try something else—anything else." Or they noted the long run of relative economic prosperity from 1983 to 1988 and said, "Whatever Reagan did, it worked. Let's keep it going by putting his vice president in office." Or, perhaps, they agreed with Clinton that Bush had failed to have a successful economic program and reasoned they should try Clinton's proposals.

Economic policies and foreign affairs issues are especially likely to be discussed in these terms because they share several characteristics. First, the outcomes are clear, and most voters can judge whether they approve of the results. Inflation and unemployment are high or low; the economy is growing or it is not. The country is at war or peace; the world is stable or unstable. Second, there is often near consensus on what the desired outcomes are; no one disagrees with peace or prosperity, with world stability or low unemployment. Third, the means to achieve these ends are often very complex, and information is hard to understand; experts as well as candidates and parties disagree over the specific ways to achieve the desired ends.

As issues, therefore, peace and prosperity differ sharply from policy areas, such as abortion and gun control, in which there is vigorous disagreement over ends among experts, leaders, and the public. On still other issues, people value means as well as ends. The classic cases often involve the question of whether it is appropriate for government to take action in that area at all. Reagan was fond of saying, "Government isn't the solution to our problems, government *is* the problem." For instance, should the government provide national health insurance? Few disagree with the end, better health care, but they do disagree over the appropriate means to achieve it. The choice of means involves some of the basic philosophical and ideological differences that have divided the Republicans from the Democrats for decades.[4] For example, in 1984 and 1988 the Democratic nominees did not argue that we were not in a period of economic prosperity or that prosperity is a bad thing. In 1984, Walter F. Mondale emphasized that Reagan's policies were unfair to the disadvantaged. Mondale, like Michael S. Dukakis, Clinton, and Perot, also claimed that Reagan's and Bush's policies, by creating such large deficits, were sowing the seeds for future woes. Disagreement was not over the ends, but over the means and the consequences that would follow from using different means to achieve the shared ends.

Two basic conditions must obtain before retrospective evaluations can affect voting choices. First, individuals must connect their concerns (for example, the problem felt to be the most important one facing the nation) with the incumbent and the actions he took in office. One might blame earlier administrations with sowing the seeds that grew into the huge deficits of the 1980s, blame a profligate Congress, or even believe that the problems are beyond anyone's control. Second, individuals, in the Downs-Fiorina view, must compare their evaluations of the incumbent's past performance with what they believe the nominee of the opposition party would do. For example, even if voters held Bush responsible for the performance of the economy, they might conclude that Clinton's programs either would not be any better or might even make things worse.

We examine next some illustrative retrospective evaluations and study their impact on voter choice. In Chapter 6 we looked at issue scales designed to measure the public's evaluations of candidates' promises. Of course, the public can evaluate not only the promises of the incumbent party but also its actions. We will compare promises with performance in this chapter, but one must remember that the distinctions are not as sharp in practice as they are in principle.[5] Of course, the Downs-Fiorina view is that past actions and projections about the future are necessarily intertwined.

Evaluations of Governmental Performance

What do you consider the most important problem facing the country, and how do you feel the government in Washington has been handling the problem? These questions are designed to measure retrospective judgments. Table 7-1 compares the respondents' evaluations of governmental performance on the problem that each respondent identified as the single most important one facing the country. We are able to track such evaluations for the past six elections.[6] The most striking finding in Table 7-1A is that in 1992, a substantial majority of respondents thought the government was doing a poor job of handling the problem they viewed as most important. These evaluations were even more negative than in 1980, the last time an incumbent president had been defeated.[7]

If the voter is a rational god of vengeance and reward, we can expect to find a strong relationship between the evaluation of government performance and the vote. Such is indeed the case for all elections, as seen in Table 7-1B. From seven to nine out of ten major party voters who thought the government was doing a good job on the most important problem voted for the incumbent party's nominee in each election. In 1992, only seven in ten of those who thought the government was doing a good job with the most important problem voted for the incumbent, a lower level of support than in most other elections, and even slightly lower than the former lowest proportion, in 1976. Bush did worse among those who thought the government was doing only a fair job than any other incumbent party nominee in this period, receiving the support of less than half of those voters. And, like other incumbent party candidates, he received the votes of only two in five major party voters who thought the government was doing a poor job with their chief concern.

According to Downs and Fiorina, it is important to know not just how things have been going but also to assess how that evaluation compares with the alternative. In recent elections, respondents have been asked which party would do a better job of solving the problem they named as the most important. Table 7-2A shows the responses to this question.[8] This question is clearly future-oriented, but it may call for judgments about past performance, consistent with the Downs-Fiorina view. It does not ask the respondent to evaluate policy alternatives, and thus responses are most likely based on a retrospective comparison of how the incumbent party had handled things with a prediction about how the opposition would fare. We therefore consider this question to be a measure of comparative retrospective evaluations.

By comparing Tables 7-1A and 7-2A, we can see that about one in eight of the respondents thought the Republican party would be better at

Table 7-1 Evaluation of Governmental Performance on Most Important Problem and Major Party Vote, 1972-1992

Government Is Doing:	1972[a]	1976	1980	1984	1988	1992
A. Evaluation of Governmental Performance on Most Important Problem						
Good job	12%	8%	4%	16%	8%	2%
Only fair job	58	46	35	46	37	28
Poor job	30	46	61	39	56	69
Total percent	100%	100%[b]	100%	101%	101%	99%[b]
(N)	(993)	(2,156)[b]	(1,319)	(1,797)	(1,672)	(1,974)[b]
B. Percentage of Major Party Vote for Incumbent Party's Nominee						
Good job	85	72	81	89	82	70
(N)	(91)	(128)[b]	(43)	(214)	(93)	(27)[b]
Only fair job	69	53	55	65	61	45
(N)	(390)	(695)[b]	(289)	(579)	(429)	(352)[b]
Poor job	46	39	33	37	44	39
(N)	(209)	(684)[b]	(505)	(494)	(631)	(841)[b]

Note: Numbers in parentheses are the totals upon which percentages are based.

[a]These questions were asked of a randomly selected half of the sample in 1972. In 1972 the question wording and responses were different. Respondents were asked whether the government was being (a) very helpful, (b) somewhat helpful, or (c) not helpful at all in solving this most important problem.

[b]Numbers are weighted.

Table 7-2 Evaluation of Party Seen as Better on Most Important Problem and Major Party Vote, 1972-1992

Party Better	1972[a]	1976	1980	1984	1988	1992
A. Distribution of Responses on Party Better on Most Important Problem						
Republican	28%	14%	43%	32%	22%	13%
No difference	46	50	46	44	54	48
Democratic	26	37	11	25	24	39
Total percent	100%	101%[b]	100%	101%	100%	100%[b]
(N)	(931)	(2,054)[b]	(1,251)	(1,785)	(1,655)	(1,954)[b]
B. Percentage of Major Party Voters Who Voted Democratic for President						
Republican	6	3[b]	12	5	5	4
(N)	(207)	(231)[b]	(391)	(464)	(295)	(185)[b]
No difference	32	35	63	41	46	45
(N)	(275)	(673)[b]	(320)	(493)	(564)	(507)[b]
Democratic	75	89	95	91	92	92
(N)	(180)	(565)[b]	(93)	(331)	(284)	(519)[b]

Note: Numbers in parentheses are the totals upon which percentages are based.

[a]These questions were asked of a randomly selected half of the sample in 1972. In 1972 respondents were asked which party would be more likely to get the government to be helpful in solving the most important problem.

[b]Numbers are weighted.

handling the most important problem, but this was a far larger proportion of respondents than thought the government was already doing a good job with it. Almost half thought neither party would do a better job, while about two in five thought the Democrats would be better at handling the most important problem. Indeed, responses in 1992 were very similar to those in 1976, a year in which the incumbent Republican lost to the Democrat. And the pattern in 1976 and 1992 is almost a mirror image of the pattern in 1980, a year in which an incumbent Democrat was defeated. But there is one similarity across all six elections. The most frequent answer is that *neither* party would do a better job handling the most important problem, and nearly half of the respondents chose that option in 1992.

As Table 7-2B reveals, the relationship between the party seen as better on the most important problem and the vote is very strong—stronger than that found in Table 7-1B, which examines voters and their perception of the government's handling of the problem. In this case, 1992 looks most like 1984 and 1988, and displays an overwhelming relationship. Over nine in ten of the major party voters who thought the Democratic party was the better bet for handling the voter's most important concern voted for the Democratic candidate, while nineteen of twenty who thought the Republican party was better suited for the task voted for its nominee. The plurality who thought there was little difference between the parties on this concern gave Bush a slight edge over Clinton. It appears that one way of winning a vote is by convincing the voter that your party will be better at handling whatever issue it is that concerns the voter the most. If neither candidate convinces the voter that his party is better, the voter apparently looks to other factors.

The data presented in Tables 7-1 and 7-2 have two limitations. First, as we saw in Chapter 6, there was considerable diversity in what problems most concerned respondents. Even though many cited the economy, respondents differed considerably on what aspect of the economy most concerned them, and many cited other domestic issues, such as health care. It is therefore hard to make comparisons and interpret the findings. Are those who expressed concern about the budget deficits, for example, similar to those who were concerned about drugs, about health care, or about some other problem? Second, the first survey question refers to "the government" and not to the incumbent president (is it the president, Congress, both, or even others—such as the bureaucracy or the courts—who are handling the job poorly?); the second question refers to the "political party" and not the candidate. So we will look more closely at the incumbent and at people's evaluations of comparable problems where there are data to permit such comparisons.

Economic Evaluations and the
Vote for the Incumbent

More than any other, economic issues have received attention as suitable retrospective issues. The impact of economic conditions on congressional and presidential elections has been studied extensively.[9] Popular evaluations of presidential effectiveness, John E. Mueller has pointed out, are strongly influenced by the economy. Edward R. Tufte suggests that because the incumbent realizes his fate may hinge on the performance of the economy, he may attempt to manipulate it, leading to what is known as a "political business cycle." [10] A major reason for Carter's defeat in the 1980 election was the perception that economic performance was weak during his administration. Reagan's rhetorical question in the 1980 debate with Carter, "Are you better off than you were four years ago?" indicates that politicians realize the power such arguments have with the electorate. Reagan owed his sweeping reelection victory in 1984 largely to the very different and more positive perception that economic performance by the end of his first term had become, after a deep recession in the middle, much stronger.

If people are concerned about economic outcomes, they might start by looking for an answer to the sort of question Reagan asked. Table 7-3A presents respondents' perceptions of whether they were financially better off than they had been one year earlier. From 1972 to 1980, about a third of the sample felt they were better off. Over that period, however, more and more of the remainder felt they were worse off. By 1980, "worse now" was the most common response. But in 1984, many felt the economic recovery, and more than two of five said they were better off than in the previous year; only a little more than one in four felt worse off. Of course, 1984 was only two years after a deep recession. Therefore, many may have seen their economic fortunes improve considerably over the prior year or so. In 1988, that recovery had been sustained. So, too, were the responses to the question. The distribution of responses to this question in 1988 is very similar to that of 1984. But, by 1992, there was a return to the feelings of the earlier period, and responses were nearly evenly divided between better, the same, and worse off—a pattern similar to that in 1976.

In Table 7-3B, responses to this question are related to the two-party presidential vote. We can see that the relationship between the respondents' financial situations and their vote is often not particularly strong. Even so, those who felt their financial status had become worse off in the last year were always the least likely to support the incumbent. Moreover, the relationship between this variable and the vote became considerably stronger in 1984 and only slightly less so in 1988. Perhaps the electorate held the Reagan administration responsible for their answer to his

Table 7-3 Assessments of Personal Financial Situation and Major Party Vote, 1972-1992

Response	1972[a]	1976	1980	1984	1988	1992
A. Distribution of Responses to the Question "Would you say that you (and your family here) are better off or worse off financially than you were a year ago?"						
Better now	36%	34%	33%	44%	42%	31%
Same	42	35	25	28	33	34
Worse now	23	31	42	27	25	35
Total percent	101%	100%	100%	99%	100%	100%
(N)	(955)	(2,828)[b]	(1,393)	(1,956)	(2,025)	(2,474)[b]
B. Percentage of Major Party Voters Who Voted for the Incumbent Party Nominee for President						
Better now	69	55	46	74	63	53
(N)	(247)	(574)[b]	(295)	(612)	(489)	(413)[b]
Same	70	52	46	55	50	45
(N)	(279)	(571)[b]	(226)	(407)	(405)	(500)[b]
Worse now	52	38	40	33	40	27
(N)	(153)	(475)[b]	(351)	(338)	(283)	(453)[b]

Note: Numbers in parentheses are the totals upon which percentages are based.

[a] These questions were asked of a randomly selected half of the sample in 1972.

[b] Numbers are weighted.

question, one they had decided in the Republicans' favor. By 1992, the relationship, if anything, strengthened even more, with a majority of major party voters who were better off voting for Bush, but barely more than one in four of those worse off voting to return him to office. Thus, it appears that Bush first was the recipient of support due to good economic conditions in 1988, and then was held responsible for bad economic circumstances in 1992.

People may "vote their pocketbooks," but people are even more likely to vote retrospectively based on their judgments of how the economy as a whole has been faring. In 1980, about 40 percent thought their own financial situation was worse than the year before, but twice as many (84 percent) thought the national economy was worse off than the year before. In the first three columns of Table 7-4A, we see that there was quite a change in the perceptions of the fortunes of the national economy over the last three elections. In 1984, the improved status of personal finances almost matched perceptions of the status of the economy as a whole. In 1988, the personal financial situation was quite like that in 1984, but perceptions of the national economy were clearly more negative. Half the sample thought the national economy was about the same in 1988 as a year earlier, nearly a third thought it was worse, and only one in five thought it had improved. In 1992, nearly three in four thought that the nation's economy had deteriorated over the past year, and under one in twenty thought it had gotten better, a far more negative assessment than respondents gave of their personal financial situations. Thus, one's perceptions of personal fortunes may be very different from those of the economy as a whole.

The next question is whether the respondents believe that the federal government and its policies have shaped these economic fortunes. The responses in 1992 were not particularly good news for Bush, as hardly anyone thought that government policies had made them better off. But the news was not that bad for the GOP, since two in three thought those policies made no difference to them. Still, three in ten thought the policies had hurt them, a larger proportion than in the two preceding elections. A larger proportion thought that the economic policies of the government had made the economy worse off than had hurt their own fortunes, and this was a far larger proportion than in earlier elections. The important point, then, is that very few thought the national economy was in good shape or that the policies of the federal government had done much good for the economy as a whole or for their own fortunes.

In Table 7-4B, we show the relationship between responses to these items and the two-party vote for president. As we can see, this relationship between these measures and the vote is always quite strong, somewhat more so in 1984 than in 1988 and 1992, but still robust in the

Table 7-4 Public's View of the State of the Economy, Government Economic Policies, and Major Party Vote, 1984-1992

	Would you say that over the past year the nation's economy has gotten:			Would you say that the economic policies of the federal government have made you:			Would you say that the economic policies of the federal government have made the nation's economy:		
	1984	1988	1992	1984	1988	1992	1984	1988	1992
A. Distribution of Responses									
Better [off]	44%	19%	4%	19%	12%	3%	38%	20%	4%
Stayed same/ have not made much difference	33	50	22	59	67	67	40	57	51
Worse [off]	23	31	73	22	22	30	22	23	45
Total percent	100%	100%	99%[a]	100%	101%	100%	100%	100%	100%[a]
(N)	(1,904)	(1,956)	(2,465)[a]	(1,891)	(1,992)	(2,435)	(1,841)	(1,895)	(2,401)[a]
B. Percentage of Major Party Voters Who Voted for the Incumbent Party Nominee for President									
Better [off]	80	77	86	86	79	71	84	83	79
(N)	(646)	(249)	(62)[a]	(282)	(153)	(53)[a]	(544)	(258)	(61)[a]
Stayed same/ have not made much difference	53	53	62	58	55	46	52	50	49
(N)	(413)	(568)	(318)[a]	(757)	(742)	(893)[a]	(457)	(606)	(671)[a]
Worse [off]	21	34	32	30	34	26	23	30	29
(N)	(282)	(348)	(981)[a]	(281)	(276)	(408)[a]	(302)	(275)	(597)[a]

Note: Numbers in parentheses are the totals upon which percentages are based.
[a] Numbers are weighted.

later two surveys. Moreover, comparing the bottom halves of Tables 7-3B and 7-4B shows that, in general, the vote is more closely associated with perceptions of the nation's economy and the role the government has been seen to play in it than it is with perceptions of one's personal economic well-being.

To this point, we have looked at personal and national economic conditions and the role of the government in shaping them. We have not yet looked at the extent to which such evaluations are attributed to the incumbent. In Table 7-5, we report responses to the question of whether people approved of the incumbent's handling of the economy from the 1980 through 1992 elections. We also include perceptions respondents held of governmental performance on inflation and unemployment in the 1972 and 1976 NES surveys. These comparisons are difficult to make because different questions were asked in the earlier surveys. Still, even with different questions, it seems quite reasonable to conclude that the public held far more positive views of Reagan's performance than of the performance of any of the three administrations that preceded his. While a majority approved of Reagan's handling of the economy in both 1984 and 1988, less than one in four held positive views of economic performance in the Nixon, Ford, and Carter years. In 1992, evaluations of Bush were very negative.

The bottom-line question is whether these views are related to voter choice. As the data in Table 7-5B show, the answer is yes. Those who held positive views of the incumbents' performance on the economy were very likely to vote for that party's candidate, and the nine of ten who backed Bush in 1992 is, if anything, even a higher proportion than is the norm. Large majorities of those with negative views voted to change administrations. Bush's loss to Clinton among major party voters, therefore, is attributable primarily to the heavily negative views of his stewardship of the economy, just as it was for Carter in 1980. In 1988, Bush had benefited primarily from the positive assessments of Reagan's handling of the economy, even though he did more poorly among those who disapproved in 1988 than he did in 1992; but he lost that advantage in 1992 because of the negative evaluations of his economic stewardship.

Other Retrospective Evaluations

Although economic concerns have been central to all recent elections and have dominated studies of retrospective voting, other retrospective judgments have also influenced voters.

Foreign affairs is another important area for retrospective evaluations. Peace and prosperity share many of the properties that make them important retrospective concerns. Bush, of course, had hoped to make peace a major part of his reelection campaign, and for good reason.

Table 7-5 Evaluations of the Government's/Incumbent's Handling of the Economy and Major Party Vote, 1972-1992

	Government Performance on Inflation/Unemployment		Approval of Incumbent's Handling of the Economy			
	1972[a]	1976[b]	1980[c]	1984[d]	1988[d]	1992[d]
A. Distribution of Responses						
Positive view	22%	15%	18%	58%	54%	20%
Neutral/balanced view	59	45	17	—	—	—
Negative view	19	39	65	42	46	80
Total percent	100%	99%	100%	100%	100%	100%
(N)	(941)	(2,664)	(1,097)	(1,858)	(1,897)	(2,425)[e]
B. Percentage of Major Party Voters Who Voted for the Incumbent Party Nominee for President						
Positive view	91	79	88	86	80	90
(N)	(149)	(247)	(130)	(801)	(645)	(310)[e]
Neutral/balanced view	68	57	60	—	—	—
(N)	(401)	(688)	(114)	—	—	—
Negative view	30	26	23	16	17	26
(N)	(122)	(597)	(451)	(515)	(492)	(1,039)[e]

[a] Questions asked of randomly selected half sample, asking whether the government had done a good (positive), fair (neutral), or poor (negative) job on handling inflation and unemployment, combined.

[b] Numbers are weighted. Two questions asked in a fashion similar to 1972. A "positive [negative] view" was good [poor] on both, or on one, "fair," on the other. Neutral/balanced was any other combination of nonmissing responses.

[c] In 1980 the questions asked whether the respondent approved or disapproved of Carter's handling of inflation [unemployment]. A positive [negative] view was approve [disapprove] on both; balanced responses were approve on one, disapprove on the other.

[d] In 1984, 1988, and 1992 responses were whether the respondent approved of Reagan's [Bush's] handling of the economy.

[e] Numbers are weighted.

Nearly seven in ten approved of "the way George Bush handled the war in the Persian Gulf," for example, and over four in ten approved strongly. In fact, over three in four said that "we did the right thing in sending U.S. military forces to the Persian Gulf." Unfortunately for Bush, however, much had happened since the Persian Gulf war. By the fall campaign, only 55 percent felt that "anything good came out of [the Persian Gulf war] for the United States," while 45 percent said nothing had.

Still, Bush was given high marks for foreign affairs generally: 62 percent approved of his handling of foreign affairs, a dramatically higher proportion than the mere 20 percent who approved of his handling of the economy. Bush's approval ratings on foreign affairs were higher than Reagan's 53 percent in 1984 and about the same as Reagan's 61 percent in 1988. Of course, Reagan also received high approval for his handling of the economy (58 percent in 1984 and 54 percent in 1988), so that, in his case, voters did not have to consider whether to support an incumbent whom they believed had done well in foreign affairs but poorly on economics.

Republicans have had an advantage over Democrats on peace issues for two decades, and 1992 was no exception. Although three in ten thought neither party would better handle foreign affairs, only slightly less than half thought the Republicans would be better, leaving only two in ten who said the Democrats would be. This partisan advantage has aided Republicans since at least 1972, and the Democrats have selected nominees who accentuated the perceptions. In 1988, Bush was fond of saying that Dukakis had never met a weapons system that he liked. That charge did not fit Clinton, nor circumstances, in 1992, but Bush hammered repeatedly on Clinton's draft record. Whether or not the public cared about Clinton's draft status of two decades earlier, most did believe that Bush would do a better job in foreign affairs; 55 percent cited Bush, 23 percent said Clinton, and 19 percent said there wouldn't be any difference.

Peace, like prosperity, seems to matter most when it is threatened. The ending of the cold war—a victory Bush claimed for himself and Reagan—had the ironic effect of reducing concern about threats to peace. In 1992 a majority (55 percent) were not worried about the threat of a nuclear war, while only 14 percent were "very worried." In 1984 and 1988, about a third had been very worried about the prospect of nuclear war. Concern about conventional war also fell. About 37 percent were "very worried" in 1988, but this fell to 11 percent in 1992, with the rest evenly divided between "somewhat worried" and "not worried at all." Even so, there was little difference between 1988 and 1992 in people's feelings about whether "the United States' position in the world had grown weaker, stayed about the same, or ... has grown stronger." The percentages choosing those responses were 28, 36, and 36 in 1992, and 24, 39, and

38 in 1988, respectively. Perhaps as a result, the Republicans in 1992 had lost the advantage they held in 1988 in being seen to be better at handling the problem of potential war. In 1988, a little more than half thought neither party would be better, but the remainder were 10 points more likely to say Republicans than Democrats. In 1992, three in five said neither party would be better, and the remainder were nearly evenly divided, with the Republicans holding a mere 1-point edge among these respondents. Thus, while Bush could claim some important credits on foreign affairs, the advantage was no longer as consistently given to the Republicans. But what was far more important, as we saw in Chapter 6, was that although peace was no longer threatened in the public's mind, prosperity was. People voted retrospectively on prosperity concerns, but not on peace concerns.

Evaluations of the Incumbent

Fiorina distinguishes between simple and mediated retrospective evaluations. By simple Fiorina means evaluations of the direct effects of social outcomes on the person, such as financial status, or direct perceptions of the nation's economic well-being. Mediated retrospective evaluations are evaluations seen through or mediated by the perceptions of political actors and institutions. Approval of Bush's handling of the economy or the assessment of which party would better handle the most important problem facing the country are examples.[11]

As we have seen, the more politically mediated the question, the more closely responses align with voting behavior. Perhaps the ultimate in mediated evaluations is the presidential approval question: "Do you approve or disapprove of the way [the incumbent] is handling his job as president?" From a retrospective voting standpoint, this evaluation is a summary of all aspects of his service in office. Table 7-6 reports the distribution of overall evaluations and their relationship to major party voting in the last six elections.[12]

As can be seen in Table 7-6A, the Republican incumbents Nixon, Ford, and Reagan enjoyed widespread approval, whereas only two respondents in five approved of Carter's and of Bush's handling of his job. This presented Carter in 1980 and Bush in 1992 with a problem. Conversely, highly approved incumbents, such as Reagan in 1984—and his vice president as beneficiary in 1988—had a major advantage. As can be seen in Table 7-6B, there is a very strong relationship between approval of the incumbent and the vote for that incumbent (and, as in 1988, his vice president). Bush held a great proportion of the major party vote among those who approved of the incumbent—and lost a vast majority of the major party vote among those who disapproved. We can see why Bush would seek to accentuate his ties to Reagan in 1988 so that

Table 7-6 Distribution of Responses on President's Handling of Job and Major Party Vote, 1972-1992

Do you approve or disapprove of the way [the incumbent] is handling his job as president?	1972	1976	1980	1984	1988	1992
A. Distribution of Responses						
Approve	71%	63%	41%	63%	60%	43%
Disapprove	29	37	59	37	40	57
Total percent	100%	100%	100%	100%	100%	100%
(N)	(1,215)	(2,439)[a]	(1,475)	(2,091)	(1,935)	(2,419)[a]
B. Percentage of Major Party Voters Who Voted for the Incumbent Party's Nominee						
Approve	83	74	81	87	79	81
(N)	(553)	(935)[a]	(315)	(863)	(722)	(587)[a]
Disapprove	14	9	18	7	12	11
(N)	(203)	(523)[a]	(491)	(449)	(442)	(759)[a]

Note: Question was asked of a randomly selected half sample in 1972. Numbers in parentheses are the totals upon which percentages are based.

[a] Numbers are weighted.

he could benefit from Reagan's high approval ratings. In 1992, he ran on his own record. While he did as well among those who approved of his performance, as other incumbents have before him, he faced virtually the same problem as Carter did in 1980; only about two in five approved of his performance. Unlike Carter in 1980, but rather like most other incumbents, he won only about one in ten votes from those who disapproved, while losing about two in ten of the smaller number who approved of his handling of the job.

The Impact of Retrospective Evaluations

Our evidence strongly suggests that retrospective voting has been widespread in all recent elections. Moreover, as far as data permit us to judge, the evidence is clearly on the side of the Downs-Fiorina view. Retrospective evaluations appear to be used to make comparative judgments. Presumably, voters find it easier, less time consuming, and less risky to evaluate the incumbent party on what its president did in the most recent term or terms in office than on the nominees' promises for the future. But few base their vote on judgments of past performance alone. Most use past judgments as a starting point for comparing the major contenders. When the incumbent's performance in 1980 and 1992 was compared with the anticipated performance of the opponent, most felt the incumbent had not done very well, but a surprisingly large number of those did not believe that the opposition party would do any better (see Table 7-2). In 1972, 1984, and 1988, many felt the incumbent had done well, and few thought the challenger's party would do better. The 1992 election was most like the 1980 election. Negative evaluations were quite severe, and if these elections had been simply a referendum on the incumbents' performance, it seems likely that the incumbents would have lost to their major party opponents by an even greater margin than they, in fact, did. At least some of those who were not happy with the incumbent stuck with him, apparently fearing that his opponent might turn out to be worse.

We can strengthen the overall assessment of retrospective voting in the last few elections by forming a combined index of retrospective evaluations common to the five most recent presidential election surveys. In Figures 7-1 and 7-2, we report the result of combining the presidential approval measure with the evaluation of the job the government has done on the most important problem and the assessment of which party would better handle that problem.[13] This creates a 7-point scale ranging from strongly supportive of the job the incumbent and his party have done to strongly opposed to that performance. For instance, those who approved of Bush's job performance, thought the government was doing a good job, and thought the Republican party would better handle the problem scored as strongly supportive of the incumbent party's nominee in their retrospective evaluations in 1992.

In Figure 7-1, we report the distribution of responses on this combined measure. As these figures make clear, respondents had very negative evaluations of the incumbent and his party in 1992. Far more of the respondents were strongly or moderately against Bush and his party than had been against the incumbent in any previous election except 1980; very few were moderately or strongly favorable toward him and his party. In 1984, there was clear support for the incumbent party, and nearly half of the respondents had a pro-incumbent orientation, while only slightly more than one in three had evaluations that favored the opposition. In both 1976, when the incumbent narrowly lost, and in 1988, when the incumbent vice president won the second closest of these elections, the electorate tended to favor the opposition, but by a relatively narrow margin. Moreover, in both 1976 and 1988, over a fifth of the electorate held a neutral position on this measure. In 1992, there was about the same percentage of neutrals as in 1980 and 1984. Overall, then, the distribution of responses was most unfavorable for the incumbent in 1992, quite like it was for Carter in 1980.

As Figure 7-2 shows, respondents who have positive retrospective evaluations of the incumbent party are much more likely to vote for that party than those who disapprove of the incumbent party's performance. In this case, the support for Bush in 1992 looks to be in between that for Carter in 1980 and the remaining elections we have analyzed. Carter, in 1980, generally fared better than Republican incumbents, especially among voters who were negatively disposed toward the Democrats; Bush in 1992 did somewhat better than previous Republican incumbents. But in 1992, as in 1980, there were far too many voters who were negatively disposed toward his party. Reagan's 1984 election can clearly be seen to result from favorable retrospective evaluations. In 1976, Ford failed to overcome the negative evaluations of governmental performance and of his party, and he narrowly lost the election. Overall evaluations were about the same in 1988, but Bush fared better than Ford among voters who were slightly favorable to the incumbent party but fared just as poorly among voters who were moderately against the incumbent. In general, however, these differences are relatively small, while the similarities are substantial—the most important being a very strong relationship between retrospective evaluations and the vote.

In sum, it would seem reasonable to conclude that the 1976 election, with its razor-thin margin going to Carter, was a very narrow rejection of Ford's incumbency, and 1980 was a clear and strong rejection of Carter's. In 1984, Reagan won in large part because he was seen as having performed well and because Mondale was unable to convince the public that he would do better. In 1988, Bush won in large part because Reagan

Figure 7-1 Distribution of Electorate on Summary Measure of Restrospective Evaluations, 1976-1992

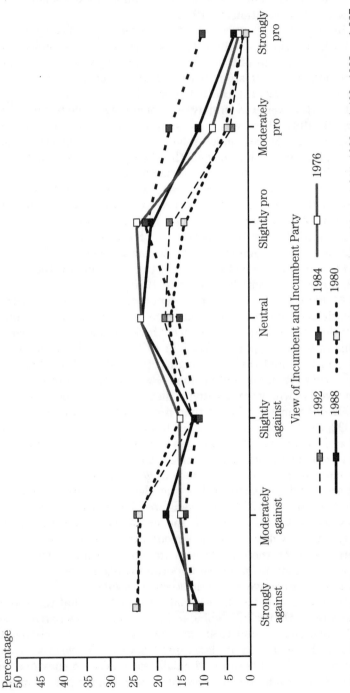

Note: The total number of cases: 1976 — 2,166(weighted); 1980 — 1,325(weighted); 1984 — 1,814; 1988 — 1,409; 1992 — 1,987 (weighted).

Figure 7-2 Percentage of Major Party Voters Who Voted for Incumbent, by Summary Measure of Retrospective Evaluations, 1976-1992

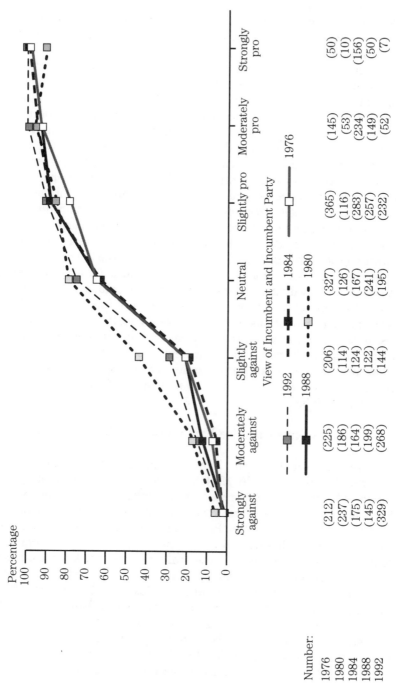

Note: Numbers in parentheses are the totals upon which the percentages are based. Weighted *N*s were used for 1976 and 1992.

was seen as having performed well—and people thought Bush would stay the course. In 1992, Bush lost because of the far more negative evaluations of his administration and of his party than had obtained in any other recent elections except 1980—including 1976, an election in which the incumbent lost the election.

There are obviously more differences between these elections than illustrated by retrospective evaluations alone. In particular, there were also prospective issues. As you may recall from Chapter 6, these issues were also clearly related to the vote. There are too few prospective issue scales in the 1992 NES survey, however, to be able to make reasonable comparisons between the balance of issues measure and the summary retrospective measure. We were able to make such comparisons for earlier elections: we found variation in how important prospective issues appeared to be, once we took retrospective evaluations into account. In the 1976 and 1980 elections, we found little relationship between prospective issues and the vote, once retrospective measures were taken into account. For 1984, we found that prospective measures had some effect on the vote. For 1988, like 1972, however, the effect of prospective measures was even more pronounced. We also found, however, that retrospective evaluations remained very important in each election, even after taking the balance of issues measure into account.[14] In 1992, retrospective evaluations were very strongly related to the vote, regardless of the voter's score on the balance of issues measure. The balance of issues measure, however, is not strongly related to the vote except for those who were neutral in their summary retrospective evaluations. In this sense, 1992 results seem more like those of earlier elections than like that of 1988.

The Retrospective Evaluations of Perot Voters

We have examined the impact of retrospective evaluations upon major party voters. In 1976, 1984, and 1988, over 98 percent of the voters supported either the Democratic or Republican presidential candidate. Even in 1980, when Anderson ran, Reagan and Carter won nearly 92 percent of the total vote. But Perot gained 19 percent of the total vote in 1992, and we can ill afford to ignore the retrospective evaluations of his supporters. We will examine those evaluations on the key measures that we use to construct our summary measure of retrospective evaluations.

Table 7-7 presents the percentage of Bush, Clinton, and Perot voters who approved of Bush's performance as president, their views about the job the government was doing solving the most important national problem, and their beliefs about which party would do a better job solving that problem. Last, Table 7-7 shows the distribution of each candidate's voters on our summary measure of retrospective evaluations.

Table 7-7 Retrospective Evaluations, by How Voted for President, 1992 (in percentages)

	Voted for		
	Bush	Clinton	Perot
Approval of Bush's job performance			
Approve	84	14	35
Disapprove	14	84	64
Don't know	2	2	1
Total percent	100	100	100
(N)	(569)	(799)	(317)
Job government is doing solving the most important problem			
Good	3	1	—ᵃ
Only fair	28	24	20
Poor	58	64	70
Don't know	11	10	11
Total percent	100	99	101
(N)	(569)	(799)	(317)
Which party would do a better job solving problem			
Republican	31	1	9
Neither	49	28	51
Democratic	7	60	28
Don't know	12	11	12
Total percent	99	100	100
(N)	(569)	(799)	(317)
Summary measure of retrospective evaluations			
Strongly Republican	1	0	0
Moderately Republican	10	0	1
Slightly Republican	41	3	13
Neutral	29	7	19
Slightly Democratic	8	14	13
Moderately Democratic	9	31	34
Strongly Democratic	2	45	21
Total percent	100	100	101
(N)	(508)	(719)	(284)

Note: Numbers are weighted.

ᵃ Less than 1 percent.

Despite Bush's low overall approval rating, more than eight out of ten Bush voters approved of his performance as president. Among Clinton voters, an equal percentage disapproved of Bush's performance. Perot voters disapproved of Bush's performance by a nearly two to one margin, but they were not as negative toward Bush as Clinton voters were. Further analysis (not shown in Table 7-7) reveals that three out of five Clinton voters strongly disapproved of Bush's performance as president, while just over one-third of the Perot voters did. This finding is understandable. Voters who strongly disapproved of Bush might have been less willing to "waste" their vote on an independent candidate who had very little chance of winning. If a voter's goal was to remove Bush from the White House, the most likely way to achieve this goal was to vote for Clinton. Indeed, among voters who strongly disapproved of Bush's job performance ($N = 620$), 5 percent voted for Bush, 77 percent voted for Clinton, and 18 percent voted for Perot. Among those who disapproved, but did not disapprove strongly ($N = 343$), Bush won 15 percent of the vote, Clinton won 58 percent, and Perot won 27 percent.

As Table 7-7 shows, even a clear majority of Bush voters thought that the government was doing a poor job of handling the most important problem facing the country. Perot voters had a somewhat more negative assessment than either Clinton or Bush voters. Seven out of ten Perot voters believed that the government was doing a poor job.

As we saw in Table 7-2, nearly half the electorate thought that neither party would do a better job solving the most important problem. Nonetheless, three out of ten Bush voters thought that the Republicans would do a better job, although half thought that neither party would do better. Among Clinton voters, three out of five thought the Democrats would do a better job, and only one out of four thought neither party would do better. Half the Perot voters thought that neither party would do a better job, about the same percentage as among Bush voters. Unlike Bush voters, the remainder of Perot voters split three to one in favor of the Democrats.

The differences on these three questions are clearly reflected in our summary measure of retrospective voting. Fifty-two percent of Bush voters were at least somewhat more supportive of the Republican party than of the Democrats, although most of them were only slightly Republican in their evaluations. Fully 90 percent of the Clinton voters were pro-Democratic, with 45 percent scoring as strongly Democratic. Among Perot voters, 14 percent scored in the Republican direction, 19 percent were neutral, and 68 percent were pro-Democratic. However, only one in five Perot voters was strongly Democratic. Once again, the findings make sense. Voters who believed that Bush was doing a poor job, that the government was doing a poor job, and that the Democrats would do a better job were very likely to want to replace Bush. Most of them would recognize that their best chance of defeating Bush was to vote for Clinton. Indeed, among such voters ($N = 388$), 2 percent voted for Bush, 83 percent voted for Clinton, and 15 percent voted for Perot. Perot did best among the group that was moderately Democratic on our summary measure. Among this group ($N = 364$), 12 percent voted for Bush, 62 percent voted for Clinton, and 26 percent voted for Perot.

In short, Perot voters were clearly negative toward Bush and the Republican party, but only a fourth of them thought that the Democratic party would do a better job of solving the most important national problem. Since most Perot voters were attracted to neither party, their vote for an independent candidate makes sense. One reason for their lack of confidence in the Democrats (or Republicans) is that Perot voters were much less likely than major party voters to be strong party identifiers, and they were more likely to be self-professed independents. Conversely, those who were most strongly Democratic in their retrospective evaluations were more likely to have a Democratic—or strong Democratic—partisan identification. We shall examine these relationships further in Chapter 8.

Conclusion

In this and the previous chapter, we have found that both retrospective and prospective evaluations were strongly related to the vote. Indeed, in 1992, dissatisfaction with Bush's performance and with his and his party's handling of the most important problem—often an economic concern—goes a long way in explaining his defeat. Those who thought the Democratic party would handle that problem were quite likely to vote for the Democratic candidate, while those who thought neither party would do better were divided in their choice between Clinton and Perot. Although it seems likely that policy voting of both sorts was very strong in 1992, the explanation remains incomplete. Most important, we have not accounted for why people hold the views they expressed on these two measures. We cannot provide a complete account of the origins of people's views, but there is one important source we can examine. Party identification, a variable we have used in previous chapters, provides a powerful means for the typical citizen to reach preliminary judgments. As we will see, partisanship is strongly related to these judgments, especially to retrospective evaluations.

Moreover, party identification plays a central role in debates about the future of American politics. Will there be a partisan realignment? A dealignment? Or will the unified government that resulted from the 1992 elections be an aberration after which the United States will return to the years of federal government under split control and "gridlock," in a situation some have called a split level realignment? Many political scientists believe that change in the political system of this magnitude can come only if there are changes in party loyalties in the electorate as well as in their voting behavior. Therefore, to understand voter choice better and to assess future partisan prospects, we must examine the role of party loyalties.

Chapter 8

Party Loyalties, Policy Preferences, and the Vote

Most Americans identify with a political party. Their party identification influences their political attitudes and, ultimately, their behavior. In the 1950s and 1960s the authors of *The American Voter*, along with other scholars, began to emphasize the role of party loyalties.[1] Although today few would deny that partisanship is central to political attitudes and behavior, many scholars question the interpretation of the evidence gathered during this period. We begin here by asking two questions: What is party identification? And how does it actually structure other attitudes and behavior? After we try to answer these questions, we examine the role that party identification played in the 1992 presidential election, and then we look at the impact of Perot's independent candidacy on voters' attitudes and behavior.

Party Identification: The Standard View

According to the authors of *The American Voter*, party identification is "the individual's affective orientation to an important group-object in his environment," in this case the political party.[2] In other words, an individual sees that there are two major political parties that play significant roles in elections and develops an affinity for one of them. Most Americans develop a preference for either the Republican or the Democratic party. (Very few identify with another party.) The remainder are mostly independents, who are not only unattached to a party but also relatively unattached to politics in general. They are less interested, less informed, and less active than those who identify with a party. Partisanship represents an evaluation of the two parties, but its implications extend to a wider variety of political phenomena. Angus Campbell and his colleagues measured partisanship by asking individuals which party they identified with and how strong that identification was.[3] If an individual does not identify with one of the parties, he or she may either "lean" toward a party or be a "pure" independent. Individuals who could not answer the party identification questions were classified as "apolitical." [4]

Partisan identification in this view becomes an attachment or loyalty not unlike that observed between the individual and other groups or organizations in society, such as a religious body, a social class, or even a favorite sports team. As with loyalties to many of these groups, partisan affiliation often begins early. One of the first political attitudes children develop is partisan identification, and it develops well before they acquire policy preferences and many other political orientations. Furthermore, as with other group loyalties, once an attachment to a party develops, it tends to endure. Some people do switch parties, of course, but they usually do so only if their social situation changes, if there is an issue of overriding concern that sways their loyalties, or if the political parties themselves change substantially.

Party identification, then, stands as a base or core orientation to electoral politics. It is formed at an early age and endures for most people throughout their lives.[5] Once formed, this core orientation, predicated on a general evaluation of the two parties, affects many other specific orientations. Democratic loyalists tend to rate Democratic candidates and officeholders more highly than Republican candidates and officeholders, and vice versa. In effect, one is predisposed to evaluate the promises and performance of one's party leaders relatively more favorably. It follows, therefore, that Democrats are more likely to vote for Democratic candidates than are Republicans, and vice versa.

Party Identification: An Alternative View

In *The Responsible Electorate*, published in 1966, V. O. Key, Jr., argued that party loyalties contributed to electoral inertia, and that many partisans voted as "standpatters" from election to election.[6] That is, in the absence of any information to the contrary, or if the attractions and disadvantages of the candidates are fairly evenly balanced, partisans are expected to vote for the candidate of their party. Voting for their party's candidates is their "standing decision," until and unless voters are given good reasons not to. In recent years, scholars have reexamined the bases of such behavior. In this new view, citizens who consider themselves Democrats have a standing decision to vote for the Democratic nominee because of the past positions of the Democrats and the Republicans and because of the parties' comparative past performances while in office. In short, this view of partisan identification presumes that it is a "running tally" of past experiences (mostly in terms of policy and performance), a sort of summary expression of political memory, according to Morris P. Fiorina.[7]

Furthermore, when in doubt about what, for example, a Democratic candidate is likely to do on civil rights in comparison to the Republican opponent, it is reasonable to assume the Democrat would be more liberal than the Republican—at least until the candidates indicate otherwise. Because the political parties tend to be consistent on the basic historical policy cleavages, summary judgments of parties and their typical candidates will not change radically or often.[8] As a result, a citizen's running tally serves as a good first approximation, changes rarely, and can be an excellent device for saving time and effort that would be spent gathering information in the absence of this "memory."

Many of the major findings used in support of the conventional interpretation of party identification are completely consistent with this more policy oriented view. We do not have the evidence to assert that one view is superior to the other. Indeed, the two interpretations are not mutually exclusive. Moreover, they share the important conclusion that party identification plays a central role in shaping voters' decisions.

In terms of the account of voting discussed in Chapter 6, both views agree that partisan identifications are long-term forces in politics. Both agree that such identifications are formed early in life for most of us; children often develop a partisan loyalty, which they usually learn from their parents, although these loyalties are seldom explicitly taught. Partisan identifications are also often closely associated with social forces, as discussed in Chapter 5, especially when a social group is actively engaged in partisan politics. An important illustration of this point is the affiliation of many labor unions with the New Deal Democratic coalition, which often reinforced the tendency of those who were in labor unions to identify with the Democratic party. Finally, both views agree that partisanship is closely associated with more immediate evaluations, including prospective and retrospective issue evaluations and evaluations of the candidates, as analyzed in Chapters 6 and 7.

The two views disagree over the nature of the association between partisanship and other attitudes such as those toward the candidates and on issues. The standard view argues that partisanship, as a long-term loyalty, affects the evaluations of issues and candidates by voters, but that it in turn is largely unaffected by such evaluations, except in such dramatic circumstances as realigning elections. In this sense, partisanship is a "filter" through which the concerns relevant to the particular election are viewed. In the alternative view, partisanship as a running tally may affect, but is also affected by, more immediate concerns. Indeed, Fiorina's definition of partisanship makes clear that the running tally includes current as well as past assessments. Distinguishing between these two views is quite difficult. Although the alternative view may see partisan identification as being open to the impact of retrospective and prospective evaluations and assessments of the candidates in the current election, such assessments will typically change an individual's identification relatively little, due to the accumulation of past experiences and the impact of initial socialization. We shall analyze the role of partisan identification in 1992 and other recent elections in ways consistent with both major views of partisan identification.

Party Identification in the Electorate

If partisan identification is a fundamental orientation for most citizens, then the distribution of partisan loyalties is of crucial importance. The National Election Studies (NES) have monitored the party loyalties of the American electorate since 1952. In Table 8-1 we show the basic distributions of partisan loyalties from 1980 through 1992. As the table shows, most Americans identify with a political party. In 1992, more than 3 in 5 claimed to think of themselves as a Democrat or as a Republican, and more than one-quarter more, who initially said they were independent or had no partisan preference, nonetheless said they felt closer to one of the major parties than to the other.[9] About 1 in 8 was purely independent of party, and barely 1 in 100 was classified as "apolitical." There was very little change in partisan loyalties between the 1984 (preelection) and 1988 surveys, and there was only slightly more change by 1992. One of the largest changes in partisanship in the electorate began in the mid-1960s, when more people claimed to be independents.[10] This growth stopped, however, in the late 1970s and early 1980s. The percentage of independents increased modestly in 1992, but it is too soon to say whether this trend will continue. Similarly, as we saw in Chapter 4, the percentage of strong partisans declined in the same period. Again, this decline reversed somewhat in the mid-1980s, before resuming again slightly by 1992.

Table 8-1 also shows that more people think of themselves as Democrats than as Republicans. Over the past forty years, the balance between the two parties has favored the Democrats by a range of about 55/45 to about 60/40. While the results from the last four presidential election years still fall within that range, they show a clear shift toward the Republicans. In the 1980 (preelection) survey, 35 percent of partisans were Republicans; in 1984, 42 percent were; by 1988, 44 percent were; and in 1992, 43 percent of partisans were Republicans. Including independents who lean toward a party would increase the percentage of Republicans from 38 percent (1980 preelection) to 45 percent (1984 preelection) to 47 percent (1984 postelection and 1988 preelection), and then to 44

Table 8-1   Party Identification in Pre- and Postelection Surveys, 1980-1992 (in percentages)

Party Identification	1980 Pre-	1980 Post-	1982 Post-	1984 Pre-	1984 Post-	1986 Post-	1988 Pre-	1990 Post-	1992 Pre-
Strong Democrat	18	17	21	17	18	18	18	20	17
Weak Democrat	24	24	25	20	22	23	18	19	18
Independent, leans Democratic	12	11	11	11	10	11	12	13	14
Independent, no partisan leanings	13	12	11	11	7	12	11	11	12
Independent, leans Republican	10	12	8	13	14	11	14	12	13
Weak Republican	14	14	15	15	15	15	14	15	15
Strong Republican	9	10	10	13	15	11	14	10	11
Total percent	100	100	101	100	101	101	101	100	100
(N)	(1,577)	(1,376)	(1,383)	(2,198)	(1,941)	(2,120)	(1,999)	(1,955)	(2,450)[a]
Apolitical	2	2	2	2	2	2	2	2	1
(N)	(35)	(26)	(28)	(38)	(32)	(46)	(33)	(31)	(23)[a]

Note: In the midterm years, 1982, 1986, and 1990, the NES conducted only a postelection survey. The 1988 and 1992 surveys measured party identification only in the preelection interview.

[a] Numbers are weighted.

percent in 1992. Thus, the Democratic advantage in loyalties in the electorate has narrowed, an edge made even smaller in practice by the tendency of the Republicans to have higher turnout than Democrats (see Chapter 4).

The partisan loyalties of the American electorate can also be analyzed through other surveys. Among these, the most useful are the General Social Surveys (GSS) conducted by the National Opinion Research Council (NORC). These surveys of about 1,500 respondents are based upon in-person interviews, and they employ the standard party identification questions developed by the authors of *The American Voter* to measure long-term attachments to the political parties. The GSS surveys have been carried out annually since 1972 (except 1979, 1981, and 1992), during February, March, and April. Like the NES surveys, the GSS reveals Republican gains. From 1972 through 1982, the percentage of party identifiers supporting the Republicans never rose above 37 percent, and even if independent leaners are included as partisan, support for the GOP never rose beyond 38 percent. The GOP made gains in 1983, and in 1984 the percentage of party identifiers who were Republican rose to 40 percent. Republican strength peaked in the 1990 GSS. Forty-eight percent of all party identifiers were Republicans, and if independents who lean toward a party are included, 49 percent were Republicans. But the Republicans made no further gains, even during the 1991 survey conducted during and shortly after the Persian Gulf war. In the most recent GSS survey, conducted in February through April of 1993, 47 percent of all identifiers were Republicans, although if independent leaners are excluded, Republican strength drops to 46 percent. However, the 1993 GSS also reveals fairly weak partisan loyalties among the electorate. Only 14 percent were strong Democrats and only 11 percent were strong Republicans. Thirteen percent were independents who felt closer to neither party. In all, 35 percent were self-proclaimed independents.[11]

The Gallup organization has studied partisan loyalties even longer than the NES, and the Gallup surveys also show Republican gains. As Michael B. MacKuen, Robert S. Erikson, and James A. Stimson demonstrate, the Gallup data provide an important measure of political change, because until recently they have been based on frequent in-person interviews, allowing scholars to study quarterly partisan results.[12] With the exception of surveys conducted in 1946, the Gallup surveys have consistently shown that there are more Democrats than Republicans. Throughout the 1960s, 1970s, and early 1980s, the Democrats generally led the Republicans by about a three to two margin. But support for the Republicans grew markedly in the third quarter of 1984, and their strength peaked in the first quarter of 1990—47 percent of the Gallup respondents who supported one of the major parties were Republican.

The most recent Gallup surveys, conducted during the second quarter of 1993, show some slippage. Thirty-nine percent were Democrats, 27 percent were Republicans, and 34 percent were independents, so that the Democrats nearly regained their three to two lead over the Republicans.[13] However, the Gallup party affiliation question is not designed to measure long-term partisan attachments. It asks respondents about their partisanship "as of today."[14] Philip E. Converse and Roy Pierce argue that responses to partisanship questions that lack a long-term focus are basically "statements of momentary vote preference, thereby obviating the whole point of the party identification measurement."[15] Although we do not agree that Gallup-type questions are merely measures of voting preference, responses to the Gallup questions are more volatile than responses to the party identification questions developed by Campbell and his colleagues.[16]

We have focused our analysis on the NES surveys, and our study reveals that the shift toward the Republican party is a phenomenon concentrated among white Americans. As we saw in Chapter 5, the sharpest social division in U.S. electoral politics is race, and this division has been reflected in partisan affiliations for decades. Moreover, the gap appears to be widening. Although the distribution of partisanship in the electorate as a whole is virtually the same in 1992 as it was in 1984, this stability masks a growth in Republican identification among whites, and, of course, a compensating growth of already strong Democratic affiliation among African-Americans. In Table 8-2 we report the party identification of whites between 1952 and 1992, and in Table 8-3 we report the affiliation of blacks. As the tables show, black and white patterns in partisan affiliation have been very different throughout this period. There was a sharp shift in black loyalties in the mid-1960s. Before then, about 50 percent of African-Americans were strong or weak Democrats; since that time, 60 percent, 70 percent, and even more blacks have considered themselves Democrats.

The party affiliations of whites have changed more slowly. Still, the percentage of self-professed Democrats among whites declined over the Reagan years, while the percentage of Republicans increased. In the 1984, 1988, and 1992 elections affiliation by race has changed with shifts among whites. In 1984, there was about an even balance among whites between the two parties, if independent leaners are included. By 1988, the shift continued. This time, the number of strong and weak Democrats and strong and weak Republicans was virtually the same, with more strong Republicans than strong Democrats for the first time. Adding in the two independent-leaning groups gave Republicans a clear advantage in identification among whites. In 1992, however, this advantage disappeared. There were slightly more strong Democrats and weak Democrats than strong and weak Republicans. Thus, in

Table 8-2   Party Identification Among Whites, 1952-1992 (in percentages)

Party Identification[a]	1952	1954	1956	1958	1960	1962	1964	1966	1968
Strong Democrat	21	22	20	26	20	22	24	17	16
Weak Democrat	25	25	23	22	25	23	25	27	25
Independent, leans Democratic	10	9	6	7	6	8	9	9	10
Independent, no partisan leanings	6	7	9	8	9	8	8	12	11
Independent, leans Republican	7	6	9	5	7	7	6	8	10
Weak Republican	14	15	14	17	14	17	14	16	16
Strong Republican	14	13	16	12	17	13	12	11	11
Apolitical	2	2	2	3	1	3	1	1	1
Total percent	99	99	99	100	100	101	99	101	100
(N)	(1,615)	(1,015)	(1,610)	(1,638)[b]	(1,739)[b]	(1,168)	(1,394)	(1,131)	(1,387)

[a] The percentage supporting another party has not been presented; it usually totals less than 1 percent and never totals more than 1 percent.
[b] Numbers are weighted.

1992, the two parties had essentially the same proportions of white identifiers.

Although the increased Republicanism of the white electorate is partly the result of long-term forces, such as generational replacement, the actual movement between 1964 and 1988 appears to result from two shorter-term increases in Republican identification. There was a 5 percentage point movement toward the GOP from 1964 through 1968, and a 10-point movement toward the GOP between 1982 and 1988. This movement waned modestly in 1992, as we saw.

Party identification among blacks is very different. In 1992, there were very few black Republicans. Ninety-four percent of strong and weak identifiers among blacks are Democrats (compared to 52 percent of whites), and, adding in leaners, 92 percent of blacks are Democrats (compared to 51 percent of whites).

These racial differences in partisanship are of long standing, and over time, changes have exaggerated this division. Between 1952 and 1962, blacks were primarily Democratic, but about one in seven supported the Republicans. Black partisanship shifted massively and abruptly even further toward the Democratic party in 1964. In that year, over half of all black voters considered themselves *strong* Democrats.

1970	1972	1974	1976	1978	1980	1982	1984	1986	1988	1990	1992
17	12	15	13	12	14	16	15	14	14	17	14
22	25	20	23	24	23	24	18	21	16	19	17
11	12	13	11	14	12	11	11	10	10	11	14
13	13	15	15	14	14	11	11	12	12	11	12
9	11	9	11	11	11	9	13	13	15	13	14
16	14	15	16	14	16	16	17	17	15	16	16
10	11	9	10	9	9	11	14	12	16	11	12
1	1	3	1	3	2	2	2	2	1	1	1
99	99	99	100	101	101	100	101	101	99	99	100[b]
(1,395)	(2,397)	(2,246)[b]	(2,490)[b]	(2,006)	(1,405)	(1,248)	(1,931)	(1,798)	(1,693)	(1,663)	(2,072)[b]

Since then, well over half have identified with the Democratic party. Black Republican identification fell to barely a trace in 1964 and has edged up only very slightly since then.

The abrupt change in black loyalties in 1964 reflects the two presidential nominees of that year. President Lyndon B. Johnson's advocacy of civil rights legislation appealed directly to black voters, and his Great Society and War on Poverty programs in general made an only slightly less direct appeal. Sen. Barry M. Goldwater, the Republican nominee, voted against the 1964 Civil Rights Act, a vote criticized even by many of his Republican peers. Party stances have not changed appreciably since then, although the proportion of blacks who were strong Democrats declined somewhat after 1968.

The proportion of blacks considered "apolitical" dropped from the teens to very small proportions, similar to those among whites, in 1964 as well. This shift can be attributed to the civil rights movement, the contest between Johnson and Goldwater, and the passage of the Civil Rights Act. The civil rights movement stimulated many blacks, especially in the South, to become politically active. Furthermore, the 1965 Voting Rights Act enabled many of them to vote for the first time.

Table 8-3   Party Identification Among African-Americans, 1952-1992 (in percentages)

Party Identification[a]	1952	1954	1956	1958	1960	1962	1964	1966	1968
Strong Democrat	30	24	27	32	25	35	52	30	56
Weak Democrat	22	29	23	19	19	25	22	31	29
Independent, leans Democratic	10	6	5	7	7	4	8	11	7
Independent, no partisan leanings	4	5	7	4	16	6	6	14	3
Independent, leans Republican	4	6	1	4	4	2	1	2	1
Weak Republican	8	5	12	11	9	7	5	7	1
Strong Republican	5	11	7	7	7	6	2	2	1
Apolitical	17	15	18	16	14	15	4	3	3
Total percent	100	101	100	100	101	100	100	100	101
(N)	(171)	(101)	(146)	(161)[b]	(171)[b]	(110)	(156)	(132)	(149)

[a] The percentage supporting another party has not been presented; it usually totals less than 1 percent and never totals more than 1 percent.
[b] Numbers are weighted.
[c] Less than 1 percent.

Party Identification and the Vote

As we saw in Chapter 4, partisanship is related to turnout. Strong supporters of either party are more likely to vote than weak supporters, and independents who lean toward a party are more likely to vote than independents without partisan leanings. Republicans are somewhat more likely to vote than Democrats. Although partisanship influences whether people go to the polls, it is more strongly related to *how* people vote.

Table 8-4 reports the percentage of white major party voters who voted for the Democratic candidate across all categories of partisanship since 1952.[17] Clearly, there is a strong relationship between partisan affiliation and choice of candidate. In every election except 1972, the Democratic nominee has received more than 80 percent of the vote of strong Democrats and majority support from both weak Democratic partisans and independent leaners. In 1992, these figures were as high as—or even slightly higher than—in the Democratic landslide of 1964, and higher than in any other election in this period. Since 1952, strong Republicans had given the Democratic candidate less than one vote in ten. In 1988, more of the weak Republicans and independents who leaned

1970	1972	1974	1976	1978	1980	1982	1984	1986	1988	1990	1992
41	36	40	34	37	45	53	32	42	39	40	40
34	31	26	36	29	27	26	31	30	24	23	24
7	8	15	14	15	9	12	14	12	18	16	14
12	12	12	8	9	7	5	11	7	6	8	12
1	3	—c	1	2	3	1	6	2	5	7	3
4	4	—c	2	3	2	2	1	2	5	3	3
0	4	3	2	3	3	0	2	2	1	2	2
1	2	4	1	2	4	1	2	2	3	2	2
100	100	100	99	100	100	100	99	99	101	101	100
(157)	(267)	(224)b	(290)b	(230)	(187)	(148)	(247)	(322)	(267)	(270)	(317)b

toward the Republican party voted for Dukakis than had for Mondale, but, even so, only about one in seven voted Democratic. In 1992, Clinton won an even larger percentage of the two-party vote from these Republicans. The pure independent vote, which fluctuates substantially, has tended to be Republican. John F. Kennedy won 50 percent of that vote in 1960, but Clinton won nearly two-thirds of the pure independents' two-party votes in 1992, short only of Johnson's three in four in 1964. Thus, at least among major party voters, Clinton won because he held his own party identifiers, carried the vote of the pure independents handily, and even did better than usual among independents who lean toward the GOP and among weak Republican identifiers. Still, the strength of the association between partisanship and the votes cast by major party voters was as strong as usual.

Among whites, then, partisanship leads to loyalty in voting. Between 1964 and 1980, the relationship between party identification and the vote was declining, but in 1984, the relationship between party identification and the presidential vote was higher than in any of the five elections from 1964 through 1980.[18] The relationship remained strong in 1988, and it was strong in 1992, at least among major party voters. Nonetheless, the partisan basis of the vote in congressional elections remained weaker than it had been in the past (see Chapter 10). Thus, the question of whether the parties are gathering new strength or whether they are weaker than in the 1950s and early 1960s cannot be answered from the 1992 election data.

Partisanship is related to the way people vote. The question, therefore, is why do partisans support their party's candidates? As we shall see, party identification affects behavior because it helps structure (and, according to Fiorina, is structured by) the way voters view both policies and performance.

Policy Preferences and Performance Evaluations

In their study of voting in the 1948 election, Bernard R. Berelson, Paul F. Lazarsfeld, and William N. McPhee discovered that Democratic voters attributed to their nominee, incumbent Harry S Truman, positions on key issues that were consistent with their own beliefs—whether those beliefs were liberal, moderate, or conservative.[19] Similarly, Republicans tended to see their nominee, Gov. Thomas E. Dewey of New York, as taking whatever positions they preferred. Since then, research has emphasized the roles of party identification in the projection onto the preferred candidate of positions similar to the voter's own views and in influencing policy preferences in the public.[20] We use four examples to illustrate the strong relationship between partisan affiliation and perceptions, preferences, and evaluations of candidates as well as other election-specific factors.

First, most partisans evaluate the job done by a president of their party more highly than do independents and, especially, more highly than do those who identify with the other party. Figure 8-1 shows the percentage of each of the seven partisan groups that approves of the way the incumbent has handled his job as president (as a proportion of those approving or disapproving) in the last six presidential elections. Strong Republicans have given overwhelming approval to all Republican incumbents, and even three of four strong Democrats gave their approval to the generally unpopular Carter presidency in 1980. Similarly, strong partisans generally give low approval ratings to incumbents of the opposite party. The other two Republican categories had given very high levels of approval to Republicans; in 1992 most, but substantially fewer than in the past, approved of Bush. A majority of weak, but not of independent, Democrats approved of Carter in 1980, but that percentage was lower than the percentage who approved of Nixon in 1972 and the same as that of those who approved of Ford in 1976. Only in 1992 were weak Democrats heavily disapproving of the incumbent. Independents who lean Democratic have not been particularly approving of any incumbent, with only Nixon being approved of by a majority of them; Carter and

Table 8-4 Percentage of White Major Party Voters Who Voted Democratic for President, by Party Identification, 1952-1992

Party Identification	1952	1956	1960	1964	1968	1972	1976	1980	1984	1988	1992
Strong Democrat	82	85	91	94	89	66	88	87	88	93	96
Weak Democrat	61	63	70	81	66	44	72	59	63	68	80
Independent, leans Democratic	60	65	89	89	62	58	73	57	77	86	92
Independent, no partisan leanings	18	15	50	75	28	26	41	23	21	35	63
Independent, leans Republican	7	6	13	25	5	11	15	13	5	13	14
Weak Republican	4	7	11	40	10	9	22	5	6	16	18
Strong Republican	2	—[a]	2	9	3	2	3	4	2	2	2

Note: To approximate the numbers upon which these percentages are based, see Table 8-2. Actual *N*s will be smaller than those that can be derived from Table 8-2 because respondents who did not vote (or who voted for a minor party) have been excluded from these calculations. Numbers also will be lower since the voting report is provided in the postelection interviews that usually contain about 10 percent fewer respondents than the preelection interviews in which party identification is measured.

[a] Less than 1 percent.

Ford were approved of by only slightly less than a majority. In 1992, only three in ten weak Democrats approved of Bush's performance. In every case, each Democratic category, including leaners, is very different from the comparable Republican category. Approval ratings, that is, are heavily partisan. The pure independents had favored the Republican incumbents on this measure until 1992, and large majorities gave their approval even to the least popular of the Republican incumbents, Ford. Bush, however, was approved of by barely three in ten pure independents, about the same low proportion as approved of Carter in 1980. Overall, partisanship is clearly not directly translated into approval or disapproval (for instance, weak Democrats consistently give higher marks to Republican incumbents than do independents who lean toward the Democratic party), but it is closely related to it.

Second, the relationship between partisanship and evaluation of presidential performance can be extended to show a strong relationship between party loyalties and approval of Reagan's handling of the economy in the 1984 and 1988 surveys, and Bush's handling of the economy in the 1992 survey.[21] Table 8-5 shows this distribution for all seven partisan categories.[22]

In 1984 and 1988, over three-quarters of each of the three Republican groups approved of Reagan's handling of the economy, while over half—and often over two-thirds—of each of the three Democratic groups disapproved. In 1984, the pure independents gave very strong approval to Reagan, and, while the level of approval declined in 1988, a clear majority of independents approved of his handling of the economy that year. In 1992, the situation altered dramatically. Over nine in ten of each of the three Democratic groups and the pure independents disapproved of Bush's handling of the economy. Even two in three weak and independent-leaning Republicans disapproved, while one in three strong Republicans did. Thus, in 1988, Bush was left with a legacy of generalized approval of Reagan among Republicans and independents, and this approval was even more important because there was widespread support for Reagan's handling of the economy. In 1992, Bush's own legacy was one of sharp disapproval, except among strong Republicans, of his handling of this critical area.

Third, partisans' policy preferences tend to put them closer to the policy positions of their party's nominee. In Table 8-6 we present the relationship between partisan affiliation and our balance of issues measure, which summarizes the overall Democratic or Republican leanings of each respondent on the issue scale questions analyzed in Chapter 6.[23] As we saw, these issues favored the Republicans in 1972, 1976, and 1980, but have worked slightly to the Democrats' favor in 1984 and 1988. The same was true for 1992, although the reader must remember that the evaluation for 1992 is based on a smaller set of issue

Figure 8-1 Approval of Incumbent's Handling of Job by Party Identification, 1972-1992 (in percentages)

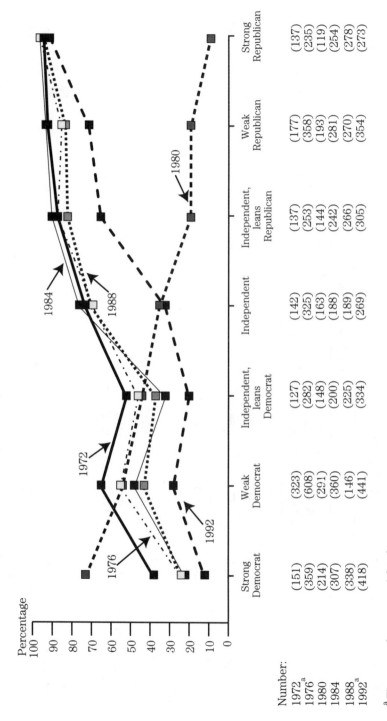

Number:	Strong Democrat	Weak Democrat	Independent, leans Democrat	Independent	Independent, leans Republican	Weak Republican	Strong Republican
1972	(151)	(323)	(127)	(142)	(137)	(177)	(137)
1976[a]	(359)	(608)	(282)	(325)	(253)	(358)	(235)
1980	(214)	(291)	(148)	(163)	(144)	(193)	(119)
1984	(307)	(360)	(200)	(188)	(242)	(281)	(254)
1988	(338)	(146)	(225)	(189)	(266)	(270)	(278)
1992[a]	(418)	(441)	(334)	(269)	(305)	(354)	(273)

[a] These numbers are weighted.

Table 8-5 Approval of Incumbent's Handling of the Economy Among Partisan Groups, 1984-1992 (in percentages)

	Party Identification							
	Strong Democrat	Weak Democrat	Independent, leans Democratic	Independent	Independent, leans Republican	Weak Republican	Strong Republican	Total
1984								
Approve	17	41	32	68	84	86	95	58
Disapprove	83	59	68	32	16	14	5	42
Total percent	100	100	100	100	100	100	100	100
(N)	(309)	(367)	(207)	(179)	(245)	(277)	(249)	(1,833)
1988								
Approve	19	35	32	57	76	79	92	54
Disapprove	81	65	68	43	24	21	8	46
Total percent	100	100	100	100	100	100	100	100
(N)	(337)	(332)	(229)	(185)	(262)	(262)	(269)	(1,876)
1992[a]								
Approve	3	9	6	9	31	34	66	20
Disapprove	97	91	94	91	69	66	34	80
Total percent	100	100	100	100	100	100	100	100
(N)	(425)	(445)	(340)	(267)	(310)	(347)	(266)	(2,401)

[a] Numbers are weighted.

scales, and therefore is not easily comparable to the results for the other years.

As the table shows, there is a clear, if moderately strong, relationship between partisanship and the balance of issues measure in the last four elections, and there was a similar relationship in 1972 and 1976. Until 1984 the relationship had been stronger among the Republicans than among the Democrats (the 1980 data in Table 8-5 are similar to those for the two preceding elections). But, in 1984 and 1988, the relationship was, if anything, stronger among the Democrats than among the Republicans. The reason for this change is very likely the change in political context. In 1980, for example, most people, Democrats as well as Republicans, were closer to the median position of Reagan than to Carter on such important issues as defense spending and cutting income taxes. Reagan pushed greatly increased defense spending and his income tax cuts through Congress in his first term, and he slowed the increases in spending for many domestic programs. By 1984, then, the public no longer favored as great an increase in defense spending and were more amenable to increased spending on domestic programs. These issues tended to divide the electorate along party lines, and in the last three elections Democrats became closer to their party's candidate than to the Republican candidate. The result is a sharper and more balanced relationship between party identification and the balance of issues measures. With the poorer measure of issues in 1992, far more fall within the neutral category, and very few were closer to the Republican incumbent. That one in four were closer to Clinton, however, demonstrates the probability of a partisan cast to prospective issues in 1992. And there is a steady decrease in the percentage closer to Clinton as one moves across the various partisan categories from the strong Democrats, through independents, to strong Republicans.

Finally, we find a strong relationship between party identification and our summary measure of retrospective evaluations in the last five elections.[24] Table 8-7 shows the basic relationships from 1976 through 1992, collapsing the summary retrospective measure into the three categories of pro-Democratic, neutral, and pro-Republican. In all years until 1992, a majority in each Republican category tended to evaluate Republican performance favorably. Even in 1976, when only about one respondent in three was favorable to the Republicans, more than 60 percent of the Republicans were favorable. And in 1976, 1984, and 1988, more than three of five Democratic identifiers assessed the Democratic party favorably. In 1980 only 20 percent of the electorate made favorable assessments of Democratic performance; but among all Democratic identifiers, 36 percent did, and 45 percent of strong Democrats did so. In 1992, no fewer than four out of five in each of the three Democratic identifying groups were pro-Democratic in their retrospective evalua-

Table 8-6 Balance of Issues Positions Among Partisan Groups, 1976-1992 (in percentages)

				Party Identification				
Issue Positions Closer to:	Strong Democrat	Weak Democrat	Independent, Leans Democrat	Independent	Independent, Leans Republican	Weak Republican	Strong Republican	Total
1976								
Democratic candidate	28	27	22	15	12	9	3	18
Neutral[a]	21	26	37	29	27	23	27	29
Republican candidate	39	47	40	55	61	67	69	53
Total percent	99	100	99	99	100	99	99	100
(N)	(422)	(655)	(336)	(416)	(277)	(408)	(254)	(2,778)
1980								
Democratic candidate	26	23	27	20	12	10	9	19
Neutral[a]	34	37	33	43	40	43	31	37
Republican candidate	40	40	40	37	48	48	60	43
Total percent	100	100	100	100	100	101	100	99
(N)	(245)	(317)	(161)	(176)	(150)	(202)	(127)	(1,378)
1984								
Democratic candidate	57	49	59	35	23	29	14	39
Neutral[a]	32	37	28	48	46	40	39	38
Republican candidate	11	14	13	17	32	32	47	23
Total percent	100	100	100	100	101	101	100	100
(N)	(331)	(390)	(215)	(213)	(248)	(295)	(256)	(1,948)
1988								
Democratic candidate	49	36	50	33	21	21	11	32
Neutral[a]	34	40	38	48	46	43	35	40
Republican candidate	17	24	12	19	33	36	53	29

Total percent	100	100	100	100	100	100	99	101
(N)	(355)	(359)	(240)	(215)	(270)	(281)	(279)	(1,999)

1992

Democratic candidate	40	36	30	26	13	13	9	25
Neutral[a]	55	57	65	70	74	77	74	67
Republican candidate	5	7	4	5	13	11	17	9
Total percent	100	100	99	101	100	101	100	101
(N)[b]	(380)	(389)	(313)	(235)	(283)	(335)	(238)	(2,192)

[a] The neutral category consists of scores of −1, 0, or +1 on the full measure, while the Republican [Democratic] category is any score greater than +1 [less than −1] on the full measure.
[b] Numbers are weighted.

Table 8-7 Retrospective Evaluations Among Partisan Groups, 1976-1992 (in percentages)

Summary Measure of Retrospective Evaluations	Party Identification							
	Strong Democrat	Weak Democrat	Independent, Leans Democrat	Independent	Independent, Leans Republican	Weak Republican	Strong Republican	Total
1976								
Democratic	80	53	62	39	16	19	6	42
Neutral[a]	11	23	24	28	28	25	23	23
Republican	10	24	15	33	56	57	71	35
Total percent	101	100	101	100	100	101	100	100
(N)[b]	(314)	(535)	(249)	(293)	(238)	(314)	(206)	(2,149)
1980								
Democratic	45	29	18	11	8	7	4	20
Neutral[a]	26	21	25	22	8	9	2	17
Republican	29	50	57	68	85	84	93	62
Total percent	100	100	100	101	101	100	99	99
(N)	(299)	(294)	(157)	(160)	(144)	(197)	(123)	(1,304)
1984								
Democratic	77	54	65	27	9	9	5	37
Neutral[a]	12	17	13	22	15	18	5	14
Republican	12	29	21	52	76	73	90	49
Total percent	101	100	99	101	100	100	100	100
(N)	(303)	(356)	(197)	(181)	(241)	(270)	(239)	(1,787)
1988								
Democratic	79	61	64	32	20	17	6	42
Neutral[a]	11	19	24	34	32	28	19	23
Republican	10	20	12	35	48	55	75	36

Total percent	100	100	100	101	100	100	100	101
(N)	(287)	(305)	(199)	(167)	(228)	(239)	(245)	(1,670)
1992								
Democratic	90	80	85	72	39	32	12	61
Neutral[a]	7	12	8	16	28	29	26	17
Republican	3	9	7	12	32	39	62	21
Total percent	100	101	100	100	99	100	100	99
(N)[b]	(339)	(340)	(267)	(207)	(245)	(268)	(221)	(1,886)

[a] The neutral category is the same as that for the full scale, while the Democratic [Republican] category is the combination of all three Democratic [Republican] categories on the full scale.
[b] Numbers are weighted.

tions, while three in four of the pure independents were. Among the independents who lean Republican and the weak Republicans, about one in three held pro-Republican retrospective evaluations, while three in five strong Republicans did.

We have seen that both party identification and retrospective evaluations are related to the vote, but the two are also strongly related to each other. Do they still both contribute independently to the vote? The answer, as can be seen in Table 8-8, is yes. In this table, we have examined the combined impact of party identification and retrospective evaluations upon voting choices in the last five presidential elections. To simplify the presentation we have regrouped party identification into the three basic categories: strong and weak Republicans, all independents, and strong and weak Democrats. We also present the results for the three basic categories of our summary measure of retrospective evaluations.

Table 8-8 shows the percentage of major party voters who voted Republican by both party identification and retrospective evaluations. Reading across the row reveals that for all elections, retrospective evaluations are strongly related to the vote, regardless of the respondent's partisanship. Reading down each column shows that in all elections, party identification is related to the vote, regardless of the respondent's retrospective evaluations. Moreover, party identification and retrospective evaluations have a combined impact upon how people voted. For example, in 1992 among Republican identifiers with pro-Republican evaluations, 99 percent voted for Bush; among Democratic identifiers with pro-Democratic evaluations, only 4 percent did. Note as well the overall similarity of the 1984, 1988, and 1992 portions of the table. The most important reason that the 1988 election was a smaller Republican victory than 1984 had been appears to be that retrospective evaluations in the electorate were less positive, while the most important reason for Clinton's victory in 1992 was the decidedly negative retrospective evaluations of the public.

In sum, partisanship appears to affect the way voters evaluate incumbents and their performance. Positions on issues are a bit different. Although partisans are likely to be closer to their party's nominee and his policy platform, and although this seems to be increasingly so, the connection of partisanship with comparisons of partisans' preferences with candidates' positions on issues is less clear. Policy-related evaluations in general are influenced partly by history and political memory and partly by the candidate's campaign strategies. Partisan attachments, then, limit the ability of candidates to control their fate in the electorate, but they are not entirely rigid. Candidates may be fairly tightly constrained by prior performance, especially that of the incumbent, as seen in partisan terms, but they are less limited by partisanship in their ability to gain support based on issues.

Table 8-8   Percentage of Major Party Voters Who Voted for the Republican Candidate, by Party Identification and Summary Measure of Retrospective Evaluations, 1976-1992

Party Identification[a]	Summary Measure of Retrospective Evaluations							
	Republican		Neutral[b]		Democratic		Total	
	%	(N)	%	(N)	%	(N)	%	(N)
A. Voted for Ford, 1976[c]								
Republican	96	(269)	90	(98)	35	(54)	87	(421)
Independent	85	(183)	73	(133)	16	(187)	56	(503)
Democratic	53	(111)	30	(96)	5	(404)	18	(611)
Total	84	(563)	65	(327)	11	(645)	49	(1,535)
B. Voted for Reagan, 1980								
Republican	100	(217)	75	(12)	33	(12)	95	(241)
Independent	82	(183)	36	(36)	24	(25)	69	(244)
Democratic	51	(135)	6	(78)	7	(140)	24	(353)
Total	81	(535)	21	(126)	11	(177)	58	(838)
C. Voted for Reagan, 1984								
Republican	99	(344)	86	(42)	39	(18)	95	(404)
Independent	91	(230)	77	(62)	10	(110)	67	(402)
Democratic	72	(97)	32	(62)	5	(333)	22	(492)
Total	93	(671)	63	(166)	8	(461)	59	(1,298)
D. Voted for Bush, 1988								
Republican	97	(277)	93	(84)	46	(37)	91	(398)
Independent	86	(124)	64	(94)	15	(131)	54	(349)
Democratic	67	(54)	27	(63)	5	(296)	16	(413)
Total	91	(455)	64	(241)	11	(464)	53	(1,160)
E. Voted for Bush, 1992								
Republican	99	(187)	83	(87)	57	(61)	89	(335)
Independent	86	(72)	83	(56)	15	(233)	40	(362)
Democratic	58	(24)	32	(41)	4	(422)	9	(487)
Total	92	(282)	75	(185)	12	(717)	41	(1,184)

Note: Numbers in parentheses are totals upon which percentages are based.

[a] Democratic (Republican) identifiers were those classified as strong and weak Democrats (Republicans). Independents include those who lean toward either party and "pure" independents.

[b] The neutral category is the same as that for the full scale, while the Democratic (Republican) category is the combination of all three Democratic (Republican) categories on the full scale.

[c] Numbers are weighted.

The Perot Candidacy

Perot differed from the other third-party and independent candidates who had enjoyed an appreciable level of success in this century. Theodore Roosevelt in 1912, Robert M. LaFollette in 1924, J. Strom Thurmond in 1948, George C. Wallace in 1968, and John B. Anderson in 1980 had all been notable figures within the two-party system before they launched their presidential candidacies. Perot was not. And, unlike his predecessors in 1968 and 1980, for whom there is survey evidence available, he did not lose support over the course of the general election campaign. He won the support of nearly one presidential voter in five, and he remains a considerable political force. In Chapter 11 we discuss how he may influence the party system. Having little information about the electorate's attitudes toward and perceptions of Perot in 1992, we cannot directly measure the source of his surprising strength in that election. We can, however, examine the views of those who voted for him.

In Table 8-9, we report how whites voted for the three candidates in 1992 according to their partisan identification, along with comparisons among the white partisan groups in voting for the three major contenders in 1968 and in 1980. Support for Wallace, Anderson, and Perot exhibits two basic similarities with regard to partisanship. First, and most important, all three drew more support from independents than from partisans. This pattern reinforces the importance of partisan loyalties for the major parties' candidates; their base of support is resistant to challenges from independent candidates as well as from the opposing party's candidates. Second, each independent candidate drew more support from those who identified with the incumbent's party than from those who were loyal to the opposition. Thus, Wallace and Anderson drew more support from Democrats than from Republicans, while Perot drew more from Republicans than from Democrats. In each case, the incumbent president was unpopular, and it seems that voters from the unpopular incumbent's party were more willing to defect, whether to the opposition party's candidate or to a more "neutral" candidate, than opposition party loyalists were to support the independent candidate.

As we saw in Chapters 6 and 7, Perot voters differ in both their issue preferences and their retrospective evaluations from Bush voters and Clinton voters. As we saw, Perot voters were more likely to think the government had done a poor job on the most important problem and thought that neither party would be better for solving that problem. While there were relatively few differences between Perot and major party voters in their assessments of their and the nation's economic performances, Perot voters were more likely to disapprove of Bush's handling of his job than were Bush voters, although they were not as

Table 8-9   How Whites Voted for President Among the Three Major Candidates, 1968, 1980, and 1992, by Party Identification (in percentages)

Party Identification	Candidate Voted For			Total Percent	(N)
	Democrat	Independent	Republican		
A. 1968	Humphrey	Wallace	Nixon		
Strong Democrat	80	10	10	100	(164)
Weak Democrat	55	17	28	100	(212)
Independent, leans Democratic	51	18	31	100	(89)
Independent, no partisan leanings	23	20	57	100	(84)
Independent, leans Republican	4	14	82	100	(101)
Weak Republican	9	8	83	100	(163)
Strong Republican	3	2	96	101	(117)
B. 1980	Carter	Anderson	Reagan		
Strong Democrat	84	3	12	99	(129)
Weak Democrat	54	9	38	101	(173)
Independent, leans Democratic	44	23	33	100	(93)
Independent, no partisan leanings	20	13	67	100	(79)
Independent, leans Republican	11	10	78	99	(106)
Weak Republican	5	9	87	101	(151)
Strong Republican	4	4	93	101	(110)
C. 1992	Clinton	Perot	Bush		
Strong Democrat	90	6	4	100	(228)[a]
Weak Democrat	65	20	16	101	(238)[a]
Independent, leans Democratic	68	26	6	100	(203)[a]
Independent, no partisan leanings	37	41	22	100	(125)[a]
Independent, leans Republican	10	29	60	99	(193)[a]
Weak Republican	14	26	61	101	(240)[a]
Strong Republican	2	11	87	100	(210)[a]

[a] Numbers are weighted.

negative as Clinton voters. Although Democrats were very negative in their summary retrospective evaluations (and Republicans were much more positive), Perot voters made up a significant proportion of those whose assessments ran from the neutral through the strongly Democratic categories. On prospective issues, Perot voters differed little from major party voters on their position on the government spending and services scale, but they were much more in favor of cutting defense spending, and they tended to oppose the government's providing jobs and a good standard of living. Thus, the average Perot voter was no closer to Clinton than the average major party voter on the first scale, closer to Clinton on the second, and farther from him on the third scale. As a result, Perot voters tended to score in the middle range ($-1, 0, +1$) on our balance of issues measure.

The partisan loyalties of Perot supporters were very different from those of Bush or Clinton supporters. This may be seen in Table 8-10, which shows the distribution of party identification among Bush, Clinton, and Perot voters. Because there are strong racial differences in partisanship, and because very few Bush or Perot voters were black, we present these results for white voters.

Half of Bush's total vote came from Republican identifiers. Three out of ten Bush voters were self-proclaimed independents, but most of these were independents who said they felt closer to the Republican party. Three out of five whites who voted for Clinton were Democratic identifiers. A third of Clinton's votes came from self-professed independents, although most of them said that they felt closer to the Democratic party. Just over a fourth of Perot's support came from Republican identifiers, but only about one out of twelve was a strong Republican. A fifth of Perot's voters were Democratic identifiers, but only one out of twenty-five Perot voters was a strong Democrat. Just over half of Perot's vote came from self-professed independents, equally divided among those who leaned Democratic, those who leaned Republican, and those who felt closer to neither party.

It thus appears that the most important characteristics of Perot voters were their relative independence of party, their dissatisfaction with the government's handling of the most important problem, and their expectation that neither major party would solve what they saw as the most important problem. In this sense, the Perot voter in 1992 stands as something of an unpredictable quantity for the future. Weakly or not at all loyal to a major party, apparently standing closer to neither party on the issues, and having been dissatisfied with the previous administration, this large bloc of voters could be wooed to Clinton's side if they view him as successful, could be wooed by the Republican nominee if they do not—or could remain with Perot if he were to run in 1996.

Table 8-10   Party Identification Among Whites, by How Voted for
President, 1992 (in percentages)

Party Identification	How Voted for President		
	Bush	Clinton	Perot
Strong Democrat	2	34	4
Weak Democrat	7	26	15
Independent, leans Democratic	2	23	17
Independent, no partisan leanings	5	8	17
Independent, leans Republican	22	3	18
Weak Republican	27	6	20
Strong Republican	34	1	8
Total percent	99	101	99
(*N*)	(531)	(600)	(306)

Note: Numbers are weighted.

Conclusion

Party loyalties affect how people vote, how they evaluate issues, and how they judge the performance of the incumbent president and his party. In recent years, research has suggested that party loyalties not only affect issue preferences, perceptions, and evaluations, but that these in turn may also affect partisanship. There is good reason to believe that the relationship between partisanship and issue preferences is more complex than any model that assumes a one-way relationship would suggest. Doubtless, evaluations of the incumbent's performance may also affect party loyalties.[25]

As we saw in this chapter, there was a substantial shift toward Republican loyalties over the 1980s, and among whites, the advantage the Democrats have enjoyed over the past four decades appears to be gone. To some extent, this shift in party loyalties must have reflected Reagan's appeal and his successful performance in office, as judged by the electorate. It also appears that Reagan was able to shift some of that appeal in Bush's direction in 1988 directly, by the connection between performance judgments and the vote, and also indirectly, through shifts in party loyalties among white Americans. And, Bush was able to lose some of the appeal he inherited by his negatively assessed performance in office, largely directly, but also indirectly, losing the slight edge in partisan loyalties the Republicans had built over the Reagan years. At the same time, the growth in independence from parties has made it possible for independent candidates to do as well as they have. Perot especially benefited from the rise in independence, as he drew heavily from the ranks of independents and came close to winning a plurality of those who were completely independent of the two major parties. It is even possible that he has contributed, or at least will contribute (should he continue as a force in electoral politics), to a further weakening of the public's attachment to the two parties.

At this point, however, it is still as true today as it was four decades ago that most Americans have a sense of identification with one or the other of the two major parties. This identification stands as a major force that connects the social affiliations of Americans with electoral politics, and it is closely related to the evaluations Americans make of the candidates, the issues, and the performance of the incumbent party in office. It thus continues to play a major role in the voting choices of most Americans.

Perhaps more than for any other recent election, our analysis presents a very simple answer to the question of why George Bush lost his bid for reelection in 1992. People were very dissatisfied with his administration. This disapproval was concentrated on his handling of the economy. His defeat was, that is, primarily a retrospective evaluation of the electorate, filtered through partisan identification, but affecting all categories of partisan identifiers, save only the relatively small number of strong Republicans. Insofar as data permit us to judge, partisan-related retrospective evaluations were used as a guide to choosing among the three major candidates, based on who (and which party) voters thought might better handle the economy. A plurality, it appears, thought that the Democratic alternative was superior. Thus, Clinton was aided by the large number of Democrats in the electorate, and their view that their party would be the best at solving that problem. All of this was accentuated by the high degree of concern expressed by the public over the economy, which accentuated Bush's greatest area of vulnerability.

In this sense, the possibility of a continuation of Perot's independent candidacy is one of the major concerns facing a Clinton reelection campaign, should he run for reelection, and facing the campaign of the Republican opponent in 1996. If one in five voters supported Perot in 1992, it is not hard to imagine that many will support him in 1996. Many of Perot's voters in 1992, and those whom he may hope to woo in 1996, also voted for candidates for other offices. And, in casting those votes they voted overwhelmingly for candidates who were Democratic or Republican—the only major options on the ballot. If Perot were to attempt to build a new major party, he would have to find some mechanism to break the stranglehold the two major parties have on access to the 535 seats in the House and Senate, something no third party has had much success with in this century. Even if a Republican wins the presidency in 1996, it is likely that he or she will face a Democratic House of Representatives. Despite substantial changes since World War II, there are somewhat more Democrats than Republicans in the electorate and there are clearly more Democrats than Republicans elected to Congress (and to most other offices). Is the very long run of Democratic majorities in the Congress a result of party-line voting for Congress or some other phenomenon? Why did the Republican presidential successes in the 1980s fail to translate into appreciable gains in Congress? To examine these questions, we turn next to congressional elections.

The 1992 Congressional Election

So far we have focused on the presidential election, the major event of the 1992 elections. But the president shares responsibility with Congress, which must enact a legislative program and approve major appointments. Having concluded our analysis of Bill Clinton's election, we now turn to the selection of the Congress that governs with him. In Part 3 we consider the selection of the 103d Congress.

There were many elections in 1992. In addition to the presidential election, there were twelve gubernatorial elections,[1] elections for thousands of state and local officials, thirty-five elections for the U.S. Senate,[2] and elections for all 435 members of the U.S. House of Representatives. Unlike the 1980 election, in which the Republicans won control of the U.S. Senate, the 1992 election held no major surprises. The Democrats had regained control of the Senate in 1986, and they held it easily during the 1988, 1990, and 1992 elections. In the 1992 Senate races, the Democrats broke even, retaining their 57 to 43 seat margin over the Republicans. Despite Bush's crushing defeat, the Republicans gained ten seats in the U.S. House, but the Democrats still held a comfortable margin of control. The Democrats won 258 seats, the Republicans won 176, and Bernard Sanders of Vermont was reelected as an independent.

By sending a Democrat to the White House, voters ended divided government, at the very least for two years. Moreover, the Democrats had now won twenty consecutive general elections for control of the U.S. House, by far the longest winning streak in U.S. electoral history. As we shall see, the Republicans got little encouragement from their small gains in the House, because they hoped that reapportionment and redistricting would lead to substantial gains. At the end of the Gulf war, they even might have dreamed of winning control of the House. Only 86 House Democrats had voted to authorize the use of force in the Gulf, and 179 had voted against. As we saw, after the Gulf war, Bush's approval rating soared, and Democrats who had opposed America's spectacular military success seemed vulnerable. Moreover, many Democrats (and many Republicans) were implicated in a scandal involving "bounced" checks at a bank run by the House of Representatives. Not only did the Republicans seem to have a string of good luck, but long-term demographic change seemed likely to help them as well. After the 1990 census, nineteen House seats were reallocated through reapportionment, and this shift seemed to favor the Republicans. Moreover, even in states that neither gained nor lost seats, congressional districts were redrawn, and the Republicans hoped to gain from redistricting as well. But Republican dreams were not to be realized.

Why were Republican gains in the House so small? Why did the Democrats once again retain control of the U.S. House? Will the end of divided government end gridlock and facilitate major policy reforms? And what are the prospects that the Republicans will end Democratic dominance of the national legislature?

Chapter 9 attempts to answer these questions by examining the election results. In 1992, only 368 incumbents sought reelection, but 325 were successful. Although 110 new members were elected to the House of Representatives, neither party was able to gain many of the seats that had been held by the other party. We examine the geographic bases of party support and show that there has been a major transformation, paralleling—though not in quite as striking a way—those we observed in presidential elections.

We examine the impact of reapportionment and redistricting and see why Republican hopes were not fulfilled. The Republicans did make some gains as a result of reapportionment and redistricting, but these gains were far smaller than they expected; we explain why. We pay special attention to the effects of scandals in the U.S. House of Representatives, in particular the House check bouncing scandal, in which forty-six sitting representatives were revealed to have written 100 or more overdrafts. We shall see that this scandal did lead to both retirements and defeats, especially in party primaries. Just over half of these forty-six members did not return to the House in the 103d Congress, although one, Barbara Boxer of California, returned to Congress as a senator. We explain why this scandal had an electoral impact, although not a major impact on the general election.

One of the major changes in the congressional races was the great increase in the representation of women and minorities. We explain why many female candidates were successful in House and Senate races, and why the minority representation, especially of African-Americans, increased.

Chapter 9 explains why incumbents usually win. Incumbency itself is a major resource, and challengers usually lack the experience and money to launch an effective campaign. Incumbents have generally been winning by increasing margins, and we discuss alternative explanations for this change. However, the trend has recently been reversed, and we discuss the reasons for this reversal.

Although the Democrats lost ten seats in the House and broke even in the Senate, their role changed dramatically because a Democrat once again controlled the White House. With a Democrat in the White House, congressional Democrats got more opportunities to enact new policies. But the Democratic House losses, though small, diminished Clinton's opportunities for influence. We attempt to assess the impact of the presidential and congressional elections upon public policy changes.

Finally, we speculate on the future of congressional elections through the beginning of the twenty-first century. As the party controlling the White House has lost strength in the House in thirty-seven of the thirty-eight midterm elections held since the Whigs first won the presidency in 1840, it seems reasonable to expect the Democrats to lose seats in 1994.[3] But how many seats are they likely to lose? We discuss several academic models that give us insight about the likely outcomes of midterm congressional elections. These models suggest that unless the economy deteriorates badly and unless Clinton's approval ratings dip to extremely low levels, the Democrats are very likely to retain control of the U.S. House and to extend their winning streak to twenty-one consecutive victories.

The battle for control of the U.S. Senate is far less predictable. Texas Republican Kay Bailey Hutchison's two-to-one victory in a special election in June 1993 to fill Lloyd Bentsen's vacated Senate seat boosted Republican hopes. But the Democrats still hold a fifty-six to forty-four margin over the Republicans, and because there is a Democratic vice president, the Republicans would need to win fifty-one seats to control the Senate.

Chapter 9 ends by explaining the reasons for Democratic dominance of U.S. House elections. Although the Republicans often argue that they are underrepresented because of gerrymandering by Democratic state legislatures and Democratic governors, we will show that their claim is unfounded. We examine the pattern of open-seat races—that is, races in which there is no incumbent running—to explore further the reasons for the Democratic pattern of House success. We also explain why the end of divided government may be a liability for congressional Democrats.

Chapter 10 explores how voters make congressional voting decisions—one of the most exciting and rapidly growing areas of research since the National Election Studies (NES) survey introduced new questions in 1978 to study congressional voting behavior. Because only a third of the Senate seats are contested in each election, our analysis focuses on the House. Chapter 10 examines how social factors influence voters' choices and compares the relationship of these factors in congressional and presidential voting. The effects of issues, party loyalties, and incumbency upon voters' choices are also assessed. We examine the ways in which congressional voting can be seen as a referendum on performance of a particular member of Congress, and we show how it can be viewed as a referendum on the president's performance. We attempt to determine whether Bill Clinton had "coattails," that is to say, whether Democrats were elected to Congress because of his presidential victory. We show that support for Clinton did have some drawing power for other Democrats, but that this effect was not very strong. Last, we present additional evidence to document the importance of campaign spending and we make further observations on the advantages of incumbency.

Chapter 9

Candidates and Outcomes

In the 1992 presidential election, the voters endorsed change by choosing the Democratic challenger over the Republican incumbent. The 1992 elections also resulted in considerable change in Congress, although only a small proportion of that change derived from the defeat of congressional incumbents in the general election. Despite the large number of new members, however, the partisan control of Congress remained unaltered.[1] The combined effect of the congressional and presidential elections was to bring an end to divided government for the first time since Ronald Reagan defeated Jimmy Carter in 1980.

In this chapter we shall look in some detail at the pattern of congressional outcomes for 1992 and how they compared with outcomes of previous years. We seek to explain why the 1992 results took the shape they did—what factors affected the success of incumbents seeking to return and what permitted some challengers to run better than others. We also discuss the likely impact of the election results on the politics of the 103d Congress. Finally, we consider the implications of the 1992 results for the 1994 midterm elections, and for subsequent elections through the beginning of the next century.

Election Outcomes in 1992

Patterns of Incumbency Success

Most races involve incumbents and most incumbents are reelected. This generalization, however, was less true in 1992 than it has been in any election for some time. Table 9-1 presents information on election outcomes for House and Senate races involving incumbents between 1954 and 1992.[2] During this period, an average of 93 percent of the House incumbents and 82 percent of the Senate incumbents who sought reelection were successful.

These data show that the 1992 results were atypical on a number of counts. For example, while the rate of reelection for senators was very close to the average rate for the twenty-election series, the House results deviated more. The reelection rate of 88.3 percent represented only the fifth time since 1954 that incumbent representatives' success had fallen below 90 percent, and it was at the lowest level since the 1974 election, which followed the Watergate scandal. Also in 1992, an unusually low number of representatives sought reelection. Previously the lowest number of incumbents running had been 382 in 1978; in 1992 only 368 ran. Finally, unlike the usual pattern, almost as many incumbents were defeated in primaries as in the general election. As we will discuss more fully below, these unusual patterns stemmed from a confluence of circumstances that jointly undermined the reelection prospects of many representatives, including scandals in the House and the redrawing of the boundaries of congressional districts after the 1990 census.

During the period covered by Table 9-1, House and Senate outcomes have sometimes followed different patterns. Between 1968 and 1980, House incumbents were notably more successful than Senate incumbents, and the rates of success of the two groups were moving in opposite directions. In the three elections between 1976 and 1980, House incumbents' success averaged more than 90 percent, while for the Senate the rate was only about 60 percent. In more recent elections, however, the patterns became much more similar, and in the two most recent years the respective results differed by no more than a few percentage points.

It appears that the variations in the comparative results from the two bodies are the consequence of at least two factors, the first primarily statistical and the second substantive. In the first place, House elections routinely involve about 400 incumbents, and Senate races usually involve fewer than 30. A comparatively small number of cases is more likely to produce volatile results over time. Thus, the proportion of successful Senate incumbents tends to jump around more than that for the House. Second, Senate races are more likely to be vigorously contested than House races. In 1990, for example, eighty House incumbents—or about 20 percent—had no opponent from the other major party, and a large share of the remainder had opponents who were inexperienced or underfunded or both. (As we will see, in 1992 the proportion of vigorously contested House races was higher than the norm.) In 1990 Senate races, by contrast, all but three of the thirty incumbents had major party opponents. Most of these opponents had previously won elective office and were reasonably well funded. Thus in recent years, a large number of

Table 9-1 House and Senate Incumbents and Election Outcomes, 1954-1992

Year	Incumbents Running (N)	Primary Defeats (N)	Primary Defeats (%)	General Election Defeats (N)	General Election Defeats (%)	Reelected (N)	Reelected (%)
House							
1954	(407)	(6)	1.5	(22)	5.4	(379)	93.1
1956	(410)	(6)	1.5	(15)	3.7	(389)	94.9
1958	(394)	(3)	0.8	(37)	9.4	(354)	89.8
1960	(405)	(5)	1.2	(25)	6.2	(375)	92.6
1962	(402)	(12)	3.0	(22)	5.5	(368)	91.5
1964	(397)	(8)	2.0	(45)	11.3	(344)	86.6
1966	(411)	(8)	1.9	(41)	10.0	(362)	88.1
1968	(409)	(4)	1.0	(9)	2.2	(396)	96.8
1970	(401)	(10)	2.5	(12)	3.0	(379)	94.5
1972	(392)	(13)	3.3	(13)	3.3	(366)	93.4
1974	(391)	(8)	2.0	(40)	10.2	(343)	87.7
1976	(383)	(3)	0.8	(12)	3.1	(368)	96.1
1978	(382)	(5)	1.3	(19)	5.0	(358)	93.7
1980	(398)	(6)	1.5	(31)	7.8	(361)	90.7
1982	(393)	(10)	2.5	(29)	7.4	(354)	90.1
1984	(411)	(3)	0.7	(16)	3.9	(392)	95.4
1986	(393)	(2)	0.5	(6)	1.5	(385)	98.0
1988	(409)	(1)	0.2	(6)	1.5	(402)	98.3
1990	(407)	(1)	0.2	(15)	3.7	(391)	96.1
1992	(368)	(20)	5.4	(23)	6.3	(325)	88.3
Senate							
1954	(27)	(0)	—	(4)	15	(23)	85
1956	(30)	(0)	—	(4)	13	(26)	87
1958	(26)	(0)	—	(9)	35	(17)	65
1960	(28)	(0)	—	(1)	4	(27)	96
1962	(30)	(0)	—	(3)	10	(27)	90
1964	(30)	(0)	—	(2)	7	(28)	93
1966	(29)	(2)	7	(1)	3	(26)	90
1968	(28)	(4)	14	(4)	14	(20)	71
1970	(28)	(1)	4	(3)	11	(24)	86
1972	(26)	(1)	4	(5)	19	(20)	77
1974	(26)	(1)	4	(2)	8	(23)	88
1976	(25)	(0)	—	(9)	36	(16)	64
1978	(22)	(1)	5	(6)	27	(15)	68
1980	(29)	(4)	14	(9)	31	(16)	55
1982	(30)	(0)	—	(2)	7	(28)	93
1984	(29)	(0)	—	(3)	10	(26)	90
1986	(27)	(0)	—	(6)	22	(21)	78
1988	(26)	(0)	—	(3)	12	(23)	88
1990	(30)	(0)	—	(1)	3	(29)	97
1992	(27)	(1)	4	(3)	11	(23)	85

House races have involved incumbents who were virtually guaranteed reelection. Had all House races been as heavily contested as Senate races were in the late 1970s, the rate of defeat of House incumbents might have been substantially higher. We will consider the substantive point again later in this chapter.

We next turn from the consideration of incumbency to party. Figure 9-1 portrays the proportion of seats in the House and Senate held by the Democrats after each election since 1952. In House elections, high rates of incumbent participation, coupled with the high rates of incumbent success, led to fairly stable partisan control. Most important, the Democrats have won a majority in the House in every election since 1954, and have now won twenty consecutive general elections. This is by far the longest period of dominance of the House by the same party in American history.[3] The Democrats' share of the House seats has been quite stable for the last six elections, varying only between 58 and 62 percent. In the more volatile Senate, however, partisan change has been greater (46 to 57 percent Democratic). Moreover, there have been two shifts in Senate control over the last twelve years (with the Republicans gaining a majority in 1980 and the Democrats regaining power in 1986). These patterns suggest that although Democratic control of the Senate may not be assured in the near future, the Democrats are very likely to retain control of the House.

The combined effect of party and incumbency in the general election of 1992 is shown in Table 9-2. Overall, the Democrats won 60 percent of the races for House seats and 57 percent of the Senate races. Despite the problems of scandals and redistricting, House incumbents of both parties who reached the general election were very successful, and Senate incumbents did almost as well. In contests for open seats, the Democrats achieved substantial success in both houses, winning more than 60 percent of the races. Since, however, most of the vacancies resulted from the departures of Democrats, this success permitted the party basically to hold its ground.

The important point from these results is that neither party in either house was able to make significant inroads into the other party's seats. By historical standards, one might argue that this was a poor showing for the Democrats because the party regained control of the presidency from the GOP, and that a party that regains the White House usually makes congressional gains. But this has not been true for Democratic victors since Franklin D. Roosevelt regained the presidency for the Democrats in 1932. With his victory, the Democrats gained ninety-seven House seats. But when John F. Kennedy regained the White House for the Democrats in 1960, the Democrats lost twenty House seats, and when Jimmy Carter regained it in 1976, the Democrats gained only a single seat. The reason for the 1960 and 1976 results is similar in both cases: the Democrats were

Figure 9-1 Democratic Share of Seats in the House and Senate, 1953-1993 (in percentages)

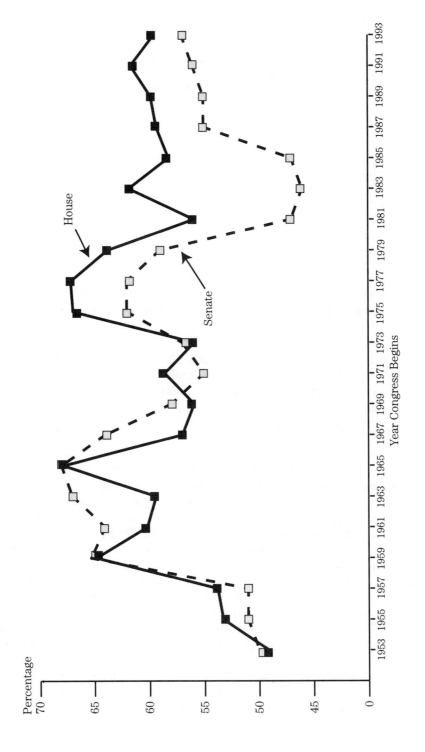

Table 9-2   House and Senate General Election Outcomes, by Party and Incumbency, 1992 (in percentages)

	Democratic Incumbent	No Incumbent	Republican Incumbent	Total
House				
Democrats	94	63	5	60
Republicans	6	37	95	40
Total Percent	100	100	100	100
(*N*)	(208)[a]	(91)	(132)[b]	(435)
Senate				
Democrats	87	67	9	57
Republicans	13	33	91	41
Total Percent	100	100	100	100
(*N*)	(15)	(9)	(11)	(35)

[a]Excludes three Democratic incumbents who were defeated by Republican incumbents.

[b]Excludes one Republican incumbent who was defeated by a Democratic incumbent.

not in a position to gain significantly because they already held a substantial majority of seats. The Republicans usually have had 50 to 100 percent more seats from which to make gains when the partisan tide swings in their direction.

Regional Bases of Power

The geographic pattern of 1992 outcomes in the House and Senate can be seen in the partisan breakdowns by region in Table 9-3.[4] For comparison we also present breakdowns for 1979 (before the Republicans took control of the Senate in Reagan's first election) and for 1953 (the last Congress in which the Republicans controlled both chambers). In the House, since the last Congress in which the Democrats held the presidency, the GOP has gained ground in every region except the Midwest. Ironically, in that region—which was historically the Republican heartland and where their party held 76 percent of the seats in 1953—Republicans lost some ground. Overall, the Democrats won a majority of seats in every region in 1992.

The pattern is only slightly different when we consider the Senate. Between 1979 and 1993 the Republicans have made small gains in the West, South, and border states, while they lost some ground in the East and Midwest. After the 1992 elections, the Democrats controlled a majority of seats in all regions but the West, where Republican strength in the mountain states yields them numerical dominance.

Table 9-3   Party Shares of Regional Delegations in the House and
Senate, 1953, 1979, and 1993

	1953			1979			1993		
Region	Demo-crats (%)	Repub-licans (%)	(N)	Demo-crats (%)	Repub-licans (%)	(N)	Demo-crats (%)	Repub-licans (%)	(N)
House									
East	35	65	(116)	66	34	(105)	57	43	(89)
Midwest	23	76	(118)[a]	51	49	(111)	57	43	(96)
West	33	67	(57)	62	38	(76)	59	41	(93)
South	94	6	(106)	71	29	(108)	62	38	(125)
Border	68	32	(38)	77	23	(35)	66	34	(32)
Total	49	51	(435)	64	36	(435)	60	40	(435)
Senate									
East	25	75	(20)	55	45	(20)	60	40	(20)
Midwest	14	86	(22)	59	41	(22)	68	32	(22)
West	45	55	(22)	46	54	(26)	42	58	(26)
South	100	0	(22)	73	27	(22)	59	41	(22)
Border	70	30	(10)	70	30	(10)	60	40	(10)
Total	49	51	(96)	59	41	(100)	57	43	(100)

[a] Includes one independent.

The 1993 results are even more interesting when viewed from the longer historical perspective. In 1953 there were sharp regional differences in party representation in both houses. In the intervening years, these differences have greatly diminished. The most obvious changes occurred in the South. The percentage of southern seats in the House held by Democrats declined from 94 percent in 1953 to 62 percent in 1993. In 1953 the Democrats held all twenty-two southern Senate seats, but in 1993 they controlled only thirteen of those seats. While the regional shift is not as dramatic as in presidential elections (see Chapter 3), the South is no longer a guaranteed Democratic stronghold for congressional candidates.

This change in the partisan share of the South's seats in Congress has had an important impact on that region's influence within the two parties. The South used to be the backbone of Democratic congressional representation. This, and the tendency of southern members of Congress to build seniority, gave southerners disproportionate power within the Democratic party in Congress. Because of the decline in Democratic electoral success within the region, the numerical strength of southern Democrats in Congress has waned. In 1947, when the Republicans were in control of both houses of Congress, southerners accounted for about half of the Democratic seats in the House and Senate. During the late 1940s and the 1950s, southern strength was fairly stable at over 40 percent. It then began to decline, and by the 1970s it had stabilized again at between 25 and 30 percent of the Democratic seats in Congress.

A consideration of the South's share of Republican congressional representation presents the reverse picture. Minuscule at the end of World War II, it steadily began to grow, reaching about 20 percent in 1980 and 27 percent in 1992. As a consequence of these changes, southern influence has declined in the Democratic party and grown in the GOP. Because southerners of both parties tend to be on average somewhat more conservative than their colleagues from other regions, these shifts in strength have tended to make the Democratic party in Congress more liberal and the Republican party more conservative.[5]

Other regional changes since 1953, while not as striking as those in the South, are also significant. In the 1953 House, the Republicans controlled the East and West by two-to-one margins, and the Midwest by a margin of three to one; in 1993, they controlled none of these regions, and the party proportions were nearly identical among the three. In the 1953 Senate, the Republicans had a massive lead in the East and Midwest and a slight lead in the West; by 1993, the Democrats had a majority of the seats in the East and Midwest, although party control was more evenly balanced, and the GOP had gained slightly in the West. On balance, what we have witnessed in the past four decades might be termed the "deregionalization" of congressional elections. The Congress of 1993 is regionally homogeneous with regard to partisan representation when compared with the Congress of 1953.

The Impact of Reapportionment and Redistricting

As we have noted, there were a number of significant influences on the congressional elections of 1992. One of these was reapportionment and redistricting. Reapportionment is the process by which the number of House seats to which each state is entitled is determined after the decennial census figures become available. By law, states with more than one representative must be divided into congressional districts, and each district elects a single member of the House. The number of House seats has been fixed at 435 since early in this century, so as population change occurs unevenly across states between censuses, the seats must be redistributed among the states after the census figures become available.[6] After the 1990 count, eight states in the South and West gained nineteen seats, while thirteen states—mostly in the East and Midwest—lost the same number. The big winners were California, Florida, and Texas (with gains of seven, four, and three seats, respectively), while the worst losers were New York (which lost three seats) and Illinois, Michigan, Ohio, and Pennsylvania (which lost two each). The Republican party had hoped to gain directly from the reapportionment, because seats were generally shifting from the "frost belt" where the party was weaker to the "sun belt" where it was stronger.

After the apportionment of seats is complete, redistricting can begin. That is the process by which the lines of congressional districts within each state are redrawn to make all of a state's districts as equal in population as possible. (This equality of districts is mandated by the U.S. Supreme Court's "one-person, one-vote" decisions.) The line drawing is generally done by state legislatures with the approval of the state's governor. In 1992, the GOP was especially hopeful that redistricting would bring the party gains in the House. The GOP had long asserted that district lines had been drawn to Republicans' disadvantage in many states where the governments were controlled by Democrats. This time they hoped for more favorable results from redistricting because they had gained certain strategic advantages.

First, Republicans were in a better political position in many states. For example, after the 1980 census the state government in California was entirely controlled by Democrats; they drew the congressional district lines in a way that was highly favorable to their party. After the 1990 census, by contrast, there was a Republican governor facing a Democratic legislature. Although the GOP could not guarantee an outcome favorable to Republicans, it could—and did—block a pro-Democratic plan. The resulting deadlock was resolved in court. This related to the second aspect of the GOP's improved political position: unlike previous redistricting years, when state and federal courts were overwhelmingly staffed by elected or appointed Democrats, in 1992 many more judges were Republicans, especially in the federal judiciary. In California, a redistricting plan was imposed by the state Supreme Court, and Republicans believed the plan would lead to a significant improvement in the party's share of seats in the nation's largest delegation.

The same pattern in which divided state government led to deadlock, and in turn to a judicial settlement, was repeated in a number of large states, including Illinois, Michigan, and Pennsylvania.[7] In other states, deadlock occurred even though government was not divided between the parties, and a court-imposed districting plan was implemented. For example, the two houses of the Florida legislature could not resolve their differences even though they were both Democrat-controlled, and a federal court drew the district lines. In all, eleven states, with a total of 170 House seats, ended up with redistricting plans that were devised by a court.[8] In other states with divided governments, the two parties compromised rather than let the courts take over the process.[9]

The Voting Rights Act gave the Republicans a second strategic advantage. The act was originally passed in 1965 to protect minorities' right to vote. When the act was renewed in 1982, amendments were included that were intended to foster the creation of legislative districts that had black or Latino majorities. (Such districts are termed "majority-minority" districts.) As interpreted by the federal Justice Department, the law requires that where it is possible to create or retain a majority-minority district, that must be done. These rules apply to the South and to a few other states with large Latino populations. In those states the Justice Department must approve any state-passed districting plan. The requirement to create such districts was supported by leaders of minority groups, who wanted more members of Congress from their ethnic or racial group. It was also supported by the Republican party, which believed that by concentrating minority voters who usually supported Democrats in a few districts, many Democratic incumbents whom those voters had supported in the past would be undermined. During the redistricting process, the Justice Department disapproved a number of state plans because they did not create enough majority-minority districts. The result was some very convoluted district lines in a number of cases.

In North Carolina, for example, after an earlier plan was disapproved, a district was created that ran from the north of the state almost all the way to the southern border in order to pick up sufficient concentrations of black residents to make up a majority of the district. It was dubbed the "I-85 district" because its lines follow the interstate highway, and at some points that road constitutes virtually the entire width of the district. In all, the redistricting process for 1992 created fifteen new districts with black majorities, and nine that were newly majority-Hispanic.[10]

Data on outcomes in 1992 House races, controlling for who redrew the district lines and for region, are presented in Table 9-4.[11] The table shows the partisan division of seats before and after the election, and the consequent net gain or loss for each party. It demonstrates that almost all of the Democrats' net loss occurred in the North, while almost all of the Republicans' net gain was made in the South.[12] Thus, from this point of view, the GOP's hopes to gain from reapportionment were partially realized. The Republicans' net gain was equal to about half of the nineteen seats shifted from the East and Midwest to the South and West.

Some of the GOP's gain in the South can be traced to the impact of the Voting Rights Act requirements. In Alabama, Georgia, and South Carolina, Democratic incumbents were weakened by the subtraction of black voters from their districts, and the combined result in these states was a loss of four seats for the Democrats and a gain of five for the

Table 9-4 The Partisan Impact of Redistricting on 1992 House Races

Who Redistricted?	Region		
	North	South	Total
Democrat-controlled state governments	(7) 20D-12R/18D-12R −2D/0R	(8) 59D-25R/60D-29R +1D/+4R	(15) 79D-37R/78D-14R −1D/4R
Split state governments	(8) 65D/40R/56D-41R −9D/+1R	(0) —	(8) 65D-40R/56D-41R −9D/+1R
Courts or commissions	(13) 97D-67R/99D-67R +2D/0R	(3) 18D-14R/17D-19R −1D/+5R	(16) 115D-81R/116D-86R +1D/+5R
Total	(28) 182D-119R/173D-120R −9D/+1R	(11) 77D-39R/77D-48R 0D/+9R	(39) 259D-158R/250D-168R −9D/+10R

Note: The number in parentheses is the number of states in the category. In the second line, the entry before the slash is the number of seats held by each party before the election; after the slash is the number after the election. The third line gives the net change for each party.

Republicans. The requirement to create majority-minority districts did not, however, always work to the Republicans' advantage. In some instances, the Democrats were able to control the redistricting process and mitigate partisan damage. In North Carolina, Texas, and Virginia, for example, four new African-American districts and one new Hispanic district were created, but the net partisan election result in those states was a gain of four seats for the Democrats and only one for the Republicans.

The results in the North show that the entire Democratic net loss is accounted for by changes in those eight states in which party control was split and compromise redistricting plans were imposed. Most of the shift was concentrated in two states, Massachusetts and New York, where the Democrats lost a total of six seats. Although these results, combined with those from the South, show some benefits from redistricting and reapportionment for the Republicans, it is clear that they gained far less than they expected. In particular, the results from northern states redistricted by courts or commissions show that the GOP had no net gain and the Democrats actually got two new seats. Here the overall result masks two contrary patterns. In three western states (Arizona, California, and Washington), the Democrats did very well, gaining nine seats while the Republicans showed no change. In the other ten states, the Democrats lost seven seats, again with no GOP net change.

The results in California and Washington may reflect the negative effect of President Bush's unpopularity in those states. In any event, the outcomes there were far from what the GOP was hoping for. Many analysts expected the new California lines to bring the Republicans a majority of the fifty-two-seat delegation. Instead the final tally was thirty seats for the Democrats and only twenty-two for the Republicans. This result raises the question of how predictable the impact of redistricting is from a partisan perspective.

Yet, one can see some general effects from the redistricting process. The redrawing of district lines is very disruptive to the patterns of support of sitting members of the House. In some cases, friendly voters are removed and are replaced by people who will be inclined toward the other party. More often, it is just that many new voters are in the incumbent's district; they are not necessarily hostile, but they are unfamiliar with the incumbent and therefore less likely to support him or her. In addition, in some instances two incumbents are placed in the same district, which presents the prospect of a much more difficult reelection campaign. These changes provide a larger than normal incentive for members to consider retirement, and the number of retirements was unusually large in 1992. These decisions created a great many open seats, and the retirees from them were disproportionately Democrats.[13] As we saw earlier, however, the Republicans were unable to take advantage of the opportunity this presented; they won only 37 percent of the open districts. We will return to a consideration of the predictability of redistricting plans and of Republican performance in open-seat races later in this chapter.

The Electoral Effects of Scandals in the House

In addition to the disruption caused by reapportionment and re-districting, many House incumbents encountered another difficulty in 1992. On September 18, 1991, the General Accounting Office revealed that in the previous year members had written 8,331 bad checks against their accounts in the House bank, and that these overdrafts had been covered by the bank without penalty or interest.[14] Initially, both the Speaker and the minority leader sought to keep secret the identities of those who had written the overdrafts, but a group of junior Republicans exerted pressure to make the names public, and the leadership eventually agreed.

In April 1992, the House Ethics Committee revealed the names of 325 current or former members who had been responsible for one or more overdrafts. Forty-six sitting representatives had written 100 or more overdrafts.[15] The scandal created a tremendous public uproar, something not needed by an institution whose approval rating was already at a low point. The check-bouncing scandal was a frequent topic of discussion on radio talk shows, where callers expressed anger at what they regarded as another abuse of power. Even though many Republicans had written overdrafts, the GOP sought to make this a partisan campaign issue. At the end of March, the National Republican Congressional Committee (NRCC) paid for a televised ad that blamed the Democrats for the scandal, and ended with the tag line: "For real change in Washington, bounce the Democrats." [16]

The Democratic leadership tried to limit the impact of the growing scandal by announcing plans to appoint a House administrator and the intent to pass a campaign finance reform bill before the election. Meanwhile, the Justice Department appointed an independent special counsel to investigate the possibility of violations of criminal law. As the congressional campaign season unfolded, opponents of incumbents who had written overdrafts used the issue as a club against them in primaries and the general election.

The check scandal appears to have produced congressional casualties in a variety of ways. First, many of those with a large number of overdrafts recognized the difficulty of their situation and retired. Of the forty-six members with more than 100 bounced checks, twelve did not seek reelection. Next, there were a large number of primary casualties, and eight of the forty-six (or 17 percent) fell in this manner. This number contrasts with the 12 of the other 389 members (3 percent) who lost in primaries. Finally, five members on the list were defeated in the general election, accounting for more than one-fifth of the incumbents who lost. Moreover, some of the other defeated incumbents had a substantial number of overdrafts, but less than 100. It is likely that the situation of many members with overdrafts was made even worse by the redistricting process, which added many new voters with whom the members did not have a longstanding relationship to draw on.

Thus overall, twenty-five of the forty-six representatives with 100 or more overdrafts did not return to the House, and many of the remainder had difficult and close reelection races.[17] The check scandal encouraged many potentially strong challengers to run against the incumbents, when in the absence of this event they might have decided to forgo the race.

Transforming the Membership: Women and Minorities in Congress

One effect of the substantial turnover in Congress in 1992 was a significant alteration in the gender and ethnic makeup of its membership. Frequently during the campaign year, 1992 was referred to as "the year of the woman," and this was not much of an exaggeration. The number of women among candidates for Congress and among members had been growing in recent years, but the inclination of women to seek a seat in Congress in 1992 appeared to have been spurred by the treatment of Anita Hill by the Senate Judiciary Committee during hearings on the confirmation of Clarence Thomas for the Supreme Court the previous year. Other issues that were on the congressional agenda, like abortion and family leave, also may have encouraged some women to run.

Whatever the reasons, the number of candidacies by women grew substantially. In all, 106 women won major party nominations for the House, and eleven won nominations to the Senate; for both chambers these were record numbers. Seventy female candidates for the House and ten of the female Senate candidates were Democrats. In some states, the representation of women among congressional candidates was remarkable. For example, they accounted for Democratic candidacies in nineteen of the fifty-two districts in California, and in seven of the twenty-three districts in Florida.

Not only were women spurred to run by "women's issues," they also apparently received funding disproportionately from women donors. We do not have systematic evidence on this point because reports on campaign donations are not routinely broken down by gender, but analysis of a few races does offer indications. For example, in the Pennsylvania U.S. Senate race involving incumbent Republican Arlen Specter and unsuccessful challenger Lynn Yeakel, 75 percent of Specter's in-state contributions and 82 percent of his contributions from out of state came from men. For Yeakel, on the other hand, 64 percent of her in-state money and 71 percent of her out-of-state money came from women.[18] In the Illinois U.S. Senate race, won by Carol Moseley-Braun, there was a similar—albeit less extreme—pattern of giving by gender.

In addition to general patterns of contributions, there was also organized gender-related giving designed to encourage candidacies by women. The most visible such effort is by an organization called EMILY's List, which gives only to female Democrats and focuses on choosing candidates early in the process. (The acronym EMILY stands for "Early Money Is Like Yeast," because early money raises the "dough" necessary to attain more funding.) This organization has existed since 1985, but it has increased the amount and range of its support in recent years. In 1992, EMILY's List gave "about $6 million to 44 candidates, three times what it gave to 14 women in the 1990 campaign." [19] Other groups that provide funding to women include WISH List (Women In the Senate and House), an organization of pro-choice Republican women, and the PAC (political action committee) of the National Organization for Women.[20]

The 1992 election results show that women were quite successful. In Senate races, four Democratic women won new seats (Dianne Feinstein and Barbara Boxer in California, Carol Moseley-Braun in Illinois, and Patty Murray in Washington), and Barbara A. Mikulski (D-Md.) was reelected. This brought the total number of women in the Senate to six, including the only Republican, Nancy Landon Kassebaum of Kansas. In the House, the number of women almost doubled, from twenty-eight to forty-seven. Of the forty-seven, twenty-three were reelected incumbents and twenty-four were newcomers. Thirty-five of the female representatives were Democrats. As women make up 52 percent of the voting-age population, and only 11 percent of the U.S. House, they are still substantially underrepresented. Even so, the gains in 1992 were significant. Moreover, women should continue to gain in Congress because they made further progress in the lower offices from which congressional candidates tend to be drawn. For example, after the 1992 election, women held over 20 percent of the seats in state legislatures. That compares with 18 percent before the election, and only 5 percent in 1971.

The 1992 election also resulted in increases in the number of minority members in the Congress. In the Senate, Carol Moseley-Braun was the first black woman elected to that body, and Ben Nighthorse Campbell (D-Colo.) was the first Native American. As we noted earlier, the Voting Rights Act had been amended in 1982 to encourage the creation of majority-minority districts. This resulted, in 1992, in the election of many new minority representatives. There are now thirty-seven black members in the House, up from twenty-six in the previous Congress. This amounts to 9 percent of the membership; African-Americans make up 11 percent of the voting population. All but one of the black representatives are Democrats.

Hispanic membership in the House increased from eleven to seventeen. Of these, fourteen are Democrats and three are Republicans. Also, one new member of Asian heritage won election, Republican Jay C. Kim of California, bringing the number of Asian-American representatives to four (the other three are Democrats). Thus, the ethnic and gender diversity of Congress increased noticeably in 1992.

Candidates' Resources and Election Outcomes

Seats in the House and Senate are highly valued posts for which candidates vigorously compete. In contests for these offices, candidates draw on whatever resources they have available. To explain the results of congressional elections we must consider the comparative advantages and disadvantages of the various candidates. In this section we will consider the most significant resources available to candidates and the impact of resources on the outcomes of congressional elections.

Candidate Quality

One major resource that candidates can draw on is the set of personal political abilities that foster electoral success. Few constituencies today offer a certain victory for one of the two major parties, so election outcomes usually depend heavily on candidate quality. A strong, capable candidate is a significant asset for a party; a weak, inept one is a liability that is difficult to overcome. In his study of the activities of House members in their districts, Richard F. Fenno, Jr., describes how members try to build support within their constituencies, establishing bonds of trust between constituents and their representative.[21] Members attempt to convey to their constituents a sense that they are qualified for their job, a sense that they identify with their constituents, and a sense of empathy with constituents and their problems. Challengers of incumbents and candidates for open seats engage in similar activities to win support. The winner of a contested congressional election will usually be the candidate who is better able to establish these bonds of support among constituents and to convince them that he or she is the person for the job.

One indicator of candidate quality is previous success at winning elective office. The more important the office a candidate has held, the more likely it is that he or she has had to overcome significant competition to obtain that office. Moreover, the visibility and reputation for performance that usually accompany public office can also be a significant electoral asset. For example, a state legislator who is running for a House seat can appeal to the electorate on the basis of the preparation for congressional service obtained in the previous office. A state legislator would also have built a successful electoral organization that could be useful in conducting a congressional campaign. Finally, previous success in an electoral arena suggests that experienced candidates are more likely to be able to run strong campaigns than candidates without previous success or campaign experience. Less adept candidates have already been screened out at lower levels of office competition. For these and other reasons, an experienced candidate tends to have an electoral advantage over a candidate who had held no previous elective office.[22] Moreover, the higher the office previously held, the stronger the candidate will tend to be in the congressional contest.

In Table 9-5, we present data that show which candidates were successful, controlling for office background, party, and incumbency.[23] The vast majority of candidates who challenged incumbents lost regardless of their office background or party, but clearly House challengers with office experience were more successful than those who had none. In Senate races there were only three defeats of incumbents in all, so it is not surprising that there is no visible relationship with challenger quality. The impact of candidate quality is most visible, however, in races without incumbents, where candidates with office experience were noticeably more successful. Given the importance of candidate quality, it is worth noting that in recent years there had been a decline in the proportion of House incumbents that faced challengers who had previously won elective office, and that this decline was reversed in 1992. In 1980, 17.6 percent of incumbents faced such challenges; in 1984, 14.7 percent did; in 1988, only 10.5 percent did; but in 1992, the proportion rose to 23.5 percent.[24] It is also important to note that in races against incumbents, Republicans were slightly more likely than Democrats to field candidates with elective-office experience (25.5 percent versus 20.5 percent). In open-seat races, however, the Democrats ran experienced candidates in 67 percent of the contests, while only 45 percent of these races included Republicans who had held previous elective office.[25] We will return to this partisan contrast in candidate quality later in the chapter.

Whether experienced politicians actually run for the House or Senate is, of course, not an accident. These are significant strategic decisions made by politicians, and they have much to lose if they make the wrong choice. The choices will be governed by a host of factors that relate to the perceived chance of success, the potential value of the new office relative to what will be lost if the candidate fails, and the costs of running.[26] The chances of success of the two major parties vary from election to election, both locally and nationally. Therefore, each election offers a different mix of experienced and inexperienced candidates from the two parties for the House and Senate.

The most influential factor in the choice of a potential candidate is whether there is an incumbent in the race. High reelection rates tend to discourage potentially strong challengers from running, which in turn

Table 9-5　Success in House and Senate Elections, Controlling for Office Background, Party, and Incumbency, 1992

Candidate's Last Office	Candidate Is Opponent of				No Incumbent in District			
	Democratic Incumbent		Republican Incumbent		Democratic Candidate		Republican Candidate	
	(%)	(N)	(%)	(N)	(%)	(N)	(%)	(N)
House[a]								
State legislature or U.S. House	15	(34)	10	(20)	78	(46)	61	(28)
Other elective office	5	(19)	29	(7)	73	(15)	38	(13)
No elective office	5	(142)	2	(93)	36	(28)	27	(45)
Senate								
U.S. House	0	(2)	0	(1)	60	(5)	0	(1)
Statewide elective office	0	(2)	0	(2)	—	(0)	100	(1)
Other elective office	0	(2)	25	(4)	100	(3)	25	(4)
No elective office	22	(9)	0	(4)	0	(1)	33	(3)

Note: Percentages show proportion of candidates in each category who won; numbers in parentheses are the totals on which percentages are based.

[a] Four races in which both parties ran incumbents are excluded.

makes it more likely that the incumbents will win. In addition to the general difficulty of challenging incumbents, factors related to specific election years will affect decisions to run. For example, the Republican party had particular difficulty recruiting strong candidates in 1986 because of fears about a potential backlash from the Iran-contra scandals. Moreover, the actions of incumbents can influence the choices of potential challengers. For example, building up a large reserve of campaign funds between elections may dissuade some possible opponents, although analysis of Senate contests (which usually involve experienced challengers) indicates that this factor does not have a systematic impact in those races.[27]

Ironically, there are times when parties do not try to recruit strong challengers. If a party's chances are not good, a strong challenger may increase turnout for the opposition and thus affect other races in the same election. For example, in Texas in 1988, the Republican party fielded no candidates against eleven Democratic House incumbents in order to hold down Democratic turnout. Of course, parties have only a limited impact on whether or not a race is contested. In any event, this tactic works against long-run efforts at party building, and so is unlikely to be pursued extensively.

As we have seen, most congressional races do not involve challengers who have previous office experience. Given their slight chance of winning, why do challengers without experience run at all? As Jeffrey S. Banks and D. Roderick Kiewiet point out, although the chances of success against incumbents may be small for such candidates, the race may be their best chance of ever winning a seat in Congress.[28] If inexperienced challengers put off their candidacies until a time when there is no incumbent, their opposition is likely to include multiple experienced candidates from both parties. Moreover, as David Canon demonstrates, previous office experience is an imperfect indicator of candidate quality, because some candidates without such experience can still have significant political assets and be formidable challengers.[29] For example, four former television journalists who had never previously held office won seats in the House in 1992, and three of them defeated incumbents. They were able to build on their substantial name recognition among voters to win nomination and election.[30]

Incumbency

One reason most incumbents win is that incumbency itself is a significant resource. Actually, incumbency is not a single resource, but rather a status that usually gives a candidate a variety of benefits. In some respects, incumbency works to a candidate's advantage automatically. For example, incumbents tend to be more visible to voters than their challengers.[31] Less automatic, but very important, is the tendency for incumbents to be viewed more favorably than challengers. Moreover, a plurality of the electorate in most districts will identify with the incumbent's political party. Incumbents can also use their status to gain advantages. Incumbents usually raise and spend more campaign funds than challengers, and they usually have a better developed and more experienced campaign organization. They also have assets, provided at public expense, that both help them perform their jobs and provide electoral benefits.

Increasing Electoral Margins. From the mid-1960s through the late 1980s, the margins by which incumbents were reelected increased (the pattern was less clear and more erratic in Senate elections than in House elections).[32] These changing patterns have interested analysts both for their own sake and because it was believed that the disappearance of marginal incumbents would mean less congressional turnover and a locking in of current members.

One explanation for the increased incumbent margins was offered by Edward R. Tufte, who argued that redistricting protected incumbents of both parties.[33] This argument seemed plausible, because the increase in margins occurred about the same time as the massive redistrictings required by Supreme Court decisions of the mid-1960s. But other analysts showed that incumbents had won by larger margins both in states that had redistricted and in those that had not, as well as in Senate contests.[34] Thus redistricting could not be the major reason for the change.

Another explanation for the increase in incumbents' margins was the growth in the perquisites of members and the greater complexity of government. Morris P. Fiorina has noted that in the post-New Deal period the level of federal services and the bureaucracy that administers them have grown tremendously.[35] More complex government means that many people will encounter problems in receiving services, and people who have problems frequently contact their representative to complain and seek help. Fiorina contended that in the mid-1960s new members of Congress placed greater emphasis on such constituency problem solving than had their predecessors. This expanded constituency service was translated into a reservoir of electoral support. Although analyses of the impact of constituency services have produced mixed conclusions, it is likely that the growth of these services offers a partial explanation for changing incumbent vote margins and for the incumbency advantage generally.[36]

The declining impact of party loyalties offers a third explanation for the growth in incumbent vote margins, either alone or in interaction with other factors. Until the mid-1960s there was a very strong linkage between party identification and congressional voting behavior: most people identified with a political party; many people identified strongly; and most voters supported the candidate of their chosen party. Since then, however, the impact of party identification has decreased, as we will see in Chapter 10. John A. Ferejohn, drawing on data from the National Election Studies (NES), showed that the strength of party ties generally weakened and that within any given category of party identification the propensity to support the candidate of one's party declined.[37] An analysis by Albert D. Cover showed that between 1958 and 1974 voters who did not identify with the party of a congressional incumbent were increasingly more likely to defect from their party and support the incumbent, while there had been no increase in defections from party identification by voters of the same party as incumbents.[38] Thus weakened party ties produce a substantial net benefit for incumbents.

The Trend Reverses. Whatever the relative importance of these factors, and the others we will discuss, in explaining the increase in incumbents' victory margins, the increase continued through the 1980s, as the data in Table 9-6 show. The average share of the vote for all incumbents was 61.7 percent in 1974; in 1980 it was 65.5. The share then continued to grow, peaking at 68.2 percent in 1986 and 1988.[39] These data

Table 9-6   Average Vote Percentages of House Incumbents, Selected Years, 1974-1992

Year	Democrats	Republicans	All Incumbents
1974	68.5	55.2	61.7
1980	64.0	67.9	65.5
1982	67.9	59.9	64.1
1984	64.2	68.2	65.9
1986	70.2	65.6	68.2
1988	68.8	67.5	68.2
1990	65.8	59.8	63.5
1992	62.2	61.6	62.0

are only for races in which both parties ran candidates. Thus they exclude contests where an incumbent ran unopposed. Such races were also increasing in number over this period; therefore, the data understate the growth in incumbents' margins.

Then, in 1990, something changed. The average share of the vote for incumbents declined by nearly 5 percentage points. The decline was, moreover, not a result of a shift of voters toward one party, as with the decline from 1980 to 1982; both parties' incumbents suffered. Rather, the shift in incumbents' electoral fortunes was apparently the result of what was called the anti-incumbent mood among the voters. Early in 1990 pollsters and commentators began to perceive stronger anti-Congress sentiments within the electorate.[40] For the first time, analysts began to question whether incumbency remained the asset it used to be.

There was, of course, nothing new about Congress being unpopular; Congress had long suffered ups and downs in approval, just as the president had. Indeed, Fenno had noted long before that candidates for Congress often sought election by running against Congress. They sought to convince voters that while most members of Congress were untrustworthy, they were different and deserved the voters' support.[41] What changed in 1990 was that Congress's unpopularity appeared to be undermining the approval of individual members by their own constituents. In July 1990, Geoff Garin, a pollster for Democratic candidates, said: "The conventional wisdom, which held that voters could hate Congress while liking their own Congressman, is rapidly becoming outdated.... The feeling is starting to seep from one over to the other." [42]

As the data presented in Table 9-1 showed, although there was a drop in the average percentage of the vote received by incumbents in 1990, the rate of reelection still reached 96 percent. The decline in vote margins was not great enough to produce a rash of defeats.

Many observers wondered, however, whether 1990 was the beginning of a new trend: Would incumbents' electoral drawing power continue to decline?

Certainly, with all of the scandals in Congress, there were apparent grounds for this speculation, and there was evidence in 1992 that incumbents still had significant political problems. In March 1992, approval of Congress's performance reached "an all-time low" according to a *Washington Post* poll. "But the news for incumbents was even more ominous. For the first time, fewer than half of those interviewed ... said they approved of the job their individual representative was doing." [43] Opponents of incumbents emphasized that they were "outsiders" and not "professional politicians" (even when they had substantial political experience), and many incumbents were induced to claim outsider status for themselves. For example, one member stopped claiming credit for all of the federal projects he had brought to his district. "We don't talk about that stuff. It makes him look like a congressman, a typical politician," his campaign manager explained.[44]

As the results from 1992 indicate, incumbents' share of the vote took another drop, from 63.5 percent to 62.0 percent (see Table 9-6). Republicans rebounded a bit from their bad 1990 showing, while Democrats fell more than 3 percentage points. This left incumbents of both parties with almost the same average share of the vote. Yet again, however, the casualty rate among incumbents who ran in the general election was lower than many expected; 93 percent were reelected.

This discussion illustrates that incumbents' vote margins and incumbents' reelection success are related but distinct phenomena. When—as was true in the 1980s—the average share of the vote received by incumbents is very high, they can lose a lot of ground before a large number of defeats is registered. What appears to have occurred in 1990, and continued even more strongly in 1992, is that many incumbents were subjected to vigorous contests for the first time in many years. Potential candidates apparently looked at the political situation and concluded that incumbents who had previously looked immovable could now be defeated, and there was a substantial increase in the number of candidates for Congress. By May 1, 891 candidates had filed to run for the House; the comparable figure for 1990 was 445.[45] These vigorous contests by challengers who were stronger than usual resulted in a decrease in the share of the vote received by many incumbents, but in most cases the decrease was not large enough to bring the challenger victory.

Campaign Spending

A third resource that has an important impact on congressional elections is campaign spending. The effects of campaign spending have received a great deal of attention in the last two decades because researchers have gained access to more dependable data than had previously been available.[46] The data on spending have consistently shown that incumbents generally outspend their challengers, often by large margins, and that the disparity has grown over time.[47] In 1990, incumbent spending averaged about $401,000, while challengers spent approximately $116,000—a ratio of 3.45 to 1. In 1992, challenger spending increased, to an average of $160,000, but the stronger challenges of that year also stimulated the incumbents to keep pace, and their spending rose to $560,000. This was a ratio of 3.50 to 1, which left challengers and incumbents in about the same relative position as they had been in two years earlier.[48]

Disparities in campaign spending are linked to the increase in incumbents' election margins. Beginning in the 1960s, congressional campaigns relied more heavily on campaign techniques that cost money—for example, media time, campaign consulting, and direct mailing—and these items have become more and more expensive. At the same time, candidates have been progressively less likely to have available pools of campaign workers from established party organizations or from interest groups, which have made using expensive media and direct mail strategies relatively more important. Most challengers are unable to raise significant campaign funds. Neither individuals nor the groups who are interested in the outcomes of congressional elections like to throw money away; before making contributions they usually need to be convinced that the candidate has a chance. Yet we have seen that few incumbents have been beaten. Thus it is difficult to convince potential contributors that their money will be well spent, and contributions are often not forthcoming. Meanwhile, incumbents build up large war chests long before a challenge is launched, keeping the money on hand, just in case. Two of the leading House fund raisers for the 1988 election were incumbents who had no serious opposition: Robert K. Dornan (R-Calif.) and Joseph P. Kennedy II (D-Mass.), each of whom raised over $1.2 million.[49] Indeed, after the 1988 election, twenty representatives already had over $515,000 on hand for 1990, and three had over $1 million.[50] Most challengers are at a strategic disadvantage, and they are unable to raise sufficient funds to wage a competitive campaign.

It is the ability to compete, rather than the simple question of relative amounts of spending, that is at the core of the issue. We have noted that incumbents have many inherent advantages that the challenger must overcome if he or she hopes to win. But often the money is not there to overcome them. In 1990, for example, over 47 percent of challengers spent $25,000 or less.[51] With so little money available, challengers are unable to make themselves visible to the electorate or to convey a convincing message. Under such circumstances, most voters—being unaware of the positions, or perhaps even the existence, of the

Table 9-7　Incumbents' Share of the Vote in the 1990 House Elections, by Challenger Campaign Spending (in percentages)

	Incumbents' share of the two-party vote					
Challenger Spending[a]	70 Percent or More	60-69 Percent	55-59 Percent	Less Than 55 Percent	Total	(N)
0-25	40.6	47.7	8.4	3.2	99.9	(155)
26-75	12.7	54.5	27.3	5.5	100.0	(55)
76-125	6.7	63.3	16.7	13.3	100.0	(30)
126-199	4.3	34.8	30.4	30.4	99.9	(23)
200 or more	4.8	19.4	29.0	46.8	100.0	(62)
All	23.4	44.0	17.8	14.8	100.0	(325)

[a] In thousands of dollars.

challenger—vote for the incumbent. This effect is mitigated somewhat in races where the voters have reasons to oppose the incumbent without regard to the positions of the challenger. This happened to a degree in 1990 and 1992, but the effect was usually not strong enough to bring down the incumbent.

Available data on campaign spending and election outcomes seem consistent with this argument. Table 9-7 shows the relationship between the incumbent's share of the vote in the 1990 House elections and the amount of money spent by the challenger. It is clear that there is a strong negative relationship between how much challengers spend and how well incumbents do. In races where challengers spent less than $26,000, almost 90 percent of the incumbents received 60 percent or more of the vote. At the other end of the spectrum, in races where challengers spent $200,000 or more, over three-fourths of the incumbents received less than 60 percent of the vote, and almost half got less than 55 percent. These results are consistent with those in earlier House elections for which comparable data are available.[52]

These findings are reinforced by other research which shows that challenger spending has a much greater influence on election outcomes than does incumbent spending.[53] This generalization has been questioned on methodological grounds,[54] but further research by Gary C. Jacobson reinforces his earlier findings. Using both aggregate and survey data, he finds that "the amount spent by the challenger is far more important in accounting for voters' decisions than is the amount of spending by the incumbent."[55] Parallel results have been found for Senate elections.[56]

It is true, of course, that challengers who appear to have good prospects will find it easier to raise money than those whose chances seem slim. Thus one might wonder whether these data are simply a reflection of the fulfillment of expectations, in which money flows to challengers who would have done well regardless of spending. Other research, however, indicates that that is probably not the case. In an analysis of the 1972 and 1974 congressional elections, Jacobson concludes, "Our evidence is that campaign spending helps candidates, particularly non-incumbents, by bringing them to the attention of the voters; it is not the case that well-known candidates simply attract more money; rather money buys attention." [57]

From this perspective, adequate funding is a necessary but not a sufficient condition for a closely fought election contest. Heavily outspending one's opponent is not a guarantee of victory; the evidence does not support the conclusion that elections can be bought. If an incumbent outspends the challenger, the incumbent can still lose if the challenger is adequately funded and runs a campaign that persuades the voters. The 1990 elections offer clear evidence of this. In fourteen of the fifteen races in which incumbents lost, the loser outspent the winner. In these contests, incumbents outspent challengers by almost 50 percent on average, and in five instances the loser spent more than twice as much. [58] Nor is a spending advantage any kind of guarantee to a challenger. In an extreme example from 1986, Republican Marc Holtzman, in the Eleventh District of Pennsylvania, spent $1.35 million in his race against Democratic incumbent Paul E. Kanjorski, who had spent about $714,000. Holtzman received only 29 percent of the vote. Based on this analysis, our view can be summarized as follows: if a challenger is to attain visibility and get his or her message across to the voters—neutralizing the incumbent's advantages in name recognition and perquisites of office—the challenger needs to be adequately funded. If both sides in a race are adequately funded, the outcome will tend to turn on factors other than money, and the relative spending of the two candidates will not matter very much.

This argument carries us full circle back to our earlier discussion and leads us to bring together the three kinds of resources that we have been considering—candidate experience, incumbency, and campaign spending. Table 9-8 presents data about these three factors in the 1990 House elections. We have categorized challenger experience as strong or weak depending on previous elective-office experience; challenger spending was classified as low or high depending on whether it was below or above $125,000. [59] The data show that each of the elements exerts an independent effect. When challengers had weak experience and low spending (over 70 percent of the races), all incumbents won, and the vast majority won with more than 60 percent of the vote. In the opposite situation, where the challenger had both strong experience and substantial spending, almost two-thirds of the races were relatively close. The combined results for the two intermediate categories fall between the extremes. Table 9-8 also reveals that it is rare for a challenger with strong experience not to be able to raise substantial funds.

This combination of factors also helps to explain the greater volatility of outcomes in Senate races. Previous analysis has shown that data on campaign spending in Senate contests are consistent with what we have found true for House races: if challenger spending is above some threshold level, the election is likely to be quite close; if it is below that level, the incumbent is likely to win by a large margin.[60] In Senate races, however, the mix of well-funded and poorly funded challengers is different. Senate challengers are more likely to be able to raise significant amounts of money than their House counterparts. Senate challengers, moreover, are also more likely to possess significant office experience. Thus, in Senate contests incumbents often will face well-funded and experienced challengers, and the stage is then set for their defeat if other circumstances work against them.

The 1986 Senate campaigns appear to provide additional evidence for the argument that if challengers have enough money to wage an adequate campaign, they will not be at a significant disadvantage if the incumbent spends considerably more. In the sixteen most competitive Senate races, the Republicans outspent the Democrats by $1 million on average—$3.8 million to $2.8 million—yet they lost eleven of the contests.[61] In some races the incumbent's advantage was much greater. Republican Mark Andrews spent $2.3 million defending his Senate seat in North Dakota, while his victorious Democratic challenger Kent Conrad spent $900,000. The lesson from this evidence appears to be captured by the statement made by David Johnson, the director of the Democratic Senatorial Campaign Committee, to Rep. Richard C. Shelby of Alabama, who was challenging Republican senator Jeramiah Denton. Shelby, who eventually won, was concerned that he did not have enough campaign funds, since Denton was outspending him two to one. Johnson responded: "You don't have as much money, but you're going to have enough—and enough is all it takes to win."[62]

The 1992 Elections: The Impact on Congress

When Ronald Reagan was first elected president in 1980, the impact of the congressional elections on Congress was substantial. The Republican party had unexpectedly taken control of the Senate from the Democrats and had gained thirty-three seats in the House of Representatives. Most of the incoming senators and representatives were very conservative, shifting the ideological balance of the Congress noticeably

Table 9-8 Incumbents' Share of the Vote in the 1990 House Elections, by Challenger Campaign Spending and Office Background (in percentages)

Challenger Experience/ Challenger Spending	Incumbents' share of the vote						Percentage of Incumbents Defeated
	70 Percent or More	60-69 Percent	55-59 Percent	Less Than 55 Percent	Total	(N)	
Weak/Low	29.9	50.6	12.6	6.9	100.1	(231)	0.0
Strong/Low	66.7	33.0	0.0	0.0	100.0	(9)	0.0
Weak/High	6.2	27.7	20.0	46.1	100.0	(65)	18.5
Strong/High	0.0	10.0	25.0	65.0	100.0	(20)	15.0

Note: Percentages read across. Strong challengers have held a significant elective office (see note 59). High-spending challengers spent more than $125,000.

to the right. The massive Reagan victory and Republican congressional gain also had an impact on the behavior of many southern Democrats. Reagan's popularity in the South led many of them to support his early policy initiatives on taxes and the budget. Southern Democratic support provided the margin of victory on those measures.

The 1992 results were very different. Turnover of membership in the House was even greater than in 1980, with 110 new members as opposed to 74. The party winning the presidency carried the lion's share of these new seats in both elections, but the Democrats' share in 1992 was only 57 percent (compared with the Republicans' 70 percent twelve years before). More important, the results meant that the Democrats had lost ground. In the Senate, turnover was twelve—less than the eighteen of 1980—and it was split seven to five for the Democrats. In partisan terms, the two parties broke even. The GOP had taken sixteen of the new seats when Reagan beat Carter, for a net gain of twelve seats, and had seized majority control.

The contrasting results in these two elections show that the pattern affects the impact the election has on the relationship between the president and Congress. In politics, appearance and interpretation are frequently more important than reality. Because the GOP made significant gains in the House and wrested control of the Senate from the Democrats while Reagan was defeating the incumbent Democratic president, many observers attributed a causal connection to these events. Specifically, many believed that Reagan's coattails had pulled into office a large share of the new Republicans, and that the voters were endorsing the conservative policy agenda that Reagan had espoused in the campaign. That this interpretation was questionable at best mattered little; its widespread acceptance helped Reagan to win congressional support for his cuts in taxes and domestic spending and for increased money for defense.

In 1992, on the other hand, the party winning the presidency did not make gains in either chamber. As a consequence, no one attributed special political potency to Clinton, and many regarded the election as merely a negative judgment on Bush rather than as a popular endorsement of the specific items on the new president's agenda. Clinton's situation was made more difficult because he was a minority president who was unable to claim a natural popular majority for his programs. Thus, despite the end of divided government in 1993, we should not be surprised that the new president had more than a little difficulty in his relations with Congress.

In part, Clinton's difficulties stemmed from the end of divided government itself, and from the increase in homogeneity in both parties over the previous decade. The Republicans in both houses were very conservative, and with a Democrat in the White House they could give free rein to their opposition to federal domestic programs and to increased taxes. In the House, activist conservatives within the GOP strengthened their hold on the leadership by replacing a comparatively moderate conference chairman (the number three leadership post) with a combative right-winger—Dick Armey of Texas. As a professional economist, Armey sees economic issues as the vehicle to unify the Republicans, and then plans to use that unity to combat the Democrats. After his election he said, "I see confrontation as a tool. . . . If it becomes necessary, I am capable of using it." [63]

Because the rules of the House permit a majority to work its will, Republican unity alone is not enough to bring the GOP victory. Indeed, after ten months the Clinton administration had been able to persuade the House to endorse most of his main agenda items. But, with the exception of the North American Free Trade Agreement (NAFTA), Clinton's proposals gained few Republican votes. The minority's unity, however, left Clinton relatively little leeway; without many Republican votes, he had to simultaneously accommodate the different segments of his own party. Even moderate and relatively conservative Democrats had little common ground with the Republicans, so there was not much chance of a cross-party coalition forming behind a policy proposal different from what the president preferred. That did not mean that there was a natural majority among the Democrats in favor of the president's position—or any other—for that matter.

Republican unity was of even more consequence in the Senate. That body is not structured to permit a majority to control outcomes; its rules contain features that allow a portion of the membership to block action. Probably the best known of these is the filibuster, whereby debate on a proposed bill can continue indefinitely—preventing supporters from bringing it to a vote—unless sixty senators are willing to end the debate. This institutional structure, coupled with the fact that the Republicans held forty-three Senate seats, meant that a completely united GOP contingent could block a vote on any Clinton proposal. For example, a Republican filibuster killed Clinton's proposed economic stimulus package early in his first year.

Of course, Bob Dole of Kansas—the Senate minority leader—was not able to hold all of his members together on every vote; but a high degree of unity within both Senate parties gave some senators tremendous leverage in the bargaining over policy proposals. Thus, in the first year of Clinton's presidency, a great deal of influence in the Senate was exercised by Dole, by moderate to conservative Democrats like David L. Boren of Oklahoma and John B. Breaux of Louisiana, and by the small group of moderate Republicans. And, as was implied by our comparison of the 1980 and 1992 results, there were not many members of Congress who had reason to believe that the people back home would exact political retribution if they did not go along with Clinton. Indeed, fifty House Democrats (thirty-one of them in the South) represented districts that Bush had carried.[64]

Turning from relations between the president and Congress to the impact of the elections on the internal politics of the House and Senate, it seems fair to say that the influx of a large number of new members has had an effect, but its magnitude will probably not be clear for a while. The 110 first-term representatives comprise more than a quarter of the membership of the House, and those numbers mean that they have the potential to affect outcomes. It does not appear, however, that they can be regarded as a bloc on any particular issue, and that will weaken their impact. They are split along party lines (sixty-three Democrats and forty-seven Republicans, which is not much different from the division in the rest of the House), and they are no more united on issues than returning members are. For example, every first-term Republican voted against Clinton's economic package, and all but three Democrats supported it.

This split is apparent even on matters like congressional reform. Both freshman party contingents came up with a set of reform proposals, and the proposals had little in common. The GOP members favored term limits on Congress and restrictions on the Democratic leadership's control over the arrangements for floor debate on bills. The Democrats supported reform of campaign finance and lobbying, and their proposals were backed by their party leaders.[65]

The new House members have expanded the share of minorities and women in the body. Because the number of African-American members was nearly doubled, the influence of the House Black Caucus increased substantially. The larger number of black members, coupled with the growing committee seniority of the returning members, will increase the caucus's influence on the content of legislation. Women will also have increased legislative clout, especially because they are concentrated disproportionately in the majority party. The new female members demonstrated that they would press their own agenda when all twenty-four first-term women held a joint press conference in December 1992 to endorse a number of legislative items, including full funding for the Head Start preschool program and a proposed family and medical leave bill.[66] One of the interesting effects of the large number of women in the class of 1993 was that the House was compelled, for the first time, to set up a special spouse-orientation reception for congressional husbands.

In the Senate, the twelve new members comprise a smaller share of the body, and they are also split along party lines; seven new Democrats and five new Republicans came in with the 103d Congress. Thus we would expect their aggregate impact to be modest. Perhaps the most noticeable effect so far stems from the tripling of the number of women in the body. Two Democratic women were placed on the Senate Judiciary

Committee, in a symbolic response to the outrage voiced by many women about the committee's treatment of Anita Hill.

The unpopularity of Congress induced both new and returning members to put a priority on congressional reform. Issues like new regulations on lobbyists, cutting the budget of the legislative branch, and reforming campaign finance all received legislative action during the first six months of the 103d Congress, although it was not clear that a satisfactory compromise on the last item could be worked out and passed.

As in many previous Congresses, the most important reforms in the House at the beginning of the 103d Congress were the consequence of actions taken by the Democratic Caucus. The caucus revised its rules to create the Speaker's Working Group on Policy Development, which was intended to assist the leadership in creating and passing a legislative agenda. New rules also increased the accountability of committee and subcommittee chairmen to the caucus by expanding the mechanisms by which they could potentially be removed. When, in June 1993, eleven subcommittee chairmen voted against the reconciliation bill that embodied Clinton's budget and tax proposals, a special meeting of the caucus was called to consider removing them from their positions. (The caucus declined to exercise its removal power when it met.)[67] The caucus also imposed new limits on the number of subcommittees each committee could have, which required the abolition of more than a dozen subcommittees.

The Senate did not adopt any major reforms at the beginning of the Congress, although Majority Leader George J. Mitchell of Maine endorsed in principle rules changes that would expedite the Senate's operations and reduce the opportunities for minorities to block action. Those ideas, and many other reform proposals for both the House and Senate, became part of the agenda of a special Joint Committee on the Operation of Congress that was created to take a comprehensive look at the organization of the institution and to propose changes in its operation. As of this writing, the committee has not completed its deliberations, but it has considered a wide range of proposals, from simple ideas designed to minimize the scheduling of conflicting meetings to radical items such as the abolition of the appropriations committees.

The 1994 Elections and Beyond

The Elections of 1994

The Democrats began to exhibit concern about the elections of 1994 soon after the 1992 results had been finalized, and their concern is well founded. There is a strong historical pattern to midterm elections: the party of the president has lost seats in the House in twenty-one of the

Table 9-9   House Seat Losses by the President's Party in Midterm
Elections, 1946-1990

All Elections	First Term of Administration	Later Term of Administration
1946: 55 Democrats	1954: 18 Republicans	1946: 55 Democrats
1950: 29 Democrats	1962: 4 Democrats	1950: 29 Democrats
1954: 18 Republicans	1970: 12 Republicans	1958: 47 Republicans
1958: 47 Republicans	1978: 11 Democrats	1966: 47 Democrats
1962: 4 Democrats	1982: 26 Republicans	1974: 43 Republicans
1966: 47 Democrats	1990: 9 Republicans	1986: 5 Republicans
1970: 12 Republicans		
1974: 43 Republicans	Average: 13.3	Average 37.7
1978: 11 Democrats		
1982: 26 Republicans		
1986: 5 Republicans		
1990: 9 Republicans		
Average: 25.5		

twenty-three midterm elections in this century. The first column in Table
9-9 shows the magnitude of these losses in midterms since World War II.
They average 25.5 seats for the president's party. There was, however,
considerable variation in the outcomes, from the fifty-five-seat loss by the
Democrats in 1946 to the four-seat Democratic loss in 1962. So, although
we can say that the Democrats are likely to lose House seats in 1994, we
have no way to predict the size of that loss.

Another consideration related to the president, however, clarifies the
context for judgment somewhat. During the first midterm election of his
presidency, the president may be able to make a plausible appeal that he
has not had enough time to bring about substantial change or to solidify
many achievements. Moreover, even if things are not going very well,
voters may not be inclined to place the blame on a president who has
served for such a short time. But four years later (if the president is
fortunate enough to face a second midterm), appeals of too little time are
likely to be unpersuasive. After six years, if the economy or foreign policy
is not going well, voters may seek a policy change by reducing the number
of the president's partisans in Congress.

The second and third columns in Table 9-9 indicate that this is what
has happened in the past. Losses by the president's party in the first
midterm election of a presidency tend to be much smaller than losses in
subsequent midterms.[68] Indeed, with the exception of the result in 1986,
the two categories yield two fairly homogeneous sets of outcomes that are

sharply different from one another. In the six midterm elections that took place during a first term, the president's party lost between four and twenty-six seats, with an average loss of fourteen. In the five elections after the first term (excluding 1986), the range of losses was between twenty-nine and fifty-five seats, with an average loss of forty-four. (We will discuss the atypical 1986 result later.)

Models of House Elections. In the last two decades, a number of scholars have constructed and tested models of congressional election outcomes, focusing especially on midterms, seeking to isolate the factors that most strongly influence the results. The first models, constructed by Tufte and by Jacobson and Samuel Kernell, focused on two variables: presidential approval and a measure of the state of the economy.[69] Tufte hypothesized a direct influence by these forces on voter choice and election outcomes. The theory was that an unpopular president or a poor economic situation would cause the president's party to lose votes and, therefore, seats in the House. In essence, the midterm elections were viewed as a referendum on the performance of the president and his party.

Jacobson and Kernell, on the other hand, saw more indirect effects of presidential approval and the economy. They argued that these forces affected election results by influencing the decisions of potential congressional candidates. If the president is unpopular and the economy is in bad shape, potential candidates will expect the president's party to perform poorly. As a consequence, strong potential candidates of the president's party will be more inclined to forgo running until a better year, and strong candidates from the opposition party will be more inclined to run because they foresee good prospects for success. According to Jacobson and Kernell, this mix of weak candidates from the president's party and strong opposition candidates will lead to a poor election performance by the party occupying the White House. To measure this predicted relationship, their model relates the partisan division of the vote to presidential approval and the economic situation early in the election year. This, they argue, is when decisions to run for office are being made, not at the time of the election, so it is not appropriate to focus on approval and the economy at that time. This view has come to be called the strategic politicians hypothesis.[70]

More recent research has built from this base. One model, developed by Alan I. Abramowitz, Albert D. Cover, and Helmut Norpoth, considered a new variable: short-term party evaluations.[71] They argued that voters' attitudes about the economic competence of the political parties affect the impact of presidential approval and economic conditions on voting decisions. If the electorate judges that the party holding the presidency is better able to deal with the problems voters regard as most serious, the negative impact of an unpopular president or a weak economy will be reduced. The authors concluded from their analysis of both aggregate votes and responses to surveys in midterm elections that there is evidence for their "party competence" hypothesis.

All of the models we have discussed used the division of the popular vote as the variable to be predicted, and they focus only on midterm elections. More recent work has merged midterm results with those of presidential years, contending that there should be no conceptual distinction between them. These efforts have sought to predict changes in seats without reference to the division of the vote. For example, a study by Bruce I. Oppenheimer, James A. Stimson, and Richard W. Waterman argued that the missing piece in the congressional election puzzle is the degree of "exposure," or "the excess or deficit number of seats a party holds measured against its long-term norm." [72] If a party wins more House seats than normal, those extra seats will be vulnerable in the next election, and the party is likely to suffer losses. Thus the party that wins a presidential election does not automatically benefit in House elections. But if the president's party does well in the House races, it will be more vulnerable in the subsequent midterm elections. Indeed, the May 1986 article by Oppenheimer and his colleagues predicted only small Republican losses for 1986 because Reagan's large 1984 victory was not accompanied by substantial congressional gains for his party. The actual result in 1986 was consistent with this prediction, for the GOP lost only five seats.

Another model of House elections was constructed by Robin F. Marra and Charles W. Ostrom, Jr.[73] They developed a "comprehensive referendum voting model" of both presidential year and midterm elections, and included factors such as foreign policy crises, scandals, unresolved policy disputes, party identification, and the change in the level of presidential approval. The model also incorporated measures reflecting hypothesized relationships in the models we discussed earlier: the level of presidential approval, the state of the economy, the strategic politicians hypothesis, exposure, and party competence. The model was tested on data from all congressional elections from 1950 through 1986.

The Marra-Ostrom analysis showed significant support for most of the predicted relationships. The results indicated that the most powerful influences affecting congressional seat changes were presidential approval (directly and through various events) and exposure. The model is striking in its statistical accuracy; the average error in the predicted change was only four seats. The average error varied little whether presidential or midterm years were predicted, and the analysis demonstrated that the usually greater losses for the president's party in second midterm years resulted from negative shifts in presidential approval, exposure, and scandals.

Drawing on the insights of these various models, we can see how these factors may influence outcomes in the 1994 House elections. How well the economy is doing and what proportion of the voters approve of Clinton's performance early in the year may encourage or discourage high quality potential challengers. The same variables close to election time may lead voters to support or oppose Democratic candidates based on their judgments of the job the Clinton administration is doing. Thus it was reasonable for the Democrats to be concerned about Clinton's low approval rating in 1993. Another ground for concern is the relatively high exposure of the Democrats, given their still substantial majority, although it is not as high as it would have been if Clinton had pulled a large increase in Democratic representatives in with him. Finally, the impact of events like crises and scandals in the Marra-Ostrom model reminds us that there are many unforeseeable events that may influence the 1994 congressional election results.

There are a few other considerations to note before turning to consider Senate races in 1994. First, recall that the margins in House contests in 1992 were closer than normal among both Democrats and Republicans. This may entice stronger candidates than usual to oppose those incumbents whose margins of victory had slipped. Second, it is not now clear how many open seats there will be. Surely the number of retirements will be lower than in 1992, but if many representatives choose to seek statewide office, the total could still be substantial. Finally, some observers believe that the full impact of the redistricting that was carried out before 1992 has not yet been felt, and that we will see GOP gains in the future as a result. We will return to these issues in the concluding section.

The Battle for Senate Control in 1994. The tendency of the president's party to lose seats is less strong in Senate races than in House contests. Despite this fact, the Democratic situation in 1994 with regard to the Senate may be volatile. The party's concern was heightened after the Democratic candidate lost, by a two to one margin, the 1993 special election to replace Sen. Lloyd Bentsen of Texas.[74] To be sure, some indicators do not look unfavorable for the Democrats. Two important considerations in assessing vulnerability are the previous margin of victory and whether the incumbent is a freshman. Although large previous margins of victory do not guarantee the next win, narrow victories frequently mean future vulnerability because the next race tends to attract strong, well-funded challengers. First-term incumbents also tend to be more vulnerable than longer-serving members, who have had greater time to solidify their political bases. As we write this, there are nine senators who are first-termers who were elected with no more than 55 percent of the vote, but Democrats only hold one more of these seats than Republicans. Five other freshmen (three Democrats and two Republicans) were elected by larger margins, and two nonfreshmen (one from each party) won with less than 55 percent of the vote. Finally, there is the matter of open seats, which are generally more vulnerable to party switches than incumbent-held seats. As of November 1993, there will be six seats without elected incumbents in 1994, three Democratic and three GOP.

Based on these indicators, the Democratic position for the Senate races of 1994 is only a little worse than that of the Republicans. This is not, however, the entire story. Most important, the Democrats have many more seats to defend overall—twenty-one versus thirteen. Moreover, many Democratic incumbents seem likely to face strong opponents.

Because Vice President Al Gore can vote to break ties, the Republicans (as of late 1993) would need a net gain of seven seats to win control of the Senate. This seems unlikely. One assessment of the Senate races lists six seats in the "toss-up" category (five Democrat and one GOP); another eleven seats are categorized as only leaning to a party—four Democratic and seven Republican.[75] If each party were to hold its leaning seats, and the toss-ups were to split evenly, the GOP would gain two seats. The Republicans would need a net gain of forty-two seats to win control of the House. Although the GOP did make gains of this magnitude in the 1946 and 1966 midterm elections (see Table 9-9), these contests followed presidential elections in which the Democrats had gained twenty-one and thirty-eight seats, respectively. Of course, a drastic erosion of Clinton's approval rating could put Democratic control of the House at risk, but, given the advantages of incumbency, it seems very unlikely that the Democrats will lose control of the House. It *is* likely, however, that they will lose some seats in both chambers, and that will make it even more difficult for the Clinton administration to secure passage of its agenda—especially in the Senate.

The Midterm of 1994 and Beyond: Continued Democratic Dominance of the House?

Senate elections are so independent of one another, and the partisan balance is sufficiently close, that it is difficult to anticipate what will occur beyond 1994 until we know the results of those elections. We will, therefore, confine our attention to the House in this concluding section. Specifically, we will try to assess the likelihood that the Republicans will be able to take over partisan control beyond 1994, considering the impact of factors like party organizations and gerrymandering of districts.

National Party Organizations.   The Republicans' supposed comparative advantage with regard to the impact of national party organizations in House elections has received a good deal of attention.[76] In the 1982 House races, for example, the Republican party outspent the Democratic party almost six to one in direct contributions to candidates and coordinated spending.[77] In 1989, the National Republican Congressional Committee (NRCC) hired Ed Rollins (who had managed Ronald

Reagan's reelection campaign in 1984) as cochairman, at a salary of $250,000 a year, to develop a strategy to win control of the House.[78]

Yet things are not so one-sided or simple as this brief summary might suggest. Even though the Republicans were the first to organize and develop their national congressional campaign organization, the Democrats have been catching up. The party has improved its fundraising and organization over the last decade. In 1992, the NRCC outspent the Democratic Congressional Campaign Committee (DCCC) by less than three to one. The Republicans' fundraising was at about the same level as two years earlier, while the Democrats showed an increase of about 32 percent. Moreover, the NRCC ended the 1992 cycle with a substantial debt—$7.9 million—while the Democrats' debt was less than $2.1 million.[79]

It is also true that a disproportionate share of the money from the party committees goes to incumbents who may not be in real electoral trouble, rather than to challengers or candidates in open-seat contests. Thus an advantage in spending by party committees may not translate into a real political advantage. In addition, the Democrats have followed other strategies that do not show up in the kind of spending figures we have cited. For example, the DCCC has concentrated on helping candidates get money from PACs, rather than simply raising it themselves and donating it to those candidates. They argue that their party controls the House and will continue to do so, so the PACs would be well advised to support their candidates. The strategy has worked well. In the 1988 election cycle, Democratic candidates received $69.4 million in PAC contributions, while Republicans raised only $30.3 million. Of course, much of this advantage occurs because there are more Democratic than Republican incumbents, and PACs tend to give to incumbents. Democrats, however, also received more PAC money in open seats ($5.8 million to $3.6 million), and Democratic challengers got $8.1 million to GOP challengers' $2.4 million.[80]

Finally, party organizations can have only a limited impact on the pattern of House election outcomes. They can provide some funds, but they cannot fully bankroll a campaign. They can and do make efforts to recruit candidates, but they cannot guarantee that those whom they persuade to run will win the nomination in a primary. Moreover, their recruitment efforts are not always successful. In 1991, after the victory over Iraq in the Persian Gulf war, House Minority Whip Newt Gingrich of Georgia pledged to recruit eighty veterans of Desert Storm to run against Democratic incumbents who had voted against authorizing President Bush to use force in the Gulf. The efforts put into the recruitment were minimal, and few veterans ran.[81]

Gerrymandering. As was noted earlier in this chapter, the Republican party has claimed that in many states congressional districts were gerrymandered against their interests. (*Gerrymandering* is the historical term for drawing district lines to benefit a particular party or group.) They assert that this has deprived them of their fair share of House seats based on their share of the national congressional vote. Citing 1984 as an example, Republicans pointed out that they got 47 percent of the vote but only 42 percent of the seats. Therefore the GOP made it a high priority to influence the districting process before 1992, in order to secure more favorable results.

To be sure, in the 1980s and earlier, districts in some states—California after 1982, for example[82]—were drawn to disadvantage Republicans. Other states, like Indiana, however, were gerrymandered in favor of the GOP, and in still others—mostly where political control was divided between the parties—districts were drawn to the advantage of incumbents of both parties.[83] This would suggest that the net effect of congressional districting was less one-sided than the Republicans claimed.

Moreover, even when one party controls the districting process, there is no guarantee that the plan they impose will bring political benefits. We have already seen that in a number of states after the 1992 districting, the GOP did not make the gains the party anticipated. The Indiana districting plan in the 1980s offers an excellent illustration of this problem. In 1981 the Republicans controlled the governorship and both houses of the legislature, and they were determined to draw the House district lines in a way that would erase the six to five Democratic advantage in House seats. Analyses of the plan they imposed anticipated a six to four, or even a seven to three, outcome in favor of the GOP.[84] (The state had lost one House seat as a result of reapportionment.) Instead, the outcome in 1982 was an even five to five split, and in 1986 the Democrats gained another seat to make it six to four Democratic. Then in 1989, the Republicans lost a special election to fill the vacancy caused by the appointment of GOP representative Dan Coats to fill Vice President Dan Quayle's former Senate seat. Finally, another Republican incumbent was defeated in 1990. Thus the "pro-Republican" plan resulted in an eight to two Democratic advantage in House seats by the end of the decade. This puts the alleged efficacy of gerrymandering in doubt, to say the least.[85]

Nor is it even clear that the basic Republican claim of bias is well supported. Norman J. Ornstein has pointed out that the gap between the share of seats and the share of the vote for the Republicans seems to be more a consequence of the single-member district system employed in this country and higher turnout by persons who live in areas that tend to vote Republican.[86] The single-member district system means that a party can win a seat with 51 percent of the vote (or less, if more than two candidates are running) as well as with 80 percent. If one party wins districts across the country by larger margins than the other party, the former party will "waste" a lot of votes even if there is no bias in the districting. Districts are, moreover, apportioned on the basis of population, not votes cast.

The Democrats do very well in districts where very few people vote, and the Republicans fare better in districts with relatively high turnout. In 1992, the Democrats won 97 percent of the thirty districts in which less than 150,000 votes were cast. They won 59 percent of the 271 districts in which there were between 150,000 and 250,000 votes, and 52 percent of the 129 districts in which over 250,000 votes were cast.[87] When these votes are added up for the nation as a whole, the total vote of the two parties is closer than it would be if turnout were equal across districts. Thus the existence of "bias" is questionable. Indeed, given that we have a district system, disparities between the *national* division of seats and the *national* division of the vote are very likely to occur. Similar patterns are found in other countries that use the single-member, plurality-vote win system to elect legislatures. For example, the British Labour party tends to benefit somewhat because it does better in districts with relatively low turnout.[88]

Open Seats. Further light can be shed on Republican electoral opportunities and the question of alleged systemic bias against the GOP by considering competition for open seats. In these instances, all GOP disadvantages that might stem from incumbency were stripped away. These races offered the Republicans their best chance for gaining ground. In an analysis of such contests between 1968 and 1988, Jacobson showed that the Democrats "have taken 27.6 percent of the Republicans' open seats while losing 19.9 percent of their own." [89] Table 9-10 presents data on open-seat races between 1983 and 1992. These data include not only contests decided in general elections, as is true of most other studies, but also special election contests to fill vacancies. A significant number of representatives were initially elected in this way, so including these races substantially improves the completeness of the data.[90]

Table 9-10 shows the partisan division of the aggregate of open seats before and after these elections. During this period, the Democrats made a net gain of two seats. Republican partisans might argue that many of these seats were gerrymandered against the GOP, so that the Democrats could hold on to a disproportionate share. Because the 1992 redistricting entailed enormous shifting of lines, it is not possible to match individual districts before and after the election, but if we confine our attention to 1983 through 1991, we can shed some light on these claims. The advantage of this time period is that all of the preelection-postelection comparisons take place within the same district lines, so changes in the outcomes cannot result from gerrymandering.[91]

Table 9-10   Partisan Outcomes in Open-Seat House Races, 1983-1992

Seats	Division Before Elections (D-R)	Division After Elections (D-R)	Net Seat Change
Including 1992 general elections			
All seats	133-108	135-106	+2D
Excluding 1992 general elections			
All seats	77-77	78-72	+5D
Democratic seats	73-0	58-15	−15D
Republican seats	0-77	20-57	+20D
Republican seats in districts won by Bush in 1988	0-71	16-55	+16D
Republican seats in districts won by Bush with 60% or more of the vote	0-41	8-36	+ 8D

In this set of races, the overall Democratic gain was five seats. To look further, we first break the districts down according to which party held the seat before the open-seat race, paralleling Jacobson's results cited earlier. The Republicans won 20.5 percent of the Democratic seats, while 26.0 percent of the GOP seats went to the Democrats. These results seriously undermine Republican claims. If most districts were gerrymandered against Republicans, GOP districts would tend to be packed with Republican voters, forcing the party to waste its votes by winning those districts by large margins. This is the only way a bias (that is, more districts for the Democrats than they would be entitled to by their share of the vote) can be created. Without such a bias, there is no gerrymander. Open Republican seats should be safely Republican. And since the GOP had already won the Republican seats in one or more races preceding the open-seat election, it is logically impossible for the GOP to claim that the districts were drawn in such a way that the party could not win them.

We can create additional subsets of these data to examine the issue of bias in more detail. First, we consider only the seventy-one seats that were held by the Republicans before the open-seat election and were carried by Bush in 1988. Thus, these districts have a double indication that the Republican party can carry them. However, Republicans lost 22.5 percent of these seats, a net loss of sixteen. Next, we show the results for the forty-one formerly Republican districts in which Bush received 60 percent or more of the vote. These districts are clearly not biased against the Republican party, but even in them the GOP lost 19.5 percent of its seats (for a net decline of eight seats).[92]

The analyses presented here strongly indicate that neither incumbency nor gerrymandering, separately or in combination, explains the Republicans' failure to win majority control of the House.[93] Instead one must look to political problems rather than these structural ones to account for the party's continued minority status. As Jacobson states, "Republicans have failed to advance in the House because they have fielded inferior candidates on the wrong side of issues that are important to voters in House elections and because voters find it difficult to assign blame or credit when control of the government is divided between the parties." [94] This reinforces the paradoxical conclusion that is implied by our earlier discussion of midterm elections: the Republicans' primary asset in seeking to make gains in the House is their party's failure to retain the presidency. With government no longer divided, if voters are not satisfied with the situation in the country and with Clinton's performance, they will be more likely to place the blame on the Democrats. They may, therefore, turn away from the Democratic party in the congressional elections, producing gains for the GOP.

Future Considerations.   Before concluding, we should say a few words about two factors that may have some potential to alter the electoral landscape we have been describing, and thus may in turn affect the pattern of outcomes: campaign finance reform and term limits. In 1992 the Congress passed a campaign finance reform bill containing provisions for the public financing of congressional elections and for spending limits on campaigns, but President Bush vetoed it. Indeed, many observers said that the only reason Congress supported the bill was because members were certain it would be vetoed.

In June 1993, the Senate passed a very different bill.[95] It imposed "voluntary" spending limits on Senate campaigns ($1.2 million to $5.5 million, depending on the state's population). Any candidate who did not voluntarily comply with the spending limit would be subject to a tax on his or her campaign contributions at the highest corporate rate (currently 34 percent). Complying candidates would also be limited to $25,000 in personal contributions to their own campaign; there is now no limit. Furthermore, the bill would ban completely PAC donations to candidates for the House or Senate, or, if the ban were declared unconstitutional, limit PAC donations to $1,000. If a complying candidate faced an opponent who did not comply, he or she would be eligible for vouchers from the government for mail and broadcast spending and would have campaign limits lifted from his or her campaign. There were no other provisions for public financing.

The House has taken no action on this bill at the time we write. Certainly, the ban on PAC donations is unlikely to be popular there. Also, many observers regard the tax on contributions to be unconstitutional. It is not clear what effect these provisions would have if they were to become law. The one reform that would very likely have a major impact is the one that is no longer included: general public financing. That would mitigate the financing disadvantage faced by challengers that we discussed at length above. The potential opponent of an incumbent would know that he or she would have some guaranteed base of funding to build on. That would almost certainly persuade stronger challengers to choose to run, and it would lead to more competitive congressional elections, especially in the House.

Term limits offer another possible alteration to the institutional arrangements governing congressional elections. As another expression of anti-Congress sentiment in 1992, fourteen states adopted laws that imposed limits between six and twelve years on members of the House. All the plans contained twelve-year limits for senators.[96] Many analysts question the constitutionality of these proposals as well, contending that the qualifications for congressional service cannot be altered except by a constitutional amendment. There should be a determination of the legal issues within a couple of years, because challenges to a number of these term restrictions have already been launched. One challenge was personally started by Democratic Speaker of the House Thomas S. Foley of Washington, one of the states that adopted a term-limit proposal. These state restrictions do not count congressional service before the limitations were passed. Therefore, a court determination may come before any sitting member would be forced out.

One major effect of term limits is likely to be a greater number of open seats, and correspondingly a smaller impact from incumbency. Another effect may be to make congressional service less attractive to potential challengers, thus further weakening the challenger pool. A third aspect of term limits is likely to have a countervailing effect to the one just cited. Many states have also imposed term limits on their state legislatures, and there is no constitutional question about these provisions. In the future, some legislators who are forced to vacate their current offices may decide to run for Congress. This would increase the strength of the overall challenger pool; it would probably not be a net benefit to the Republicans because Democrats hold more seats in state legislatures across the country.

It appears that the Republicans have little reason to anticipate an alteration of their minority status except from a potential negative reaction by the voters to the Clinton administration and to the Democrats generally. This will make the congressional elections of 1994 and 1996 particularly interesting.

Chapter 10

The Congressional Electorate

In the preceding chapter we viewed congressional elections at the district and state level and saw how those outcomes come together to form a national result. In this chapter we consider congressional elections from the point of view of the individual voter, using the same National Election Studies (NES) surveys we employed to study presidential voting. We discuss how social forces, issues, partisan loyalties, incumbency, and evaluations of congressional and presidential performance influence the decisions of voters in congressional elections. We also try to determine the existence and extent of presidential coattails and to shed additional light on the effects of adequate or inadequate campaign resources on the part of challengers.

Social Forces and the Congressional Vote

In general, social forces relate to the congressional vote the same way they do to the presidential vote (Table 10-1).[1] But in 1992 Democratic congressional candidates did better than their presidential candidate, Bill Clinton, in many of the categories used in the presidential vote analysis (see Table 5-1).[2] This is true mainly because Clinton faced not only a Republican opponent, but also a significant independent challenger, while most House members had at most one serious opponent.

Consider, for example, the relationship between voting and Hispanic identification. Among white voters who identify as Hispanic, Democratic House candidates ran 40 percentage points ahead of Republicans, while the comparable figure for Clinton versus Bush was 36 points. Similarly, among whites who do not identify as Hispanic, Democratic House

Table 10-1 How Social Groups Voted for Congress, 1992 (in percentages)

Social Group	Democratic	Republican	Total Percent	(N)
Total electorate	58	42	100	(1,385)
Electorate, by race				
African-American	89	11	100	(141)
White	55	45	100	(1,210)
Whites, by Hispanic identification				
Identify as Hispanic	70	30	100	(65)
Do not identify	54	46	100	(1,145)
Whites, by gender				
Females	57	43	100	(625)
Males	52	48	100	(585)
Whites, by region				
New England and Mid-Atlantic	54	46	100	(252)
North Central	54	46	100	(371)
South	50	50	100	(234)
Border	58	42	100	(88)
Mountain and Pacific	61	39	100	(265)
Whites, by birth cohort				
Before 1924	63	37	100	(160)
1924-1939	57	43	100	(236)
1940-1954	55	45	100	(346)
1955-1962	47	53	100	(276)
1963-1970	55	45	100	(151)
1971-1974	56	44	100	(41)
Whites, by social class				
Working class	58	42	100	(443)
Middle class	51	49	100	(601)
Farmers	48	52	100	(60)
Whites, by occupation of head of household				
Unskilled manual	55	45	100	(124)
Skilled, semiskilled manual	60	40	100	(319)
Clerical, sales, other white collar	58	42	100	(190)
Managerial	49	51	100	(227)
Professional and semiprofessional	48	52	100	(185)

(Table continues)

Table 10-1 Continued

Social Group	Democratic	Republican	Total Percent	(N)
Whites, by level of education				
Eight grades or less	76	24	100	(46)
Some high school	55	45	100	(67)
High school graduate	61	39	100	(393)
Some college	53	47	100	(309)
College graduate	41	59	100	(241)
Advanced degree	58	42	100	(124)
Whites, by annual family income				
Less than $10,000	64	36	100	(76)
$10,000 to $14,999	69	31	100	(95)
$15,000 to $19,999	65	35	100	(72)
$20,000 to $24,999	66	34	100	(92)
$25,000 to $29,999	62	38	100	(81)
$30,000 to $34,999	57	43	100	(95)
$35,000 to $39,999	45	55	100	(93)
$40,000 to $49,999	60	40	100	(171)
$50,000 to $59,999	49	51	100	(119)
$60,000 to $74,999	47	53	100	(133)
$75,000 to $89,999	46	54	100	(62)
$90,000 and over	29	71	100	(86)
Whites, by union membership[a]				
Member	63	37	100	(232)
Nonmember	53	47	100	(974)
Whites, by religion				
Jewish	77	23	100	(31)
Catholic	60	40	100	(333)
Protestant	49	51	100	(686)
None, no preference	65	35	100	(142)
White Protestants, by whether born again				
Not born again	54	46	100	(373)
Born again	42	58	100	(294)
White Protestants, by religious commitment				
Medium or low	52	48	100	(197)
High	51	49	100	(385)
Very high	37	63	100	(104)

(Table continues)

Table 10-1 Continued

Social Group	Democratic	Republican	Total Percent	(N)
White Protestants, by religious tradition				
Mainline	49	51	100	(302)
Evangelical	46	54	100	(271)
Whites, by social class and religion				
Working-class Catholics	61	39	100	(118)
Middle-class Catholics	56	44	100	(181)
Working-class Protestants	56	44	100	(263)
Middle-class Protestants	44	56	100	(320)

Note: Numbers are weighted. Respondents for whom direction of vote was not ascertained or who voted for candidates who were neither Republicans nor Democrats have been excluded from these analyses.

[a] Whether respondent or family member belongs to a trade union.

candidates ran 8 points ahead of Republicans, while Clinton led Bush by 3 points within that group. (Except for the discussion of voting and race, the analysis here, as in Chapter 5, is limited to white voters.)

Keeping in mind this difference in relative support, we find that presidential and congressional voting patterns are similar not only with respect to Hispanic heritage, but also within many other social categories, including race, gender, social class, education, income, union membership, and Protestant and Catholic categories of religion. For both the presidential and the congressional vote, African-Americans were substantially more likely to vote Democratic. Among major party voters, the difference was 41 points for the presidential race and 34 points in House contests. Members of union families were 10 percentage points more likely to vote Democratic for the House than voters from nonunion families; working-class voters were 7 points more Democratic than middle-class voters. Catholics were 11 points more likely to vote Democratic than Protestants, and among Protestants, those who did not claim to be "born again" were 12 points more Democratic than those who claimed that status. Religious commitment was also related to congressional voting preferences, although the relationship was not as strong as that between religious commitment and presidential voting choices. Even so, just over a third of the white Protestants who had very high levels of religious commitment voted Democratic, while Protestants who did not score very high split their vote evenly between the two major parties.

There are some differences in the ways the presidential and congressional vote relate to income categories, but it is likely that these differences reflect the small number of cases in those categories. The overall patterns are similar and consistent: the propensity to vote Democratic is considerably greater in lower categories of income.

Of particular interest is the relationship between House voting and gender. In 1988, there was a small gender gap in the presidential vote (about 3 points), with women more likely to vote Democratic than men, but there was no gap in the House vote. In 1992, however, the gender gap was more pronounced in the vote both for the president and for representatives; the major party share of the vote was 7 points more Democratic for women in the former case and 5 points more Democratic in the latter.

There are, however, some differences worth noting in the way social forces relate to the two types of votes. One is with respect to region; for Clinton the best regions were the New England and Mid-Atlantic states, while the South and North Central states were the worst for him. In the House vote, Democrats did better in the West than in any other region, although for Congress the South was also the worst region for Democrats. This is a shift from 1988, when the South was the worst region for the Democrats in the presidential race, but not for Democrats in the congressional contests. There are also some differences with regard to both cohort and occupation, but these are modest and may also reflect the small number of cases in certain categories. Overall, then, the relationship of social forces to the 1992 congressional vote was quite similar to their relationship to the 1992 presidential vote.

Issues and the Congressional Vote

In Chapter 6 we analyzed the impact of issues on the presidential vote in 1992. Any attempt to conduct a parallel analysis for congressional elections is hampered by limited data. One interesting perspective on issues in the congressional vote is gained by asking whether voters are affected by their perceptions of where candidates stand on the issues. Previous analysis has demonstrated a relationship between a voter's perception of House candidates' position on a liberal-conservative issue scale and the voter's choice.[3] Unfortunately, the 1992 NES survey does not contain similar questions on the perceived position of House candidates on issues. We can, however, draw on other research to shed further light on this question. In two articles, Alan I. Abramowitz used NES surveys to demonstrate a relationship between candidate ideology and voter choice in both House and Senate elections.[4] For the 1978 Senate election, Abramowitz classified the contests according to the clarity of the ideological choice the two major party candidates offered to voters. He found that the higher the ideological clarity of the race, the more likely voters were to perceive some difference between the candidates on a liberalism-conservatism scale, and the stronger the relationship was between voters' positions on that scale and the vote. Indeed, in races with a very clear choice, ideology had approximately the same impact on the vote as party identification. In an analysis of House races in 1980 and 1982, Abramowitz found that the more liberal the voter was, the more likely the voter was to vote Democratic; but the relationship was statistically significant only in 1982.

Another point of view is offered in an analysis by Robert S. Erikson and Gerald C. Wright.[5] They examined the positions of 1982 House candidates on a variety of issues (expressed in response to a CBS News/*New York Times* poll) and found that, on most issues, most of the districts were presented with a liberal Democrat and a conservative Republican. They also found that moderate candidates did better in attracting votes than more extreme candidates. In a more recent study, involving the 1990 House elections, Erikson and Wright show that both the issue stands of incumbents (measured by positions on roll call votes) and the district's ideology (measured by the district's propensity to vote for Dukakis in the previous presidential election) are strongly related to the congressional vote.[6]

We examined the relationships between issues and congressional voting choices in 1992, analyzing the issues we studied in Chapter 6. For the most part, the relationship between issue preferences and congressional vote choices were weak and inconsistent, and these relationships were even weaker when we controlled for the tendency of Democratic party identifiers to have liberal positions on these issues and of Republicans to have conservative issue preferences. However, partisan loyalties clearly affect congressional voting, even when we take issue preferences into account. Therefore, before considering the effects of other factors we will provide more information about the effects of party identification on House voting.

Party Identification and the Congressional Vote

As our discussion in the preceding chapters demonstrates and data presented here indicate, party identification has a significant effect on voters' decisions. Table 10-2, which corresponds to Table 8-4 on the presidential vote, reports the percentage of whites voting Democratic for the House across all categories of partisanship from 1952 through 1992. Even a casual inspection of the data reveals that the proportion of voters who cast ballots in accordance with their party identification has declined substantially over time.

Consider first the strong identifier categories. In every election from 1952 through 1964, at least nine strong party identifiers out of ten supported the candidate of their party. After that, the percentage dropped, falling to four out of five in 1980, then fluctuating through 1992. The relationship between party and voting among weak party identifiers shows a more erratic pattern, although in most years defection rates tend to be higher since the 1970s than earlier. Note that the tendency to defect is stronger among Republicans, which reflects the Democrats' greater number of incumbents, as discussed in Chapter 9. We consider this further in the next section.

Despite this increase in defections from party identification since the mid-1960s, strong party identifiers continue to be more likely to vote in accord with their party than weak identifiers. In most years, weak Republicans are more likely to vote Republican than independents who lean toward the Republican party, although in 1992 these groups were equally likely to vote Republican. Weak Democrats were more likely to vote Democratic than independents who leaned Democratic in most of the elections from 1952 through 1978, although in a number of elections since then this pattern has been reversed. In 1992, however, weak Democrats were more likely to vote Democratic than independents who leaned Democratic. In general, then, the relationship between party identification and the vote was strongest in the 1950s and early 1960s, and less strong thereafter. This is especially true in the ability of Democratic congressional candidates to win votes from the various Republican-identifying groups. On the other hand, partisanship is still strongly related to the vote in the more recent period. There are few signs, however, of a restrengthening of this relationship at the congressional level.

As we saw in Chapters 4 and 8, however, the proportion of the electorate that strongly identifies with either political party has declined. Thus, strong Democrats, for example, not only are less likely to vote Democratic than before, but also fewer voters identify themselves as strong Democrats. The impact of party on voting, therefore, has suffered a double weakening.

If party identifiers have been defecting more frequently in House elections, to whom have they been defecting? As one might expect from the preceding chapter, the answer is: to incumbents.

Incumbency and the Congressional Vote

In Chapter 9 we mentioned Albert D. Cover's analysis of congressional voting behavior from 1958 through 1974.[7] Cover compared the

Table 10-2   Percentage of White Major Party Voters Who Voted Democratic for the House, by Party Identification, 1952-1992

Party Identification	1952	1954	1956	1958	1960	1962	1964	1966	1968
Strong Democrat	90	97	94	96	92	96	92	92	88
Weak Democrat	76	77	86	88	85	83	84	81	72
Independent, leans Democratic	63	70	82	75	86	74	78	54	60
Independent, no partisan leanings	25	41	35	46	52	61	70	49	48
Independent, leans Republican	18	6	17	26	26	28	28	31	18
Weak Republican	10	6	11	22	14	14	34	22	21
Strong Republican	5	5	5	6	8	6	8	12	8

Notes: To approximate the numbers upon which these percentages are based, see Table 8-2. Actual *N*s will be smaller than those that can be derived from Table 8-2 because respondents who did not vote (or who voted for a minor party) have been excluded from these calculations. Numbers also will be lower for the presidential election years because

rates of defection from party identification among voters who were of the same party as the incumbent and those who were of the same party as the challenger. The analysis showed no systematic increase over time in defection among voters who shared identification with incumbents, and the proportions defecting varied between 5 percent and 14 percent. Among voters who identified with the same party as challengers, however, the rate of defection—that is, the proportion voting for the incumbent instead of the candidate of their own party—increased steadily from 16 percent in 1958 to 56 percent in 1972, then dropped to 49 percent in 1974. Thus the decline in the strength of the relationship between party identification and House voting appears to be due in large measure to increased support for incumbents. Because there are more Democratic incumbents, this tendency is consistent with the higher defection rates among Republican identifiers, as seen in Table 10-2.

Data on the percentage of respondents who voted Democratic for the House and Senate in 1992, controlling for party identification and incumbency, are presented in Table 10-3, and confirm this view. In House voting we find the same relationship as Cover did. As we present the percentage of major party voters who voted Democratic, the defection

Table 10-2   Continued

1970	1972	1974	1976	1978	1980	1982	1984	1986	1988	1990	1992
91	91	89	86	83	82	90	87	91	86	91	87
76	79	81	76	79	66	73	66	71	80	80	81
74	78	87	76	60	69	84	76	71	86	79	73
48	54	54	55	56	57	31	59	59	66	60	53
35	27	38	32	36	32	36	39	37	37	33	36
17	24	31	28	34	26	20	33	34	29	39	35
4	15	14	15	19	22	12	15	20	23	17	16

the voting report is provided in the postelection interviews that usually contain about 10 percent fewer respondents than the preelection interviews in which party identification was measured. The 1954 survey measured voting intention shortly before the election. Except for 1954, the off-year election surveys are based upon a postelection interview.

rate for Democrats is the reported percentage subtracted from 100 percent. Among Republicans, the percentage reported in the table percentage is the defection rate. (By definition, independents cannot defect.) The proportion of voters defecting from their party identification is low when that identification is shared by the incumbent: 7 percent among Democrats and 10 percent among Republicans.[8] When, however, the incumbent belongs to the other party, the rates are much higher: 40 percent among Democrats and 41 percent among Republicans. Note also that the support of the independents is skewed sharply in favor of the incumbent. When there was an incumbent Democrat running, nearly three-fourths of the independents voted Democratic; when there was an incumbent Republican, nearly three-fourths of the independents voted Republican. This finding is quite different from independents' voting choices for president, as both Clinton and Perot benefited because many independents voted *against* the incumbent, as we saw in Chapter 8.

A similar pattern is apparent from the data on Senate voting, although the pull of incumbency appears to be somewhat weaker. When given the opportunity to support a Republican House incumbent, 40 percent of the Democratic identifiers defected. Faced with the opportunity to support an incumbent Republican senator, only 27 percent

Table 10-3   Percentage That Voted Democratic for the House and
Senate, 1992, by Party Identification and Incumbency

| | Party Identification | | | | | |
| | Democrat | | Independent | | Republican | |
Incumbency	*(%)*	*(N)*	*(%)*	*(N)*	*(%)*	*(N)*
House						
Democrat	93	(311)	73	(231)	41	(173)
None	83	103)	48	(78)	27	(86)
Republican	60	(80)	28	(127)	10	(128)
Senate						
Democrat	88	(119)	64	(73)	32	(68)
None	87	(120)	59	(107)	24	(98)
Republican	73	(121)	47	(125)	16	(143)

Note: Numbers in parentheses are totals upon which percentages are based. Numbers are weighted.

defected. Because the proportion of the electorate that has the chance to vote for Democratic and Republican senatorial candidates will vary greatly from election to election, it is difficult to make generalizations about the overall effects of incumbency in Senate contests. But the results in Table 10-3 show that in House elections the Democrats are the clear beneficiaries of the tendency to support incumbents. Over two-fifths of all Republican identifiers lived in a district in which a Democratic incumbent was seeking reelection. On the other hand, just about one-sixth of the Democratic identifiers lived in a district in which a Republican incumbent was running. Among independents, 53 percent lived in a district in which a Democratic incumbent was seeking reelection, and 29 percent lived in a district with a Republican incumbent. In the remainder of this chapter we explore this relationship among party identification, incumbency, and congressional voting.

The Congressional Vote as a Referendum

In Chapter 7 we analyzed the effect of perceptions of presidential performance on the vote for president in 1992, more or less viewing that election as a referendum on Bush's job performance, especially about the most salient concern among voters: the economy. A similar conception can be applied here, employing different perspectives. On the one hand, a congressional election can be considered as a referendum on the performance of a particular member of Congress in office; on the other hand, it can be viewed as a referendum on the performance of the president. We will consider both possibilities here.

As we noted in Chapter 9, for some time, public opinion surveys have shown that the approval ratings of congressional incumbents are very high, even when judgments on the performance of Congress as an institution are not. While traveling with House incumbents in their districts, Richard F. Fenno, Jr., noted that the people he met overwhelmingly approved of the performance of their own representative, although at the time the public generally disapproved of the job the institution was doing.[9] Data in the 1992 NES survey again indicate widespread approval of House incumbents: among respondents who had an opinion, an average of 85 percent endorsed their member's job performance. Approval was widespread, regardless of the party identification of the voter or the party of the incumbent. Indeed, an examination of all combinations of these two variables shows that the lowest approval rate for incumbents is the 64 percent level achieved by Republican members among Democratic party identifiers.

Further evidence indicates, moreover, that the level of approval has electoral consequences. Table 10-4 shows the level of proincumbent voting among voters who share the incumbent's party and among those who are of the opposite party, controlling for whether they approve or disapprove of the incumbent's job performance. If voters approve of the member's performance and share his or her party identification, support is overwhelming. At the opposite pole, among voters from the opposite party who disapprove, support is negligible. In the mixed categories, 50 to 60 percent of the voters support the incumbent. Because approval rates are very high even among voters of the opposite party, most incumbents are reelected by large margins even in a difficult year like 1992.[10]

In Chapter 9 we pointed out that midterm congressional elections were influenced by public evaluations of the president's job performance. Voters who think the president is doing a good job are more likely to support the congressional candidate of the president's party. Less scholarly attention has been given to this phenomenon in presidential election years, but the 1992 NES survey provides us with the data needed to explore the question.

On the surface at least, there would appear to be a strong relationship. Among voters who approved of Bush's job performance, only 35 percent voted Democratic for the House; among those who disapproved of the president's performance, 75 percent supported Democrats. In 1980 there was a similar relationship between the two variables, but when controls were introduced for party identification and incumbency, the relationship all but disappeared.[11] Approval of Carter increased the Democratic House vote by a small amount among Democrats, but had

Table 10-4   Percentage of Voters Who Supported Incumbents in House Voting, 1992, by Party and Evaluations of Incumbent's Performance

| | Voters' Evaluation of Incumbent's Job Performance | | | |
| | Approve | | Disapprove | |
	(%)	(N)	(%)	(N)
Incumbent is of same party as voter	97	(332)	49	(16)
Incumbent is of opposite party	59	(137)	3	(54)

Note: Numbers in parentheses are totals upon which percentages are based. Numbers are weighted. The total number of cases is markedly lower than for previous tables because we have excluded respondents who did not evaluate the performance of the incumbent and those who live in a district that had no incumbent running.

virtually no effect among independents and Republicans. In 1992, however, the results are very different. Table 10-5 presents the relevant data on House voting, controlling for party identification, incumbency, and evaluation of Bush's job performance. We found that even with these controls, evaluations of the president's job had a noticeable impact on House voting. To be sure, Democrats were still more likely both to disapprove of Bush and to vote Democratic than were Republicans. Yet even after controlling for the pull of incumbency, within each party identification category, those who disapproved of Bush's job performance were noticeably more likely to vote Democratic for the House than were those who approved, and the difference in five of the six categories was larger than the corresponding difference in 1980. The results for 1992 are similar to those for the 1984 and 1988 elections. Further research is necessary to reconcile these conflicting findings.

Presidential Coattails and the Congressional Vote

Another perspective on the congressional vote, somewhat related to the presidential referendum concept we have just considered, is the impact of the voter's presidential vote decision, or the length of a presidential candidate's coattails. That is, does a voter's decision to support a presidential candidate make him or her more likely to support a congressional candidate of the same party, so that the congressional candidate, as the saying goes, rides into office on the president's coattails?

Table 10-5 Percentage That Voted Democratic for the House, 1992, Controlling for Evaluation of Bush's Performance, Party Identification, and Incumbency

Party Identification	Evaluation of Bush's Job							
	Incumbent Is Republican				Incumbent Is Democrat			
	Approve		Disapprove		Approve		Disapprove	
	(%)	(N)	(%)	(N)	(%)	(N)	(%)	(N)
Democrat	51	(13)	62	(67)	88	(51)	94	(253)
Independent	11	(52)	41	(72)	58	(77)	80	(150)
Republican	7	(99)	20	(28)	36	(142)	66	(31)

Note: Numbers in parentheses are totals upon which percentages are based. Numbers are weighted.

Expectations regarding presidential coattails have been shaped in substantial measure by the period of the New Deal realignment. Franklin D. Roosevelt won by landslide margins in 1932 and 1936 and swept enormous congressional majorities into office with him. Research has indicated, however, that such strong pulling power by presidential candidates may have been a historical aberration, and in any event, that candidates' pulling power has declined in recent years.[12] In an analysis of the coattail effect since 1868, Randall L. Calvert and John A. Ferejohn pointed out that the effect is a combination of two factors: how many voters a presidential candidate can pull to congressional candidates of his party and how many congressional seats can be shifted between the parties by the addition of those voters.[13] (The second aspect is called the seats/votes relationship, or the swing ratio.)

Ferejohn and Calvert discovered that the relationship between presidential voting and congressional voting from 1932 through 1948 was virtually the same as it was from 1896 through 1928 and that the impact of coattails was strengthened by an increase in the swing ratio. In other words, the same proportion of votes pulled in by a presidential candidate produced more congressional seats in the New Deal era than in the past. After 1948, they argued, the coattail effect declined because the relationship between presidential and congressional voting decreased. Analyzing data from presidential elections from 1956 through 1980, Ferejohn and Calvert reached similar conclusions about the length of presidential coattails.[14] They found that although every election during the period exhibited significant coattail voting, over time the extent of such voting probably declined. More recently, James E. Campbell and Joe A.

Table 10-6 Percentage of Respondents Who Voted Democratic for House and Senate, 1992, Controlling for Party Identification and Presidential Vote

Presidential Vote	Party identification					
	Democrat		Independent		Republican	
	(%)	(N)	(%)	(N)	(%)	(N)
House						
Bush	68	(38)	32	(136)	20	(282)
Clinton	88	(404)	73	(187)	64	(34)
Perot	78	(50)	52	(107)	39	(69)
Senate						
Bush	56	(27)	21	(77)	16	(228)
Clinton	86	(293)	83	(137)	50	(49)
Perot	74	(40)	41	(86)	33	(49)

Note: Numbers in parentheses are totals upon which percentages are based. Numbers are weighted.

Sumners concluded from an analysis of Senate elections that presidential coattails exert a modest but significant influence on the Senate vote.[15]

Data on the percentage of respondents who voted Democratic for the House and Senate in 1992, controlling for their presidential vote and their party identification, are presented in Table 10-6. For both houses, a strong relationship is apparent. Within each party identification category, the proportion of Bush voters who supported Democratic congressional candidates is substantially lower than the proportion of Clinton voters who supported Democratic candidates. Moreover, the proportion of Perot voters who voted Democratic falls between the proportions for the supporters of the two major party candidates in every instance, although fewer "Perot-Democrats" defected from their party in congressional races than "Perot-Republicans."

Because we know that this apparent relationship could be just an accidental consequence of the distribution of different types of voters among Democratic and Republican districts, in Table 10-7 we present the same data on House voting in 1992, but this time controlling for the party of the House incumbent. Despite this additional control, the relationship holds up very well. Within every category for which comparisons are possible, Bush voters supported Democratic candidates at substantially lower rates than did Clinton voters. Democratic and Republican identifiers who voted for Perot were as likely to vote for Democratic incumbents

Table 10-7 Percentage of Respondents Who Voted Democratic for the House, 1992, Controlling for Presidential Vote, Party Identification, and Incumbency

Party Identification	Voted for Bush		Voted for Clinton		Voted for Perot	
	(%)	(N)	(%)	(N)	(%)	(N)
		Incumbent Is Democrat				
Democrat	83	(23)	94	(255)	93	(32)
Independent	51	(69)	88	(105)	68	(52)
Republican	34	(133)	67	(15)	64	(24)
		Incumbent Is Republican				
Democrat	—	(5)	66	(61)	52	(13)
Independent	4	(42)	49	(47)	28	(37)
Republican	3	(82)	38	(12)	16	(33)

Note: Numbers in parentheses are totals upon which percentages are based. Numbers are weighted. No percentage is reported where the total *N* is less than 10.

as were those who voted for Clinton. Among other categories, Perot voters fell between Clinton voters and Bush voters. These data are consistent with the interpretation that the presidential vote exerted some influence on the congressional vote, although not as strong an influence as partisanship and congressional incumbency. The results in both Table 10-6 and Table 10-7 are very similar to the corresponding data for 1980, 1984 and 1988: within the various categories of party identification and congressional incumbency, the relationship between presidential voting and congressional voting seems to be substantially the same in these four elections.[16]

Incumbency and Candidate Resources Revisited

In Chapter 9 and this chapter, we have consistently seen the impact of incumbency both on congressional election outcomes and on the decisions of individual voters. In Chapter 9 we discussed the relationship between incumbency and candidate resources and argued that the larger margins of victory of House incumbents, observed since the mid-1960s, may be primarily the consequence of the challengers' inability to raise enough money to compete effectively. The 1992 election study contains a number of questions that provide further support for this position.

Table 10-8   Percentage That Supported House Incumbents, 1992, Controlling for Party of Voter and Incumbent and for Contact by Incumbent and Challenger

| | Voter Was Contacted by | | | | | |
| | Only the Incumbent | | Both Candidates | | Neither Candidate | |
Voter Is	(%)	(N)	(%)	(N)	(%)	(N)
Same party as incumbent	98	(185)	91	(156)	85	(61)
Independent	89	(106)	66	(193)	75	(27)
Opposite party from incumbent	62	(73)	30	(142)	54	(21)

Note: Numbers in parentheses are totals upon which percentages are based. Numbers are weighted.

Respondents in the 1992 NES survey were asked a number of questions about contacts they had with incumbents and challengers in House races.[17] Recalling our earlier discussion of incumbency and resources, we would expect most voters to have been contacted in some way by their House incumbent, but not by challengers, because many of the challengers lacked the resources to do so. There are as many as 400,000 persons of voting age in each district, and contacting them is expensive. The survey data bear out this expectation. Among congressional voters who lived in contested districts with incumbents running, 37 percent reported some contact with both candidates, but an additional 50 percent remembered only contact with the incumbent. Eleven percent of the voters reported no contact with either candidate, and less than 2 percent reported being contacted only by the challenger.

The next step is to assess whether these patterns of contact have electoral consequences. Table 10-8 presents data on voters' support for incumbents, controlling for party identification and contacts between voters and congressional candidates. (Because there were so few cases in which voters were contacted only by the challenger, this category is excluded.) The results appear to be fairly strong and consistent with our expectations. When voters share partisanship with the incumbent, support rates tend to be very high across all categories, although there is some slippage when the incumbent and the challenger both fail to contact the voter. Among independents and voters who identify with the same party as the challenger, however, the variations across categories are substantial. When only the incumbent contacts independent voters, the incumbent wins nearly nine out of ten votes. But incumbents win only two-thirds of the votes when both candidates contact the voters, although they win three out of four votes among the few respondents contacted by neither candidate. Similarly, among voters of the challenger's party, the defection rate is 62 percent when only the incumbent has contacted the voter, but it is half that when both candidates have contacted the voter. These results seem to support our hypothesis that a significant part of the electoral advantage of House incumbents comes from the inability of challengers to get their message across to voters.

Conclusion

In this chapter we have considered a variety of possible influences on voters' decisions in congressional elections. We found that social forces have some impact on that choice. There is evidence from the work of other researchers that issues also have an effect.

Incumbency has a major and consistent impact on voters' choices. It solidifies the support of the incumbent's partisans, attracts independents, and leads to defections by voters who identify with the challenger's party. Incumbent support is linked to a positive evaluation of the representative's job by the voters and apparently also to greater contact with voters. The tendency to favor incumbents appears to be of particular benefit to the Democratic party in House races. Within the context of this incumbency effect, voters' choices also seem to be affected by their evaluations of the job the president is doing and by their vote for president. Partisanship has some direct impact on the vote, even after controlling for incumbency. The total effect of partisanship is, however, larger, because most incumbents represent districts that have more partisans of their party than of the opposition. Thus, the long-term advantage of Democrats in congressional elections is built on a three-part base: There are more Democrats than Republicans in the electorate; most incumbents of both parties achieve high levels of approval in their constituencies; and the incumbents have resources that make it possible for them to create direct contacts with voters.

PART 4

The 1992 Elections in Perspective

A careful analysis of past voting patterns provides evidence for speculating about future elections. But no analysis can predict the behavior of individuals. There was no way to predict that George Bush would squander enormous political assets by reacting passively to deteriorating economic conditions. For, although the economic problems were serious, Bush compounded them with political blunders. In some respects, the economy in 1992 was healthy—inflation was under control and interest rates were relatively low. But the 1992 recession was hurting the middle class more than earlier postwar downturns had. With health care costs rising far faster than the rate of inflation, and with health care tied to employment, Americans were worried about the dangers of unemployment. Bush reacted with amazing ineptitude—buying socks at a J. C. Penney store to boost the economy, expressing amazement over an electronic scanner at a supermarket checkout counter, and continually denying that the economic downturn was anything more than a short-term problem. By the time he made proposals for serious reform at the Detroit Economic Club in the summer of 1992, few were willing to listen.

On the other hand, Bill Clinton, who had serious liabilities, ran a highly effective campaign. Clinton had learned from Michael S. Dukakis's 1988 defeat, whereas Bush seemed to have learned nothing from his own 1988 victory. The Clinton team responded immediately to every negative charge, remained focused on the economy, and designed a strategy to win the 270 electoral votes needed to secure victory. Clinton ran a brilliant campaign, baiting Jesse Jackson seriously enough to make him protest but not enough to lead him to sit out the campaign entirely. Clinton attempted to win the votes of African-Americans at minimal cost, while directing his resources to converting Reagan and Bush voters into Clinton voters.

His choice of Al Gore as his running mate was also a brilliant maneuver, just as Bush's choice of Dan Quayle in 1988 had been a blunder. Gore could be seen as another moderate, despite charges that he was an environmental extremist. Moreover, Gore was a Vietnam veteran, a status that helped to stem the charges that Bill Clinton was a draft dodger. Bill Clinton was an opponent of the Vietnam War who had avoided military service, whereas Dan Quayle was a supporter of the war who had avoided combat by joining the Indiana National Guard. The choice of Sen. Bob Kerrey of Nebraska would have provided Clinton with a genuine war hero as a running mate, but Gore's selection seemed to anticipate the Republican suggestion that the Democrats did not represent family values. Kerrey had two children, but he had divorced and never remarried. Gore was married and had four children; his wife, Tipper, had earlier campaigned to require labels on rock music recordings warning of profanity.

Although there had been strong independent and third-party candidates in the past, H. Ross Perot was unique. By election day, Perot's campaign appeared to cost Bush and Clinton equally. Our analyses suggest that had Perot not reentered the campaign on October 1, Clinton would have easily been elected with a popular vote majority. But during his early undeclared candidacy—before announcing on July 16 that he would not run—Perot focused on Bush's failures. After he entered the race on October 1, he was far more forgiving toward Clinton than toward Bush. He claimed that Clinton, as the governor of a small state, did not have the experience to be president. But he explicitly dismissed Clinton's lack of military service during Vietnam as irrelevant. On the other hand, he not only blamed Bush for mismanaging the economy, but he also accused the Republicans of having secret plans to disrupt his daughter's wedding.

Although the behavior of individuals cannot be predicted, the U.S. government has constitutional features that make its politics more predictable than most other democracies'. According to Arend Lijphart, the United States is the only democracy with a pure presidential system.[1] Unlike parliamentary democracies, in which no one can predict when elections will be held, congressional elections and presidential elections are held at fixed intervals. Indeed, even if the president must be replaced, no election is held to fill the position.[2] Thus, we know that all 435 seats in the U.S. House of Representatives will be filled in 1994 and again in 1996. In each of these years a third of the Senate seats will be filled. Moreover, we know that Clinton's first term is scheduled to end on January 20, 1997. Although election dates are not constitutionally fixed, we can be confident that a midterm election will be held on

November 8, 1994, and that a presidential election will be held on November 5, 1996.

The Republicans are very likely to gain House seats in 1994. But they are unlikely to win control of the House unless the economy suffers badly and unless there is widespread disapproval of Clinton's performance as president. Since there are relatively few Senate seats, and since Senate elections are much more competitive than House elections, the Republicans have a greater chance of winning control of the Senate. Unlike the upper house in other bicameral democracies, the U.S. Senate has power equal to that of the House. Divided government would return even if the GOP won only the Senate. Nonetheless, unified government may continue at least through 1996.

But what will occur in the next presidential election and thereafter? In Chapter 11 we consider alternative possibilities. First, we examine the prospects that the Democrats will again establish themselves as the majority party. We then examine the prospects for a Republican return to power, noting that the Republicans have internal divisions that may create difficulties in the 1996 election. We next examine the prospects for the formation of a new political party, paying particular attention to the chances that Perot will form one. Last, we consider the prospects for continued electoral volatility, the pattern that has prevailed in postwar presidential politics.

Chapter 11

The 1992 Elections and
the Future of American Politics

In his classic study of political parties, Maurice Duverger argued that in some democracies there is clearly a dominant political party. Despite competitive elections, a single party consistently is at the center of political power. A party, Duverger wrote, "is dominant when it holds the majority over a long period of political development." Although a dominant party may occasionally lose an election, it remains dominant because "it is identified with an epoch" and because "its doctrines, ideas, methods, its style, so to speak, coincide with those of the epoch." One reason a party dominates is because it is believed to be dominant. "Even the enemies of the dominant party, even citizens who refuse to give it their vote," Duverger wrote, "acknowledge its superior status and its influence; they deplore it but admit it." [1]

Duverger's concept of the dominant party provides insights about the decline of the Democratic party after 1964. Students of comparative politics provide at least four clear examples of dominant parties:[2] Mapai (Israel Worker's Party), the Christian Democrats (DC) in Italy,[3] the Swedish Social Democratic Party,[4] and the Liberal Democratic Party (LDP) in Japan.[5] But Duverger argued that if a country had free elections, a dominant party was always in peril. "The dominant party wears itself out in office, it loses its vigour, its arteries harden." And, he concluded, "every domination bears within itself the seeds of its own destruction." [6]

Duverger appears to be prophetic.[7] Mapai was the dominant party even before Israel attained statehood in 1948, and it remained dominant until 1977, when an electoral "upheaval" drove the Alignment (the successor to Mapai) from office, and it did not become the leading party in a political coalition again until 1992. In Italy, the DC, with American assistance, won nearly half the vote in 1948, when Italy held its first postwar parliamentary elections. It lost power more gradually than Mapai, but it suffered a major loss in the 1983 election, which brought Italy's first Socialist prime minister to power.[8] By 1993, the entire Italian party system seemed to be crumbling. The Swedish Social Democratic party came to power in 1932, and, although it was forced into opposition by elections in 1976 and 1979, it returned to power in 1982. But in 1991 the nonsocialist parties won an absolute majority of the vote, and the dominance of the Swedish Social Democratic Party appears to have ended. Since its formation in 1955, the Liberal Democratic Party consistently held a majority in the Japanese House of Representatives; but in 1993, in the face of mounting scandals, the LDP split, the LDP prime minister dissolved the House of Representatives and called an election, the party lost its majority, and, although it was still the single largest party, it was excluded from the coalition government formed after the election. Perhaps the LDP will return to power, but so many of its leaders have broken from it that a return to dominance will be difficult.

Writing in 1958, Duverger argued that Democrats were the dominant party in the United States, even though Dwight D. Eisenhower, running as a Republican, had been elected president in both 1952 and 1956. Duverger viewed Eisenhower's election as a personal victory that did not change the balance of partisan power.[9] Indeed, scholars writing after the 1964 elections might have seen the Democratic party as even more dominant. The Democrats had won the White House under Franklin D. Roosevelt in 1932, then had won six of the next eight presidential elections. In 1964, under Lyndon B. Johnson, the Democrats won by a landslide over the Republican Barry Goldwater, and gained thirty-eight seats in the U.S. House of Representatives. The only Republican victories had come under a former general, Eisenhower, who had been courted by both the Democratic and Republican parties. The Republicans, much like the Whigs, who ran William Henry Harrison in 1840 and Zachary Taylor in 1848, defeated the Democrats by choosing a war hero as their standard bearer. Both of the generals elected by the Whigs died shortly after taking office, whereas Eisenhower served two full terms. However, like the Whigs, the Republicans seldom controlled the U.S. Congress. Between the 73d Congress, elected in 1932, and the 89th Congress, elected in 1964, the Republicans held a majority for only four years (the 80th, elected in 1946, and the 83d Congress, elected in 1952).

In retrospect, it is easy to see that the Democratic party had within it the "seeds of its own destruction," although the seeds for the party's decline are to be found in the composition of the coalition that supported it.[10] The New Deal coalition drew votes from northern blacks and southern whites, and this coalition was sustainable only as long as discrimination against African-Americans in the South was not a major political issue. After the civil rights movement began in the mid-1950s, ignoring racial injustice in the South became untenable. By backing the Civil Rights Act of 1964 and the Voting Rights Act of 1965, Johnson chose a position that, we believe, was morally correct. Johnson may well have had strategic goals in mind as well, but his decision to aggressively seek African-American votes helped to end Democratic dominance in presidential elections. With hindsight, the seeds of future Democratic defeats can be seen in Johnson's landslide over Goldwater, for in addition to winning his home state of Arizona, Goldwater carried Alabama, Georgia, Louisiana, Mississippi, and South Carolina. By the end of the 1960s African-Americans in these states were able to vote, and, as Johnson expected, they voted heavily Democratic. Even so, in most subsequent presidential elections these states, as well as the remaining southern states, have voted Republican. Virginia has voted Republican in all seven presidential elections held after 1964.

The Republicans, after losing control of the U.S. House of Representatives in 1954, were never able to regain the Congress. But several political scientists, writing after the 1988 election, believed that the Republicans had become the dominant party in U.S. presidential elections.[11] From 1968 through 1988, the Republicans had won five of six presidential elections, and the only Democratic victory came after the Watergate scandal in which Richard Nixon was forced to resign, when the Democrats narrowly defeated Gerald R. Ford, the man who had pardoned him. If Bill Clinton fails as president, the Republicans may once again become the party that dominates presidential elections.

But the Reagan coalition, too, may have had within it the seeds of its own destruction. Reagan created a coalition of social conservatives for whom the fight against abortion and the right to hold prayers in public schools were important issues, and economic conservatives who believed that less government was the key to economic growth. Although Reagan and Bush mainly paid lip service to conservative social values, they also provided tangible benefits to social conservatives by a series of court appointments, especially to the U.S. Supreme Court, that put *Roe v. Wade* in jeopardy. When Republican economic policies no longer appeared to provide economic growth, a large number of the economic conservatives, and some social conservatives, deserted Bush, although many turned to H. Ross Perot instead of to Clinton.

With no clear majority party in the United States, it would be unwise to predict the future of the American party system. But we can rely upon what we have learned to evaluate alternative possibilities. First, we discuss prospects for the Democrats once again to become the majority party, perhaps through a new partisan realignment. Second, we discuss future Republican prospects. Third, we discuss the prospects for a new political party, the most likely possibility being an outgrowth of Perot's United We Stand America. Last, we discuss the prospects for continued electoral volatility.

Prospects for the Democrats

Can Clinton and a Democratic Congress once again make the Democrats a majority party, and perhaps the dominant force in American politics for decades to come? In the face of the collapse of dominant parties throughout the world, this seems unlikely. All the same, unified government provides opportunities. For the first time since Jimmy Carter's administration ended in January 1981, the same party controls both houses of Congress and the presidency. In principle, unified government provides a chance for the Democrats to enact new policies that will be so attractive to a majority of the electorate that the party recovers its majority, forcing the GOP into the political backwaters. But, as we saw in Chapter 9, unified government has electoral risks.

Let us begin with a best case scenario for the Democrats. Let us suppose that in the wake of the Clinton budget package, approved by a Democratically controlled Congress in the face of unanimous Republican opposition, the economy becomes robust, unemployment falls, and inflation remains low. Let us further suppose that, because of this robust economy, the annual budget deficit falls. Although economic growth puts upward pressure on interest rates, the federal government itself has less need to borrow, and interest rates increase only marginally, or remain stable.

With this much economic prosperity, most Americans would forgive Clinton for reneging on his pledge of a tax cut for the middle class (scarcely the centerpiece of his campaign, as Bush's "Read my lips—no new taxes" pledge had been in 1988). Few would resent paying four cents more per gallon of gasoline; and even wealthy Americans, who would pay higher taxes, might think it better to continue with the Democrats.

Suppose, too, Clinton succeeds in enacting major health care reform, and that this reform is popular. And, let us further suppose that, as a consequence of economic recovery, crime diminishes, and domestic tranquility prevails. And let us further suppose that Clinton avoids major foreign policy blunders.

Under such circumstances, it is difficult to imagine a Clinton defeat except by a scandal far more dramatic than his alleged affair with Gennifer Flowers. The Democrats' grip on congressional power would be even more secure. The Republicans would be viewed as obstructionists who did their best to derail the Clinton economic miracle, and Perot would become politically irrelevant. The Democratic party would be invincible.

Let us not try to imagine a worst case scenario, which might involve massive unemployment, hyperinflation, and a civil war in the former Soviet Union. But it is not difficult to envisage a bad case scenario in which inflation and unemployment both rise to double-digit levels, in which health care reform is not enacted, and in which the United States becomes involved in costly peacekeeping operations throughout the world. Under such circumstances Clinton would have to be extremely lucky to be reelected, perhaps by facing a split Republican party or a three-candidate contest in which the third candidate draws more from the Republican challenger than from Clinton.

In this bad case scenario, even the Democratic control of Congress would be jeopardized. As we saw in Chapter 9, Gary C. Jacobson effectively demonstrates that in some respects Republican presidents were electoral assets for Democrats who sought election to Congress.[12] Under divided government, it was difficult for Americans to place blame for the nation's problems on congressional Democrats, and especially on Democratic incumbents from their own districts. As we saw in Chapter 9, despite reapportionment, redistricting, a major congressional scandal, and a Democratic presidential candidate who drew only 43 percent of the popular vote, the Republicans gained merely ten seats in the U.S. House of Representatives. Republicans could chant "sweep the House" at their 1992 convention in Houston, but voters who wanted change knew that the easiest way to bring it about was to elect a new president. But with the Democrats in control of the House, the Senate, and the presidency, blame becomes much easier to fix. If Clinton's approval ratings are low in the fall of 1994, many Democratic incumbents may run for cover, distance themselves from Clinton, and, as usual, attack Congress itself. But, under such circumstances, many Democrats might still be defeated. The Republicans might regain the Senate and might even end the Democratic winning streak in the House. If Clinton were still viewed as a failure in the fall of 1996, a united Republican party might easily regain the White House, and perhaps win control of Congress as well.

Even with a reasonably good case scenario for the Democrats, a new Democratic majority would not look much like the New Deal coalition. Apart from African-Americans, Clinton won a majority of the white vote only among Hispanics, Jews, those with low levels of formal education and the poor. He fell short of a majority among union households. In his successful fight to win congressional support for the North American Free Trade Agreement (NAFTA), Clinton directly challenged union leaders, and he may find it difficult to gain their support in 1996. It is hard to visualize what a winning Democratic coalition would look like in the twenty-first century. But if a good case scenario for the Democrats comes about, it seems likely that Clinton and his Democratic successors could create a coalition that will be viable for some time to come.

Prospects for the Republicans

The hopes for Republican success are the mirror image of the Democratic fears of failure. We expect the Republicans to gain seats in the 1994 midterm election, and it is easy to imagine them capturing the White House two years later. But to win an election, a party must have a candidate, and that candidate will be chosen mainly by voters in the Republican primaries to be held from February through early June of 1996. We expect many Republicans to vie for the GOP nomination, especially if Clinton is widely perceived as a failed president, and the contest may be brutal.

The most important conflict may be between social conservatives and economic conservatives. The goals of the social conservatives who dominated the Republican party convention in Houston are far different from those of economic conservatives. The Christian Coalition, a vestige of Pat Robertson's 1988 presidential campaign, has the explicit goal of winning control of the Republican party. If Clinton is in trouble in 1996, the scent of victory might ultimately unite the Republican party. But even the chance of winning might not matter much to partisans who see politics as religious warfare. Writing about the Republican party convention in Houston, Jack W. Germond and Jules Witcover argued that despite occasional extremism at past Republican conventions—most notably during Goldwater's 1964 nomination in San Francisco—the basic argument among Republicans has usually been about the right approach to government. "It had usually been possible for conservatives and liberals to behave with civility and even good humor toward those with whom they totally disagreed. . . . But the delegates of the religious right were a different breed of activists who believed that those who disagreed with them were not just wrong, but evil." [13]

Because Clinton's approval ratings fell faster during the first six months of his presidency than had those of any previous president since Gallup polls began to systematically measure approval during the Eisenhower administration, the Republicans might gloat about his vulnerability.[14] But many look forward to the 1996 nomination contest with considerable foreboding. This pessimism was expressed well by former U.S. Representative Bill Frenzel of Minnesota, the chairman of the Conference for a Republican Majority, one of many new groups seeking to advise the Republican party. When asked in the summer of 1993 about the future of the Republican party, he replied, "I've heard there used to be one." [15]

Surely, Frenzel is too pessimistic, even though Republican hopes must be heavily pinned on the chance of a failed Clinton presidency. Nor can we discount the possibility that Perot could run for the Republican presidential nomination, win it, and lead the GOP to victory. If he does seek the Republican nomination, however, he will face considerable opposition, especially from social conservatives who oppose his pro-choice views on abortion. And many Republican leaders blame Perot for Bush's defeat; for, even if Perot did not draw more votes from Bush than from Clinton on election day, he helped to create the political climate that defeated him. But, as we saw in Chapter 1, presidential nomination contests are decided mainly by competing for support among the electorate. Unlike most democracies, in which upstarts such as Perot could easily be denied the party leadership by party leaders, the U.S. nomination system is so open that party leaders have little control over the process.

Prospects for a New Political Party

Third parties in the United States face many obstacles, the most formidable of which are the rules through which candidates win office. With the exception of Maine and Nebraska, all the states and the District of Columbia have a winner-take-all system for allocating their electors. To win the electoral votes of these states a presidential candidate (or, to be more specific, the slate of electors pledged to a presidential candidate) must win a plurality of the votes within the state. Perot, as we saw, did not win a single electoral vote. He came in second in only two states, Maine and Utah. But even in these states he did not come within striking distance of beating the major party winner, trailing Clinton by 8 percentage points in Maine and Bush by 16 points in Utah. The only third parties actually to win electoral votes since World War II have been parties of the political right—the States' Rights Democrats in 1948 and the American Independent Party in 1968, and all their votes came in the states of the old Confederacy. As we saw in Chapter 3, there was some regional variation in Perot's support, but he had no regional base.

Third parties have a difficult time getting on the ballot, although recent court decisions have made access to the ballot much easier than it was before George C. Wallace's 1968 candidacy. Independent or third-party candidates also have financial problems, and federal election laws place an additional burden upon their ability to raise money. Democratic and Republican candidates are guaranteed federal funding, whereas third-party candidates receive funding only if they win 5 percent of the vote, and only after the general election.

If Perot chooses to run for president again in 1996, he will not face the problem of raising money. Using his personal wealth he could run without federal funding, as he did in 1992, thereby exempting himself from federal spending rules. As he ran as an independent in 1992, his success in the 1992 election would probably not automatically qualify him to be on the ballot in most states, but getting on the ballot in all fifty states and the District of Columbia would be a negligible obstacle, for, as in 1992, he could spend his own money, if necessary, to collect signatures. But if there is widespread support for Perot in the public opinion polls, he might not need to spend any of his own money to gain access to the ballot in 1996.

But Perot (or any other third-party or independent candidate) would face many other problems that money cannot so easily solve. First, as we saw through our analysis of the National Election Studies (NES) surveys in Chapter 8, despite the decline in party loyalties since World War II, strong partisans provide overwhelming electoral support for their party's presidential candidate. Lacking an established political party, Perot would have no base of strong party identifiers upon which he could rely for support. Just by relying upon strong party identifiers alone, Democratic and Republican presidential candidates are each assured of well over 10 million votes.[16] Second, Perot might find few political leaders who are willing to endorse him, which might undermine his credibility. If Clinton fails to govern with a Democratic Congress, voters may wonder how Perot would govern with a Congress in which he can rely on support from neither major party.

As of the summer of 1993, some Perot supporters were attempting to form new political parties on a state-by-state basis, but Perot had not lent them his support. His organization, United We Stand America, could provide the framework for a national political party. Establishing a national party might prove helpful, but it might also be costly. At present, United We Stand is not a party, so a voter can join it by paying fifteen dollars and still remain a Democrat or a Republican. Indeed, there are Republican members of Congress who have announced that they have joined United We Stand. But a political party is not merely an organization that collects dues and distributes a newsletter. As Joseph A. Schlesinger reminds us, a political party in a democracy is an organized attempt to gain public office by winning elections.[17] If United We Stand does not become a party, it will not provide direct access for Americans seeking public office, except for Perot and his running mate. When the Republican party emerged in 1854, it ran candidates for office at every level in the nonslave states. Ambitious Whigs, as well as former members of the Free Soil Party and the Know Nothing Party, could become Republicans and seek office for state legislatures, Congress, and governorships. In the 34th Congress, the first to be chosen after the Republican party was founded, 108 of the 234 congressmen were Republicans. The Republican party promised the collective good of limiting slavery, but it also provided selective incentives for individual men seeking elective office. Politically ambitious Americans may want selective incentives, as well as the opportunity of working for the collective good of electing Perot.[18]

But if United We Stand (or any other political organization) were to become a political party, it would have to field candidates. How it would get these candidates on the ballot would vary somewhat from state to state, because the provisions for getting a new party on the ballot are largely a matter of state law. If United We Stand became a party after the 1994 midterm election, it could probably avoid choosing candidates in primaries and attempt to get them on the ballot through petitions. Some incumbent members of Congress who wanted United We Stand support would simply send a check to Dallas, announce their commitment to Perot, display their canceled check, and then run as either a Republican or a Democrat. Such a declaration would not necessarily earn them Perot's endorsement, and it might jeopardize their chances of winning a major party nomination. To announce membership in United We Stand after gaining a major party nomination might be viewed as duplicitous.

Let us suppose Perot were to create a slate of 435 House candidates and 34 Senate candidates.[19] Perot created a slate of 538 presidential electors in 1992, but that is not the same thing as choosing candidates for Congress. An elector (who *cannot* be a member of Congress) has a largely honorary job. Perot supporters who were not chosen to be on his slate of electors might have felt slighted, but not being selected did not affect their political careers. If running as a United We Stand candidate is seen as a viable way to win a congressional seat, there will be many members in most congressional districts who will want to run on the United We Stand ticket. Those who seek office and who are denied the party label are likely to be disaffected.

Many former Perot supporters claim that he is displacing true volunteers with handpicked loyalists. Perot claims that these charges have been made by a handful of disgruntled malcontents. Regardless of the merits of these arguments, an American political party cannot be run like a private fiefdom. Unless there were some consultation process for United We Stand members within each congressional district, one would have, in effect, 435 House candidates and 34 Senate candidates handpicked by Perot and his central headquarters in Dallas. If there were a consultation process, it might lead to considerable conflict.

Admittedly, one can be a political leader in a democracy without being a party member. Charles de Gaulle, the president of the French Fifth Republic from 1958 through 1969, for example, claimed to be "above the parties," even though there was a Gaullist party (the Union for the New Republic) that supported him in the National Assembly. But de Gaulle was a former general who had refused to surrender after France was defeated by Germany in 1940, was the leader of the French resistance during World War II, and had served as the provisional leader of France after it was liberated. Even so, he came to power only during a national emergency in 1958 because the leaders of the French Fourth Republic believed that he was the best leader to end a threatened coup against the government by army units and French colonists in Algeria.

As part of his price for accepting the last premiership of the Fourth Republic, de Gaulle was authorized to draft a new constitution that greatly increased the power of the French president and substantially weakened the power of the national legislature. When that new constitution was ratified by a referendum in the fall of 1958, the Fourth Republic ended and the Fifth Republic began. De Gaulle was then elected president of the Fifth Republic. As president, he held four additional referenda, each time threatening to resign the presidency if he were not supported by the electorate. In 1969, when the final referendum to further weaken the power of the politically weak Senate was defeated, de Gaulle resigned. Twice during his presidency de Gaulle dissolved the National Assembly to force new legislative elections.

There are many differences between the French presidential system and the American presidential system, including the inability of the American president to call for a direct popular vote to support his policies or to dissolve the U.S. Congress and force new congressional elections. Nor would it be easy for an American president to enact a new constitution that weakened Congress, if only because the ratification process would be far more complicated than it was in France.[20] So while governing a democracy without claiming ties to a political party is possible, at least in a presidential system, it may be possible only in exceptional circumstances. It remains to be seen whether or not American circumstances are so exceptional as to lead to a Perot presidency and, if they are, whether Perot proves able to implement his policies in the American political system.

Prospects for Continued Electoral Volatility

For the moment *dealignment* seems to be an accurate term for the American political scene. The old party system seems in disarray, but nothing seems to have replaced it. Dreams of a pro-Republican realignment have been shattered, at least for now, but the Democrats do not seem secure as a majority party. Moreover, unlike most 1968 Wallace voters, who clearly seemed to be potential Nixon voters for 1972,[21] the sources of the Perot vote are so diverse that it is difficult to predict what his voters will do in 1996.

There are many reasons to expect high levels of volatility, with massive swings in party support from election to election. The most obvious reason is the large vote for Perot. Over 19 million Americans voted for a candidate who had a negligible chance of winning, even though Clinton's margin in the polls was not large enough for voters to assume that he was certain to be elected. Sixty-three percent of the voters cast their ballots against an incumbent president, a percentage surpassed only by the 77 percent who voted against another Republican incumbent, William Howard Taft, in 1912.

Our analysis in Chapter 5 reveals that the Perot voters came from a broad spectrum of American society, although relatively few African-Americans, southern whites, or Jews voted for him. As we saw in Chapter 6, Perot voters did not have distinctive issue preferences, but were very likely to believe that neither the Republican nor the Democratic party would do a better job of solving the nation's problems (see Chapter 7). As we saw in Chapter 8, about half of Perot's vote came from self-professed independents.

Part of Perot's success came from the weak party loyalties of the American electorate. Although the strength of American partisan attachments is somewhat greater than it was at its postwar low in 1978, partisan strength is considerably weaker than it was from 1952 through 1964, the years Philip E. Converse views as the "steady-state" period in American party loyalties.[22] During that period, 22 percent of the electorate was classified as independents. In the 1992 NES survey, 39 percent was. Although some self-professed independents may be "hidden partisans," [23] claiming to be an independent does reveal a lack of strong commitment to a party.[24] Moreover, although the percentage of strong partisans is somewhat greater than the postwar low reached in 1978, it is substantially lower than it was during the steady-state period. From 1952 through 1964, 36 percent of the electorate claimed to have strong partisan ties; in 1992, only 28 percent did. Weak partisans and self-professed independents are much more volatile in their voting choices than individuals who claim strong party ties.

Last, as we saw in Chapters 5 and 10, social forces (other than race) have less and less influence on voting behavior—a trend that is likely to contribute to electoral volatility. Today few voters feel bound to a political party by social class, ethnicity, or religion. This lack of affiliation increases the proportion of the electorate that is likely to switch from election to election.

In the early 1990s the party systems of many democracies appeared to be in disarray. But the American electoral system, like that in Britain, provides a check against new political parties and considerable protection for the two major established parties. Ultimately, however, the people in a democracy can displace a major party, although this has not happened in the United States since the 1850s or in Britain since the 1920s. The ability of the Democratic and Republican parties to maintain their duopoly ultimately depends on the abilities of their leaders to solve the nation's problems.

Notes

Introduction to Part 1

1. See, for example, Benjamin Ginsberg and Martin Shefter, *Politics by Other Means: The Declining Importance of Elections in America* (New York: Basic Books, 1990). See also many of the essays in Benjamin Ginsberg and Alan Stone, eds., *Do Elections Matter?* 2d. ed. (New York: Sharpe, 1991).
2. Everett Carll Ladd, "The 1992 Vote for President Clinton: Another Brittle Mandate?" *Political Science Quarterly* 108 (Spring 1993): 2.
3. R. W. Apple, Jr., "Clinton Is Pulled Back from the Brink. He'll Be Back," *New York Times*, August 8, 1993, E-1.
4. See Ginsberg and Stone, *Do Elections Matter?*
5. John H. Aldrich and Thomas Weko, "The Presidency and the Election Process: Campaign Strategy, Voting, and Governance," in *The Presidency and the Political System*, 2d ed., ed. Michael Nelson (Washington, D.C.: CQ Press, 1988), 251-267.
6. Phil Gailey, "Republicans Start to Worry about Signs of Slippage," *New York Times*, August 25, 1985, E5.
7. V. O. Key, Jr., "A Theory of Critical Elections," *Journal of Politics* 17 (February 1954): 4.
8. V. O. Key, Jr., "Secular Realignment and the Party System," *Journal of Politics* 21 (May 1958): 198.
9. These two states were, and still are, the most heavily Roman Catholic states. Both of these states had voted Republican in seventeen of the eighteen presidential elections from 1856 through 1924, voting Democratic only when the Republican party was split in 1912.
10. V. O. Key, Jr., *Politics, Parties, and Pressure Groups*, 5th ed. (New York: Thomas Y. Crowell, 1964), 186.
11. James L. Sundquist, *Dynamics of the Party System: Alignment and Realignment of Political Parties in the United States*, rev. ed. (Washington, D.C.: Brookings Institution, 1983), 4; Lawrence G. McMichael and Richard J. Trilling, "The Structure and Meaning of Critical Realignment: The Case of Pennsylvania," in *Realignment in American Politics: Toward a Theory*, ed. Bruce A. Campbell and Richard J. Trilling (Austin: University of Texas Press, 1980), 25.
12. In addition to the eleven states that later formed the Confederacy (Alabama, Arkansas, Florida, Georgia, Louisiana, Mississippi, North Carolina, South Carolina, Tennessee, Texas, and Virginia), Delaware, Kentucky, Maryland, and Missouri were also slave states. There were fifteen free states in 1848

(Connecticut, Illinois, Indiana, Iowa, Maine, Massachusetts, Michigan, New Hampshire, New Jersey, New York, Ohio, Pennsylvania, Rhode Island, Vermont, and Wisconsin). By 1860, three additional free states (California, Minnesota, and Oregon) had been admitted into the Union.

13. Michael Nelson, "Constitutional Aspects of the Elections," in *The Elections of 1988*, ed. Michael Nelson (Washington, D.C.: CQ Press, 1989), 197.

14. Ronald Inglehart and Avram Hochstein, "Alignment and Dealignment of the Electorate in France and the United States," *Comparative Political Studies* 5 (October 1972): 343-372; Russell J. Dalton, Paul Allen Beck, and Scott C. Flanagan, "Electoral Change in Advanced Industrial Democracies," in *Electoral Change in Advanced Industrial Democracies: Realignment or Dealignment?* ed. Dalton, Flanagan, and Beck (Princeton, N.J.: Princeton University Press, 1984), 14.

15. Russell J. Dalton and Martin P. Wattenberg, "The Not So Simple Act of Voting," in *Political Science: The State of the Discipline II*, ed. Ada W. Finifter (Washington, D.C.: American Political Science Association, 1993), 202.

16. Martin P. Wattenberg, *The Rise of Candidate-Centered Politics: Presidential Elections of the 1980s* (Cambridge, Mass.: Harvard University Press, 1991); Dalton and Wattenberg, "The Not So Simple Act of Voting," 204.

17. See, for example, Joel H. Silbey, "Beyond Realignment and Realignment Theory: American Political Eras, 1789-1989," in *The End of Realignment? Interpreting American Electoral Eras*, ed. Byron E. Shafer (Madison: University of Wisconsin Press, 1991), 3-23; Everett Carll Ladd, "Like Waiting for Godot: The Uselessness of 'Realignment' for Understanding Change in Contemporary American Politics," in *The End of Realignment?* 24-36; and Byron E. Shafer, "The Notion of an Electoral Order: The Structure of Electoral Politics at the Accession of George Bush," in *The End of Realignment?* 37-84. Shafer's book also contains an excellent bibliographical essay. See Harold F. Bass, Jr., "Background to Debate: A Reader's Guide and Bibliography," in *The End of Realignment?* 141-178.

18. Walter Dean Burnham, "Critical Realignment: Dead or Alive?" in *The End of Realignment?* 101-139.

19. Gerald M. Pomper, "The Presidential Election," in *The 1992 Election: Reports and Interpretations*, Gerald M. Pomper et al. (Chatham, N.J.: Chatham House, 1993), 150.

20. Donald E. Stokes and John J. DiIulio, Jr., "The Setting: Valance Politics in Modern Elections," in *The Elections of 1992*, ed. Michael Nelson (Washington, D.C.: CQ Press, 1993), 6.

21. Guy Molyneux and William Schneider, "Ross Is Boss," *Atlantic*, May 1993: 85-86.

22. James Ceaser and Andrew Busch, *Upside Down and Inside Out: The 1992 Elections and American Politics* (Lanham, Md.: Rowman and Littlefield, 1993).

23. He could also win by converting voters who supported Bush in 1992, but these voters may be harder for him to win than former Perot supporters. Future Democratic success also depends upon retaining most 1992 Clinton voters.

24. The Republicans won control of the House in eight consecutive elections between 1894 and 1908, far short of the current series of twenty consecutive Democratic victories.

25. If the chances that either the Republicans or the Democrats will win control of the U.S. House of Representatives were 50-50, the probability that a given

party would win twenty consecutive elections would be .5²⁰, or .000000954. The odds against a given party's winning twenty elections in a row are somewhat over 1 million to one.

26. Because we are usually analyzing responses to key questions measured only in the postelection interview (for example, how respondents said they voted for president or Congress), we often restrict our analysis to the 2,255 respondents in the 1992 NES postelection interview.

27. For a brief nontechnical introduction to polling, see Herbert Asher, *Polling and the Public: What Every Citizen Should Know*, 2d ed. (Washington, D.C.: CQ Press, 1992).

28. For a brief description of the procedures used by the SRC to carry out its sampling, see Paul R. Abramson, *Political Attitudes in America: Formation and Change* (San Francisco: Freeman, 1983), 18-23. For a more detailed analysis, see Survey Research Center, *Interviewer's Manual*, rev. ed. (Ann Arbor, Mich.: Institute for Social Research, 1976).

29. The probability of sampling error is partly a function of the result for any given question. The probability for error is greater for proportions near 50 percent and diminishes somewhat for proportions above 70 percent or below 30 percent. The probability of error diminishes markedly for proportions above 90 percent or below 10 percent. For the sake of simplicity, we report the confidence level for percentages near 50 percent.

30. For an excellent table that allows us to evaluate differences between groups, see Leslie Kish, *Survey Sampling* (New York: Wiley, 1965), 580. Kish defines the difference between two groups to be significant if the results are two standard errors apart.

31. About 55 percent of the 1992 NES respondents were originally interviewed as part of the 1990 NES survey. In order to compensate for differential attrition among respondents originally interviewed in 1990, a weighting factor must be employed to obtain a representative sample. Thus, our results for the 1992 NES (as well as the 1958, 1960, 1974, and 1976 NES surveys) report the "weighted" number of cases. The weighting factor for 1992 was designed so that the weighted number will be close to the actual number of cases.

   Our results were weighted by variable (V3008), which is the best weighting variable to yield representative results for the 1992 survey. However, the data set released by the ICPSR in October 1993 included an additional weight (V7000) for making comparisons with earlier NES surveys. On September 10, Santa Traugott provided us with the information necessary to analyze the 1992 NES survey with the newly added "time series weight." We conducted numerous tests to determine whether using the new weight would lead to different results. We found that the results using this new weight differ only marginally from those employing V3008. With the exception of our analysis of the decline of electoral participation in Chapter 4, we employ V3008 to weight the results.

Chapter 1: The Nomination Struggle

1. This percentage was reached in a March 9-11 poll conducted by the *Los Angeles Times*, as reported in *The Election of 1992: Reports and Interpretations*, Gerald M. Pomper et al. (Chatham, N.J.: Chatham House, 1993), 40.

2. Cuomo waited to announce his decision not to run until December 21, 1991, the last day on which a candidate could file for the New Hampshire presidential primary.

3. Jackson announced his decision not to run on November 2, 1991, Gephardt on July 17, 1991, Gore on August 21, 1991, and Rockefeller on August 7, 1991.
4. "The Bush Barometer," *American Enterprise*, March/April 1992: 98-99.
5. Rep. Shirley Chisholm (N.Y.) had run in 1972, while Jackson ran in 1984 and 1988.
6. *Newsweek*, Election Special, November/December 1992, 28.
7. Joseph A. Schlesinger, *Ambition and Politics: Political Careers in the United States* (Chicago: Rand McNally, 1966); see also his *Political Parties and the Winning of Office* (Ann Arbor: University of Michigan Press, 1991).
8. Brown had retired after the traditional two terms as governor of California. This retirement was tarnished by his failed attempt to win a Senate seat against the mayor of San Diego, Pete Wilson, losing by a 52 to 45 percent margin. Tsongas had retired from the Senate to fight cancer, a most unfavorable circumstance in his life, but the decision was not based on concerns about electoral defeat or otherwise negative political circumstances. For more on these sorts of considerations and their relationship to the likelihood of running for president, see Paul R. Abramson, John H. Aldrich, and David W. Rohde, "Progressive Ambition among United States Senators: 1972-1988," *Journal of Politics* 49 (February 1987): 3-35.
9. For a discussion of the way nominating conventions began, see Byron E. Shafer, *Bifurcated Politics: Evolution and Reform in the National Party Convention* (Cambridge, Mass.: Harvard University Press, 1988), 9-17.
10. In 1992, Buchanan did not meet the complicated filing procedures for the New York presidential primary, and no Republican contest was held.
11. At least, this form is the most common one in the Democratic party. There are many variations. In most Republican caucuses, all Republicans in the state can attend their precinct caucus and "vote" for their favored presidential candidate. The delegates chosen do not have to reflect the proportion of presidential preferences expressed in the caucuses, although they often do so imperfectly.
12. North Dakota held party primaries on June 9, after the so-called window of dates permitted by the Democratic party had closed. For that reason, the primary did not count for delegate selection.
13. This count includes the District of Columbia, which held primaries for both parties. It excludes "beauty contest" primaries that record the public's preferences for candidates but do not select delegates. Although no Republican primary was held in New York, as noted, the GOP did hold primaries in Minnesota, Washington, Idaho, and North Dakota. The Democratic primaries in these states were not honored by the national Democratic party. All four states used caucuses to choose delegates to the Democratic national convention.
14. See John H. Aldrich, *Before the Convention: Strategies and Choices in Presidential Nomination Campaigns* (Chicago: University of Chicago Press, 1980), and Larry M. Bartels, *Presidential Primaries and the Dynamics of Public Choice* (Princeton, N.J.: Princeton University Press, 1988).
15. Many have argued that these reforms have weakened the parties. See Nelson W. Polsby, *Consequences of Party Reform* (Oxford: Oxford University Press, 1983); David S. Broder, *The Party's Over: The Failure of Politics in America* (New York: Harper & Row, 1972); and William Crotty and John S. Jackson III, *Presidential Primaries and Nominations* (Washington, D.C.: CQ Press, 1985). Howard L. Reiter, however, has made a strong argument that the decline of party predated the reforms. See his *Selecting the President: The*

Nominating Process in Transition (Philadelphia: University of Pennsylvania Press, 1985).

16. See Paul R. Abramson, John H. Aldrich, and David W. Rohde, *Change and Continuity in the 1984 Elections*, rev. ed. (Washington, D.C.: CQ Press, 1987), 25-26.

17. New Hampshire state law requires that its primary be held before any other in the nation.

18. For a detailed look at the impact of Super Tuesday in 1988, see Barbara Norrander, *Super Tuesday: Regional Politics and Presidential Primaries* (Lexington: University of Kentucky Press, 1992).

19. Thus, March 10 was the closest to a Super Tuesday in 1992. Texas, which held both a primary and a caucus on that day, is counted only once.

20. Most election contests in the United States are "winner-take-all," typically with the plurality-vote winner being elected. In forty-eight states and the District of Columbia the plurality winner of the presidential vote receives all of the electoral votes from that state.

21. For more detailed analysis of these reforms, see Crotty and Jackson, *Presidential Primaries.*

22. His opponents, Buchanan and Duke, virtually conceded delegations selected by caucus to the incumbent president. Our discussion of the Republican contest, therefore, focuses on the primary elections.

23. In what might have been a rather ominous sign of problems to come for the Bush campaign, Buchanan received over one-quarter of the vote in California on June 2.

24. *Newsweek*, Election Special, 63.

25. For a list of governors, lieutenant governors, and some mayors who endorsed his candidacy, see Charles D. Hadley and Harold W. Stanley, "Surviving the 1992 Presidential Nomination Process," in *America's Choice: The Election of 1992*, ed. William Crotty (Guilford, Conn.: Dushkin, 1993), 37-38.

26. Kerrey won the second primary in South Dakota. The lack of media attention and campaign effort by the now leading candidates there made the primary all but a nonevent in 1992, as was the case in 1988. See Abramson, Aldrich, and Rohde, *Change and Continuity in the 1988 Elections*, 22.

27. Hadley and Stanley, "Surviving," 33.

28. For demonstration of his greater support among the more highly educated in primaries, see "The 1992 Campaign: While Others Shrank from Race, Clinton Clung to Dream of Presidency," *New York Times*, July 12, 1992, 18. Poll evidence reported there indicates that Tsongas received nearly twice as large a percentage of the votes from those who had graduated from college or gone on to postgraduate education than from those who had not finished high school or who had earned no more than a high school diploma.

29. Ross K. Baker, "Sorting Out and Suiting Up The Presidential Nominations," in *The Election of 1992: Reports and Interpretations*, 69.

30. This is based on a combined sample of exit polls conducted by Voter Research and Surveys in twenty-nine states, as reported in "Road to Nomination," *New York Times*, July 12, 1992, 18.

31. *Congressional Quarterly Weekly Report*, July 18, 1992, 2131; quoted in *The Election of 1992*, 59.

32. Media attention has become harder to be certain of, however. With the convention having become largely ceremonial, network coverage has been reduced from its earlier "gavel to gavel" coverage. There is too little

information to justify from a news perspective and too little excitement to justify from a ratings perspective.

33. Although this unconventional choice appeared to have aided Clinton's presidential chances, there is no definitive way to assess how much difference this choice made on the electoral outcome. But the National Elections Studies (NES) preelection survey shows that the electorate preferred Gore to Quayle by nearly a 2 to 1 margin. Using the "feeling thermometers" to assess the respondents' overall evaluations of the two vice-presidential candidates (these scales are also employed in Chapter 6—see Figure 6-1), we found that among the 2,082 respondents who rated both Gore and Quayle, 57 percent rated Gore more favorably than Quayle, 29 percent rated Quayle over Gore, and 14 percent gave them the same score (405 others did not rate one or both of these candidates on the thermometer scales).

34. According to Jack W. Germond and Jules Witcover, key Bush operatives read a draft of Buchanan's speech two days before it was delivered. Their major concern was that Buchanan endorse Bush. According to Germond and Witcover, "None of the Bush insiders ... saw the pitfalls in the harsh language Buchanan was planning to use to attack Bill and Hillary Clinton and make his case that a religious war was under way." See Germond and Witcover, *Mad as Hell: Revolt at the Ballot Box, 1992* (New York: Time Warner, 1993), 411.

35. The quotation is taken from the text of his speech as reported in *Congressional Quarterly Weekly Report*, August 22, 1992, p. 2544.

36. "The Legacy of George Bush," in *The Election of 1992: Reports and Interpretations*, 15.

Chapter 2: The General Election Campaign

1. We consider only the elections from 1972 on to avoid having to discuss the third-party candidacy of George C. Wallace in 1968. None of the following arguments would be materially different if that race were included.

2. The source for this account of the Democrats' strategy is Jules Witcover, "Democrats Crafted Winning Blueprint," *Lansing State Journal*, November 6, 1992, 3A.

3. Quoted in Jack W. Germond and Jules Witcover, "Clinton Campaign Does It the GOP Way," *National Journal*, September 5, 1992, 2030.

4. See Garry Wills, "Clinton's Hell-Raiser," *New Yorker*, October 12, 1992, 101.

5. Quoted in the *Washington Post*, August 18, 1992, A15.

6. *Congressional Quarterly Weekly Report*, August 22, 1992, 2544.

7. Quoted in the *Washington Post*, September 22, 1992, A1.

8. Ibid., September 23, 1992, A13.

9. See Ann Devroy, "Bush Camp Apparently Planned Attack," *Washington Post*, October 9, 1992, A16.

10. Howard Kurtz, "Bush's Negative Ads Appear to Be Backfiring," *Washington Post*, October 10, 1992, A12.

11. Michael Kelly, "Clinton Says Bush Is Afraid of Debating 'Man to Man,'" *New York Times*, September 19, 1992, 6.

12. Quoted in the *Washington Post*, September 10, 1992, A12; ibid., September 12, 1992, A10.

13. Quoted in the *Washington Post*, October 9, 1992, A1.

14. Quoted in the *Washington Post*, September 23, 1992, A12.

15. All quotations from the first debate are taken from the transcript published in the *Washington Post*, October 12, 1992, A14-A15.
16. The polls were rolling two- or three-day samples of about 1,000 registered voters. The data are taken from *Public Perspective*, November/December 1992, 101.
17. Quotations in this section are from the transcript published in the *Washington Post*, October 14, 1992, A14-A15.
18. Quotations from this debate are taken from excerpts published in *USA Today*, October 16, 1992, 4A-5A.
19. Judy Keen, "Voters Take Fight out of Bush," *USA Today*, October 16, 1992, 5A.
20. Quotations from this debate are from the transcript published in the *Washington Post*, October 20, 1992, A22-A25.
21. Quoted in the *Washington Post*, October 20, 1992, A25.
22. Quoted in the *New York Times*, October 23, 1992, A1.
23. Ibid., October 28, 1992, A1.
24. Richard L. Berke, "Perot Leads in $40 Million TV Ad Blitz," *New York Times*, October 27, 1992, A11.
25. Quoted in the *New York Times*, October 27, 1992, A1.
26. Quoted in the *Washington Post*, October 30, 1992, A1.
27. Quoted in the *Washington Post*, October 30, 1992, A1.
28. Ibid., November 3, 1992, A1.
29. For a discussion of the concept of party identification, see Chapter 8. For the questions used to measure party identification, see Chapter 4, note 54. The question used to measure the point at which the respondent decided how to vote was asked in the postelection interview and reads as follows: "How long before the election did you decide that you were going to vote the way you did?" As with our subsequent analysis of the presidential vote, we exclude six respondents who voted for other presidential candidates. It should be noted that the reported share of the vote for Clinton is somewhat higher than his actual share, and Bush's share is lower. This issue is discussed in Chapter 5.
30. For analyses of presidential vote choices in the 1980, 1984, and 1988 elections, by time of vote decision controlling for party identification, see Paul R. Abramson, John H. Aldrich, and David W. Rohde, *Change and Continuity in the 1980 Elections*, rev. ed. (Washington, D.C.: CQ Press, 1983), 39; Abramson, Aldrich, and Rohde, *Change and Continuity in the 1984 Elections*, rev. ed. (Washington, D.C.: CQ Press, 1987), 62; and Abramson, Aldrich, and Rohde, *Change and Continuity in the 1988 Elections*, rev. ed. (Washington, D.C.: CQ Press, 1991), 53. All of these analyses reveal that defections from party identification are more likely among partisans who report making their vote decision late in the campaign. Unlike Perot, however, John B. Anderson, the major independent candidate in 1980, tended to fare somewhat worse among voters who made up their minds late in the campaign.
31. These totals are taken from *The Finish Line: Covering the Campaign's Final Days*, a report by the Research Group of the Freedom Forum Media Studies Center, Columbia University, 125.

Chapter 3: The Election Results

1. We report the results for 1980 in Paul R. Abramson, John H. Aldrich, and David W. Rohde, *Change and Continuity in the 1980 Elections*, rev. ed.

(Washington, D.C.: CQ Press, 1983), 52-53; we report the results for 1984 in Abramson, Aldrich, and Rohde, *Change and Continuity in the 1984 Elections*, rev. ed. (Washington, D.C.: CQ Press, 1987), 52-53; and we report the results for 1988 in Abramson, Aldrich, and Rohde, *Change and Continuity in the 1988 Elections*, rev. ed. (Washington, D.C.: CQ Press, 1991), 58-59. The results are widely available in other sources as well. For the popular vote for president, by state, between 1824 and 1988 see *Presidential Elections Since 1789*, 5th ed. (Washington, D.C.: Congressional Quarterly Inc., 1991), 100-141.

2. In the disputed election of 1876, records suggest that Samuel J. Tilden, the Democrat, won 51.0 percent of the popular vote and that Rutherford B. Hayes, the Republican, won 48.0 percent. In 1888, Grover Cleveland, the incumbent Democratic president, won 48.6 percent of the vote, and the Republican challenger, Benjamin Harrison, won 47.8 percent.

3. The twelve winners prior to Clinton were James K. Polk (Democrat) in 1844 with 49.5 percent; Zachary Taylor (Whig) in 1848 with 47.3 percent; James Buchanan (Democrat) in 1856 with 45.3 percent; Abraham Lincoln (Republican) in 1860 with 39.8 percent; James A. Garfield (Republican) in 1880 with 48.3 percent; Grover Cleveland (Democrat) in 1884 with 48.5 percent; Cleveland in 1892 with 46.1 percent; Woodrow Wilson (Democrat) in 1912 with 41.8 percent; Wilson in 1916 with 49.2 percent; Harry S Truman (Democrat) in 1948 with 49.5 percent; John F. Kennedy (Democrat) in 1960 with 49.7 percent; and Richard M. Nixon (Republican) in 1968 with 43.4 percent.

4. Britain provides an excellent example of the effects of the plurality-vote win system upon third parties. In Britain, like the United States, candidates for the national legislature run in single-member districts, and in all British parliamentary districts the plurality-vote winner is elected. Since the 1935 general election, the Liberal party (and more recently the Alliance and the Liberal Democrats) has always received a far smaller share of the seats in the House of Commons than they win in the popular vote. In the British general election of 1992, for example, the Liberal Democrats won 17.8 percent of the popular vote, but they won only 20 of the 651 seats in the House of Commons, only 3.1 percent of the total representation.

5. A third-party candidate will not always be underrepresented in the electoral college. In 1948, for example, J. Strom Thurmond, the States Rights Democrat, won only 2.4 percent of the popular vote, but he won 7.3 percent of the electoral votes. Thurmond won 55 percent of his total popular vote in the four states that he carried (Alabama, Louisiana, Mississippi, and South Carolina), all of which had very low turnout. He received no popular votes at all in thirty-one of the forty-eight states.

6. Maurice Duverger, *Political Parties: Their Organization and Activity in the Modern World*, trans. Barbara and Robert North (New York: Wiley, 1963), 217. In the original, Duverger's formulation is: "le scrutin majoritaire à un seul tour tend au dualisme des partis." Duverger, *Les Partis Politiques*, 3d ed. (Paris: Armand Colin, 1958), 247. *Political Parties*, 218. For a discussion of Duverger's law, see William H. Riker, "The Two-party System and Duverger's Law: An Essay on the History of Political Science," *American Political Science Review* 76 (December 1982): 753-766. As Riker notes, Duverger's law was understood by some scholars for over a century before Duverger's formulation. For a more recent statement of Duverger's views, see "Duverger's Law: Forty Years Later" in *Electoral Laws and Their Political Consequences*, ed. Bernard Grofman and Arend Lijphart (New York:

Agathon Press, 1986), 69-84. For an extensive discussion of the effects of electoral rules upon election outcomes, see Rein Taagepera and Matthew Soberg Shugart, *Seats and Votes: The Effects and Determinants of Electoral Systems* (New Haven, Conn.: Yale University Press, 1989).

7. William H. Riker, *The Art of Political Manipulation* (New Haven, Conn.: Yale University Press, 1986), 79.

8. Gerald M. Pomper, "The Presidential Election," in *The Election of 1992: Reports and Interpretations*, Gerald M. Pomper et al. (Chatham, N.J.: Chatham House, 1993), 135.

9. Whether a runoff election would have been necessary would depend upon the rules, as well as the strategies of the candidates and the strategic choices of the voters. In the French Fifth Republic, the president is directly elected by the popular vote, and an absolute majority of the vote is required to win. All five presidential contests held under these direct election rules (1965, 1969, 1974, 1981, and 1988) have required a runoff election. Proponents of direct presidential election have often suggested that a candidate be required to win 40 percent of the vote to be elected without a runoff. As Clinton won 43 percent, he would have met this threshold. But Clinton might not have won 40 percent of the vote if a direct election system had been used. As James Ceaser and Andrew Busch point out, Perot might have appealed to his supporters to vote for him, if only to force a runoff between Clinton and Bush. As they write, "Perot down the stretch would no doubt have appealed to voters to send the election to a second round, where he and his volunteers could then have played a deciding role." James Ceaser and Andrew Busch, *Upside Down and Inside Out: The 1992 Elections and American Politics* (Lanham, Md.: Rowman and Littlefield, 1993), 120.

10. The Marquis de Condorcet (1743-1794) was a French philosopher. For a discussion of his principles of social choice, see Duncan Black, *The Theory of Committees and Elections* (Cambridge: Cambridge University Press, 1958).

11. In a three-candidate contest, there may be no Condorcet winner; even if there were one, he or she might not be elected in a plurality-vote win electoral system. Condorcet argued that, if there were such a candidate, that candidate *should* be elected. There is abundant evidence that Clinton would have defeated Bush in a two-person contest. It is less clear whether Clinton would have defeated Perot in a two-person contest, but we present evidence later (see Chapter 6) to demonstrate that he probably would have defeated Perot.

12. For an analysis of agenda setting during this era, see William H. Riker, *Liberalism Against Populism: A Confrontation Between the Theory of Democracy and the Theory of Social Choice* (San Francisco: Freeman, 1982), 213-232. See also Riker, *The Art of Political Manipulation*, 1-9.

13. Michael Nelson, "Constitutional Aspects of the Elections," in *The Elections of 1988*, ed. Michael Nelson (Washington, D.C.: CQ Press, 1989), 195-196.

14. Although the U.S. Bureau of the Census considers several border states and the District of Columbia to be southern, we use an explicitly political definition, the eleven states of the old Confederacy, which are Alabama, Arkansas, Florida, Georgia, Louisiana, Mississippi, North Carolina, South Carolina, Tennessee, Texas, and Virginia.

15. U.S. Department of Commerce, Bureau of the Census, *Statistical Abstract of the United States*, 101st ed. (Washington, D.C.: U.S. Government Printing Office).

16. According to the U.S. Bureau of the Census, the West includes thirteen states: Alaska, Arizona, California, Colorado, Hawaii, Idaho, Montana,

Nevada, New Mexico, Oregon, Utah, Washington, and Wyoming. But, as Walter Dean Burnham points out, for presidential elections the 96th meridian of longitude provides a dividing line. See Walter Dean Burnham, "The 1980 Earthquake: Realignment, Reaction, or What?" in *The Hidden Election: Politics and Economics in the 1980 Presidential Campaign*, ed. Thomas Ferguson and Joel Rogers (New York: Pantheon, 1981), 111. For our discussion in this chapter, we therefore also consider Kansas, Nebraska, North Dakota, Oklahoma, and South Dakota to be western. Even though Texas lies mainly to the west of the 96th meridian, we have classified it as southern since it was a former Confederate state.

17. Arizona, Colorado, Idaho, Montana, Nevada, New Mexico, Utah, and Wyoming are considered the mountain states. During the postwar years, these states have been the most strongly Republican in presidential elections.

18. See Joseph A. Schlesinger, *Political Parties and the Winning of Office* (Ann Arbor: University of Michigan Press, 1991), Figure 5-1, 112. Schlesinger does not report the exact values in his figure, but he has provided them to us in a personal communication. Schlesinger treats each state as an equal unit. His key value for each state is the percentage of voters who voted Democratic, and his overall measure for each election is the standard deviation on the percentage of the Democratic vote among the states. The standard deviation measures the extent to which all states differ from the average (mean) level of Democratic voting in a given election. The standard deviation is considered the best measure of the extent to which the values are dispersed. (The formula for computing the standard deviation is available in many social statistics textbooks, and the computation can be performed on many desk calculators.) Including the District of Columbia, which has voted only since the 1964 election, increases the standard deviation, since it is always more Democratic than the most Democratic state. We report only Schlesinger's results for states, not the alternative results that include D.C. The postwar election with the lowest variation was 1960, with a state-by-state standard deviation in the Democratic vote of only 5.42 percentage points.

19. V. O. Key, Jr., *Southern Politics in State and Nation* (New York: Alfred A. Knopf, 1949), 5.

20. There have been many studies of partisan change in the postwar South. For an excellent study that presents state-by-state results, see Alexander P. Lamis, *The Two Party South*, 2d expanded ed. (New York: Oxford University Press, 1990). For two other excellent studies, see Earl Black and Merle Black, *Politics and Society in the Postwar South* (Cambridge, Mass.: Harvard University Press, 1987); and Black and Black, *The Vital South: How Presidents Are Elected* (Cambridge, Mass: Harvard University Press, 1991).

21. Alabama, Georgia, Louisiana, Mississippi, and South Carolina are generally considered to be the five Deep South states. These are also the five southern states with the highest percentage of African-Americans.

22. Southern politicians also suffered additional setbacks at the 1948 Democratic presidential nomination convention. Their attempts to weaken the civil rights plank of the party platform were defeated. In addition, Hubert H. Humphrey, then mayor of Minneapolis, argued that the proposed civil rights plank was too weak, and offered an amendent to the platform for a stronger statement. Humphrey's amendment was passed by 651½ to 582½ vote margin.

23. Since World War II there has been substantial migration of northern whites to the South, and, more recently, there has been some migration of blacks from the North to the South. The importance of this migration of whites to

the South in weakening the Democratic party is a subject of debate. Raymond E. Wolfinger, for example, argues that migration was a major factor in weakening the Democratic party. See for example, Wolfinger, "Dealignment, Realignment, and Mandates in the 1984 Election," in *The American Elections of 1984*, ed. Austin Ranney (Durham, N.C.: Duke University Press, 1985), 289. John R. Petrocik, on the other hand, argues that migration has played a negligible role. See Petrocik, "Realignment: New Party Coalitions and the Nationalization of the South," *Journal of Politics* 49 (May 1987): 346-375. In our view, the evidence suggests that immigration to the South contributed somewhat to Republican strength, but that change among native white southerners was more important.

24. Kennedy made a symbolic gesture that helped him win African-American votes. Three weeks before the election, Martin Luther King, Jr., was arrested in Atlanta for taking part in a sit-in demonstration. Although all of the other demonstrators were released, King was held on a technicality and sent to the Georgia State Penitentiary. Kennedy telephoned King's wife to express his concern, and his brother, Robert F. Kennedy, made a direct plea to a Georgia judge, which led to King's release on bail. This incident received little notice in the press but had a major impact in the African-American community. For an account, see Theodore H. White, *The Making of the President, 1960* (New York: Atheneum, 1961), 321-323.

25. Marjorie Randon Hershey, "The Campaign and the Media," in *The Election of 1988: Reports and Interpretations*, 74.

26. Michael Nelson, "Constitutional Aspects of the Elections," in *The Elections of 1988*, 193-195; James C. Garand and Wayne T. Parent, "Representation, Swing, and Bias in U.S. Presidential Elections: 1872-1988," *American Journal of Political Science* 35 (November 1991): 1011-1031.

27. For an interesting, if alarmist, discussion of this possibility, see David W. Abbott and James P. Levine, *Wrong Winner: The Coming Debacle in the Electoral College* (New York: Praeger, 1991).

28. In fact, the Democrats lost both these contests mainly because their popular vote majority in 1876 and their popular vote plurality in 1888 were built by winning southern states by very large margins.

29. The fourth possible combination does not exist, since Clinton carried all the states that Dukakis had won four years earlier.

Introduction to Part 2

1. This estimate of the size of the voting-age citizen population is based upon a personal communication from Walter Dean Burnham, June 21, 1993.

2. For an excellent collection of articles dealing with some of the major controversies, see Richard G. Niemi and Herbert F. Weisberg, *Controversies in Voting Behavior*, 3d ed. (Washington, D.C.: CQ Press, 1993). For another excellent summary of the research in this area, see Russell J. Dalton and Martin P. Wattenberg, "The Not So Simple Act of Voting," in *Political Science: The State of the Discipline II*, ed. Ada W. Finifter (Washington, D.C.: American Political Science Association, 1993), 193-218.

3. Paul F. Lazarsfeld, Bernard Berelson, and Hazel Gaudet, *The People's Choice: How the Voter Makes Up His Mind in Presidential Campaigns*, 2d ed. (New York: Columbia University Press, 1948), 27. See also Bernard R. Berelson, Paul F. Lazarsfeld, and William N. McPhee, *Voting: A Study of Opinion Formation in a Presidential Campaign* (Chicago: University of

Chicago Press, 1954).

4. See Robert R. Alford, *Party and Society: The Anglo-American Democracies* (Chicago: Rand McNally, 1963); Richard F. Hamilton, *Class and Politics in the United States* (New York: Wiley, 1972); and Seymour Martin Lipset, *Political Man: The Social Bases of Politics*, exp. ed. (Baltimore: Johns Hopkins University Press, 1981). For an interesting recent book that uses this perspective, see Chandler Davidson, *Race and Class in Texas Politics* (Princeton, N.J.: Princeton University Press, 1990).

5. Angus Campbell et al., *The American Voter* (New York: Wiley, 1960).

6. For the single best essay summarizing Converse's views on voting behavior, see Philip E. Converse, "Public Opinion and Voting Behavior," in *Nongovernmental Politics*, ed. Fred I. Greenstein and Nelson W. Polsby, vol. 4 of *Handbook of Political Science* (Reading, Mass.: Addison-Wesley, 1975), 75-169. For an excellent summary of research from a social-psychological point of view, see Donald R. Kinder and David O. Sears, "Public Opinion and Political Action," in *Special Fields and Applications*, 3d ed., ed. Gardner Lindzey and Elliot Aronson, vol. 2 of *Handbook of Social Psychology* (New York: Random House, 1985), 659-741. For an alternative approach to the study of political psychology, see Paul M. Sniderman, Richard A. Brody, and Philip E. Tetlock, with others, *Reasoning and Choice: Explorations in Political Psychology* (Cambridge: Cambridge University Press, 1991). See also Sniderman, "The New Look in Public Opinion Research," in *Political Science: The State of the Discipline II*, ed. Ada W. Finifter (Washington, D.C.: American Political Science Association, 1993), 219-245. For another provocative discussion, see John R. Zaller, *The Nature and Origins of Mass Opinion* (Cambridge: Cambridge University Press, 1992).

7. Anthony Downs, *An Economic Theory of Democracy* (New York: Harper & Row, 1957); William H. Riker, *The Theory of Political Coalitions* (New Haven, Conn.: Yale University Press, 1962).

8. See, for example, William H. Riker and Peter C. Ordeshook, "A Theory of the Calculus of Voting," *American Political Science Review* 62 (March 1968): 25-42; John A. Ferejohn and Morris P. Fiorina, "The Paradox of Not Voting: A Decision Theoretic Analysis," *American Political Science Review* 68 (June 1974): 525-536; and Morris P. Fiorina, *Retrospective Voting in American National Elections* (New Haven, Conn.: Yale University Press, 1981). For a summary of much of this research, see James M. Enelow and Melvin J. Hinich, *The Theory of Spatial Voting: An Introduction* (New York: Cambridge University Press, 1984). For an interesting perspective that combines rational choice and psychological perspectives, see Samuel L. Popkin, *The Reasoning Voter: Communication and Persuasion in Presidential Campaigns* (Chicago: University of Chicago Press, 1991).

Chapter 4: Who Voted?

1. For two excellent discussions of why electoral participation is lower in the United States than in other industrialized democracies, see G. Bingham Powell, Jr., "American Voter Turnout in Comparative Perspective," *American Political Science Review* 80 (March 1986): 17-43, and Robert W. Jackman, "Political Institutions and Voter Turnout in the Industrial Democracies," *American Political Science Review* 81 (June 1987): 405-423.

2. This chapter focuses on only one form of political participation, voting. For a discussion of other forms of political participation in the United States, as

well as a different perspective on electoral participation, see M. Margaret Conway, *Political Participation in the United States*, 2d ed. (Washington, D.C.: CQ Press, 1991).

3. During the 1916 election women had full voting rights only in Arizona, California, Colorado, Idaho, Kansas, Montana, Nevada, Oregon, Utah, Washington, and Wyoming. Only 10 percent of the U.S. population lived in these states. For a provocative discussion of the struggle for women's right to vote, see Alan P. Grimes, *The Puritan Ethic and Woman Suffrage* (New York: Oxford University Press, 1967).

4. See J. Morgan Kousser, *The Shaping of Southern Politics: Suffrage Restrictions and the Establishment of the One-Party South, 1880-1910* (New Haven, Conn.: Yale University Press, 1974). For a more general discussion of the decline of turnout in the late nineteenth century, see Paul Kleppner, *Who Voted? The Dynamics of Electoral Turnout, 1870-1980* (New York: Praeger, 1982), 55-82.

5. There has been a great deal of disagreement about the reasons for and the consequences of registration requirements. For some of the more interesting arguments, see Walter Dean Burnham, "The Changing Shape of the American Political Universe," *American Political Science Review* 59 (March 1965): 7-28; Philip E. Converse, "Change in the American Electorate," in *The Human Meaning of Social Change*, ed. Angus Campbell and Philip E. Converse (New York: Russell Sage, 1972), 266-301; and Burnham, "Theory and Voting Research: Some Reflections on Converse's 'Change in the American Electorate,'" *American Political Science Review* 68 (September 1974): 1002-1023. For another provocative discussion, see Frances Fox Piven and Richard A. Cloward, *Why Americans Don't Vote* (New York: Pantheon, 1988), 26-95.

6. For a rich source of information about the introduction of the Australian ballot and its effects, see Jerrold G. Rusk, "The Effect of the Australian Ballot Reform on Split Ticket Voting: 1876-1908," *American Political Science Review* 64 (December 1970): 1220-1238.

7. For example, see Burnham's estimates of turnout among the voting-age citizen population, which include results through 1984. These appear in Burnham, "The Turnout Problem," in *Elections American Style*, ed. A. James Reichley (Washington, D.C.: Brookings Institution, 1987), 113-114. Burnham estimates that 52.7 percent of the voting-age citizen population voted in the 1988 presidential election and that turnout increased to 56.9 percent in 1992. The 1992 figure is based upon Burnham's estimate that the citizen component of the total voting-age population was 183,500,000 (personal communication, June 21, 1993).

Because Burnham's turnout denominator is smaller than ours, his estimates of turnout are always somewhat higher. Although there are advantages to Burnham's calculations, we use the voting-age population as our base for two reasons. First, it is very difficult to estimate the size of the noncitizen population, and official estimates by the U.S. Bureau of the Census use the voting-age population as the turnout denominator. Second, even though only citizens can vote in present-day U.S. elections, citizenship is not a constitutional requirement for voting. National legislation determines how long it takes to become a citizen and state law imposes citizenship as a condition of voting.

8. The estimate for turnout among the politically eligible population is based upon Burnham, "The Turnout Problem," 114.

9. Based upon their analysis of NES surveys, Steven J. Rosenstone and John Mark Hansen argue that lower levels of participation among older women resulted from the failure of party leaders to mobilize them. (See *Mobilization, Participation, and Democracy in America* [New York: Macmillan 1993], 168.)

10. Eight respondents who said that they voted in the election, but that they did not vote for president, have been classified as nonvoters. We have excluded four respondents who said they did not remember whether or not they voted. When the time series weight (see introduction to Part 1, note 31) is employed, 74.8 percent report voting for president. Although this percentage is only 1.4 percentage points lower than turnout employing the weighting factor we use throughout our book, the results using the time series weight lead to slightly more conservative estimates of the contribution of demographic and attitudinal changes to the decline of turnout. We employ the time series weight in the section of this chapter entitled "Why Has Turnout Declined?"

11. Respondents are asked the following question: "In talking to people about elections, we often find that a lot of people were not able to vote because they weren't registered, they were sick, or they just didn't have time. How about you—did you vote in the elections this November?"

12. Vote validation checks were conducted after the 1964, 1976, 1980, 1984, and 1988 presidential election and after the 1978, 1986, and 1990 midterm elections. As of this writing, there has been no decision about whether to conduct a similar study for the 1992 NES. Even if a study is not conducted, these past studies provide considerable information about the sources of bias in overreports of voting.

    Most analyses that compare results of reported turnout with turnout as measured by the vote validation studies suggest that *relative* levels of turnout among most social groups can be measured using reported turnout. However, research also suggests that blacks are consistently more likely than whites to falsely report voting. As a result, turnout differences between the races are always greater when turnout is measured by the vote validation studies. For results between 1964 and 1988, see Paul R. Abramson and William Claggett, "Racial Differences in Self-Reported and Validated Turnout in the 1988 Presidential Election," *Journal of Politics* 53 (February 1991): 186-197. Similar differences are found in the 1990 NES survey. Our analysis of the 1990 postelection survey shows that whites were only 9 percentage points more likely to report voting than blacks; however, according to the 1990 vote validation study, whites were 15 percentage points more likely to vote than blacks.

    For an extensive discussion of factors that contribute to false reports of voting, see Brian D. Silver, Barbara A. Anderson, and Paul R. Abramson, "Who Overreports Voting?" *American Political Science Review* 80 (June 1986): 613-624.

13. See Michael W. Traugott and John P. Katosh, "Response Validity in Surveys of Voting Behavior," *Public Opinion Quarterly* 43 (Fall 1979): 359-377; and Barbara A. Anderson, Brian D. Silver, and Paul R. Abramson, "The Effects of Race of the Interviewer on Measures of Electoral Participation by Blacks in SRC National Election Studies," *Public Opinion Quarterly* 52 (Spring 1988): 53-83.

14. Results for the 1992 Census Bureau survey are reported in Jerry T. Jennings, *Voting and Registration in the Election of November 1992*, ser. P-20, no. 466 (Washington, D.C.: U.S. Government Printing Office, 1993).

15. Another factor that may contribute to relatively lower turnout is that the Census Bureau does not interview respondents before the election. The bureau's procedures for classifying respondents as nonvoters also contribute to lower reported turnout. Nonrespondents and persons who said they did not know whether or not they voted are classified as nonvoters.

16. The NES and the Census Bureau surveys sample different populations. The census surveys are based upon the total noninstitutionalized civilian voting-age population, and the NES surveys are based upon the total noninstitutionalized politically eligible civilian population.

17. The census surveys ask respondents to report information about registration and voting for all voting-age respondents in the household. Studies by the bureau indicate that relying upon information about whether other adults voted leads to no significant biases. We are grateful to Martin O'Connell of the U.S. Bureau of the Census for giving us details about the size of the sample.

18. The vote validation studies are not free from error, for some true voters may be classified as nonvoters if no record can be found of their being registered to vote or if the voting records incorrectly fail to show that they voted. The voting records where blacks tend to live are not as well maintained as those where whites are more likely to live. However, it seems unlikely that the finding that blacks are more likely than whites falsely to report voting results from the poorer quality of black voting records. See Paul R. Abramson and William Claggett, "The Quality of Record Keeping and Racial Differences in Validated Turnout," *Journal of Politics* 54 (August 1992): 871-880.

19. The results for 1964 compare whites with nonwhites.

20. See Katherine Tate, "Black Political Participation in the 1984 and 1988 Presidential Elections," *American Political Science Review* 85 (December 1991): 1159-1176. For a more extensive discussion, see Tate, *From Protest to Politics: The New Black Voters in American Elections* (Cambridge, Mass.: Harvard University Press, 1993).

21. In addition to the eleven states of the Old Confederacy, the census surveys classify Delaware, the District of Columbia, Kentucky, Maryland, Oklahoma, and West Virginia as southern.

22. Hispanics may be of any race, but far more Hispanics are white than black. Among the 212 respondents classified as Hispanic in the NES survey, 81 percent were white and only 3 percent were black. Among Hispanics, respondents are classified as Mexican, Puerto Rican, Cuban, Latin American, Central American, Spanish, and other. However, the total number of Hispanics sampled was too small to permit detailed analysis of their political behavior.

23. In comparing 1992 turnout with 1988 turnout we rely upon the U.S. Department of Commerce, Bureau of the Census, *Voting and Registration in the Election of November 1988*, ser. P-20, no. 440 (Washington, D.C.: U.S. Government Printing Office, 1989).

24. As we explain in Chapter 3, we consider the South to include the eleven states of the Old Confederacy. In our analysis of NES surveys, however, we do not classify residents of Tennessee as southern, because the University of Michigan Survey Research Center samples Tennessee to represent the border states. In the following analysis, as well as analyses of regional differences using NES data later in our book, we classify the following ten states as southern: Alabama, Arkansas, Florida, Georgia, Louisiana, Mississippi, North Carolina, South Carolina, Texas, and Virginia. Table 4-3 actually shows

turnout to be lowest among whites in the border states, but this finding results from the relatively small sample from this region.

25. See Raymond E. Wolfinger and Steven J. Rosenstone, *Who Votes?* (New Haven, Conn.: Yale University Press, 1980), 93-94.

26. Ibid., 46-50.

27. We use this distinction mainly because it allows us to make comparisons over many elections, and is especially valuable for studying change over the entire postwar period, as we do in Chapter 5. However, since the 1988 presidential election survey, the NES surveys have not designated whether the respondent is the head of household. In all of our previous analyses, we classified respondents according to the head of household's occupation. Classification according to head of household's occupation is generally considered a more valid measure of a married woman's social class than her own occupation. Many women employed at relatively unskilled nonmanual jobs are married to manually employed men. Their social and political behavior appears to be affected more by their husband's occupations than by their own. In both the 1988 and 1992 surveys we classified married woman according to their husband's occupation. A reanalysis of the 1984 NES survey suggests that we came very close to replicating our earlier measure, which was based directly upon the occupation of the head of household.

28. Our measure of family income is based upon the respondent's estimate of his or her family's 1991 annual family income before taxes. For respondents who refused to answer this question and for those whom the interviewers thought were answering dishonestly, we relied upon the interviewer's assessment of family income.

29. See Wolfinger and Rosenstone, *Who Votes?* 13-36.

30. Protestants, Catholics, and other Christians were asked, "Would you call yourself a born-again Christian; that is, have you personally had a conversion experience related to Jesus Christ?"

31. David C. Leege and Lyman A. Kellstedt and others, *Rediscovering the Religious Factor in American Politics* (Armonk, N.Y.: M. E. Sharpe, 1993). We are grateful to Leege for providing us with detailed information about the procedures used to construct this variable. We constructed the measure as follows: respondents who prayed several times a day received 2 points, those who prayed less often received 1 point, and those who never prayed received 0 points; those who attended religious services at least once a week received 2 points, those who attended less frequently received 1 point, and those who never attended received 0 points; those who said religion provided "a great deal" of guidance in their daily lives received 2 points, those who said it provided "quite a bit" of guidance received 1 point, and those who said it provided "some" guidance received 0 points; respondents who said that the Bible was literally true or the "word of God" received 2 points, and those who said it was "written by men and is not the word of God" received 0 points. Respondents received 1 point for each don't know, ambiguous, or not ascertained response, but those with more than two such responses were excluded from our analyses. In principle, scores on this measure range from 0 to 8 points, but no white Protestant actually received a score below 1 point. In regrouping this variable into three categories, respondents with 8 points were classified as "very high," those with 6 to 7 points were classified as "high," and those with a score below 6 were classified as having "low or medium" levels of religious commitment.

32. Kenneth D. Wald, *Religion and Politics in the United States*, 2d ed.

(Washington, D.C.: CQ Press, 1992), 75.

33. R. Stephen Warner, *New Wine in Old Wineskins: Evangelicals and Liberals in a Small-Town Church* (Berkeley: University of California Press, 1988), 33, 34.

34. We are grateful to Leege for providing us with the specific NES codes used to classify Protestants into these religious traditions. These codes are based upon the religious denomination variable. Categories 50, 60, 70, 100 through 109, 120 through 149, 160 through 219, 221, 222, 223, 231, 232, 233, 250 through 269, 271 through 275, 280, 282, 289, 292, and 293 were classified as Evangelicals; categories 80, 90, 110, 150 through 159, 220, 229, 230, 249, 270, 279, 281, 290, and 291 were classified as mainline.

35. Wolfinger and Rosenstone, *Who Votes?* 13-36.

36. Silver, Anderson, and Abramson's analysis of the 1964, 1976, and 1980 vote validation studies shows that respondents with high levels of formal education do have very high turnout. However, their analysis also shows that persons with high levels of education who did not actually vote are more likely falsely to claim to have voted than nonvoters with lower levels of formal education. (See Silver, Anderson, and Abramson, "Who Overreports Voting?") Our analysis shows a similar pattern with the 1978, 1984, 1986, 1988, and 1990 vote validation studies. We cannot determine whether a similar pattern holds for the 1992 NES survey, but if it does, the results in Table 4-3 may somewhat exaggerate educational differences in voting participation.

37. Richard A. Brody, "The Puzzle of Political Participation in America," in *The New American Political System*, ed. Anthony King (Washington, D.C.: American Enterprise Institute, 1978), 287-324.

38. Walter Dean Burnham, "The 1976 Election: Has the Crisis Been Adjourned?" in *American Politics and Public Policy*, ed. Walter Dean Burnham and Martha Wager Weinberg (Cambridge, Mass.: MIT Press, 1978), 24; Thomas E. Cavanagh, "Changes in American Voter Turnout, 1964-1976," *Political Science Quarterly* 96 (Spring 1981): 53-65.

39. Ruy A. Teixeira, *The Disappearing American Voter* (Washington, D.C.: Brookings Institution, 1992), 66-67. Teixeira is skeptical about the findings from NES surveys that show that turnout did not decline among college graduates.

40. Jan E. Leighley and Jonathan Nagler, "Socioeconomic Class Bias in Turnout 1964-1988: The Voters Remain the Same," *American Political Science Review* 86 (September 1992): 728-730.

41. For estimates of the effects of generational replacement between 1956 and 1980, see Paul R. Abramson, *Political Attitudes in America: Formation and Change* (San Francisco: Freeman, 1983), 56-61.

42. This procedure assumes that overall educational levels were the same in 1992 as they were in 1960, but that reported turnout within each educational level was the same level actually observed in the 1992 survey.

43. Teixeira, *The Disappearing American Voter*, 46-47.

44. Rosenstone and Hansen, *Mobilization, Participation, and Democracy*, 214-215.

45. Teixeira, *The Disappearing American Voter*, 47.

46. Rosenstone and Hansen, *Mobilization, Participation, and Democracy*, 215.

47. Warren E. Miller, "The Puzzle Transformed: Explaining Declining Turnout," *Political Behavior* 14, no. 1 (1992): 1-43.

48. Teixeira, *The Disappearing American Voter*, 75-81. Rosenstone and Hansen, *Mobilization, Participation, and Democracy*, 136-141. Teixeira provides an

explicit critique of Miller's analysis.

49. George I. Balch, "Multiple Indicators in Survey Research: The Concept 'Sense of Political Efficacy,'" *Political Methodology* 1 (Spring 1974): 1-43. For an extensive discussion of feelings of political efficacy, see Abramson, *Political Attitudes in America*, 135-189.

50. Teixeira, *Why Americans Don't Vote: Turnout Decline in the United States, 1960-1984* (New York: Greenwood Press, 1987). In his more recent study, Teixeira develops a measure of party-related characteristics that includes strength of party identification, concern about the electoral outcome, perceived differences between the parties, and knowledge of the parties and candidates. (*The Disappearing American Voter*, 40-42.)

51. See Paul R. Abramson, John H. Aldrich, and David W. Rohde, *Change and Continuity in the 1980 Elections*, rev. ed. (Washington, D.C.: CQ Press, 1983), 85-87. For a more detailed analysis using probability procedures to estimate the impact of these attitudinal changes, see Abramson and Aldrich, "The Decline of Electoral Participation in America," *American Political Science Review* 76 (September 1982): 502-521.

52. Paul R. Abramson, John H. Aldrich, and David W. Rohde, *Change and Continuity in the 1984 Elections*, rev. ed. (Washington, D.C.: CQ Press, 1987), 115-118. See also Teixeira, *Why Americans Don't Vote*, 115-123.

53. Paul R. Abramson, John H. Aldrich, and David W. Rohde, *Change and Continuity in the 1988 Elections*, rev. ed. (Washington, D.C.: CQ Press, 1991), 103-106.

54. Respondents are asked, "Generally speaking, do you usually think of yourself as a Republican, a Democrat, an independent, or what?" Persons who call themselves Republicans or Democrats are asked, "Would you call yourself a strong (Republican, Democrat) or a not very strong (Republican, Democrat)?" Respondents who call themselves independents, answer "no preference," or name another party are asked, "Do you think of yourself as closer to the Republican Party or to the Democratic Party?" Respondents who have no partisan preferences are usually classified as independents. They are classified as "apoliticals" only if they have low levels of political interest and involvement.

55. Angus Campbell et al. *The American Voter* (New York: Wiley, 1960), 120-167.

56. This expectation follows from a rational choice perspective. For the most extensive discussion of party identification from this point of view, see Morris P. Fiorina, *Retrospective Voting in American National Elections* (New Haven, Conn: Yale University Press, 1981), 84-105. For a recent discussion of turnout from this perspective, see John H. Aldrich, "Rational Choice and Turnout," *American Journal of Political Science* 37 (February 1993): 246-278; for a comment on Aldrich's essay, see Robert W. Jackman, "Rationality and Political Participation," *American Journal of Political Science* 37 (February 1993): 279-290.

57. Respondents who disagreed with both of these statements were scored as highly efficacious; those who disagreed with one but agreed with the other were scored as medium; and those who agreed with both responses were scored as low. Respondents who scored "don't know" or "not ascertained" on one question were scored high or low depending upon responses to the remaining question, and those with "don't know" or "not ascertained" responses to both questions were excluded from the analysis. In both 1988 and 1992, respondents were asked whether they agreed strongly, agreed,

neither agreed nor disagreed, disagreed, or disagreed strongly with these statements. For both years, we classified respondents who responded neither agree nor disagree to both statements as medium on this measure. The scoring decision has little effect on our results, as only 3 percent of the respondents in 1988 and only 2 percent in 1992 answered "neither agree or disagree" to both of the statements.

58. This finding is consistent with those of Bruce E. Keith and his colleagues that independents who feel closer to one of the major parties are as politically involved as weak partisans are. See Bruce E. Keith et al., *The Myth of the Independent Voter* (Berkeley: University of California Press, 1992), 38-59.

59. The calculation is based upon the assumption that each partisan strength category and each sense of political efficacy category was the same as that observed in 1960, but that reported turnout was the same as that observed in 1992. For a full explanation of this technique, see Abramson, *Political Attitudes in America*, 296.

60. Our estimates used our algebraic standardization procedures. To simplify our analysis, we combined whites with an eighth-grade education or less with those who had not graduated from high school and combined weak partisans with independents who leaned toward a party.

61. Teixeira, *The Disappearing American Voter*, 47. We disagreed with Teixeira's classification of declining media involvement as an attitudinal variable. We argued that reading about campaigns in newspapers, a key component of this measure, was a form of political participation. (See Abramson, Aldrich, and Rohde, *Change and Continuity in the 1988 Elections*, rev. ed., 117-118.) Teixeira replies to our criticism in *The Disappearing American Voter*, 42-43.

62. Rosenstone and Hansen, *Mobilization, Participation, and Democracy*, 215, 216.

63. Respondents are asked, "The political parties try to talk to as many people as they can to get them to vote for their candidate. Did anyone from one of the political parties call you up or come around and talk to you about the campaign this year?"

64. As with earlier elections, Americans who said they were contacted by a political party were much more likely to vote than those who were not contacted. Among whites who said they were contacted by a political party ($N = 403$), 92 percent said that they voted; among those who had not been contacted ($N = 1,471$), 74 percent said that they voted. Rosenstone and Hansen acknowledge that contacts by the political parties declined between 1988 and 1992, but argue that other forms of mobilization may have increased. See Rosenstone et al, "Voter Turnout: Myth and Reality in the 1992 Election" (Paper presented at the Annual Meeting of the American Political Science Association, Washington, D.C., 1993).

65. "How the Nation Voted," *New York Times*, November 5, 1992, B4.

66. Respondents are first asked who they think will be elected president. Those who name a candidate are asked, "Do you think the Presidential race will be close, or will [the candidate named] win by quite a bit?" Those who say they do not know who will win are asked, "Do you think the Presidential race will be close or will one candidate win by quite a bit?"

67. See John H. Aldrich, "Some Problems in Testing Two Rational Models of Participation," *American Journal of Political Science* 20 (November 1976): 713-733.

68. Orley Ashenfelter and Stanley Kelley, Jr., "Determinants of Participation in

Presidential Elections," *Journal of Law and Economics* 18 (December 1975): 721.

69. As with our other analyses of the presidential vote, we have excluded six voters who supported other presidential candidates. As we noted in Chapter 2 (note 29), the percentage who report voting for Clinton in the 1992 NES is somewhat higher than the percentage he actually won. We discuss this issue in Chapter 5.

70. Respondents were asked, "Generally speaking, would you say that you personally care a good deal who wins the presidential election this fall, or that you don't care very much who wins?" This question is not comparable with previous NES questions about concern with the election outcome, which ask whether the respondent is concerned with which *party* will win the election. Although this change in wording is understandable given the three-candidate contest in 1992, it also means that we cannot compare levels of concern in 1992 with levels of concern in previous elections.

71. See Abramson, *Political Attitudes in America*, 225-238. For more recent results, see Warren E. Miller and Santa A. Traugott, *American National Election Studies Data Sourcebook, 1952-1986* (Cambridge, Mass.: Harvard University Press, 1989), 261-263, 273-274.

72. Respondents are asked, "How much of the time do you think you can trust the government in Washington to do what is right—just about always, most of the time, or only some of the time?"

73. For an insightful discussion of the increase in trust in 1984, see Jack Citrin and Donald Philip Green, "Presidential Leadership and the Resurgence of Trust in Government," *British Journal of Political Science* 16 (October 1986): 431-453.

74. Respondents are asked, "Would you say that the government is pretty much run by a few big interests looking out for themselves, or that it is run for the benefit of all the people?"

75. James Ceaser and Andrew Busch, *Upside Down and Inside Out: The 1992 Elections and American Politics* (Lanham, Md.: Rowman and Littlefield, 1993), 172.

76. James DeNardo, "Turnout and the Vote: The Joke's on the Democrats," *American Political Science Review* 74 (June 1980): 406-420.

77. See Abramson, Aldrich, and Rohde, *Change and Continuity in the 1980 Elections*, rev. ed., 88-92; Abramson, Aldrich, and Rohde, *Change and Continuity in the 1984 Elections*, rev. ed., 119-124; and Abramson, Aldrich, and Rohde, *Change and Continuity in the 1988 Elections*, rev. ed., 108-113.

78. The results we report for the 1980, 1984, and 1988 elections are based upon the responses of people whose voting was verified through a check of voting and registration records. However, the Republican turnout advantage was also found when reported electoral participation was studied.

79. The only substantial difference is found in comparisons of respondents who scored +2 on the measure with respondents who were scored −2. Those who were pro-Republican were 14 percentage points more likely to vote than those who were pro-Democratic. However, only sixty respondents were scored as +2 on our measure, and readers should treat even this 14-point difference with considerable caution.

80. First, respondents were asked: "In 1988 George Bush ran on the Republican ticket against Michael Dukakis for the Democrats. Do you remember for sure whether or not you voted in that election?" Respondents who remembered voting were asked, "Which one did you vote for?"

81. Of course, some of the respondents who said that they voted in 1992 were actually nonvoters. But we do not know how these biases are distributed across the two reports. In the discussion in this paragraph, our estimates of the share of Clinton and Perot's votes that came from 1988 Bush voters take into account that the 1988 vote report exaggerates Bush's share of the two-party vote.

82. See Robert Axelrod, "Where the Votes Come From: An Analysis of Electoral Coalitions, 1952-1968," *American Political Science Review* 61 (March 1972): 11-20.

83. For a recent study comparing the political attitudes of voters and nonvoters, see Stephen Earl Bennett and David Resnick, "The Implications of Nonvoting for Democracy in the United States," *American Journal of Political Science* 34 (August 1990): 771-802.

84. Piven and Cloward, *Why Americans Don't Vote,* 21. For similar arguments, see Walter Dean Burnham, "Shifting Patterns of Congressional Voting Participation," in *The Current Crisis in American Politics,* ed. Walter Dean Burnham (New York: Oxford University Press, 1982), 166-203.

85. See Seymour Martin Lipset, *Political Man: The Social Bases of Politics,* exp. ed. (Baltimore: Johns Hopkins University Press, 1981), 226-229. Lipset emphasizes the dangers of sudden increases in political participation.

86. Gerald M. Pomper, "The Presidential Election," in *The Election of 1980: Reports and Interpretations,* Gerald M. Pomper et al. (Chatham, N.J.: Chatham House, 1981), 86.

Chapter 5: Social Forces and the Vote

1. The basic social categories used in this chapter are the same as those used in Chapter 4. The variables are described in notes to that chapter. For similar tables showing presidential voting by social groups in 1980, 1984, and 1988, see Paul R. Abramson, John H. Aldrich, and David W. Rohde, *Change and Continuity in the 1980 Elections,* rev. ed. (Washington, D.C.: CQ Press, 1983), 98-99; Abramson, Aldrich, and Rohde, *Change and Continuity in the 1984 Elections,* rev. ed. (Washington, D.C.: CQ Press, 1987), 136-137; and Abramson, Aldrich, and Rohde, *Change and Continuity in the 1988 Elections,* rev. ed. (Washington, D.C.: CQ Press, 1991), 124-125.

2. For a discussion of problems of exaggerating support for winning candidates in NES surveys, see Gerald C. Wright, "Errors in Measuring Vote Choice in the National Election Studies, 1952-88" *American Journal of Political Science* 37 (February 1993): 291-316. One way to overcome this problem for the 1992 NES survey is to standardize the Democratic share of the vote by multiplying the reported major party vote for Clinton by 0.916 (53.5 ÷ 58.4). We decided not to employ standardization procedures because the bias in the Clinton vote has relatively little effect on the relationships we discuss in this book.

3. Unless otherwise indicated, our reports of this exit poll are from "Portrait of the Electorate," *New York Times,* November 5, 1992, B9. In this survey, 43 percent reported voting for Clinton, 38 percent for Bush, and 19 percent for Perot.

   Exit polls have three main advantages. First, they are less expensive than the multistage probability samples conducted by the University of Michigan Survey Research Center. Second, partly because of their lower cost, a large number of people can be sampled. Third, because persons are selected to be interviewed shortly after they leave the voting stations, the vast majority have actually voted for president.

Despite their large size, these surveys have four disadvantages. First, the questionnaires must be fairly brief. Second, it is difficult to supervise the field work and to ensure that interviewers are using the proper procedures to select respondents. Third, there is some evidence that Republican voters are less likely than others to agree to participate. Last, these surveys are of little value in studying turnout, since persons who do not go to the polls are not sampled.

For a discussion of the procedures used to conduct exit polls, as well as of some of the limitations, see Albert H. Cantril, *The Opinion Connection: Polling, Politics, and the Press* (Washington, D.C.: CQ Press, 1991). For a discussion of problems with the 1992 exit polls, see "Problems in Exit Polling: Interviews with Warren J. Mitofsky and John Brennan," *The Public Perspective* 4 (January/February 1993), 19-23.

4. Our report of this poll is based on "1992 Presidential Campaign: November," *Gallup Poll Monthly*, November 1992, 9. In this survey, 44 percent supported Clinton, 37 percent supported Bush, 14 percent supported Perot, and 5 percent supported other candidates or were undecided.

Although Gallup surveys do not ask as many politically relevant questions as the NES surveys, they provide valuable information about change from 1952 through 1992. Gallup polls were conducted as early as 1936, but the quality of the sampling improved markedly after the 1948 election.

5. This brief discussion cannot do justice to the complexities of black electoral behavior. For an important study based upon the Black National Election Study survey conducted by the Center for Political Studies of the University of Michigan in 1984, see Patricia Gurin, Shirley J. Hatchett, and James S. Jackson, *Hope and Independence: Blacks' Response to Electoral and Party Politics* (New York: Russell Sage Foundation, 1989). For an important study that used both the 1984 Black National Election Study and the 1988 follow-up study, see Katherine Tate, *From Politics to Protest: The New Black Voters in American Elections* (Cambridge, Mass.: Harvard University Press, 1993). Tate provides an excellent list of recent literature about research on black voting behavior.

6. According to our analyses of the 1992 NES survey, 23 percent of Clinton's total vote came from black voters. However, our recalculations based upon the VRS exit poll suggest that only 15 percent of his vote came from African-Americans.

7. We have examined the results for blacks for all of the categories presented in Table 5-1, but we do not present them. Given the relatively small number of blacks sampled, the number of blacks in some of these categories is too small to present meaningful results. No black Jews were included in the 1992 NES survey. Given the small number of African-Americans in the 1992 NES survey, we report results based upon the VRS exit poll. However, for all three results we discuss, we find similar results using the 1992 NES survey.

8. For a review of recent political science research on Hispanics, as well as research on African-Americans and other racial minorities, see Paula D. McClain and John D. Garcia, "Expanding Disciplinary Boundaries: Black, Latino, and Racial Minority Groups in Political Science," in *Political Science: The State of the Discipline II*, ed. Ada W. Finifter (Washington, D.C.: American Political Science Association, 1993), 247-279.

9. For an extensive review of the research literature on women and politics, see Susan J. Carroll and Linda M. G. Zerilli, "Feminist Challenges to Political

Science," in *Political Science: The State of the Discipline II*, 55-76.
10. Everett Carll Ladd, "The 1992 Vote for President Clinton: Another Brittle Mandate?" *Political Science Quarterly* 108 (Spring 1993): 1-28. See also Michael X. Delli Carpini and Ester R. Fuchs, "The Year of the Woman? Candidates, Voters, and the 1992 Elections," *Political Science Quarterly* 108 (Spring 1993): 29-36.
11. The NES survey reports six types of marital status: married and living with spouse, never married, divorced, separated, widowed, and partners who are not married. In this paragraph we compare the first two of these groups.
12. Paul R. Abramson, "Generations and Political Change in the United States," *Research in Political Sociology* 4 (1989): 235-280; Helmut Norpoth, "Under Way and Here to Stay: Party Realignment in the 1980s?" *Public Opinion Quarterly* 51 (Fall 1987): 376-391; and Ladd, "The 1992 Vote for President Clinton," 8.
13. Philip E. Converse, *The Dynamics of Party Support: Cohort-Analyzing Party Identification* (Beverly Hills, Calif.: Sage, 1976), 121-142; Paul R. Abramson, *Political Attitudes in America: Formation and Change* (San Francisco: Freeman, 1983) 119-126; and Abramson, "Generations and Political Change," 263-270.
14. See, for example, Walter Dean Burnham, *Critical Elections and the Mainsprings of American Politics* (New York: Norton, 1970); Everett Carll Ladd, Jr., with Charles D. Hadley, Jr., *Transformations of the American Party System: Political Coalitions from the New Deal to the 1970s*, 2d ed. (New York: Norton, 1978).
15. For the best summary of the impact of religious differences in American political life, see Kenneth D. Wald, *Religion and Politics in the United States*, 2d ed. (Washington, D.C.: CQ Press, 1992).
16. The results for white Catholics are presented in Ladd, "The 1992 Vote for President Clinton," 4. Given that only 391 white Catholic voters were sampled in the NES survey, we do not have adequate data to explore the impact of differing religious beliefs or differing levels of religious involvement among Catholics. For an important discussion of the political impact of religious beliefs among Roman Catholics, see David C. Leege and Michael R. Welch, "Religious Roots of Political Orientations: Variation Among Catholic Parishioners," *Journal of Politics* 51 (February 1989): 137-162.
17. Ross K. Baker, "Sorting Out and Suiting Up: The Presidential Nominations," in *The Election of 1992: Reports and Interpretations*, Gerald M. Pomper et al. (Chatham, N.J.: Chatham House, 1993), 67.
18. David C. Leege and Lyman A. Kellstedt, with others, *Rediscovering the Religious Factor in American Politics* (Armonk, N.Y.: M. E. Sharpe, 1993).
19. Robert Axelrod, "Where the Votes Come From: An Analysis of Electoral Coalitions, 1952-1968," *American Political Science Review* 66 (March 1972): 11-20. Axelrod continued to provide updates of his estimates through the 1984 election. For his update of the 1984 results, which includes the cumulative results from 1952 through 1984, see Robert Axelrod, "Presidential Election Coalitions in 1984," *American Political Science Review* 80 (March 1986): 281-284.
20. John R. Petrocik, *Party Coalitions: Realignment and the Decline of the New Deal Party System* (Chicago: University of Chicago Press, 1981).
21. Harold W. Stanley, William T. Bianco, and Richard G. Niemi, "Partisanship and Group Support Over Time: A Multivariate Analysis," *American Political Science Review* 80 (September 1986): 969-976. Stanley and his colleagues

assess the independent contribution that group memberships make toward Democratic party loyalties after controls are introduced for membership in other pro-Democratic groups. For an update and extension, see Stanley and Niemi, "Partisanship and Group Support, 1952-1988," *American Politics Quarterly* 19 (April 1991): 189-210. For an alternative approach, see Robert S. Erikson, Thomas D. Lancaster, and David W. Romero, "Group Components of the Presidential Vote, 1952- 1984," *Journal of Politics* 51 (May 1989): 337-346.

22. For a discussion of the importance of working-class whites to the Democratic presidential coalition, see Paul R. Abramson, *Generational Change in American Politics* (Lexington, Mass.: Heath, 1975).

23. See Axelrod, "Where the Votes Come From."

24. The NORC survey, based upon 2,564 civilians, used a quota sample that does not follow the probability procedures used by the University of Michigan Survey Research Center. Following quota procedures common at the time, southern blacks were not sampled. Because the NORC survey overrepresented upper income groups and the middle and upper middle classes, it cannot be used to estimate the contribution of social groups to the Democratic and Republican presidential coalition.

25. Abramson, *Generational Change in American Politics,* 65-68.

26. The percentage difference index is designed to measure social cleavages in the two-party vote, but it can be used in multiparty systems when the parties can be classified into two basic types (for example, left parties versus right parties). In our earlier analysis of the effects of the Wallace vote and the Anderson vote, we had little question that Wallace and Anderson voters could reasonably be regrouped with the Republican voters to produce alternative measures of social cleavage (see Abramson, Aldrich, and Rohde, *Change and Continuity in the 1980 Elections,* rev. ed., 102-115). Wallace was clearly to the right of Nixon. Although Anderson was a centrist, he was a former Republican who had unsuccessfully competed for the 1980 Republican presidential nomination before launching his independent candidacy.

Classifying the Perot vote is more problematic. Ladd argues strongly that the Perot vote came mainly from Republican supporters. He writes: "Perot's voters came disproportionately from groups—defined both in terms of social status and political outlook—that have been giving the Republicans strong support in recent presidential elections. They hadn't changed their stance on most major political issues in 1992, and in general they differed sharply from Clinton backers" ("The 1992 Vote for President Clinton," 22). We should also note that despite very substantial differences between the Wallace, Anderson, and Perot candidacies, they were similar in one basic respect. None drew very much support from African-Americans—although, of course, Anderson and Perot won more black votes than Wallace. Race is by far the sharpest social division in American politics, and in all three elections racial differences are greater if votes for these third-party or independent candidates are regrouped with the Republicans' vote. The data presented in Table 5-1 allow readers to calculate their own measures, and it is easy to create measures that include Perot voters with Clinton voters.

27. As we explained in Chapter 3, we consider the South to include the eleven states of the old Confederacy. Because we could not use our definition of the South with either the 1944 NORC survey or the 1948 University of Michigan Survey Research Center survey, we have not included these years in our analysis of regional differences among the white electorate.

28. Our recalculations, based upon the VRS poll, suggest that 27 percent of Clinton's total southern vote came from blacks. This lower total results from the VRS's estimate that only 13 percent of the total southern vote was cast by black voters. Even though the VRS poll uses a broader definition of the South, which includes some border states, this estimate seems low. It seems likely to us that at least a third of Clinton's total vote in the states of the Confederacy were cast by African-Americans.

29. Clinton carried Georgia by only 13,714 votes, Louisiana by 82,585 votes, and Tennessee by 92,221 votes. There are 1,235,000 voting-age blacks in Georgia, 852,000 in Louisiana, and 551,000 in Tennessee. The vast majority of blacks who voted in these states supported Clinton. It seems certain, therefore, that Bush won more of the white vote in these states than Clinton did.

30. See Robert R. Alford, *Party and Society: The Anglo-American Democracies* (Chicago: Rand McNally, 1963); Seymour Martin Lipset, *Political Man: The Social Bases of Politics*, exp. ed. (Baltimore: Johns Hopkins University Press, 1981); and Ronald Inglehart, *Culture Shift in Advanced Industrial Society* (Princeton, N.J.: Princeton University Press, 1990).

31. The variation in class voting is smaller if one focuses on class differences in the congressional vote, but the trend clearly shows a gradual decline in class voting between 1952 and 1984. See Russell J. Dalton, *Citizen Politics in Western Democracies: Public Opinion and Political Parties in the United States, Great Britain, West Germany, and France* (Chatham, N.J.: Chatham House, 1988), 156-157.

32. See Mark N. Franklin, "The Decline of Cleavage Politics," in *Electoral Change: Responses to Evolving Social and Attitudinal Structures in Western Countries*, Mark N. Franklin, Thomas T. Mackie, and Henry Valen, with others (New York: Cambridge University Press, 1992), 383-405.

33. According to our calculations, based upon the published VRS results, there were about 550 major party Jewish voters sampled, and 87 percent of them voted for Clinton.

34. See *Statistical Abstract of the United States 1992*, 112th ed. (Washington, D.C.: U.S. Government Printing Office), 60. We list these states in descending order of the estimated number of Jews. The estimates of the number of Jews in each state are based mainly upon estimates by local Jewish organizations.

35. Based on results in "Portrait: How New Yorkers Voted," *New York Times*, November 5, 1992, B8. The survey was based upon 1,953 respondents.

36. Robert Huckfeldt and Carol Weitzel Kohfeld, *Race and the Decline of Class in American Politics* (Urbana: University of Illinois Press, 1989).

37. For evidence on this point, see Abramson, *Political Attitudes in America*, 94-96.

38. Edward G. Carmines and James A. Stimson, *Issue Evolution: Race and the Transformation of American Politics* (Princeton, N.J.: Princeton University Press, 1989).

39. James Ceaser and Andrew Busch, *Upside Down and Inside Out: The 1992 Elections and American Politics* (Lanham, Md.: Rowman and Littlefield, 1993), 168-171.

Chapter 6: Candidates, Issues, and the Vote

1. See, for example, Wendy M. Rahn et al., "A Social-Cognitive Model of Candidate Appraisal," *Information and Democratic Processes*, ed. John A. Ferejohn and James H. Kuklinski (Urbana: University of Illinois Press, 1990),

136-159, and sources cited therein.

2. For explication of the theory and tests in various electoral settings, see Paul R. Abramson et al., " 'Sophisticated' Voting in the 1988 Presidential Primaries," *American Political Science Review* 86 (March 1992): 55-69; Jerome H. Black, "The Multicandidate Calculus of Voting: Application to Canadian Federal Elections," *American Journal of Political Science* 22 (August 1978): 609-638; and Bruce E. Cain, "Strategic Voting in Britain," *American Journal of Political Science* 22 (August 1978): 639-655.

3. William H. Riker, *Liberalism Against Populism: A Confrontation Between the Theory of Democracy and the Theory of Social Choice* (San Francisco: Freeman, 1982): 85-88.

4. For a more detailed analysis of the 1980 election, see Paul R. Abramson, John H. Aldrich, and David W. Rohde, *Change and Continuity in the 1980 Elections*, rev. ed. (Washington, D.C.: CQ Press, 1983), 172-184.

5. About 40 percent of the preelection respondents were interviewed before Perot reentered the race on October 1, 1992. Among preelection respondents interviewed after Perot reentered the contest, 5 percent failed to rate Perot, 2 percent did not rate Clinton, and 1 percent did not rate Bush on the scale. Among these same respondents, 24 percent rated Perot at the midpoint, whereas 14 percent rated Clinton at the midpoint and 15 percent rated Bush at the midpoint.

6. Black, "The Multicandidate Calculus of Voting;" Cain, "Strategic Voting in Britain."

7. See Abramson et al., " 'Sophisticated' Voting in the 1988 Presidential Primaries."

8. Gordon S. Black and Benjamin D. Black, " 'Perot Wins!': The Election That Could Have Been," *Public Perspective* 4 (January/February 1993): 15-16. Black and Black's conclusions were based upon questions listed at the end of the exit poll ballot. Respondents were asked to check statements that applied to them. One of them was, "Would you have voted for Ross Perot if he had a chance to win?" Black and Black report that 36 percent of the respondents said they would have voted for Perot, and that another 4 percent who did not answer the question had voted for Perot. Larry Hugic argues that it is highly questionable to infer that Perot actually would have won the votes of all the respondents who answered yes to this question. See "A Response to Gordon and Benjamin Black: Perot's Own Actions Determined His Fate," *Public Perspective* 4 (January/February 1993): 17-18.

9. See Duncan Black, *The Theory of Committees and Elections* (Cambridge: Cambridge University Press, 1958), for a summary of Condorcet's writings on the subject. See also Riker, *Liberalism Against Populism.*

10. For more on the strategies of the candidates in the 1980, 1984, and 1988 elections, see Abramson, Aldrich, and Rohde, *Change and Continuity in the 1980 Elections*, chap. 2; Abramson, Aldrich, and Rohde, *Change and Continuity in the 1984 Elections*, rev. ed. (Washington, D.C.: CQ Press, 1987), chap. 2; and Abramson, Aldrich, and Rohde, *Change and Continuity in the 1988 Elections*, rev. ed. (Washington, D.C.: CQ Press, 1991), chap. 2.

11. For an analysis of how the candidates' campaign strategies in 1988 shaped the voters' decisions, see Thomas Weko and John H. Aldrich, "The Presidency and the Election Process: Framing the Choice in 1988," *The Presidency and the Political System*, 3d ed. Michael Nelson (Washington, D.C.: CQ Press, 1990), 263-286.

12. Each respondent in the survey is asked the question in the text and

encouraged to give up to three responses. Then, if more than one problem is raised, the respondent is asked which one is the single most important. The responses in Table 6-3 are from the latter question. Looking at the full array of responses, we find a broader range of alternatives suggested, yet the same outlines are apparent.

13. We have coded international economic issues, such as trade and American competitiveness, in the economic category. About as many cited such a concern as cited another foreign policy concern; therefore, if we had included these in the foreign concerns category, the percentage citing a foreign concern as most important would increase to 4 percent.

14. Problems associated with the family were cited by 1 percent. Thus, the Bush-Quayle and Republican National Convention theme of relating to such "public order" concerns found a receptive audience in the public, but too small an audience to materially affect Republican chances.

15. A much smaller number (only 19 respondents) expressed concern with taxes or the level of government spending in 1992 than had done so in 1984 and 1988.

16. These measures were first used in the NES survey of the 1968 election. They were used extensively in presidential election surveys beginning in 1972. The issue measures used in Chapter 7 were also used extensively beginning in the 1970s. Therefore, in this and the next two chapters, we restrict our attention to the last six elections.

17. The median is based on the assumption that respondents can be ranked from most conservative to most liberal. The number of respondents who are more liberal than the median (or who see a candidate as more liberal than the median) is equal to the number who are more conservative (see the candidate as more conservative) than the median. Because there are only 7 points on these scales, and because many respondents will choose any given point, the median is computed using a procedure that derives a median for grouped data.

18. The NES relies upon in-person interviews using printed survey instruments. The problems associated with changing the questions in the middle of a survey are formidable.

19. The wordings for the remaining issue scales are as follows:

> "Some people think that the government should provide fewer services, even in areas such as health and education in order to reduce spending. . . . Other people feel it is important for the government to provide many more services even if it means an increase in spending;"
>
> "Some people believe that we should spend much less money for defense. Others feel that defense spending should be greatly increased."

After each of these statements, respondents were asked, "Where would you place yourself on this scale, or haven't you thought much about this?" Those who placed themselves on the issue scale were asked, "Where would you place George Bush on this scale?" Then they were asked about Bill Clinton and then about other political actors or groups.

Note that "1" is the most conservative response on the government services and spending scale, but it the most liberal response on the other two scales. To increase comparability, we have "reversed" the government services and spending scale, so that "1" in the text, tables, and figures corresponds to the response, "Other people feel that it is important for the government to provide many more services even if it means an increase in spending," while "7" corresponds to the other endpoint.

20. This scale has been used in every NES survey, beginning in 1972. The average self-placement has been virtually constant, with the 4.2 average placement of 1984 being the most "liberal," and the average placement of 4.5 in 1988 being the most "conservative." See Abramson, Aldrich, and Rohde, *Change and Continuity in the 1988 Elections*, rev. ed., 162.

21. Angus Campbell et al., *The American Voter* (New York: Wiley, 1960), 168-187.

22. The NES interviewers did not ask those who failed to place themselves on an issue scale where they thought the candidates stood. Therefore, those who failed to meet the first criterion were not able to meet any of the remaining ones. Although some people who express no preference on an issue might know the positions of one or both candidates, it is difficult to see how they could vote based on those perceptions if they had no opinion of their own.

23. The arguments made by Campbell and his colleagues in *The American Voter* about issue voting criteria are critiqued by Morris P. Fiorina, *Retrospective Voting in American National Elections* (New Haven, Conn.: Yale University Press, 1981), 9-11. Although many scholars have interpreted failure to meet these criteria as akin to failing a test, he argues that the criteria imply no such thing. We agree. Failure to satisfy these criteria in no way impugns the citizen. As we will see, "failure" to satisfy these criteria is related to the strategies followed by the candidates in the campaign.

24. For details, see Abramson, Aldrich, and Rohde, *Change and Continuity in the 1980 Elections*, rev. ed., Table 6-3, 130; *Change and Continuity in the 1984 Elections*, rev. ed., Table 6-2, 174; and *Change and Continuity in the 1988 Elections*, rev. ed., Table 6-2, 165.

25. Although this is evidence that most people *claim* to have issue preferences, it does not demonstrate that they *do*. For example, evidence indicates that some use the midpoint of the scale (point 4) as a means of answering the question even if they have ill-formed preferences. See John H. Aldrich et al., "The Measurement of Public Opinion about Public Policy: A Report on Some New Issue Question Formats," *American Journal of Political Science* 26 (May 1982): 391-414.

26. These findings suggest that respondents are better able to answer the questions asked about these three issues than about other issues. It is reasonable to conclude that these three are central and longstanding bases of partisan cleavages at the elite and the mass levels.

27. Fiorina, *Retrospective Voting*.

28. We use "apparent issue voting" to emphasize several points. First, voting involves too many factors to infer that closeness to a candidate on any one issue was the cause of the voter's choice. The issue similarity may have been purely coincidental, or it may have been only one of many reasons the voter supported that candidate. Second, we use the median perception of the candidates' positions rather than the voter's own perception. Third, the relationship between issues and the vote may be caused by rationalization. Voters may have decided to support a candidate for other reasons and may also have altered their own issue preferences or misperceived the positions of the candidates to align themselves more closely with their already favored candidate. See Richard A. Brody and Benjamin I. Page, "Comment: The Assessment of Policy Voting," *American Political Science Review* 66 (June 1972): 450-458.

29. Ibid.

30. It is possible that the lower salience of foreign and defense issues in 1992 (see

Table 6-3) meant greater defections from the incumbent as voters believed more and more should be cut; there was little difference in support across the remaining categories of this scale. It may be that those who favored reductions in defense spending hoped the government would use the savings on more pressing domestic concerns, whether that meant to increase spending on domestic programs, to reduce taxes, or to reduce the deficit.

31. This procedure counts every issue as equal in importance. It also assumes that what matters is that the voter is closer to the candidate on an issue; it does not consider how much closer the voter is to one candidate or the other.

32. Because the balance of issues measure in 1992 is based on only three issue scales, it would be inappropriate to compare this measure in 1992 to those created in earlier studies, which are based on a larger number of issue scales. For analysis and comparisons for the elections from 1972 through 1988, see Abramson, Aldrich, and Rohde, *Change and Continuity in the 1980 Elections*, rev. ed., 135-138; Abramson, Aldrich, and Rohde, *Change and Continuity in the 1984 Elections*, rev. ed., 179-183; and Abramson, Aldrich, and Rohde, *Change and Continuity in the 1988 Elections*, rev. ed., 169-173.

33. Most scores will be odd numbers, given only three issue scales. Those with even numbers will typically have not placed themselves on one of the three scales.

34. Bush continued this ban, even though critics of the ban pointed to the promise that research using fetal tissue appeared to hold for curing Alzheimer's disease. His argument was that such research would encourage women to have abortions. Bush was willing to allow federal funding for research with fetal tissue that was derived from miscarriages. Such tissue is hard to obtain, however, because women do not normally have miscarriages under conditions where fetal tissue can be stored for medical research.

35. Thirty-eight respondents who did not choose one of the four basic options have been excluded from this analysis.

36. Three respondents who said Bush had some "other" position were excluded, because we cannot ascertain if they saw Clinton as more pro-choice than Bush.

37. The survey did include a 7-point scale on which respondents were asked to place themselves, Bush, Clinton, and Perot on a scale that ran from liberal to conservative. But because we do not know what respondents meant by these terms, we cannot use the questions to measure issue preferences.

Chapter 7: Presidential Performance and Candidate Choice

1. V. O. Key, Jr., *Politics, Parties, and Pressure Groups*, 5th ed. (New York: Crowell, 1964), 568. Key's theory of retrospective voting is most fully developed in *The Responsible Electorate: Rationality in Presidential Voting, 1936-1960* (Cambridge, Mass.: Harvard University Press, 1966).

2. Anthony Downs, *An Economic Theory of Democracy* (New York: Harper and Row, 1957).

3. Morris P. Fiorina, *Retrospective Voting in American National Elections* (New Haven, Conn.: Yale University Press, 1981), 83.

4. See Benjamin I. Page, *Choices and Echoes in Presidential Elections: Rational Man and Electoral Democracy* (Chicago: University of Chicago Press, 1978). He argues that "party cleavages" distinguish the party at the candidate and mass levels.

5. Arthur H. Miller and Martin P. Wattenberg, "Throwing the Rascals Out:

Policy and Performance Evaluations of Presidential Candidates, 1952-1980,"
American Political Science Review 79 (June 1985): 359-372.

6. Each respondent assesses governmental performance on the problem he or
she considers the most important. In the five most recent surveys, respondents were asked, "How good a job is the government doing in dealing with
this problem—a good job, only fair, or a poor job?"

7. Negative evaluations are not surprising. After all, if you thought the
government had been doing a good job with the problem, then it probably
would not be your major concern. This reasoning seems to underlie the very
low proportions in every survey who thought the government was doing a
good job with their most important concern.

8. Since 1976, this question has been worded as follows: "Which party do you
think would be the most likely to get the government to do a better job in
dealing with this problem—the Republicans, the Democrats, or wouldn't
there be much difference between them?"

9. See Gerald H. Kramer, "Short-Term Fluctuations in U.S. Voting Behavior,
1896-1964," *American Political Science Review* 65 (March 1971): 131-143;
Fiorina, *Retrospective Voting*; M. Stephen Weatherford, "Economic Conditions and Electoral Outcomes: Class Differences in the Political Response to
Recession," *American Journal of Political Science* 22 (November 1978): 917-
938; D. Roderick Kiewiet and Douglas Rivers, "A Retrospective on Retrospective Voting," *Political Behavior* 6, no. 4 (1984): 369-393; Kiewiet, *Macroeco-
nomics and Micropolitics: The Electoral Effects of Economic Issues*
(Chicago: University of Chicago Press, 1983); and Michael S. Lewis-Beck,
Economics and Elections: The Major Western Democracies (Ann Arbor:
University of Michigan Press, 1988).

10. John E. Mueller, *War, Presidents and Public Opinion* (New York: Wiley,
1973); Edward R. Tufte, *Political Control of the Economy* (Princeton, N.J.:
Princeton University Press, 1978). For a perceptive critique of the business
cycle formulation, see James E. Alt and K. Alec Chrystal, *Political Economics*
(Berkeley: University of California Press, 1983).

11. Fiorina, *Retrospective Voting*.

12. In the 1984 and 1988 surveys, this question was asked in both the preelection
and the postelection waves of the survey. Since attitudes held by the public
before the election are what counts in influencing their choice, we use the first
question. In both surveys, approval of Reagan's performance was more
positive in the postelection interview: 66 percent approved of his performance
in 1984, and 68 percent approved in 1988.

13. To construct this measure, we awarded respondents 2 points if they approved
of the president's performance, 1 if they had no opinion, and 0 if they
disapproved. Second, respondents received 2 points if they thought the
government was doing a good job in handling the most important problem
facing the country, 1 if they thought the government was doing only a fair job,
and 0 if they thought it was doing a poor job. Finally, respondents received 2
points if they thought the incumbent president's party would do a better job
at handling the most important problem, 1 point if they thought there was no
difference between the parties, and 0 if they thought the challenger's party
would do a better job. For all three questions, "don't know" and "not
ascertained" responses were scored as 1, but respondents with more than one
such response were excluded from the analysis. Scores on our measure were
the sum of the individual values for the three questions, and thus ranged from
a low of 0 (strongly against the incumbent's party) to 6 (strongly for the

incumbent's party). Thus, the measure has seven possible values, corresponding to the seven categories in Figure 7-1.

14. For data from the 1976 and 1980 elections, see Paul R. Abramson, John H. Aldrich, and David W. Rohde, *Change and Continuity in the 1980 Elections*, rev. ed., 155-157, Table 7-8; for data from the 1984 elections, see Abramson, Aldrich, and Rohde, *Change and Continuity in the 1984 Elections*, rev. ed., 203-204, Table 7-8; and for data from the 1988 elections, see Abramson, Aldrich, and Rohde, *Change and Continuity in the 1988 Elections*, rev. ed., 195-198, Table 7-7.

Chapter 8: Party Loyalties, Policy Preferences, and the Vote

1. Angus Campbell et al., *The American Voter* (New York: Wiley, 1960). For the most recent statement of the "standard" view of party identification, see Warren E. Miller, "Party Identification, Realignment, and Party Voting: Back to the Basics," *American Political Science Review* 85 (June 1991): 557-568.

2. Campbell et al., *The American Voter*, 121. See also Morris P. Fiorina, *Retrospective Voting in American National Elections* (New Haven, Conn.: Yale University Press, 1981), 85-86.

3. For the full wording of the party identification questions, see Chapter 4, note 54.

4. Most "apoliticals" were African-Americans living in the South. As they were disenfranchised, questions about their party loyalties were essentially meaningless to them. For the most detailed discussion of how the NES creates its summary measure of party identification, see Arthur H. Miller and Martin P. Wattenberg, "Measuring Party Identification: Independent or No Partisan Preference?" *American Journal of Political Science* 27 (February 1983): 106-121.

5. For evidence of the relatively high level of partisan stability among individuals over time, see M. Kent Jennings and Gregory B. Markus, "Partisan Orientations over the Long Haul: Results from the Three-Wave Political Socialization Panel Study," *American Political Science Review* 78 (December 1984): 1000-1018.

6. V. O. Key, Jr., *The Responsible Electorate: Rationality in Presidential Voting 1936-1960* (Cambridge, Mass.: Harvard University Press, 1966).

7. Morris P. Fiorina, "An Outline for a Model of Party Choice," *American Journal of Political Science* 21 (August 1977): 601-625; Fiorina, *Retrospective Voting*.

8. Benjamin I. Page provides evidence of this. See *Choices and Echoes in Presidential Elections: Rational Man and Electoral Democracy* (Chicago: University of Chicago Press, 1978). Anthony Downs, in *An Economic Theory of Democracy* (New York: Harper and Row, 1957) develops a theoretical logic for such consistency in party stances on issues and ideology over time.

9. There is some controversy over how to classify these independent leaners. Some argue that they are mainly "hidden" partisans who should be considered identifiers. For the strongest statement of this position, see Bruce E. Keith et al., *The Myth of the Independent Voter* (Berkeley: University of California Press, 1992). In our view, however, the evidence on the proper classification of independent leaners is mixed. On balance, the evidence suggests that they are more partisan than independents with no partisan leanings, but less partisan than weak partisans. See Paul R. Abramson,

Political Attitudes in America: Formation and Change (San Francisco: Freeman, 1983), 80-81, 95-96. For an excellent discussion of this question, see Herbert B. Asher, "Voting Behavior Research in the 1980s: An Examination of Some Old and New Problem Areas," in *Political Science: The State of the Discipline*, ed. Ada W. Finifter (Washington, D.C.: American Political Science Association, 1983), 357-360.

10. See, for example, Martin P. Wattenberg, *The Decline of American Political Parties, 1952-1988* (Cambridge, Mass.: Harvard University Press, 1990).

11. With the exception of the 1993 GSS results, all of our calculations are based upon the codebooks provided by the Roper Center for Public Opinion Research at the University of Connecticut. The 1993 results were provided directly by Tom Smith of NORC.

12. See Michael B. MacKuen, Robert S. Erikson, and James A. Stimson, "Macropartisanship," *American Political Science Review* 83 (December 1989): 1125-1142.

13. Most of these Gallup data are available through the Roper archives or are published in the *Gallup Report*. The most recent Gallup results were provided to us directly by the Gallup organization.

14. The basic Gallup partisanship question asks, "In politics, as of today, do you consider yourself a Republican, a Democrat, or an Independent?" The Gallup surveys do not ordinarily ask respondents about the strength of their attachment or about which party independents lean toward.

15. Philip E. Converse and Roy Pierce, *Political Representation in France* (Cambridge, Mass.: Harvard University Press, 1986), 73.

16. This point was first made by Philip E. Converse in *The Dynamics of Party Support: Cohort-Analyzing Party Identification* (Beverly Hills, Calif.: Sage, 1976), 35-36. For more systematic evidence, see Paul R. Abramson and Charles W. Ostrom, Jr., "Macropartisanship: An Empirical Reassessment," *American Political Science Review* 85 (March 1991): 181-192. For a controversy between MacKuen, Erikson, and Stimson on the one hand, and Abramson and Ostrom on the other, see "Question Wording and Macropartisanship," *American Political Science Review* 86 (June 1992): 475-486. For a recent experimental study that strongly suggests that responses to the Gallup party affiliation question are more changeable than responses to the standard SRC party identification questions, see Abramson and Ostrom, "Question Wording and Partisanship: Change and Continuity in Party Loyalties During the 1992 Election Campaign," *Public Opinion Quarterly* (Spring 1994): 21-48.

17. As we saw in Chapter 5, blacks have voted overwhelmingly Democratic since 1964. For that reason, there is no meaningful relationship between partisanship and the vote. We therefore analyze the relationship between party identification and the vote among whites only.

18. For details, see Paul R. Abramson, John H. Aldrich, and David W. Rohde, *Change and Continuity in the 1984 Elections*, rev. ed. (Washington, D.C.: CQ Press, 1987), 216. Note that there was a sizable third-party vote for president in the 1968 and the 1980 elections, and, of course, an even larger vote for Perot in 1992. Since Table 8-4 excludes such voters, it tends to exaggerate the impact of party identification.

19. Bernard R. Berelson, Paul F. Lazarsfeld, and William N. McPhee, *Voting: A Study of Opinion Formation in a Presidential Campaign* (Chicago: University of Chicago Press, 1954).

20. See Richard A. Brody and Benjamin I. Page, "Comment: The Assessment of

Policy Voting," *American Political Science Review* 66 (June 1972): 450-458; Page and Brody, "Policy Voting and the Electoral Process: The Vietnam War Issue," *American Political Science Review* 66 (September 1972): 979-995; and Fiorina, "An Outline for a Model of Party Choice."

21. In 1972, 1976 and 1980, we found nearly as strong a relationship between partisanship and perceptions of which party would better handle the economy. See Paul R. Abramson, John H. Aldrich, and David W. Rohde, *Change and Continuity in the 1980 Elections*, rev. ed. (Washington, D.C.: CQ Press, 1983), 170, Table 8-6, 173.

22. This question measuring approval of the president's handling of economic policy was not asked in NES surveys before 1984. In our study of these earlier elections, an alternative measure of economic retrospective evaluations was created and shown to be nearly as strongly related to party identification. See Abramson, Aldrich, and Rohde, *Change and Continuity in the 1984 Elections*, rev. ed., Table 8-6, 221.

23. For a description of this measure, see Chapter 6. Since this measure uses the median placement of the candidates on the issue scales in the full sample, much of the projection effect is eliminated. For the relationship between party identification and the balance of issues measure in 1972, see Abramson, Aldrich, and Rohde, *Change and Continuity in the 1980 Elections*, rev. ed., Table 8-5, 171.

24. Recall that the summary measure of retrospective evaluations includes the presidential approval measure, the job the government is doing in handling the most important problem the respondent sees facing the country, and which party is better at handling that problem. This measure could not be created from the 1972 election data. The presidential approval measure was asked of a different half of the sample than the most important problems questions in that survey.

25. For two important articles assessing some of these relationships, see Gregory B. Markus and Philip E. Converse, "A Dynamic Simultaneous Equation Model of Electoral Choice," *American Political Science Review* 73 (December 1979): 1055-1070, and Benjamin I. Page and Calvin C. Jones, "Reciprocal Effects of Policy Preferences, Party Loyalties and the Vote," *American Political Science Review* 73 (December 1979): 1071-1089. For a brief discussion of these articles, see Richard G. Niemi and Herbert F. Weisberg, *Controversies in Voting Behavior*, 2d ed. (Washington, D.C.: CQ Press, 1984), 89-95. For an excellent discussion of complex models of voting behavior and the role of party identification in these models, see Asher, "Voting Behavior Research in the 1980s," 341-354. For another excellent introduction to some of these issues, see Richard G. Niemi and Herbert F. Weisberg, "Is Party Identification Stable?" in *Controversies in Voting Behavior*, 3d ed., ed. Niemi and Weisberg (Washington, D.C.: CQ Press, 1993): 268-283.

Introduction to Part 3

1. As Steven J. Rosenstone and John Mark Hansen point out, between 1952 and 1988, seventeen states rescheduled their gubernatorial election from presidential election years to nonpresidential years. They estimate that in 1952, nearly half of the electorate could vote in a presidential election in which a governor was also being selected. In the 1988 presidential election, according to their estimates, only 12 percent of the electorate lived in states with a competitive gubernatorial election. See Rosenstone and Hansen, *Mobilization, Participa-*

tion, and Democracy in America (New York: Macmillan, 1993), 183. In all twelve gubernatorial elections in 1992, both major parties ran candidates. According to our estimates, 12 percent of the U.S. voting-age population lived in these states. Rosenstone and Hansen argue that this change in the scheduling of gubernatorial elections is a major factor in the decline of electoral participation.

2. California held two Senate races, and both were won by Democrats. Barbara Boxer won the six-year term for the seat vacated by the retirement of Democrat Alan Cranston, and Dianne Feinstein won the race to fill the remainder of the term that resulted from Republican Pete Wilson's resignation from the Senate after he was elected governor of California in 1990. The Georgia Senate election required a runoff because Georgia's election rules specify that the winner must receive a majority of the popular vote. The incumbent Democrat, Wyche Fowler, Jr., received a plurality of the vote, but fell short of a majority, and he was defeated by a narrow margin by Republican Paul Coverdell in an election held on November 24.

3. The only exception was in 1934, when the Democrats increased their share of the House seats during Franklin D. Roosevelt's first term.

Chapter 9: Candidates and Outcomes

1. The independent was Bernard Sanders of Vermont, who was first elected to the House in 1990. He had previously been elected mayor of Burlington, Vermont, running as a socialist. For convenience in presenting results, we will count Sanders as a Democrat throughout this chapter. This seems reasonable since he received 58 percent of the vote in 1992 in a three-way race, while the Democratic candidate got only 8 percent. Moreover, Sanders voted with the Democrats 92 percent of the time on party unity votes on the House floor in 1992, while he joined with the GOP on only 8 percent (see *Congressional Quarterly Weekly Report*, December 19, 1992), 3908.

2. *Incumbents* here is used only for elected incumbents. This includes all members of the House because the only way to become a representative is by election. In the case of the Senate, however, vacancies may be filled by appointment. We do not count appointed senators as incumbents. In the 1992 election, the only appointed senator running in his or her first election was John Seymour (R-Calif.), who lost.

   Special mention also needs to be made of the treatment of the Louisiana House races. Louisiana has an unusual open primary system in which candidates from all parties run against one another in a single primary. If no candidate receives a majority, the two top vote getters, regardless of party, face each other in a runoff in November. We count the last round in each district as the controlling race. If that round involved only candidates of a single party, that race is counted as a primary and the winner as unopposed in the general election. If candidates of both parties were involved in the final round, it is treated as a general election.

3. The Republicans won control of the House in eight consecutive elections from 1894 through 1908, far short of the current series of Democratic successes.

4. The regional breakdowns used in this chapter are as follows: East: Connecticut, Delaware, Maine, Massachusetts, New Hampshire, New Jersey, New York, Pennsylvania, Rhode Island, and Vermont; Midwest: Illinois, Indiana, Iowa, Kansas, Michigan, Minnesota, Nebraska, North Dakota, Ohio, South Dakota, and Wisconsin; West: Alaska, Arizona, California, Colorado, Hawaii,

Idaho, Montana, Nevada, New Mexico, Oregon, Utah, Washington, and Wyoming; South: Alabama, Arkansas, Florida, Georgia, Louisiana, Mississippi, North Carolina, South Carolina, Tennessee, Texas, and Virginia; and Border: Kentucky, Maryland, Missouri, Oklahoma, and West Virginia. This classification differs somewhat from the one we used in earlier chapters (and in Chapter 10), but it is commonly used for congressional analysis.

5. Over the years changes in the southern electorate have also made southern Democratic constituencies more like northern Democratic constituencies, and less like Republican constituencies, North or South. These changes also appear to have enhanced the homogeneity of preferences within the partisan delegations in Congress. See David W. Rohde, *Parties and Leaders in the Postreform House* (Chicago: University of Chicago Press, 1991), and Rohde, "Electoral Forces, Political Agendas, and Partisanship in the House and Senate," in *The Postreform Congress*, ed. Roger H. Davidson (New York: St. Martin's, 1992), 27-47.

6. The size of the House is fixed by legislation. The constitution requires that there can be no more than one representative for every 30,000 inhabitants, although each state is entitled to at least one representative. Based on the 1990 census, the average House district has about 570,000 inhabitants. The U.S. has larger single-member districts than any other democracy with the exception of India. Moreover, the redistricting process is much more political than the process of redrawing legislative districts in other democracies. For a comparative perspective, see David Butler and Bruce Cain, *Congressional Redistricting: Comparative and Theoretical Perspectives* (New York: Macmillan, 1992), 117-139.

7. The Republicans could not depend on political control of the redistricting process to make gains. They controlled both the state legislature' and the governorship in only two states that had more than a single House seat: New Hampshire and Utah, which had a total of five seats.

8. In addition to the states named above, these were: Alabama, Arizona, Colorado, Minnesota, Oregon, and South Carolina. There were also five states in which redistricting was done by a neutral commission: Connecticut, Hawaii, Idaho, New Jersey, and Washington.

9. There were eight of these: Indiana, Iowa, Kansas, Massachusetts, Missouri, New York, Ohio, and Wisconsin.

10. See *Congressional Quarterly Weekly Report*, April 24, 1993, 1035.

11. Only thirty-nine states are included in Table 9-4. Omitted states include the seven that have only one House seat (Alaska, Delaware, Montana, North Dakota, South Dakota, Vermont, and Wyoming), Nebraska (which has a nonpartisan legislature), Maine (which did not redistrict until 1993), and the two states controlled by the GOP. States that were redistricted by courts or commissions, and by split state governments, were listed in the preceding note. The remaining fifteen states were redistricted by Democratic-controlled state governments.

12. The remaining lost Democratic seat, which is not included in the table, occurred in a single-seat state.

13. In some cases, no one chooses to retire in the multiple-incumbent districts, which increases the incidence of primary or general election defeats. In 1992, five incumbents were defeated by another incumbent in the primaries, and there were four such cases in the general election.

14. The operation was not an actual bank, but was a depository for the paychecks of representatives only, against which they could write checks. It was run by

the sergeant at arms of the House.

15. For a list of representatives who wrote overdrafts, see *Congressional Quarterly Weekly Report*, April 18, 1992, 1006-1007.

16. Quoted in *Roll Call*, March 30, 1993, 3.

17. One particularly interesting case among those on the list of forty-six who escaped significant harm was Rep. Barbara Boxer (D-Calif.), who succeeded in winning a vacant Senate seat despite having written 143 overdrafts.

18. *Congressional Quarterly Weekly Report*, October 17, 1992, 3270. The analysis covers only contributions received through July 15.

19. Charles R. Babcock, "Women Are Filling Coffers of Female Candidates," *Washington Post*, October 22, 1992, A1.

20. *Washington Post*, November 22, 1992, A4.

21. Richard F. Fenno, Jr., *Home Style: House Members in Their Districts* (Boston: Little, Brown, 1978).

22. Analysis of Senate races in 1988 indicates that both the political quality of the previous office held by a challenger and the challenger's political skills had an independent effect on the outcome of the race. See Peverill Squire, "Challenger Quality and Voting Behavior in U.S. Senate Elections," *Legislative Studies Quarterly* 27 (May 1992): 247-263. For systematic evidence on the impact of candidate quality in House races, both open seats and those involving incumbents, see Gary C. Jacobson, *The Electoral Origins of Divided Government: Competition in U.S. House Elections, 1946-1988* (Boulder, Colo.: Westview Press, 1990), chap. 4.

23. The data on office backgrounds was taken from *Congressional Quarterly Weekly Report*, October 24, 1992, 3415-3430.

24. Data on earlier years come from analyses for our studies of previous national elections.

25. Note that the figures in this paragraph include races in which both parties ran candidates and races in which only one party was represented.

26. See Jacobson, *The Electoral Origins of Divided Government*; Jon R. Bond, Cary Covington, and Richard Fleischer, "Explaining Challenger Quality in Congressional Elections," *Journal of Politics* 47 (May 1985): 510-529; and David W. Rohde, "Risk-Bearing and Progressive Ambition: The Case of Members of the United States House of Representatives," *American Journal of Political Science* 23 (February 1979): 1-26.

27. See Peverill Squire, "Preemptive Fund-raising and Challenger Profile in Senate Elections," *Journal of Politics* 53 (November 1991): 1150-1164.

28. Jeffrey S. Banks and D. Roderick Kiewiet, "Explaining Patterns of Candidate Competition in Congressional Elections," *American Journal of Political Science* 33 (November 1989): 997-1015.

29. David Canon, *Actors, Athletes, and Astronauts: Political Amateurism in the United States Congress* (Chicago: University of Chicago Press, 1990).

30. See Kenneth J. Cooper, "Riding High Name Recognition to Hill," *Washington Post*, December 24, 1992, A4.

31. See Thomas E. Mann and Raymond E. Wolfinger, "Candidates and Parties in Congressional Elections," *American Political Science Review* 74 (September 1980): 617-632.

32. See David R. Mayhew, "Congressional Elections: The Case of the Vanishing Marginals," *Polity* 6 (Spring 1974): 295-317; Robert S. Erikson, "The Advantage of Incumbency in Congressional Elections," *Polity* 3 (Spring 1971): 395-405; Robert S. Erikson, "Malapportionment, Gerrymandering, and Party Fortunes in Congressional Elections," *American Political Science*

Review 66 (December 1972): 1234-1245; Warren Lee Kostroski, "Party and Incumbency in Postwar Senate Elections: Trends, Patterns, and Models," *American Political Science Review* 67 (December 1973): 1213-1234; and Donald Gross and David Breaux, "Historical Trends in U.S. Senate Elections" (Paper delivered at the Annual Meeting of the Midwest Political Science Association, Chicago, April 13-15, 1989).

33. Edward R. Tufte, "Communication," *American Political Science Review* 68 (March 1974): 211-213. The communication involved a discussion of Tufte's earlier article, "The Relationship Between Seats and Votes in Two-Party Systems," *American Political Science Review* 67 (June 1973): 540-554.

34. See John A. Ferejohn, "On the Decline of Competition in Congressional Elections," *American Political Science Review* 71 (March 1977): 166-176; Albert D. Cover, "One Good Term Deserves Another: The Advantage of Incumbency in Congressional Elections," *American Journal of Political Science* 21 (August 1977): 523-541; and Albert D. Cover and David R. Mayhew, "Congressional Dynamics and the Decline of Competitive Congressional Elections," in *Congress Reconsidered*, 2d ed., ed. Lawrence C. Dodd and Bruce I. Oppenheimer (Washington, D.C.: CQ Press, 1981), 62-82.

35. Morris P. Fiorina, *Congress: Keystone of the Washington Establishment*, 2d ed. (New Haven, Conn.: Yale University Press, 1989), esp. chaps. 4-6.

36. See several conflicting arguments and conclusions in the following articles published in the *American Journal of Political Science* 25 (August 1981): John R. Johannes and John C. McAdams, "The Congressional Incumbency Effect: Is It Casework, Policy Compatibility, or Something Else? An Examination of the 1978 Election" (512-542); Morris P. Fiorina, "Some Problems in Studying the Effects of Resource Allocation in Congressional Elections" (543-567); Diana Evans Yiannakis, "The Grateful Electorate: Casework and Congressional Elections" (568-580); and McAdams and Johannes, "Does Casework Matter? A Reply to Professor Fiorina" (581-604). See also Johannes, *To Serve the People: Congress and Constituency Service* (Lincoln: University of Nebraska Press, 1984), esp. chap. 8; and Albert D. Cover and Bruce S. Brumberg, "Baby Books and Ballots: The Impact of Congressional Mail on Constituent Opinion," *American Political Science Review* 76 (June 1982): 347-359. The evidence in Cover and Brumberg for a positive electoral effect is quite strong, but the result may be applicable only to limited circumstances.

37. Ferejohn, "On the Decline of Competition," 174.

38. Cover, "One Good Term," 535.

39. The data for 1974-1990 were taken from "House Incumbents' Average Vote Percentage," *Congressional Quarterly Weekly Report*, November 10, 1990, 3800. The figures for 1992 were computed by the authors.

40. For example, a late-1989 poll for the American Medical Association PAC showed that the approval rating for Congress had dropped 9 points over the previous year, from 62 percent to 53 percent (*Cook Political Report*, March 20, 1990): 3.

41. Fenno, *Home Style*, 163-169.

42. Quoted in Susan B. Glasser, "Anti-Incumbent Sentiment Runs Strong," *Roll Call*, July 16, 1990, 21.

43. Richard Morin and Helen Dewar, "Approval of Congress Hits All-Time Low," *Washington Post*, March 20, 1992, A17.

44. Quoted in Kenneth J. Cooper, "Incumbency: A Dreaded Word in '92," *Washington Post*, October 21, 1992, A1.

45. *Roll Call*, May 7, 1992, 23.
46. The body of literature on this subject has grown to be quite large. Some salient examples, in addition to those cited later, are: Gary C. Jacobson, *Money in Congressional Elections* (New Haven, Conn.: Yale University Press, 1980); Jacobson, "Parties and PACs in Congressional Elections," in *Congress Reconsidered*, 4th ed., ed. Lawrence C. Dodd and Bruce I. Oppenheimer (Washington, D.C.: CQ Press, 1989), 117-152; Jacobson and Samuel Kernell, *Strategy and Choice in Congressional Elections*, 2d ed. (New Haven, Conn.: Yale University Press, 1983), and John A. Ferejohn and Morris P. Fiorina, "Incumbency and Realignment in Congressional Elections," in *The New Direction in American Politics*, ed. John E. Chubb and Paul E. Peterson (Washington, D.C.: Brookings Institution, 1985), 91-115.
47. See Jacobson, *The Electoral Origins of Divided Government*, 63-65.
48. The 1990 data were taken from *Politics in America 1990: The 101st Congress*, ed. Phil Duncan (Washington, D.C.: CQ Press, 1989); the data on 1992 are from the *Washington Post*, May 26, 1993, A17. For both elections the data include all incumbents, not just those who had major party opposition.
49. *Roll Call*, November 13, 1988, 5. The figures are through September 20, 1988.
50. "Congressional War Chests," *Washington Post*, February 13, 1989, A21.
51. The last election for which full data on contributions and expenditures were available at the time this analysis was conducted was 1990. Data were taken from *Politics in America 1992: The 102d Congress*, ed. Phil Duncan (Washington, D.C.: CQ Press, 1991). Our analysis excludes races with no major party opposition.
52. See Paul R. Abramson, John H. Aldrich, and David W. Rohde, *Change and Continuity in the 1988 Elections*, rev. ed. (Washington, D.C.: CQ Press, 1991), 242-246, and the earlier work cited there.
53. See Jacobson, *The Electoral Origins of Divided Government*, 54-55, and the work cited in note 46.
54. Donald Philip Green and Jonathan S. Krasno, "Salvation for the Spendthrift Incumbent: Reestimating the Effects of Campaign Spending in House Elections," *American Journal of Political Science* 32 (November 1988), 884-907.
55. Gary C. Jacobson, "The Effects of Campaign Spending in House Elections: New Evidence for Old Arguments," *American Journal of Political Science* 34 (May 1990): 334-362.
56. Alan I. Abramowitz, "Explaining Senate Election Outcomes," *American Political Science Review* 82 (June 1988): 385-403.
57. Gary C. Jacobson, "Campaign Spending and Voter Awareness of Congressional Candidates" (Paper presented at the Annual Meeting of the Public Choice Society, New Orleans, May 11-13, 1977), 16.
58. *Roll Call*, March 4, 1991, 8.
59. Challengers were categorized as having strong experience if they had been elected U. S. representative, to statewide office, to the state legislature, or to countywide or citywide offices (for example, mayor, prosecutor, and so on).
60. Paul R. Abramson, John H. Aldrich, and David W. Rohde, *Change and Continuity in the 1980 Elections*, rev. ed. (Washington, D.C.: CQ Press, 1983), 202-203.
61. Thomas B. Edsall, "GOP's Cash Advantage Failed to Assure Victory in Close Senate Contests," *Washington Post*, November 6, 1986, A46.
62. Quoted in Angelia Herrin, "Big Outside Money Backfired in GOP Loss of Senate to Dems," *Washington Post*, November 6, 1986, A46.

63. *Congressional Quarterly Weekly Report*, December 12, 1992, 3782.
64. *National Journal*, May 29, 1993, 1285-1286.
65. See *Congressional Quarterly Weekly Report*, April 3, 1993, 808-809.
66. *National Journal*, December 12, 1992, 2843.
67. See *Congressional Quarterly Weekly Report*, June 12, 1993, 1451-1452.
68. Earlier research indicated that for these purposes voters may tend to regard a president whose predecessor either died or resigned from office as a continuation of the first president's administration. Therefore, these data are organized by term of administration, rather than term of president. See Abramson, Aldrich, and Rohde, *Change and Continuity in the 1980 Elections*, rev. ed., 252-253.
69. Edward R. Tufte, "Determinants of the Outcomes of Midterm Congressional Elections," *American Political Science Review* 69 (September 1975): 812-826; and Tufte, *Political Control of the Economy* (Princeton, N.J.: Princeton University Press, 1978); Gary C. Jacobson and Samuel Kernell, *Strategy and Choice in Congressional Elections*, 2d ed. (New Haven, Conn.: Yale University Press, 1983).
70. The Jacobson-Kernell hypothesis was challenged by Richard Born in "Strategic Politicians and Unresponsive Voters," *American Political Science Review* 80 (June 1986): 599-612. Born argued that economic and approval data at the time of the election were more closely related to outcomes than were parallel data from earlier in the year. Jacobson, however, offered renewed support for the hypothesis in an analysis of both district-level and aggregate data. See Gary C. Jacobson, "Strategic Politicians and the Dynamics of House Elections, 1946-86," *American Political Science Review* 83 (September 1989): 773-793.
71. Alan I. Abramowitz, Albert D. Cover, and Helmut Norpoth, "The President's Party in Midterm Elections: Going from Bad to Worse," *American Journal of Political Science* 30 (August 1986): 562-576.
72. Bruce I. Oppenheimer, James A. Stimson, and Richard W. Waterman, "Interpreting U. S. Congressional Elections: The Exposure Thesis," *Legislative Studies Quarterly* 11 (May 1986): 228.
73. Robin F. Marra and Charles W. Ostrom, Jr., "Explaining Seat Change in the U.S. House of Representatives 1950-86," *American Journal of Political Science* 33 (August 1989): 541-569.
74. Bentsen resigned from the Senate after his confirmation to be Clinton's Secretary of the Treasury. Kay Bailey Hutchison's victory over the appointed Democratic senator, Bob Kreuger, reduced the number of Democrats in the Senate from fifty-seven to fifty-six. With her election there are now seven female senators—five Democrats and two Republicans.
75. Charles E. Cook, "Just a Few Races Hold Key to Who Controls the Senate," *Roll Call*, July 29, 1993, 8.
76. See, for example, Gary C. Jacobson and Samuel Kernell, "Party Organization and the Efficient Distribution of Campaign Resources: Republicans and Democrats in 1982" (Paper presented at the Weingart-Caltech Conference on the Institutional Context of Elections, California Institute of Technology, Pasadena, February 16-18, 1984); and Jacobson, "The Republican Advantage in Campaign Finance," in *The New Direction in American Politics*, ed. Chubb and Peterson, 143-173.
77. Jacobson, "The Republican Advantage in Campaign Finance," 156.
78. Rollins was forced to resign in 1991 after conflicts with the Bush administration over strategy.

79. See Tim Curran, "NRCC Reports Huge Debt in 1992, But GOP Still Outraised Democrats," *Roll Call*, March 15, 1993, 12.

80. These data were reported in "PACs: The Givers and the Takers," *Washington Post*, April 10, 1989, A7.

81. See Tim Curran, "A Year After War, Gingrich's Plan to Recruit 80 Gulf Vets as GOP Candidates Falls Short," *Roll Call*, January 20, 1992, 12.

82. See Bruce E. Cain, "Assessing the Partisan Effects of Redistricting," *American Political Science Review* 79 (June 1985): 320-333; and Cain, *The Reapportionment Puzzle* (Berkeley: University of California Press, 1984).

83. For a discussion of the 1982 redistricting, see Abramson, Aldrich, and Rohde, *Change and Continuity in the 1980 Elections*, rev. ed., 256-263.

84. Christopher Buchanan, "Classic Gerrymander by Indiana Republicans," *Congressional Quarterly Weekly Report*, October 17, 1981, 2017-2022.

85. Even the vaunted California gerrymander can be questioned. As Jacobson states, Republican governor George Deukmejian, running for reelection in 1986, carried twenty of the twenty-seven Democratic House districts. His analysis of district outcomes since World War II found no evidence of a pro-Democratic bias from redistricting (see *The Electoral Origins of Divided Government*, 93-96). Gary King and Andrew Gelman concluded, in a more complex analysis, that the electoral system has been biased in favor of the Republicans when the incumbency advantage has been controlled for. See their "Systemic Consequences of Incumbency Advantage in U.S. House Elections," *American Journal of Political Science* 35 (February 1991): 110-138.

86. See Norman J. Ornstein, "The Permanent Democratic Congress," *Public Interest* 100 (1990): 33-36. For a more extensive analysis of this issue, see James E. Campbell, "Divided Government, Partisan Bias and Turnout in Congressional Elections: Do Democrats Sit in the 'Cheap Seats'?" (Paper presented at the Annual Meeting of the American Political Science Association, Washington, D.C., August 29-September 1, 1991).

87. See "1992 Results, Turnout," *Congressional Quarterly Weekly Report*, April 17, 1993, 967. This tabulation excludes four districts in Louisiana and one in Florida in which no result was tallied for the general election because the seat had been won in a primary. Because districts are similar in size, especially in an election held just after reapportionment and redistricting, the total number of votes cast can be used as an indirect measure of turnout.

88. See John Curtice and Michael Steed, "Appendix 2: The Results Analysed," in *The British General Election of 1992*, by David Butler and Dennis Kavanagh (New York: St. Martin's, 1992), 322-362.

89. Jacobson, *The Electoral Origins of Divided Government*, 33.

90. Only special elections that were held independently from the regular general election are included. Two of these elections involved the wives of deceased members and they were also excluded, as was the 1983 race in Texas when Phil Gramm, who had been elected as a Democrat, resigned and won election as a Republican. For regular elections in the 1983-1991 period (when the occupant of their seat before the election can be identified), seats in which the incumbent was defeated in a primary are not counted as open, since the opposing party could not anticipate the vacancy, a circumstance that affected the selection of its candidate.

91. Actually, eleven states redrew some or all of their district line after 1982, but most of the changes were minimal, and none substantially affected the districts in the open-seat set.

92. By comparison, the Democrats did not lose even one of the fourteen open Democratic seats that Bush lost with less than 40 percent of the vote.
93. We did note earlier in the chapter that one aspect of districting in 1992 actually appeared to benefit the Republicans: the creation of majority-minority districts under the requirements of the Voting Rights Act. Now that advantage may be in jeopardy. In June 1992, the Supreme Court ruled (in a case involving the North Carolina plan we discussed) that such districts *may* violate the rights of nonminority voters, especially if the shape of the districts is peculiar as in this instance. The case was sent back to the federal district court for a decision on the merits of the particular plan.
94. Jacobson, *The Electoral Origins of Divided Government*, 105. Also see his chapter 6 for evidence in support of this view.
95. See *Congressional Quarterly Weekly Report*, June 19, 1993, 1533-1540.
96. See *Congressional Quarterly Weekly Report*, November 7, 1992, 3593-3595.

Chapter 10: The Congressional Electorate

1. As we saw in Chapter 5 (see footnote 2 and the discussion it relates to), the 1992 NES survey results overreported the Democratic share of the presidential vote. There is a similar pro-Democratic bias in the House vote. According to the 1992 NES survey, the Democrats received 58.5 percent of the major party vote; official results show they actually received only 52.7 percent. See "Counting the Vote: 1992 Totals," *Congressional Quarterly Weekly Report*, April 17, 1993, 965. To simplify the presentation, we have eliminated from consideration votes for minor party candidates in all the tables in this chapter. Furthermore, to ensure that our study of choice is meaningful, in all tables except Tables 10-1 and 10-2 we include only voters who lived in congressional districts in which both major parties ran candidates.
2. We will confine our attention in this section to voting for the House because this group of voters is more directly comparable to the presidential electorate. We here employ the same definitions for social and demographic categories as used in Chapters 4 and 5.
3. Paul R. Abramson, John H. Aldrich, and David W. Rohde, *Change and Continuity in the 1980 Elections*, rev. ed. (Washington, D.C.: CQ Press, 1983), 213-216.
4. Alan I. Abramowitz, "Choices and Echoes in the 1978 U.S. Senate Elections: A Research Note," *American Journal of Political Science* 25 (February 1981): 112-118; and Abramowitz, "National Issues, Strategic Politicians, and Voting Behavior in the 1980 and 1982 Congressional Elections," *American Journal of Political Science* 28 (November 1984): 710-721.
5. Robert S. Erikson and Gerald C. Wright, "Voters, Candidates, and Issues in Congressional Elections," in *Congress Reconsidered*, 3d ed., ed. Lawrence C. Dodd and Bruce I. Oppenheimer (Washington, D.C.: CQ Press, 1985), 91-116.
6. Robert S. Erikson and Gerald C. Wright, "Voters, Candidates and Issues in Congressional Elections," in *Congress Reconsidered*, 5th ed., ed. Lawrence C. Dodd and Bruce I. Oppenheimer (Washington, D.C.: CQ Press, 1993), 104-108.
7. Albert D. Cover, "One Good Term Deserves Another: The Advantage of Incumbency in Congressional Elections," *American Journal of Political Science* 21 (August 1977): 523-541. Cover includes in his analysis not only strong and weak partisans, but also independents with partisan leanings.
8. It should be noted that the 1992 NES survey may contain biases that inflate

the percentage who report voting for House incumbents (see note 17 below).

9. Richard F. Fenno, Jr., "If, As Ralph Nader Says, Congress Is 'The Broken Branch,' How Come We Love Our Congressmen So Much?" in *Congress in Change: Evolution and Reform*, ed. Norman J. Ornstein (New York: Praeger, 1975), 277-287. This theme is expanded and analyzed in Richard F. Fenno, Jr., *Home Style: House Members in Their Districts* (Boston: Little, Brown, 1978).

10. This may seem surprising in light of the House banking scandal, enthusiasm for term limits, and the other indicators of dissatisfaction with Congress that, as we noted in Chapter 9, seem to be spreading to affect evaluations of individual members. Recall, however, that many more incumbents than usual retired or were defeated in primaries. Thus, the incumbents who made it to the general election stage were likely to be disproportionately those who were approved of more highly by the voters.

11. Abramson, Aldrich, and Rohde, *Change and Continuity in the 1980 Elections*, 220-221. For the 1984 results, see Abramson, Aldrich, and Rohde, *Change and Continuity in the 1984 Elections*, rev. ed. (Washington, D.C.: CQ Press, 1987), 272. For the 1988 results, see Abramson, Aldrich, and Rohde, *Change and Continuity in the 1988 Elections*, rev. ed. (Washington, D.C.: CQ Press, 1991), 273.

12. Opinion on this last point is not unanimous, however. See Richard Born, "Reassessing the Decline of Presidential Coattails: U.S. House Elections from 1952-80," *Journal of Politics* 46 (February 1984): 60-79.

13. John A. Ferejohn and Randall L. Calvert, "Presidential Coattails in Historical Perspective," *American Journal of Political Science* 28 (February 1984): 127-146.

14. Randall L. Calvert and John A. Ferejohn, "Coattail Voting in Recent Presidential Elections," *American Political Science Review* 77 (June 1983): 407-419.

15. James E. Campbell and Joe A. Sumners, "Presidential Coattails in Senate Elections," *American Political Science Review* 84 (June 1990): 513-524.

16. See Abramson, Aldrich, and Rohde, *Change and Continuity in the 1980 Elections*, 222-223, for the corresponding data on 1980; Abramson, Aldrich, and Rohde, *Change and Continuity in the 1984 Elections*, rev. ed., 273-275, for the data on 1984; and Abramson, Aldrich, and Rohde, *Change and Continuity in the 1988 Elections*, rev. ed., 272-275, for 1988 data.

17. Researchers have argued that the NES surveys from 1978 through 1982 have a built-in bias among the respondents in favor of incumbents because the question on congressional voting is preceded by a set of questions about the respondent's perceptions of and contacts with the incumbent, and in many of these questions the incumbent is mentioned by name. See Robert B. Eubank and David John Gow, "The Pro-Incumbent Bias in the 1978 and 1980 National Election Studies," *American Journal of Political Science* 27 (February 1983): 122-139; and David John Gow and Robert B. Eubank, "The Pro-Incumbent Bias in the 1982 National Election Study," *American Journal of Political Science* 28 (February 1984): 224-230. This problem was alleviated in the 1984 survey because the incumbent perception and contact questions were asked after the voting behavior questions. In the 1986 and 1988 surveys, however, questions about contacts by the incumbent preceded the questions about congressional voting behavior. In 1992, a few contact questions precede the vote question, but those specifically about the incumbent come after.

Introduction to Part 4

1. Arend Lijphart, *Democracies: Patterns of Majoritarian and Consensus Government in Twenty-One Countries* (New Haven, Conn.: Yale University Press, 1984). Finland and France could also be considered to have presidential systems, but in Finland the president and prime minister have roughly equal powers. Since Lijphart's book was published, experience has shown that France is not as much of a presidential system as he thought. Lijphart wrote, "The French president . . . is not only the head of state but also the real head of the government; the prime minister is merely the president's principal adviser and assistant" (See p. 73). This appeared to be true in 1984, but after the 1986 legislative election it became clear that the president's power is diminished substantially if he does not have political support in the National Assembly.
2. In France, a new election is held to elect a president to a full seven-year term. This has occurred twice: in 1969, when de Charles de Gaulle resigned, and in 1974, when Georges Pompidou died in office.

Chapter 11: The 1992 Elections and the Future of American Politics

1. Maurice Duverger, *Political Parties: Their Organization and Activity in the Modern World*, trans. Barbara and Robert North (New York: Wiley, 1963), 308-309. In this book, we have used the term *majority* to mean winning over half of the vote. It is clear that Duverger uses *majorité* to mean what we would call a plurality of the vote, that is, more votes than any other party received.
2. There are other democracies that might also be classified as having, or having had, a dominant party. These include Denmark, Norway, Iceland, Chile, India, Venezuela, and Columbia. The four countries we discuss here are the four democracies discussed extensively in a recent book, edited by T. J. Pempel, *Uncommon Democracies: The One-Party Dominant Regimes* (Ithaca, N.Y.: Cornell University Press, 1990).
3. See Alan Arian and Samuel H. Barnes, "The Dominant Party System: A Neglected Model of Democratic Stability," *Journal of Politics* 36 (August 1974): 592-614. In 1968, Mapai merged with two small parties to become the Israel Labor Party, and between 1969 and 1984 joined an electoral coalition called the Alignment. That coalition fell apart after the 1984 election, and the party is now generally referred to as the Labor party.
4. See Gósta Esping-Andersen, "Single-Party Dominance in Sweden: The Saga of Social Democracy," in *Uncommon Democracies*, 33-57.
5. See Scott C. Flanagan et al., *The Japanese Voter* (New Haven, Conn.: Yale University Press, 1991).
6. Duverger, *Political Parties*, 312.
7. Duverger was also vague about the reasons dominant parties tend to fall. He suggests that they lose dominance because they become too bureaucratized to govern effectively. Although dominant parties lost their dominance in Israel, Italy, Sweden, and Japan, a variety of factors led to their decline.
8. For an analysis of the gradual decline of the Christian Democrats, see Sidney Tarrow, "Maintaining Hegemony in Italy: 'The softer they rise, the slower

they fall!' " in *Uncommon Democracies*, 306-332.

9. Duverger, *Les Partis Politiques*, 3d ed. (Paris: Armand Colin, 1958), 342. The English-language translation appeared in 1963 (see note 1).

10. For a discussion of the logic of coalition structures, and why large coalitions are often at risk, see William H. Riker, *The Theory of Political Coalitions* (New Haven, Conn.: Yale University Press, 1962).

11. See, for example, Michael Nelson, "Constitutional Aspects of the Elections," in *The Elections of 1988*, ed. Michael Nelson (Washington, D.C.: CQ Press, 1989), 181-209; Byron E. Shafer, "The Election of 1988 and the Structure of American Politics: Thoughts on Interpreting an Electoral Order," *Electoral Studies* 8 (April 1989): 5-21.

12. Gary C. Jacobson, *The Electoral Origins of Divided Government* (Boulder, Colo.: Westview Press, 1990).

13. Jack W. Germond and Jules Witcover, *Mad as Hell: Revolt at the Ballot Box, 1992* (New York: Times Warner, 1993), 412, 413.

14. For a comprehensive compilation of Gallup presidential approval results between 1952 and 1988, see George C. Edwards III with Alec M. Gallup, *Presidential Approval: A Sourcebook* (Baltimore: Johns Hopkins University Press, 1990).

15. Quoted in Richard L. Berke, "Conservatives Struggle for Something to Say," *New York Times*, August 1, 1993, 4E.

16. See Paul R. Abramson, John H. Aldrich, and David W. Rohde, *Change and Continuity in the 1988 Elections*, rev. ed. (Washington, D.C.: CQ Press, 1991), 299. Because the percentage of strong Republicans has declined somewhat between 1988 and 1992, and because the proportion of strong Democrats declined marginally, our estimates require revision. We now estimate that a Democratic presidential candidate can count on about 14 million votes from strong Democratic identifiers and that a Republican presidential candidate can count on about 11 million votes from strong Republican identifiers.

17. Joseph A. Schlesinger, *Political Parties and the Winning of Office* (Ann Arbor: University of Michigan Press, 1991).

18. For a discussion of the political importance of the difference between selective incentives and the collective good, see Mancur Olson, Jr., *The Logic of Collective Action: Public Goods and the Theory of Groups* (Cambridge, Mass.: Harvard University Press, 1965). See also Terry M. Moe, *The Organization of Interests: Incentives and the Internal Dynamics of Political Interest Groups* (Chicago: University of Chicago Press, 1980).

19. Some incumbent Democrats and Republicans might seek to run on both a United We Stand and a major party ticket. To the best of our knowledge, New York is the only state that facilitates such dual candidacies.

20. As we noted in note 1 to the introduction to Part 4, since 1986 it has become clear that the French president is severely limited if he does not have support in the National Assembly.

21. This was clearly seen by Walter Dean Burnham shortly after the election. See Burnham, "Election 1968—The Abortive Landslide," *Trans-Action* 6 (December 1968): 18-24. See also Kevin P. Phillips, *The Emerging Republican Majority* (New Rochelle, N.Y.: Arlington House, 1969).

22. See Philip E. Converse, *The Dynamics of Party Support: Cohort-Analyzing Party Identification* (Beverly Hills, Calif.: Sage, 1976).

23. This thesis is advanced most forcefully by Bruce E. Keith et al., *The Myth of the Independent Voter* (Berkeley: University of California Press, 1992).

24. For the strongest evidence supporting this conclusion, see Martin P. Wattenberg, *The Decline of American Political Parties: 1952-1988* (Cambridge, Mass.: Harvard University Press, 1990), 36-49. See also Wattenberg, *The Rise of Candidate-Centered Politics: Presidential Elections of the 1980s* (Cambridge, Mass.: Harvard University Press, 1991), 31-46.

Suggested Readings

(Readings preceded by an asterisk include discussion of the 1992 elections.)

Chapter 1: The Nomination Struggle

Abramson, Paul R., John H. Aldrich, Phil Paolino, and David W. Rohde. " 'Sophisticated' Voting in the 1988 Presidential Primaries." *American Political Science Review* 86 (March 1992): 55-69.

Abramson, Paul R., John H. Aldrich, and David W. Rohde. "Progressive Ambition among United States Senators: 1972-1988." *Journal of Politics* 49 (February 1987): 3-35.

Aldrich, John H. *Before the Convention: Strategies and Choices in Presidential Nomination Campaigns.* Chicago: University of Chicago Press, 1980.

*Baker, Ross K. "Sorting Out and Suiting Up: The Presidential Nominations." In *The Election of 1992: Reports and Interpretations*, by Gerald M. Pomper, with colleagues. Chatham, N.J.: Chatham House, 1993, 39-73.

Bartels, Larry M. *Presidential Primaries and the Dynamics of Public Choice.* Princeton, N.J.: Princeton University Press, 1988.

Brams, Steven J. *The Presidential Election Game.* New Haven, Conn.: Yale University Press, 1978, 1-79.

*Ceaser, James, and Andrew Busch. *Upside Down and Inside Out: The 1992 Elections and American Politics.* Lanham, Md.: Rowman and Littlefield, 1993, 29-85.

*Germond, Jack W., and Jules Witcover. *Mad as Hell: Revolt at the Ballot Box, 1992.* New York: Warner Books, 1993, 20-416.

*Hadley, Charles D., and Harold W. Stanley. "Surviving the 1992 Presidential Nomination Process." In *America's Choice: The Election of 1992*, edited by William Crotty. Guilford, Conn.: Dushkin, 1993, 31-44.

Polsby, Nelson W., and Aaron Wildavsky. *Presidential Elections: Contemporary Strategies of American Electoral Politics*, 8th ed. New York: Free Press, 1991, 97-175.

Shafer, Byron. *Bifurcated Politics: Evolution and Reform in the National Party Convention.* Cambridge, Mass.: Harvard University Press, 1988.

Wayne, Stephen J. *The Road to the White House, 1992: The Politics of Presidential Elections.* New York: St. Martin's Press, 1992, 87-170.

Chapter 2: The General Election Campaign

Aldrich, John H., and Thomas Weko. "The Presidency and the Election Process: Campaign Strategy, Voting, and Governance." In *The Presidency and the Political System*, 2d ed., edited by Michael Nelson. Washington, D.C.: CQ Press, 1988, 251-267.

*Arterton, F. Christopher. "Campaign '92: Strategies and Tactics of the Candidates." In *The Election of 1992: Reports and Interpretations*, by Gerald M. Pomper, with colleagues. Chatham, N.J.: Chatham House, 1993, 74-109.

Asher, Herbert B. *Presidential Elections and American Politics: Voters, Candidates, and Campaigns Since 1952*, 5th ed. Pacific Grove, Calif.: Brooks/Cole, 1992, 239-340.

Brams, Steven J. *The Presidential Election Game*. New Haven, Conn.: Yale University Press. 1978, 80-133.

*Ceaser, James, and Andrew Busch. *Upside Down and Inside Out: The 1992 Elections and American Politics*. Lanham, Md.: Rowman and Littlefield, 1993, 87-126.

*Feigert, Frank B. "The Ross Perot Candidacy and Its Significance." In *America's Choice: The Election of 1992*, edited by William Crotty. Guilford, Conn.: Dushkin, 1993, 77-87.

*Germond, Jack W., and Jules Witcover. *Mad as Hell: Revolt at the Ballot Box, 1992*. New York: Warner Books, 1993, 1-19; 417-518.

Kessel, John H. *Presidential Campaign Politics*, 4th ed. Pacific Grove, Calif.: Brooks/Cole, 1992, 68-256.

*Mileur, Jerome M. "The General Election Campaign: Strategy and Support." In *America's Choice: The Election of 1992*, edited by William Crotty. Guilford, Conn.: Dushkin, 1993, 45-60.

Polsby, Nelson W., and Aaron Wildavsky. *Presidential Elections: Contemporary Strategies of American Electoral Politics*, 8th ed. New York: Free Press, 1991, 176-270.

*Quirk, Paul J., and Jon K. Dalager, "The Election: A 'New Democrat' and a New Kind of Presidential Election." In *The Elections of 1992*, edited by Michael Nelson. Washington, D.C.: CQ Press, 1993, 57-88.

Wayne, Stephen J. *The Road to the White House, 1992: The Politics of Presidential Elections*. New York: St. Martin's Press, 1992, 173-242.

Chapter 3: The Election Results

America Votes 20: A Handbook of Contemporary American Election Statistics, compiled and edited by Richard M. Scammon and Alice V. McGillivray. Washington, D.C.: Congressional Quarterly Inc., 1993.

Black, Earl, and Merle Black. *The Vital South: How Presidential Elections Are Won*. Cambridge, Mass.: Harvard University Press, 1992.

Burnham, Walter Dean. *Critical Elections and the Mainsprings of American Politics*. New York: Norton, 1970.

Clubb, Jerome M., William H. Flanigan, and Nancy H. Zingale. *Partisan Realignment: Voters, Parties, and Government in American History*. Beverly Hills, Calif.: Sage, 1980.

Kelley, Stanley, Jr. *Interpreting Elections*. Princeton, N.J.: Princeton University Press, 1983.

Lamis, Alexander P. *The Two-Party South*, 2d expanded ed. New York: Oxford University Press, 1990.

*Nardulli, Peter F., and Jon K. Dalager. "The Presidential Election of 1992 in Historical Perspective." In *America's Choice: The Election of 1992*, edited by William Crotty. Guilford, Conn.: Dushkin, 1993, 149-167.

*Pomper, Gerald M. "The Presidential Election." In *The Election of 1992: Reports and Interpretations*, Gerald M. Pomper, with colleagues. Chatham, N.J.: Chatham House, 1993, 132-156.

Presidential Elections Since 1789, 5th ed. Washington, D.C.: Congressional Quarterly Inc., 1991.

Schlesinger, Joseph A. *Political Parties and the Winning of Office.* Ann Arbor: University of Michigan Press, 1991.

Sundquist, James L. *Dynamics of the Party System: Alignment and Realignment of Political Parties in the United States*, rev. ed. Washington, D.C.: Brookings Institution, 1983.

Chapter 4: Who Voted?

Aldrich, John H. "Rational Choice and Turnout." *American Journal of Political Science* 37 (February 1993): 246-278.

Burnham, Walter Dean. "The Turnout Problem." In *Elections American Style*, edited by A. James Reichley. Washington, D.C.: Brookings Institution, 1987, 97-133.

Conway, M. Margaret. *Political Participation in the United States*, 2d ed. Washington, D.C.: CQ Press, 1991.

*Jennings, Jerry T. *Voting and Registration in the Election of November 1992*, U.S. Department of Commerce: Bureau of the Census, series P20, no. 466. Washington, D.C.: U.S. Government Printing Office, 1993.

Kleppner, Paul. *Who Voted?: The Dynamics of Electoral Turnout, 1870-1980.* New York: Praeger, 1982.

Leighley, Jan E., and Jonathan Nagler. "Socioeconomic Class Bias in Turnout: 1964-1988: The Voters Remain the Same." *American Political Science Review* 86 (September 1992): 725-736.

Piven, Frances Fox, and Richard A. Cloward. *Why Americans Don't Vote.* New York: Pantheon, 1988.

Powell, G. Bingham, Jr. "American Voter Turnout in Comparative Perspective." *American Political Science Review* 80 (March 1986): 17-43.

Rosenstone, Steven J., and John Mark Hansen. *Mobilization, Participation, and Democracy in America.* New York: Macmillan, 1993.

Tate, Katherine. *From Protest to Politics: The New Black Voters in American Elections.* Cambridge: Harvard University Press, 1993.

Teixeira, Ruy A. *The Disappearing American Voter.* (Washington, D.C.: Brookings Institution, 1992).

Wolfinger, Raymond, and Steven J. Rosenstone, *Who Votes?* New Haven: Yale University Press, 1980.

Chapter 5: Social Forces and the Vote

Alford, Robert R. *Party and Society: The Anglo-American Democracies.* Chicago: Rand McNally, 1963.

Axelrod, Robert. "Where the Votes Come From: An Analysis of Electoral Coalitions, 1952-1968. *American Political Science Review* 66 (March 1972): 11-20.

*Delli Carpini, Michael X., and Ester R. Fuchs. "The Year of the Woman? Candidates, Voters, and the 1992 Elections." *Political Science Quarterly* 108 (Spring 1993): 29-36.

Hamilton, Richard F. *Class and Politics in the United States.* New York: John Wiley, 1972.

Huckfeldt, Robert, and Carol Weitzel Kohfeld. *Race and the Decline of Class in American Politics.* Urbana: University of Illinois Press, 1989.

Leege, David C., and Lyman A. Kellstedt, with others. *Rediscovering the Religious Factor in American Politics.* Armonk, N.Y.: M. E. Sharpe, 1993.

Lipset, Seymour Martin. *Political Man: The Social Bases of Politics*, expanded ed. Baltimore: Johns Hopkins University Press, 1981.

Stanley, Harold W., William T. Bianco, and Richard G. Niemi. "Partisanship and Group Support Over Time: A Multivariate Analysis." *American Political Science Review* 80 (September 1986): 969-976.

Stanley, Harold W., and Richard G. Niemi. "Partisanship and Group Support, 1952-1988." *American Politics Quarterly* 19 (April 1991): 189-210.

Wald, Kenneth D. *Religion and Politics in the United States*, 2d ed. Washington, D.C.: CQ Press, 1992.

Chapter 6: Issues, Candidates, and Voter Choice

Asher, Herbert B. *Presidential Elections and American Politics Issues, Candidates, and Campaigns Since 1952*, 5th ed. Pacific Grove, Calif.: Brooks/Cole, 1992, 122-195.

Campbell, Angus, Philip E. Converse, Warren E. Miller, and Donald E. Stokes. *The American Voter*. New York: Wiley, 1960, 168-265.

Carmines, Edward G., and James A. Stimson. *Issue Evolution: Race and the Transformation of American Politics*. Princeton, N.J.: Princeton University Press, 1989.

*Elshtain, Jean Bethke. "Issues and Themes: Spiral of Delegitimation or New Social Covenant?" In *The Elections of 1992*, edited by Michael Nelson. Washington, D.C.: CQ Press, 1993, 109-124.

Enelow, James M., and Melvin J. Hinich, *The Spatial Theory of Voting: An Introduction*. New York: Cambridge University Press, 1984.

Kessel, John H. *Presidential Campaign Politics*, 4th ed. Pacific Grove, Calif.: Brooks/Cole, 1992, 258-289.

*Frankovic, Kathleen A. "Public Opinion in the 1992 Campaign." In *The Election of 1992: Reports and Interpretations*, by Gerald M. Pomper, with colleagues. Chatham, N.J.: Chatham House, 1993, 110-131.

Page, Benjamin I. *Choices and Echoes in Presidential Elections: Rational Man and Electoral Democracy*. Chicago: University of Chicago Press, 1978.

Popkin, Samuel L. *The Reasoning Voter: Communication and Persuasion in Presidential Campaigns*. Chicago: University of Chicago Press, 1991.

Stimson, James A. *Public Opinion in America: Moods, Cycles, and Swings*. Boulder, Colo.: Westview Press, 1991.

Chapter 7: Presidential Performance and Candidate Choice

Brace, Paul, and Barbara Hinckley. *Follow the Leader: Opinion Polls and the Modern Presidents*. New York: Basic Books, 1993.

Brody, Richard A. *Assessing the President: The Media, Elite Opinion, and Public Support*. Stanford, Calif.: Stanford University Press, 1991.

Downs, Anthony. *An Economic Theory of Democracy*. New York: Harper and Row, 1957.

Edwards, George C., III, with Alec M. Gallup. *Presidential Approval: A Sourcebook*. Baltimore: Johns Hopkins University Press, 1990.

Fiorina, Morris P. *Retrospective Voting in American National Elections*. New Haven, Conn.: Yale University Press, 1981.

Key, V. O., Jr. *The Responsible Electorate: Rationality in Presidential Voting, 1936-1960*. Cambridge, Mass.: Harvard University Press, 1966.

Kiewiet, D. Roderick. *Macroeconomic and Micropolitics: The Electoral Effects of Economic Issues*. Chicago: University of Chicago Press, 1983.

Lewis-Beck, Michael S. *Economics and Elections: The Major Western Democra-*

cies. Ann Arbor, Mich.: University of Michigan Press, 1988.

Riker, William H. *Liberalism Against Populism: A Confrontation Between the Theory of Democracy and the Theory of Social Choice*. San Francisco: W. H. Freeman, 1982.

Tufte, Edward R. *Political Control of the Economy*. Princeton, N.J.: Princeton University Press, 1978.

Chapter 8: Party Loyalties, Policy Preferences, Performance Evaluations, and the Vote

Abramson, Paul R. *Political Attitudes in America: Formation and Change*. San Francisco: W. H. Freeman, 1983.

Asher, Herbert B. "Voting Behavior Research in the 1980s: An Examination of Some Old and New Problem Areas." In *Political Science: The State of the Discipline*, edited by Ada W. Finifter (Washington, D.C.: American Political Science Association, 1983), 339-388.

Beck, Paul Allen. "The Dealignment Era in America." In *Electoral Change in Advanced Industrial Democracies: Realignment or Dealignment?* edited by Russell J. Dalton, Scott C. Flanagan, and Paul Allen Beck. Princeton, N.J.: Princeton University Press, 1984, 240-266.

Campbell, Angus, Philip E. Converse, Warren E. Miller, and Donald E. Stokes. *The American Voter*. New York: Wiley, 1960, 120-167.

Jennings, M. Kent, and Gregory B. Markus. "Partisan Orientations over the Long Haul: Results from the Three-Wave Political Socialization Panel Study." *American Political Science Review* 78 (December 1984): 1000-1018.

Keith, Bruce E., David B. Magleby, Candice J. Nelson, Elizabeth Orr, Mark Westlye, and Raymond E. Wolfinger. *The Myth of the Independent Voter*. Berkeley: University of California Press, 1992.

Kinder, Donald R., and David O. Sears. "Public Opinion and Political Action." In *Special Fields and Applications*, vol. 2 of *Handbook of Political Psychology*, 3d ed., edited by Gardner Lindzey and Elliot Aronson. New York: Random House, 1985, 659-741.

Miller, Warren E. "Party Identification, Realignment, and Party Voting: Back to the Basics." *American Political Science Review* 85 (June 1991): 557-568.

Wattenberg, Martin P. *The Decline of American Political Parties: 1952-1988*. Cambridge, Mass.: Harvard University Press, 1990.

———. *The Rise of Candidate-Centered Politics: Presidential Elections of the 1980s*. Cambridge: Harvard University Press, 1991.

Chapter 9: Candidates and Outcomes

Campbell, James E. "Predicting Seat Gains from Presidential Coattails." *American Journal of Political Science* 30 (February 1986): 165-183.

*Ceaser, James, and Andrew Busch. *Upside Down and Inside Out: The 1992 Elections and American Politics*. Lanham, Md.: Rowman and Littlefield, 1993, 127-158.

Fenno, Richard F., Jr. *Home Style: House Members in Their Districts*. Boston: Little, Brown, 1978.

Fiorina, Morris P. *Congress: Keystone of the Washington Establishment*, 2d ed. New Haven, Conn.: Yale University Press, 1989.

*Hershey, Marjorie Randon. "The Congressional Elections." In *The Election of 1992: Reports and Interpretations*, by Gerald M. Pomper, with colleagues. Chatham, N.J.: Chatham House, 1993, 157-189.

*Jacobson, Gary C. "Congress: Unusual Year, Unusual Election." In *The Elections of 1992*, edited by Michael Nelson. Washington, D.C.: CQ Press, 1993, 153-182.

*Jackson, John S., III. "The Congressional Races." In *America's Choice: The Election of 1992*, edited by William Crotty. Guilford, Conn.: Dushkin, 1993, 88-110.

Rohde, David W. " 'Something's Happening Here; What It Is Ain't Exactly Clear.': Southern Democrats in the House of Representatives." In *Home Style and Washington Work: Studies in Congressional Politics*, edited by Morris P. Fiorina and David W. Rohde. Ann Arbor: University of Michigan Press, 1989, 137-163.

———. *Parties and Leaders in the Postreform House*. Chicago: University of Chicago Press, 1991.

Schlesinger, Joseph A. *Ambition and Politics: Political Careers in the United States*. Chicago: Rand McNally, 1966.

———. "The New American Political Party." *American Political Science Review* 79 (December 1985): 1152-1169.

Simon, Dennis M., Charles W. Ostrom, Jr., and Robin F. Marra. "The President, Referendum Voting, and Subnational Elections in the United States." *American Political Science Review* 85 (December 1991): 1177-1192.

Chapter 10: The Congressional Electorate

Abramowitz, Alan I., and Jeffrey A. Segal. *Senate Elections*. Ann Arbor: University of Michigan Press, 1992.

Born, Richard. "Reassessing the Decline of Presidential Coalitions: U.S. House Elections from 1952-80," *Journal of Politics* 46 (February 1984): 60-79.

Calvert, Randall L., and John A. Ferejohn. "Coattail Voting in Recent Presidential Elections." *American Political Science Review* 77 (June 1983): 407-419.

Erikson, Robert S., and Gerald C. Wright, Jr. "Voters, Candidates, and Issues in Congressional Elections." In *Congress Reconsidered*, 3d ed., edited by Lawrence C. Dodd and Bruce I. Oppenheimer. Washington, D.C.: CQ Press, 1985, 87-108.

Fenno, Richard F., Jr. "If, as Ralph Nader Says, Congress Is 'the Broken Branch,' How Come We Love Our Congressmen So Much? In *Congress in Change: Elections and Reform*, edited by Norman J. Ornstein. New York: Praeger, 1975, 227-287.

Ferejohn, John A., and Randall L. Calvert. "Presidential Coattails in Historical Perspective." *American Journal of Political Science* 28 (February 1984): 127-146.

Franklin, Charles H. "Eschewing Obfuscation? Campaigns and the Perceptions of U.S. Senate Incumbents." *American Political Science Review* 85 (December 1991): 1193-1214.

Hurley, Patricia A. "Partisan Representation and the Failure of Realignment in the 1980s." *American Journal of Political Science* 33 (February 1989): 240-261.

Jacobson, Gary C. *The Politics of Congressional Elections*, 3d ed. New York: Harper Collins, 1991.

Jacobson, Gary C. *The Electoral Origins of Divided Government: Competition in U.S. House Elections, 1946-1988*. Boulder, Colo.: Westview Press, 1990.

Chapter 11: The 1992 Elections and the Future of American Politics

*Burnham, Walter Dean. "The Legacy of George Bush: Travails of an Understudy." In *The Election of 1992: Reports and Interpretations*, by Gerald M. Pomper, with colleagues. Chatham, N.J.: Chatham House, 1993, 1-38.

*Ceaser, James, and Andrew Busch. *Upside Down and Inside Out: The 1992 Elections and American Politics.* Lanham, Md.: Rowman and Littlefield, 1993, 1-28, 159-187.

*Ladd, Everett Carll. "The 1992 Vote for President Clinton: Another Brittle Mandate?" *Political Science Quarterly* 108 (Spring 1993): 1-28.

*Lipset, Seymour Martin. "The Significance of the 1992 Election." *PS: Political Science and Politics* 26 (March 1993): 7-16.

*Nelson, Michael. "Conclusion: Some Things Old, Some Things New." In *The Elections of 1992*, edited by Michael Nelson. Washington, D.C.: CQ Press, 1993, 183-192.

*____. "The Presidency: Clinton and the Cycle of Politics and Policy." In *The Elections of 1992*, edited by Michael Nelson. Washington, D.C.: CQ Press, 1993, 125-152.

*McWilliams, Wilson Carey. "The Meaning of the Election." In *The Election of 1992: Reports and Interpretations*, by Gerald M. Pomper, with colleagues. Chatham, N.J.: Chatham House, 1993, 190-218.

*Stokes, Donald E., and John J. DiIulio, Jr., "The Setting: Valence Politics in Modern Elections," In *The Elections of 1992*, edited by Michael Nelson. Washington, D.C.: CQ Press, 1993, 1-20.

Index

Abbott, David W., 341*n*27
ABC News, 67
Abortion, 2, 3, 50, 189-191, 325, 359*n*34
Abramowitz, Alan I., 287, 301, 368*n*56, 369*n*71, 371*n*4
Abramson, Paul R., 333*n*28, 334*n*8, 335*nn*16, 26, 337*n*30, 337-338*n*1, 344*nn*12, 13, 345*n*18, 347*nn*36, 41, 348*nn*51-53, 349*n*61, 350*nn*71, 77, 351*n*1, 353*nn*12, 13, 354*nn*22, 25, 26, 355*n*37, 356*nn*2, 4, 7, 10, 358*n*24, 359*n*32, 361*nn*4, 9, 362*n*16, 18, 363*nn*21-23, 368*nn*52, 60, 369*n*68, 370*n*83, 371*n*3, 372*nn*11, 16
Adams, John Quincy, 167
Afghanistan, 177
African-Americans
    appeals to, 38, 87, 88, 158, 229, 315, 341*n*24
    congressional representation, 264, 266, 269, 284
    contribution to Democratic presidential coalition, 81, 144, 149, 150, 160, 352*n*6, 355*n*28
    party identification of, 227-231, 361*n*4
    sampling of, 11, 105, 106, 354*n*24
    turnout of, 38, 81, 98, 100, 104, 106, 109, 123, 129, 144, 147, 152, 154, 157, 160, 229
    and the vote, 38, 87, 131, 135-137, 139, 144-147, 149, 150, 152, 154, 156-158, 160, 163, 300, 320, 321, 323, 354*n*26, 362*n*17
Age
    and party identification, 138, 139
    and turnout, 106, 109, 110, 116
    and the vote, 126-128, 138, 301
Agnew, Spiro T., 16
Agrin, Larry, 18
Alabama, 74, 81, 87, 88, 264, 321, 338*n*5, 340*n*21
Alaska, 74, 80
Aldrich, John H., 331*n*5, 334*nn*8, 14, 335*nn*16, 26, 337*n*30, 337-338*n*1, 348*nn*51-53, 56, 349*nn*61, 67, 350*n*77, 351*n*1, 354*n*26, 356*nn*4, 10, 11, 358*nn*24, 25, 359*n*32, 361*n*14, 362*n*18, 363*nn*21-23,

368*nn*52, 60, 369*n*68, 370*n*83, 371*n*3, 372*nn*11, 16, 374*n*16
Alford, Robert R., 93, 342*n*4, 355*n*30
Alt, James E., 360*n*10
American Independent Party, 325
The American Voter, 164, 179, 221, 226, 358*n*23
Anderson, Barbara A., 344*nn*12, 13, 347*n*36
Anderson, John B., 73-75, 147, 149, 150, 152, 156, 165, 167, 216, 244, 337*n*30, 354*n*26
Andrews, Mark, 280
Apple, R. W., Jr., 4, 331*n*3
Arian, Alan, 373*n*3
Arizona, 266, 321, 340*n*17
Arkansas, 50, 61, 72, 81, 87, 88
Armey, Dick, 283
Aronson, Elliot, 342*n*6
Ashenfelter, Orley, 121, 349*n*68
Asher, Herbert B., 333*n*27, 362*n*9
Asian-Americans, 270
Australian ballot, 100
Axelrod, Robert, 143, 351*n*82, 353*n*19, 354*n*23

Babcock, Charles R., 366*n*19
Baker, James, 44, 142
Baker, Ross K., 33, 141, 335*n*29, 353*n*17
Balch, George I., 116, 348*n*49
Banks, Jeffrey S., 273, 366*n*28
Barkley, Alben W., 12
Barnes, Samuel H., 373*n*3
Bartels, Larry M., 334*n*14
Bass, Harold F., Jr., 332*n*17
Beck, Paul Allen, 7, 332*n*14
Bennett, Stephen Earl, 351*n*83
Bentsen, Lloyd, 253, 289, 369*n*74
Berelson, Bernard R., 93, 232, 341*n*3, 362*n*19
Berke, Richard L., 374*n*15
Bianco, William T., 144, 353*n*21
Black, Benjamin D., 167, 356*n*8
Black, Duncan, 339*n*10, 356*n*9
Black, Earl, 340*n*20
Black, Gordon S., 167, 356*n*8